The Contributors

Graham Birtwell B.Ed (Hons), DASE, M.Ed., Dip. Psycho is a Deputy Principal of a residential school, which provides educational services.

Andy Bowly Cert. CYD, M.A. is a Senior Practitioner with a Barnardo's Scheme in the North-West of England. The Scheme is a joint funded project between Barnardo's N.W. region and a local Social Services Directorate, which provides programmes of intervention to young people who sexually abuse others.

Martin C. Calder M.A., CQSW is a Child Protection Co-ordinator and Reviewing Officer with the City of Salford Community and Social Services Directorate. He has written around work with young people who sexually abuse and adult sex offenders, and is driven to write to provide practical frameworks for operational use. He also has interests in the areas of post-registration work and child protection theory.

Mark S. Carich Ph.D. is currently employed with the Illinois Department of Corrections at Big Muddy River Correctional Center and is on the faculty of the Adler School of Professional Psychology in Chicago. He is currently co-ordinating the Sexually Dangerous Persons Sex Offender Program under the programme administrator. He currently works with sex offenders and for the last 9 years has worked with the Sexually Dangerous Persons of Illinois. Dr Carich has authored, edited, co-authored, and co-edited a number of publications on sex offenders, regarding assessment and treatment, and on psychology, regarding hypnosis, therapy techniques, relapse prevention, and cybernetics. Dr Carich has also developed a number of inventories and scales for sex offender assessment. Dr Carich can be contacted, with comments, at 439 Chapel Drive, Collinsville, Illinois 62234, USA. Tel: 618 344 5879 (h) or 618 437 5300 (w).

Kevin J. Epps is currently Principal Psychologist, Glenthorne Youth Treatment Centre (Department of Health) and Honorary Lecturer in Psychology, University of Birmingham. He has 14 years experience of working with children and young people in a variety of residential, community and psychiatric settings. He is currently involved at Glenthorne with the care and treatment of young people detained in secure accommodation, most of whom have committed serious offences. He has developed a particular interest in the management and treatment of aggressive and violent adolescents. This interest is reflected in his clinical, teaching, and research activities. He has published in various journals, contributed to several edited books, and has worked on several national and local working groups concerned with young offenders. Address for correspondence: Glenthorne Youth Treatment Centre, Kingsbury Road, Erdington, Birmingham, England. B24 9SA. Tel: 0121 623 1700; Fax: 0121 623 1710.

Jane F. Gilgun Ph.D., LICSW, is Professor at the School of Social Work, University of Minnesota, Twin Cities. She has published extensively on adult sex offenders, resilience, and more recently in relation to working with client strengths. All correspondence can be sent to School of Social Work, University of Minnesota, 224 Church St., SE, Minneapolis MN 55455, USA. Tel: 612 624 0082; Fax: 612 626 0395.

Matthew C. Lampley B.S. is currently working for the Illinois Department of Corrections, where he is completing his graduate internship with their offender unit. He is also a Masters candidate at Southern Illinois University at Carbondale, Illinois. He has been with the department for 6 years.

Dr. Rachel Leheup is a Child and Adolescent Psychiatrist at the Thorneywood Unit of Nottingham N.H.S. Health Care Trust. She has considerable experience of working within the child psychiatry field and has developed an interest and expertise in working with young people who sexually abuse. This has included direct therapeutic work; reports for court; training social workers; as groupwork consultant; research and establishing the Young Abusers Project.

Kevin Lenehan CQSW is a Child Protection Officer working with the NSPCC at Craigavon Child Protection Team. With the setting up of the Juvenile Perpetrators Project Team, he was seconded on a full-time basis to the Project, undertaking individual assessment and treatment work with the young people referred and co-working the Group programme. Prior to this, he was involved in child protection work in terms of investigations, assessment and treatment/recovery work. Before joining the NSPCC, he had been a Field Social Worker in family and child care within social services, having moved from working with adolescents in a residential unit.

Meg Lindsay OBE, M.A., M.Sc., Diploma in Applied Social Studies. Meg qualified as a social worker in 1971, and worked in a range of settings, including 10 years managing residential care at a variety of levels. Since 1994, she has been Director of The Centre for Residential Child Care, established by the Scottish Office. The objective of the Centre has been to improve the quality of residential child care via information, networking, training, research, consultancy, and the exchange of good practice, and has achieved an international reputation in the field. Meg has published extensively via The Centre and elsewhere on a range of topics related to residential care.

Frank J. MacHovec Ph.D. is a Licensed Clinical Psychologist and Associate Professor of Psychiatric Medicine at the University of Virginia; Senior Lecturer at Christopher Newport University; formerly supervising psychologist at 2 residential juvenile sex offender treatment programmes.

Gerard McCarthy is currently Principal Clinical Child Psychologist with the Child and Adolescent Service of the Western Area Health Trust, Weston-Super-Mare, North Somerset. He previously worked as a research scientist for the Medical Research Council at the MRC Child Psychiatry Unit at the Institute of Psychiatry, London. His interests include the clinical implications of attachment theory and the links between children's experiences and adult psychological functioning.

Jacqui McGarvey B.A. (Hons), CQSW. Jacqui is currently employed as a manager with the NSPCC (NI) managing a number of projects in children's services. She has developed and co-ordinated a multi-disciplinary inter-agency project working with young people who sexually abuse and their families. Prior to this role, she gained extensive experience working with this population of young people by individual and group work. She is involved in training, consultancy and has presented at regional, national and international conferences.

Kieran McGrath B.C.L., CQSW, M.Soc.Sc. took a law degree at University College, Dublin, before choosing a career in social work. Since 1988 he has been senior social worker attached to St Clare's child sexual abuse unit in Dublin. He was a founding member of NIAP in 1991 and previously worked in a sexual abuse treatment agency in Sacramento, California. He is also editor of *Irish Social Worker* and is a frequent contributor to both professional journals and mass media publications in Ireland on social issues, particularly child protection.

Jeannie McIntee M.Sc., C. Psychol., A.F.B.Ps.S., Dip. Psychotherapy, is a Consultant Clinical and Forensic Psychologist. She is the Director of the Chester Therapy Centre, an independent psychology and psychotherapy service providing specialist assessment, expert witness and therapeutic intervention to individuals, families and organisations. The majority of work is provided to the courts, social and health services, probation and the police. Ms McIntee has worked with trauma for the last 20 years and has specialised in this area for the past 13 years and has written several articles and books around this topic.

First published in 1999 by:
Russell House Publishing Limited
4 St. George's House
The Business Park
Uplyme Road
Lyme Regis
Dorset DT7 3LS

British Library Cataloguing-in-Publication Data:
A catalogue record for this manual is available from the British Library.

ISBN: 1-898924-46-5

Text design and layout by The Hallamshire Press Limited, Sheffield

Printed by Cromwell Press, Trowbridge

To
Janet and Stacey Laura Calder
for
Being there for me all the time.

Working with Young People who Sexually Abuse:
New Pieces of the Jigsaw Puzzle

Contents

Acknowledgements

To Janet for her unstinting love and support.

Thanks to the continuing diligence of the staff at Leigh Library for providing materials to source this book.

To each of the contributors for sticking to the time scales and for providing chapters of such quality.

To Geoffrey Mann at RHP for his continuing encouragement.

To the practitioners involved in this work for their pioneering work and vision of the future which has motivated this collection of papers.

Martin C. Calder

Loretto McKeown M.A., MFCC. Loretto is a Family Therapist in private practice in Newry, Northern Ireland. In addition to her work as a Family Therapist she does recovery work with children and young people who are victims of abuse and also with adults molested as children. She is currently co-therapist for the Support Disciplinary Inter-agency Project Team working with young people who abuse and their carers.

Stuart J. Mulholland graduated from Glasgow University with an honours degree in English Literature and Politics and went on to complete a Diploma in Social Work in 1990. Since then, he has worked in both the child protection and criminal justice systems, specialising for the last five in devising and delivering treatment programmes for adults, adolescents, and children who exhibit problematic or aggressive sexual behaviours. He has conducted training and consultancy for criminal justice, child care and residential staff in many local authorities, and is an associate member of the Centre for the Child and Society at the University of Glasgow. He currently works for Glasgow City Council social work department as a member of the Halt Project.

Michael Murray B.S.Sc., CQSW, MSW, M.Med.Sc. is currently a Project Manager in Barnardo's, implementing computerised records. He has previously worked as a Project Leader in Windsor Avenue Family Centre in Belfast. His interest in research on adolescent sexual abusers developed from a 3 year period from 1993 to 1996 when he worked as a Senior Social Work Practitioner in the Young People's Centre, Belfast. He has a keen interest in Psycho-analytical Theory and Practice. He is currently undertaking part-time postgraduate research in the Department of Social Work, Queen's University, Belfast, on Paternal Deprivation in Young People who Sexually Abuse.

Steve Myers is Senior Lecturer in Social Work at the Manchester Metropolitan University. He has a background in youth justice and child protection with a particular interest in young abusers, which included the establishment of systems and interventions in a local authority to manage this issue. He is involved in research and training around young people who sexually abuse with a particular emphasis on the social construction of sexual offending.

Kate O'Boyle B.S.E. (Hons) P.G.C.E., C.S.S is a Child Protection Officer with NSPCC, Craigavon, Northern Ireland. She left a career in teaching and subsequently retrained as a social worker in family and childcare. Her current work includes risk assessment, comprehensive assessment and treatment/recovery work with victims of sexual abuse. She has been involved since 1994 in individual work and in the group work programme with young people who sexually abuse. Experience in contemporary dance has led to successful completion of the Laban Guilds Leadership in Community Dance and has promoted a commitment to developing body based therapy work.

David O'Callaghan, B.A. (Hons) CQSW qualified as a social worker at Lancaster University in 1982 and has worked as a child care practitioner and guardian ad litem in the West Midlands and the North West. He is currently the Programme Director of G-MAP, an independent project providing assessment and therapeutic services to young people who sexually abuse. G-MAP works with young people across the ability spectrum though it is noted for the development of service to young people with learning disabilities. David has published on a number of aspects of work with young abusers and provides staff training and consultancy nationally. He is contactable at Suite 10, 1 Roebuck Lane, Sale, Cheshire M33 7SY. Tel: 0161 976 4414; Fax: 0161 976 4474.

Lynne Peyton is Regional Director for Northern Ireland with the NSPCC. At the time of writing, Lynne was Assistant Director of Social Services with the Southern Health and Social Services Board and led the Board's multi-disciplinary commissioning group for children's services. Lynne has extensive experience of assessing the need for and planning a wide range of services and projects. She has served on two ACPCs, a number of cross border partnerships and chaired the N.I. Joint Investigation Protocol Group.

Spencer Santry is currently concluding his doctoral research at the Tizard Centre at the University of Kent. His areas of interest include the attachment and intimacy of young people and adults who sexually abuse, and the methodologies employed for the assessment of attachment and intimacy, as well as other related constructs. The current piece of research examines the attachment and intimacy experience of men with learning disabilities who have sexually abusive behaviour.

Audrey Sheridan, M.A., M.Psych. Sc. works as a senior clerical psychologist with the Lucena Clinic Child and Adolescent Mental Health Service, Dublin. Since 1990, she has worked in both rural and urban communities, providing assessment and therapy for a broad range of developmental problems. Her special interest is in child protection and she has worked with victims and perpetrators of sexual abuse. As a member of NIAP between 1993 and 1997, she devised research and assessment protocols for NIAP, was involved in direct therapeutic work, and promoted the goals of NIAP at national and international conferences.

Introduction

How to Begin
the Assembly Process

Martin C. Calder

How to Begin the Assembly Process

In 1997, I argued that it was 'make or break' time for the problem of young people who sexually abuse in the UK: it could either be elevated to the national agenda and due attention paid to consolidating and extending the knowledge and practice base; or it could fall, without trace, leaving with it tragic consequences (Calder, 1997, p10). I also accepted that there was much left to learn in such an embryonic area of work. In the interim, there have been some developments. The Department of Health has published some of their commissioned research (see Farmer and Pollock, 1998; Monck and New, 1996; Skuse *et al.*, 1998) and there is a gradual increase in the number of publications reflecting the blend of research, theory and practice wisdom development. However, there remains no substantial central guidance, consolidation of best practice to allow ACPCs to fill the void, or any move towards a National Task Force akin to that in the USA. The concern remains, therefore, that we are at a watershed, particularly as we will soon be responding to the implications of the Crime and Disorder Bill with young people. The best way forward is to collate and utilise the important, but all too frequently, fragmented pieces of work which are undertaken by enthusiastic individuals. This book aims to achieve some of this and to challenge the isolated practice, which has allowed us for too long to allow individuals to forge their own path.

The aim of this collection of papers from England, Scotland, Northern and Southern Ireland and the United States is to make available new thinking, research and practice to a wider audience. There is too much territorial practice - which has the problem of forcing the same wheel to be unnecessarily re-invented; as well as preventing skills and ideas to be shared and harnessed collectively to find new ways of managing this emerging and significant problem. This book thus aims to provide new pieces of the jigsaw puzzle. All puzzles have clues, and each chapter offers us either a new piece of the jigsaw or some clues as to how it may be constructed. We must try to complete the jigsaw as best we can in order to provide the most informed and tested interventions in the best possible way. This can be done even if some bits are missing, although the risk of a distorted overall view is higher.

Defining sexually abusive behaviour by young men is not straightforward, and this is evident from the range of terms and definitions used by the different contributors. What is clear is that definitions are very important: if they are too narrow, they restrict our understanding as well as our intervention threshold. Conversely, if they are too broad, they are all embracing and often detract from focusing on the highest risk cases (Calder, 1999, p10). I would argue that few individual definitions are adequate in themselves, but collectively have much to offer if they provide a baseline for workers. It is important that we do succeed in defining the concept as it carries with it implications for solutions to the problem, and more specifically determines which acts are dealt with, and in what ways (Haugaard and Reppucci, 1988, p 14). The task of communicating about an issue remains much more difficult when the same term does not convey identical meaning across professionals and in the local community. I have previously proposed (Calder, 1997, p 11) the following definition of young people who sexually abuse which now appears to have been adopted by several programmes and is reflected in the chapters:

> *Young people (below the age of 18 years) who engage in any form of sexual activity with another individual, that they have powers over by virtue of age, emotional maturity, gender, physical strength, intellect and where the victim in this relationship has suffered a sexual exploitation and betrayal of trust. Sexual activity includes sexual intercourse (oral, anal or vaginal), sexual touching, exposure of sexual organs, showing pornographic material, exhibitionism, voyeurism, obscene communication, frottage, fetishism,*

Understanding the problem: what is required of a theory of adolescent sexual offending?

Normal and abnormal sexual development

It is difficult to identify the characteristics of adolescent sex offenders that distinguish them from other young people, the 'non-sex offenders'. It is generally accepted that there is no 'typical' adolescent sex offender, and no particular personality profile that is associated with sexual offending. Although some sex offenders present with a variety of characteristics that may increase the risk of sexual offending, such as deviant sexual arousal ('preference offenders'), others do not ('situational offenders'). Male sexual aggression forms a graded continuum, ranging from the coerciveness of subtle pressure to overtly violent assault. An adequate theory of adolescent sex offending must be able to accommodate this blurred boundary, and encompass the processes associated with 'normal' sexual development and behaviour (Moore and Rosenthal, 1993).

Characteristics of juvenile sex offenders

Despite the poor quality of much of the research in this area, especially the lack of comparative studies, a variety of psychosocial problems have been found in juvenile sex offenders whose offences come to light. An adequate theory of juvenile sexual offending must somehow explain the association of these characteristics with sexual offending behaviour.

A recent British study (Richardson *et al.*, 1995) presented data on the characteristics of 100 sexually abusive male adolescents aged between 11 and 18 years, and concluded that they were consistent with those found in the North American literature. Typical psychosocial problems found in groups of adolescent sex offenders who are referred for assessment include: low self-esteem; poor social skills; peer relationship difficulties; social isolation and loneliness; emotional problems; shyness and timidity; educational and academic problems; intellectual and neurological impairments; psychiatric problems; gender-identity confusion; feelings of confused masculinity; problems arising from sexual and physical victimisation; sexual deviancy and sexual dysfunction; substance abuse; and family problems. Many also have a history of childhood conduct disorder and juvenile delinquency, often with convictions for non-sexual offences. The extent to which these problems are also associated with sexual offending in juveniles whose offences never come to light is not clear.

Types of offence

A satisfactory theory of juvenile sexual offending must also account for the wide variety of sexual offending behaviours. Fehrenbach *et al.*, (1986), describing the offence behaviour of 279 male juvenile offenders, found that fondling was the most common type of sexual behaviour (59 per cent), then rape (23 per cent), exhibitionism (11 per cent), and other non-contact behaviours (7 per cent). In a similar study, Wasserman and Kappel (1985) found that some form of penetration occurred in 59 per cent of offences, of which 52 per cent were penetration by the penis, while 31 per cent involved intercourse, 12 per cent oral-genital contact, and only 16 per cent genital fondling. It appears that intercourse becomes more common as the age of both offender and victim increases. Further, there seems to be a higher incidence of offences involving penetration in imprisoned samples of juvenile sex offenders. It seems likely that offences that involve physical contact, especially those resulting in tissue damage, are more likely to be detected and recorded. A range of offence-related variables could be used to place adolescent sex offenders into subgroups. These include:

Age of victim

James and Neil (1996) found that the average age of the victim was 9.8 years, with a wide range from less than 2 years to 23 years. Interestingly, they found a bi-modal distribution of victims' ages, with an early peak around 4 years, and a later peak of 14 years. In addition, offenders were consistent in selecting victims of a similar age. Although this study is based on a relatively small sample, this finding lends support to the idea that there may be three distinct groups of juvenile sex offenders: those that target children (child molesters), those that offend against adolescent girls and women (sexual assaulters), and those that offend against both children and adults. Richardson *et al.* (1995) also found significant differences between the sexual behaviour of the child molesters and the sexual assaulters in their sample of 100 adolescent abusers. The sexual assaulters were more likely to offend against strangers, and in public places. There was also a higher frequency of non-contact offences, such as exhibitionism, and more evidence of unsuccessful, or attempted, penetration. The authors suggest that the higher rate of successful penetration in offences committed against children may be explained by the fact that the offender often has greater access to the victim over a prolonged period of time and encounters less victim resistance.

Gender of victim

Some adolescent child molesters tend to abuse either boys or girls, whilst others abuse both groups. It seems that the majority (69 per cent to 84 per cent) of the victims of juvenile sex offenders are female. However, as the age of the victim decreases, the victim is more likely to be male.

Relationship to victim

Most of the victims of child abuse are known to the offender and are usually friends, relatives, or neighbours. Some offenders, perhaps those who are more sophisticated in their abuse, tend to prefer victims who are less familiar, perhaps to avoid detection. The proportion of stranger victims varies from study to study, ranging from 17 per cent to 48 per cent. Some studies have found that juveniles who offend against women and peer-aged girls are more likely to chose stranger victims than those who molest children. Almost all the juvenile child molesters described by Awad and Saunders (1989, 1991) knew their victims, either as relatives, children of friends of the parents, or children the offenders had been babysitting. In contrast, in a sample of adolescent sexual assaulters (rapists), Vinogradov *et al.* (1988) found that only one-third knew their victims before the assault took place. However, studies

into college populations of sexual assaulters produce different findings, indicating that the victims are frequently acquaintances rather than strangers. Koss (1988), for example, reported that 84 per cent of the rapists she surveyed knew their victims; 61 per cent of the rapes occurred on dates; and 84 per cent of the rapes involved one offender. Further, it seems that when a young man rapes an acquaintance he uses less force and is less likely to use a weapon (Koss *et al.*, 1988). Several studies indicate that first dates are riskier than later dates (Muehlenhard and Linton, 1987), though others have suggested that sexual aggression is more likely to occur in long-term relationships (Russell, 1984; Weis and Borges, 1973).

Use of force and violence

Overall, juvenile sex offenders use less coercion, force, and violence than adult sex offenders and seem to cause fewer injuries to their victims. A significant minority of offences, however, do involve violence, especially offences such as rape and indecent assault perpetrated against female peers and women. Groth (1977) reported that 43 per cent of offences against a peer or older victim involved a weapon, whereas when the victim was a much younger child no weapons were used. Nevertheless, some offences against children are accompanied by force and violence. Some juvenile sex offenders even abduct their victim. There is some evidence to suggest that adult sex offenders who abduct children tend to be more sadistic, deriving pleasure from placing the victim in fear of pain. The extent to which this may be true of juvenile offenders is not known; there has been scant research into the more serious forms of juvenile sex offender. Certainly there are examples of juvenile sex offenders who experience sadistic sexual fantasies involving bondage, torture, mutilation, and murder (Epps, 1996b).

Typologies of adolescent sex offenders

Despite the lack of coherent research several attempts have been made to develop taxonomic systems for the categorisation and classification of juvenile sexual offenders, a necessary prerequisite for the development of theory. Using the notion of 'preference' versus 'situational' offenders, Becker (1988) made a

Theory Becker

distinction between juvenile sex offenders who have deviant recurrent sexual fantasies and a preference for deviant sexual activity and those whose sexual offending appears to be part of a wider repertoire of delinquent activity. Groth (1977) has suggested that the dynamics of the juvenile sex offender parallel those of adult offenders. He proposed that there should be power and anger rapist subtypes, as well as a passive, fixated child molester type. However, the fact that these have not proved to be optimal subdivisions in adult sex offender research has led Knight and Prentky (1993) to cast doubt on their usefulness in developing taxonomic boundaries in juvenile sex offenders.

Psychiatric systems of classification and diagnosis have been of limited use because most adolescent sex offenders are not considered to be psychiatrically abnormal, and sexual deviance in children and juveniles below the age of 16 is not recognised as a psychiatric disorder. Thus, there is no diagnostic category for paedophilia within either DSM-IV (American Psychiatric Association, 1994) or ICD-10 (World Health Organisation, 1992). However, it has recently been suggested that the creation of a new disorder 'Sexual Arousal Disorder of Childhood' would help to identify vulnerable sexually aroused children and target resources towards early prevention of abuser behaviours (Vizard et al., 1996).

Perhaps the most well-known system is the descriptive typology proposed by O'Brien and Bera (1986), which has found its way into clinical practice despite the lack of supporting empirical data. In this typology O'Brien and Bera described seven types of juvenile sex offender: naïve experimenter, group influenced, disturbed impulsive, low social competence, early childhood abuse, impulsive life-style, and sexual preoccupation and compulsivity. One of the difficulties inherent in this kind of descriptive system is that some juvenile sex offenders can be placed in more than one category. More recently, Knight and Prentky (1993) proposed another taxonomic system, based on the system developed from their work with 564 adult sex offenders. The results indicated that those who had committed offences prior to age nineteen were defined by low social competence and higher life-style impulsivity and criminal activity. Clearly this typology has yet to be empirically

validated on juvenile sex offenders. It seems likely, however, that the population of juvenile sex offenders is every bit as heterogeneous as the population of adult sex offenders (see Knight Rosenberg and Schneider, 1985).

Theoretical Models

At some time or another most theoretical models of human behaviour have been explored in an attempt to understand juvenile sexual offending. Marshall and Eccles (1993) propose that the extant research literature is inadequate to allow for the development of a comprehensive theoretical model of adolescent sexual offending. Further, there is now widespread agreement that no single theoretical model can currently provide an adequate understanding of juvenile sexual offending. Nevertheless, it is accepted that some models have more to offer than others, and that it may be possible to develop some form of integrative theory. Marshall and Eccles, however, suggest that a comprehensive theory of adolescent sexual offending may not be possible. Rather, they propose that specific theories are needed for different types of sexual offence, each emphasising different processes. Clearly this cannot take place until some agreement is reached on how to classify and group adolescent sex offenders. Only then will it be possible to look at which processes are associated with which types of offence.

Before looking at the integrative theories that have been proposed, it is necessary to briefly review the various single theories. Despite their limitations each theory makes a useful contribution to understanding at least some types of sexual offending, and some have had a significant impact on the management and treatment of adolescent sex offenders. Ultimately, all behaviour is mediated through the brain and involves an interaction between the individual and the environment. Some theories have more to say about what happens inside the individual (internal factors), at either a biological level (genetics, brain and body chemistry) or psychological level (conscious and unconscious thoughts, fantasies, and feelings). Other theories are more concerned with what happens outside the individual (external, 'environmental' factors) and the effect these experiences have on thinking, feeling and behaviour. Through various learning processes human behaviour is especially open to influence from external sources. Parents, other primary care-givers, and family members play a particularly important role in helping to shape behaviour and attitudes during early childhood, whilst the effect of the peer group, the media, and the values and beliefs held in wider society are most likely to have an impact during later childhood and adolescence.

Single-theory models

Biological (or medical) theories

All behaviour, perception, thought, and feeling, is mediated through the brain. In turn, the structure and functioning of the brain, and its effects on body chemistry through the action of hormones and other body chemicals, is influenced by genetics and the effects of external factors such as nutrition and physical injury (e.g. brain damage). The relationship between genetics, brain and behaviour, is extremely complex and poorly understood. Research into non-human primates and humans has established that whilst aggression and sexual behaviour have strong biological determinants, their expression is shaped by experience and learning. It is not altogether surprising, therefore, that very little is known about the relationship between human biology and sexual offending behaviour, especially in juveniles. The role of biological factors has been implicated in several 'medical theories' of juvenile sex offending. Attempts to find a link between **genetic** (inherited) factors and criminal behaviour has a long history in psychiatry. Crime, including sexual offending, is more common among men. This has led to investigation into the biological differences between men and women, one of which is the 'Y' chromosome. This helps to determine male characteristics, including the presence of the male hormone, testosterone, in the male body. However, not all men sexually offend, even though they have the 'Y' chromosome. The presence of chromosomal abnormalities, especially an extra 'Y' chromosome (the 'supermale' syndrome), has also been linked to criminal and sexual offending behaviour, although the evidence is inconclusive (Day, 1993). There has also been speculation about the role of **physiological** factors. Specifically, that sex offenders suffer from some form of brain damage (neurological problems) or a hormonal imbalance (e.g. too much testosterone) that leads to an increase in aggressive and sexual behaviour. High levels of testosterone have been found in some men convicted of violent rape (Rada, Laws and Kellner, 1976). However, the relationship between testosterone and aggressive and sexual behaviour is extremely complex and poorly understood (Mazur, 1983). Some male adult sex offenders receive medical treatment to reduce their levels of sexual arousal, usually in the form of drug treatment (e.g. cyproterone acetate). Although there are reports of this being used with juvenile offenders, its benefits are unclear, and concern has been expressed about its effects on sexual and physical development.

The idea that sex offenders are **mentally ill** was also prevalent for many years. However, research in Britain and the United States is consistent in showing that very few juvenile sex offenders are mentally ill. The British study by Dolan *et al.* (1996) is especially significant because they looked at the psychosocial characteristics of 121 juvenile sex offenders referred to an adolescent forensic psychiatric service over a 7-year period. Whilst previous psychiatric contact was documented in 48 (39.6 per cent) of the cases, only one adolescent had a diagnosis of mental illness (obsessive-compulsive disorder). Conduct disorder or mixed emotional conduct disorder was the most common diagnosis (111), and only 10 were left undiagnosed. Similar findings were reported in another British study, by Richardson *et al.* (1995). They found that none of their sample of 100 sexually abusive adolescents had been previously or currently diagnosed as suffering from a major psychiatric illness, and there was no evidence to suggest that any were mentally disordered at the time they perpetrated their sexually abusive acts.

Although any one of these biological theories cannot offer a complete explanation, all behaviour has biological roots. It therefore seems reasonable to speculate that biological factors play an indirect role in some sexual offences. However, the nature of this role remains unclear. It may be that some males are more predisposed toward aggression or violence of any kind, lacking emotional understanding and the ability to empathise, associated with a tendency to impulsive behaviour. Some forms of sexual aggression may be a natural extension of this type of antisocial personality problem. Alternatively, some individuals may be predisposed to developing a sexual preference for specific stimuli that are different to the norm, such as violence or children (Quinsey *et al.*, 1993). Some rapists, for example, are sexually aroused to violence.

Psychodynamic theories

Freud trained as a neurologist, and his ideas about the workings of the human mind and personality development, and their influence on behaviour, are rooted in biological concepts. Behaviour is seen to be the result of inner drives and forces (especially 'sexual drive' and 'aggressive drive') which develop during early childhood and become 'fixed' around the age of 5 years. Consequently, Freud considered sexually deviant behaviour to be a perversion of 'character' or personality resulting from deep-seated intra-psychic conflicts that are largely unconscious and resistant to change (Freud, 1953). According to Freud, treatment requires the restructuring of personality, which can be achieved only through the long and arduous process of psychoanalysis (psychoanalytic therapy).

The writings of Freud had an enormous impact on psychiatry, psychology and social work. Although his ideas have since been developed and modified, leading to the establishment of alternative 'schools' of psychoanalytical theory and therapy, the idea that sexual deviancy is the result of an abnormal personality did little to advance the treatment of sex offenders and for many years they were often considered untreatable.

Nevertheless, it is important to draw a distinction between **psychoanalytical therapy** and **psychodynamic theory**. It is difficult to avoid the conclusion that there is an unconscious and that individuals are often not aware of the various influences on their behaviour. Psychodynamic theory can shed light on the nature and origin of these unconscious processes (see Hodges *et al.*, 1994). Childhood memories and experiences are stored away, and particularly distressing

emotional experiences may be partly shielded from awareness through the use of various psychological **'defence mechanisms'**. Everybody uses defence mechanisms to some extent. They become problematic, however, when they are used too often or to extreme levels, especially from an early age, thereby allowing deviant patterns of thought and behaviour to develop.

In some sex offenders there is clear evidence that defence mechanisms have contributed to the development of their unacceptable sexual behaviour. Defence mechanisms include denial ('I haven't got a problem'), projection ('I only did what most men really want to do'), rationalisation ('sex with children is allowed in some countries, it doesn't do any harm'), and displacement ('I had to get rid of my sexual urges somehow, after all I am a man'). These processes may be particularly pronounced in sex offenders who have been subject to traumatic experiences during childhood, such as sexual abuse, who may not be fully aware of the relationship between their own victimisation and their offending behaviour (see Lanyado *et al.*, 1995). Similarly, they may be more pronounced in juvenile offenders who are especially anxious about their sexual development and do not want to be considered as 'abnormal'. Although many sex offenders are unwilling to enter into an intensive therapeutic relationship to explore their behaviour, psychodynamic theory can nevertheless provide an insight into some types of sexual offences, especially where offending has a compulsive element and seems to be an expression of powerful psychological processes which have no clear origin.

Behavioural theories

In many ways, behavioural theory is the antithesis of psychodynamic theory. According to behavioural theory behaviour is determined largely by the influence of the external environment. From the moment of birth, behavioural responses, and patterns of thought and feeling, are learned through various learning processes. A complex range of processes help to determine what is learned. The most basic type of learning occurs when an organism makes a connection between two events in the external world, known as 'associative learning'. A simple type of associative learning, termed '**classical conditioning**', occurs when an organism (e.g. a human baby) notices that two **stimuli** go together (e.g. sight of breast or bottle and taste of milk). It has traditionally been assumed that classical conditioning sometimes occurs below the level of conscious thought, particularly the conditioning of simple physiological responses (e.g. salivation, muscle tension, release of stomach acid, penile erection). This view has been subject to criticism, on the grounds that various 'cognitive' (thinking) processes mediate between stimulus and response (Rescorla, 1988; Zinbarg, 1990).

One theory of sexual offending suggests that some sexual offences are the direct result of sexually deviant behaviours (e.g. sexual arousal to children) that have been classically conditioned through direct experience, and reinforced by fantasy and masturbation (McGuire, Carlisle and Young, 1965). There is certainly evidence that sexual arousal in men is subject to conditioning, and this may explain the development of sexual deviations such as 'fetish disorders' in which the individual can sustain sexual arousal (penile erection) only in the presence of particular non-sexual objects, for example a stiletto shoe. However, Marshall and Eccles (1993) note that deviant sexual behaviour and thinking often occurs in the absence of direct experience. They suggest that cognitive processes, such as imagery and fantasy, play a particularly significant role, allowing deviant sexual behaviour to be conditioned in the absence of direct experience. The dramatic increase in sexual arousal ('libido') during puberty may make adolescent boys especially sensitive to conditioning in this way. Deviant patterns of sexual behaviour and thinking that begin during this period may quickly become established due to the intensity of sexual activity and experience (e.g. fantasy, masturbation) during early adolescence. Once established, these patterns may become entrenched and difficult to change.

According to Marshall and Eccles (1993), some adolescent males, as a result of their developmental history, are particularly attracted to deviant, alternative, '**sexual scripts**' (i.e. recurrent fantasies, thoughts, images). These scripts are often based on themes of control and power and allow the young person to compensate for feelings of low self-esteem, poor social competence and associated psychological problems. Use of these sexual scripts, however, also increases the risk of engaging in sexually deviant behaviours and sexual offending.

Treatment programmes using classical conditioning techniques (e.g. orgasmic reconditioning) in isolation have not been particularly successful in changing patterns of sexual arousal, although they have been used successfully in conjunction with other intervention methods. Their use with juvenile sex offenders seems to be more limited. However, Becker and Kaplan (1993) describe a conditioning technique called 'verbal satiation' which they used successfully with a number of juveniles with a history of serious sexual offending.

A more complex type of associative learning is known as '**operant conditioning**'. This is especially important in understanding complex human behaviour, and is concerned with the way the external world (people, objects) **responds** to particular behaviours (behavioural consequences). Those behaviours that result in satisfying, pleasurable consequences are more likely to be repeated, a process termed '**reinforcement**'. In contrast, behaviours that lead to unpleasant consequences are less likely to occur again, and are considered to have been 'punished'. During the course of development complex patterns of behaviour, associated with particular thoughts and feelings, are established or 'shaped'. It is important to note that the terms reinforcement and punishment are defined according to the effect they have on behaviour. There may be inherent individual differences in the way people respond to the same consequences. For example, some people may be more sensitive to pain and therefore go to greater lengths to avoid this experience.

Although modern behavioural theory recognises the significance of thoughts and feelings, these are seen to be less influential than the effects of the external environment in shaping and determining behaviour. Thus, behavioural therapies place most emphasis on changing the external environment, especially the patterns of reinforcement and punishment. The term '**behaviour modification**' generally refers to treatment programmes which alter the environment around the individual. Thus, in a residential setting staff may be required to reward specific desirable behaviours and ignore other, undesirable, behaviours. This technique may be used where the individual is unwilling or unable to take an active role in personal change. More often, however, the individual being treated is directly involved in the treatment process and works with the therapist to achieve behavioural change through the process of **'behavioural therapy'**. For example, the therapist may help a juvenile sex offender to learn conversational skills to evoke a different, more rewarding, response from female peers and women. This skill may allow him to build personal and sexual relationships, and develop emotional understanding, thereby reducing the risk of further incidents of sexual aggression.

Social-cognitive theories

Social-cognitive theories have their roots in social learning theory, introduced by Rotter (1954) and developed by Bandura (1977, 1986). These theories have their roots in behavioural theory and, like behavioural theories, generally place most emphasis on behavioural interventions which alter the external environment. However, they attach much more significance to the role of **'cognitive processes'**. The term 'cognition' is often used synonymously with 'thought', although it actually refers to a wide range of mental structures, processes, and products, including perceptions, appraisals, beliefs, attitudes, memories, goals, standards and values, expectations, and attributions, in addition to current thoughts and self-statements (i.e. what individuals 'say to themselves'). Cognitive functioning is to some extent determined by inherent factors (e.g. temperament and intellectual ability) and past learning (e.g. encouragement for achieving goals).

Bandura developed an elaborate theory, based on experimental studies, in which he demonstrated that individuals learn not only through operant processes (i.e. through the effects of their behaviour) but also through observational learning. Indeed, much human learning, including sexual behaviour and attitudes, occurs through observation, from parents, siblings, peers, other adults, and the media (e.g. television, videos). Individuals who have been exposed to an 'abnormal' learning environment during childhood may develop a range of 'dysfunctional' (i.e. unhelpful)

behaviours and styles of thinking. For example, some juvenile sex offenders consider it perfectly acceptable to have sexual contact with siblings. Others are unable to control or manage their emotional states, or have not been encouraged to think about the consequences of their behaviour.

Bandura also recognised that various cognitive processes affect learning and behaviour. Individuals **'regulate'** their own behaviour by paying attention to some events more than others ('selective attention'), by setting goals and rewarding or punishing themselves. Individuals also differ in the extent to which they believe they can achieve certain goals (**'self-efficacy'**). An adolescent boy who believes that he will never have a girlfriend and achieve consensual sexual intercourse, for example, may be more at risk of finding alternative sources of sexual and emotional gratification, perhaps with a child or through the use of violence and aggression.

Social-emotional developmental theories

This area of theoretical development is poorly understood and has yet to be pulled together into a useful theoretical framework. It incorporates a number of different theories concerned with emotional development and the factors which affect the ability to form and maintain close interpersonal emotional attachments. Compared to psychological investigation into cognitive development, this area has been relatively neglected. In recent years Marshall and his colleagues have been pursuing this line of investigation in their research into adult male sex offenders, recognising that many male sex offenders find it difficult to form intimate relationships with women and often have little emotional understanding of others (Marshall, 1989; Marshall *et al.*, 1993). They suggest that treatment programmes need to pay more attention to helping offenders to develop appropriate intimate relationships.

It is generally accepted within psychology that human emotional development begins at birth and underpins later cognitive and social development. The emotional parts of the brain are separate from the parts concerned with thinking and other cognitive processes. As such, adverse factors, such as early separation from primary care-givers and failure to form at least one consistent and lasting emotional attachment to an adult, may have long-lasting consequences which detrimentally affect later learning and behaviour. The ideas expressed in attachment theories of sexual offending are similar to those enshrined in psychodynamic theories, although there is more emphasis on structuring theoretical proposals in a way which allows them to be investigated through empirical research.

Cognitive theories

Cognitive psychology as an academic discipline has flourished during the past twenty years. This expansion owes much to the development of **'cognitive therapy'**, based on the ideas of Beck (1976). He noticed that many of his depressed and anxious patients had 'errors of thinking' which helped to maintain their dysfunctional emotional state. In common with behavioural therapies, cognitive therapy is concerned with the 'here-and-now' and does not seek to delve too deeply into childhood experiences. It is based on the assumption that an individual's thought processes, beliefs, and styles of thinking ('cognitive schemes') have a direct influence on emotions (e.g. anger) and behaviour (e.g. aggression) and should therefore be a focus for intervention. Thus, in contrast to behaviour therapy, the focus in cognitive therapy is on altering habitual styles of thinking and belief systems, based on the assumption that changes in these 'covert' (internal) factors will lead to changes in overt behaviour. It is this issue, above all others, that causes conflict between radical behaviourists and cognitive therapists.

Although cognitive therapy techniques such as 'cognitive restructuring' and 'thought stopping' have been used with juvenile sex offenders, cognitive techniques tend to be combined with behavioural techniques to form a hybrid **'cognitive-behavioural'** (CBT) treatment programme. Kendall (1991) defines CBT as techniques that 'use enactive performance-based procedures as well as cognitive interventions to produce changes in thinking, feeling and behaviour' (p 5). The use of cognitive and behavioural techniques together combines the advantages of both theoretical models. Attention to cognitive variables is especially important in developing an understanding of sexual offending

behaviour from the perspective of the offender. One of the objectives of CBT assessment is to identify the meaning or **'function'** of the behaviour for the offender and the extent to which the behaviour is seen to be rewarding. This depth of understanding enables treatment programmes to be tailored to the needs of the individual offender. For example, some violent sex offenders gain pleasure (i.e. reinforcement) from inflicting pain and humiliation on their victims (sadistic offenders). In contrast, other violent sex offenders are convinced that the victim does not suffer (the result of cognitive distortions), but nevertheless gain satisfaction from other aspects of their sexual offending behaviour. They may be convinced that the victim somehow benefits from the experience, or that they have established some kind of meaningful relationship with the victim (see Canter, 1994).

Compared to other types of intervention CBT seems to be most effective in reducing rates of reoffending in groups of offenders (see Hollin, 1990; Lipsey, 1991, 1995; Losel, 1996). Most treatment programmes for sex offenders, both adult and juvenile, now utilise CBT techniques, focusing on three main areas of functioning: attitudinal and cognitive distortions (to modify unhelpful thoughts, attitudes, and beliefs), deviant sexuality (to reduce sexual arousal to deviant sexual acts or partners and to enhance or establish arousal to appropriate partners or acts), and social competency (to improve interpersonal behaviour and skills and to improve the ability to develop and maintain intimate relationships).

Trauma theories

The role of traumatic experiences in the development of dysfunctional behaviour and thinking in children has received increased attention during the past few years (Conte and Berliner, 1988; LeDoux, 1994; Pynoos and Nader, 1993; Yule, 1993). That severe trauma, such as sexual or physical abuse, or witnessing extreme violence (e.g. the murder of a parent), should have an effect on emotional and cognitive development and behaviour is not entirely surprising. It has recently been proposed that some types of severe trauma can permanently alter the neurochemistry of the brain, resulting in long-term psychological and behavioural consequences (Perry, 1994). Clinicians working with the victims and perpetrators of sexual abuse have also developed psychological models linking trauma and victimisation to sexual offending behaviour. Psychodynamic theory has proved particularly useful as a way of trying to understand the effects of trauma on the developing mind, especially in very early childhood (before age 5), when language and other cognitive processes are poorly developed.

It has been hypothesised that the sexual aggression of at least some juveniles and adults may be due in part to the recapitulation of their own sexual victimisation. Several mechanisms have been proposed to explain why some boys who have been sexually abused go on to repeat the abuse they suffered, a phenomenon termed the **'cycle-of-abuse'** (see Woods, 1997). These explanations include simple re-enactment of the abuse, through social-learning and modelling; that abusive acts are an attempt to achieve mastery over conflicts about sexuality resulting from negative sexual experiences; and that sexual arousal becomes conditioned to sexually abusive fantasies as a result of past abusive experiences which, in turn, lead to sexually abusive behaviour.

The **'traumagenic dynamics'** model developed by Finkelhor and colleagues (Finkelhor, 1984; Finkelhor and Browne, 1986) has been particularly useful in understanding the psychological effects of sexual abuse and their relationship to sexual offending behaviour. Within this model the consequences of sexual abuse are examined under four headings: traumatic sexualisation, powerlessness, betrayal, and stigmatisation. Of these, the notion of traumatic sexualisation has most relevance to understanding the progression from victim-to-abuser. This refers to the process in which abusive experiences are re-enacted cognitively (e.g. 'flashbacks') and behaviourally (e.g. engaging other children in sexual acts). Preoccupation with sexual behaviour, combined with a desire to gain control over distressing feelings of fear and helplessness, may lead the child to victimise other children, placing himself in the powerful abuser role rather than the helpless victim role ('identification with the aggressor').

However, whilst trauma clearly plays an important role in the development of sexual offending behaviour in some individuals, and requires sensitive, skilled treatment, it is unlikely to account for all sexual offending. Many sex offenders seem not to have experienced significant trauma and research is consistent in showing that many juvenile sex offenders have not been sexually abused. The role of physical abuse is particularly uncertain. Research has often failed to distinguish between the various degrees of physical maltreatment experienced by juvenile sex offenders. Thus, boys who have been severely and repeatedly beaten with objects, causing serious injury, are sometimes placed in the same category as those who have been smacked by a parent on one occasion.

Family theories

Most children are born into a family context or 'system' which immediately begins to exert an influence over development and behaviour. The effects of the various theoretical models outlined earlier are, to a greater or lesser extent, mediated through the family, particularly the parents. It is the parents who nurture, or hinder, physical, emotional, cognitive, and behavioural development (see Frude, 1991). There is overwhelming evidence that the family often plays a significant role in the development of criminal behaviour (Farrington, 1995, 1996). The extent to which this is true of sexual offending is unclear. The research and clinical literature on the relationship between family life and behaviour can be separated into several broad theoretical categories, including social learning models (e.g. parental modelling, patterns of social interaction, styles of discipline), structural models (e.g. composition of family, communication and boundaries between family members), and functional models (e.g. ability to provide care, protection and independence, and adapt to change).

Some family variables clearly have a direct influence on the development of sexual offending behaviour. Being sexually abused by family members, witnessing others being abused, or being exposed to pornography, for example. Other family factors, however, may have an indirect effect. For example, family breakdown leading to blurred family roles and boundaries, marital violence and physica[1] abuse, poor care and neglect, and lack of parental supervision. It is possible that different clusters of family factors are associated with different types of sexual offending. For example, the families of juvenile sex offenders whose offences occur within the family setting (e.g. incest) may be different in structure and functioning compared to those whose sexual offending takes place outside the family as part of a wider spectrum of antisocial, delinquent behaviour. It follows that family-focused treatment initiatives should be based on an assessment of family structure and functioning. Some families may benefit more from behavioural family therapy (e.g. behavioural contracting, parent-management training), whilst others may require some form of functional or systemic family therapy.

Sociological theories

Finally, several theories explore the effects of wider social and cultural factors on individual and family functioning and their relationship to sexual crime. Many of the social and economic factors that are the concern of criminological research, such as poverty, deprivation, and social inequality, probably influence the rate of sexual offending. Social changes that lead to a reduction in the overall level of antisocial, delinquent behaviour should also result in a decrease in sexual crime, especially sexual offending which is part of a wider pattern of antisocial, aggressive behaviour.

Several sociological theories, however, appear to have particular relevance to sexual offending, especially sexual violence toward women. **Feminist theory** has concerned itself with the role of women in society and the effect this has on the sexual and physical behaviour of men toward women (see Brownmiller, 1975). Several studies have demonstrated a relationship between sexual aggression in adult males and the endorsement of rape myths and negative, hostile attitudes toward women. However, there is also evidence that n̶ ̶ve and stereotypical attitudes toward ̶ ̶ are commonplace among men and ̶ ̶s and are not specific to sex ̶ ̶e role of anger, aggression and ̶ ̶d women is central to the ̶ ̶proposed by Groth and his ̶ ̶1979; Groth, Burgess and

Holstrom, 1977). According to this hypothesis rape is a 'pseudo-sexual' act dominated by either power needs or anger needs. Sex is viewed as a weapon and, not surprisingly, anger rapists not only use excessive force whilst perpetrating rape but are often physically assaultive toward women in other contexts. Unfortunately there has been scant research into the influence of feelings of power, control, dominance, and anger on juvenile sex offending. Interestingly, however, Van Ness (1984) found problems in controlling anger to be more than twice as common in a sample of incarcerated adolescent rapists than in a non-sex offender sample.

Research into sexual aggression among male college students by Koss and her colleagues has also implicated the role of **peers**. White and Koss (1993) suggested that there may be individual differences in attitudes, personality, motives for sex and domination, and opportunities for sexual aggression that explain why young men in similar circumstances differ in the likelihood of committing a sexually aggressive act. More recently, Schwartz and DeKeseredy (1997) proposed a male peer-support model to explain the high levels of sexual aggression on North American college campuses. They argue that the college campus provides fertile ground for young men who share 'rape-supportive' attitudes to congregate and to support and maintain sexually coercive behaviour toward women.

Lisak and colleagues (Lisak, 1991; Lisak and Roth, 1990) have suggested that a particularly unhelpful form of masculine identity, termed **'defensive masculinity'** (see Chodorow, 1978), may be exacerbated when the male does not experience an adequate relationship with his father. They suggest that the presence of a father figure eases the process of 'masculinisation' by supplying a vivid model of 'masculinity' for the son to follow. Without such a model, some boys may exaggerate what they perceive to be masculine attitudes and behaviours and reject characteristics they perceive to be 'feminine', including the experience and expression of important emotional states that are important in establishing intimate relationships. Father-absent adolescents are over-represented in sex offender and non-sex offender delinquent samples. There is also evidence that self-esteem in male adolescents and adults is especially closely linked to the development of sexual identity and sense of masculinity, and that some types of sexual identity may be less adaptive than others. Specifically, that an overly masculine sexual identity may be less suited to the formation and development of intimate relationships. As noted earlier, Marshall (1989) has suggested that failure to develop intimate relationships may have important aetiological significance for the development of sexual offending.

Some empirical support for the role of the father in the development of defensive masculinity comes from cross-cultural research into child-rearing practices. For example, Coltrane's (1988, 1992) analysis of 90 pre-industrial societies demonstrated a relationship between father-distant child rearing and relatively high levels of institutionalised misogyny and the dis-empowerment of women. Men were less prone to exaggerated masculine ('hypermasculine') behaviour and women were less likely to be socially disempowered in societies in which fathers participated more in child rearing. Similarly, Whiting (1965), in an analysis of six societies, suggested that father-distant child rearing is associated with 'protest masculinity' which, in turn, is associated with male-perpetrated interpersonal violence.

Further support for the 'gender-socialisation' theory of male sexual aggression comes from studies looking at masculine identity in sexually aggressive men. Several studies have found that they are more likely than non-aggressive men to have experienced negative relationships with their fathers. They also score higher on a variety of psychometric measures designed to assess for the presence of 'hostile masculinity', 'hypermasculinity', and 'gender role stress', and 'emotional disconnection'. In addition, several studies have found that sexually aggressive men also score lower on measures of femininity (e.g. Lisak and Roth, 1990).

In recent years there has been renewed interest in the role of the father in child development and delinquency (Johnson, 1987; Lamb, 1997; Phares, 1996), an area that has traditionally been neglected in the research literature. Interestingly, in their study of 100 British adolescent sex offenders, Richardson *et al.* (1995) found that 50 per cent had no contact

with a natural father and came from families where parents had separated with a history of parental violence toward the children.

Integrated theories
Four-factor model (Finkelhor, 1984)

Finkelhor's model was developed in relation to male adult sexual offending against children, although it has also had a significant impact on work with adolescent sex offenders. Finkelhor proposed that four conditions need to be met before a sexual offence can take place. The offender must: (1) be motivated to abuse sexually (e.g. be sexually aroused to children); (2) overcome his internal inhibitions (e.g. feelings of guilt); (3) overcome external inhibitions (e.g. parental protection); and (4) overcome victim resistance (e.g. use of bribes, threats, violence). Finkelhor recognised that each factor may be the result of independent processes, each requiring an explanation. Thus, the model does not explain why some men develop a sexual interest in children, or why some men have less self-control over their sexual behaviour. Nevertheless, the model provides a useful framework for managing and treating sexual offenders, and suggests areas that warrant further research and investigation.

Offender cycle model (Wolf, 1985)

The basic assumption underlying Wolf's model is that sexual offending is a behaviour that is deeply rooted in the thinking and fantasy of the offender which, over time and through experience, becomes 'compulsive' in nature. According to Wolf, early experiences combined with certain personality features (which he termed 'potentiators') predispose some individuals to developing deviant sexual interests. The model proposes that offence-related thinking and behaviour become closely inter-related until they form a regular, predictable sequence or 'cycle' of events, which underpin offending behaviour. Before an offence the offender progresses through the sequence, each step taking him closer to the point at which he actually commits the offence. Offenders develop an individualised cycle which must be explored in treatment. However, Wolf proposed that particular themes are common to most cycles, beginning with negative self-image and progressing through feelings of rejection (distorted thinking); social withdrawal (inappropriate behaviour); escapist, 'compensatory', sexually deviant fantasies which allow the offender to achieve a sense of control; offence planning in which the offender begins to move from fantasy to reality (e.g. 'grooming' potential victims); sexual offending behaviour; feelings of guilt, shame and anxiety which follow the behaviour; and unsuccessful attempts to alleviate guilt and anxiety through various type of distorted thinking ('defence mechanisms') which bring him back to the beginning of the cycle, in which his feelings of guilt and 'failure' only serve to further undermine his self-esteem and the illusion of being in control. The cycle then repeats itself.

Wolf's model has a simplistic appeal, providing a neat summary of several independent social, behavioural and psychological processes. Like Finkelhor's model, it also has direct implications for the management and treatment of the sex offender. It has had an enormous influence on practice in this area, sitting comfortably within the cognitive-behavioural framework that informs most sex-offender treatment programmes (see Lane and Zamora, 1985). However, despite its practical applications, Wolf's model has been subject to surprisingly little empirical research. On the one hand this is understandable: the model summarises a variety of complex psychological and behavioural processes which, as seen earlier in this chapter, are poorly understood. On the other hand, however, there are inherent risks associated with the use of a model which has not been more fully investigated. Of particular concern is the assumption that all sex offenders have an offence cycle which must be explored in treatment. This belief can result in an aggressive, confrontational approach to treatment in an attempt to reveal the cycle. It is possible that some offenders do not have a well-developed cycle, especially 'situational offenders' whose offending is of recent origin or part of a wider spectrum of anti-social behaviour.

Young Abusers Project (YAP) integrated perspectives model

Hawkes et al. (1997) describe a clinical model which they employ in their work with male

adolescent abusers who sexually offend against children. The abusers seen at the YAP seem to be a particularly traumatised group of young people, with high levels (91 per cent) of sexual, physical and emotional abuse. In common with other integrated theoretical models, the YAP approach combines a variety of single theories (reviewed earlier in the present chapter) into a framework that can be used to inform assessment and treatment. Hawkes et al. place the various theories into five 'levels of explanation':

1. Individual (medical, psychodynamic, trauma, behavioural, cognitive)

2. Family based

3. Peer group

4. Formal societal structure (feminist, attitudes to sexual behaviour, cultural)

5. Wider perspectives (pornography, media).

The damaging effects of trauma on child development is central to the model, with each 'level' of explanation offering a different perspective on the long-term consequences and its relationship to sexual offending. Whilst the model provides a useful framework for clinical assessment, it does not suggest specific treatment or research strategies.

Developmental vulnerability models

Becker and Kaplan (1988) suggested three potential pathways a juvenile sex offender may take after having engaged in inappropriate sexual behaviour: the 'dead-end path', where he no longer commits any further sexual offences; the 'delinquency path', where he continues to commit sexual as well as non-sexual offences; and the 'sexual interest path', where the adolescent continues to commit sex crimes and often develops a paraphilic (sexually deviant) arousal pattern. Although these developmental pathways have not been empirically validated, it seems likely that each may be associated with different clusters of developmental and psychological problems which may be related to types of sexual offence. The vulnerability model of juvenile sexual offending, in which deviant 'sexual scripts' appeal to some adolescent males (Marshall and Eccles, 1993), has been described earlier in this chapter. Williams and New (1996) formulated a similar multi-factorial developmental model, based on their research investigating potential risk factors associated with sexual offending. The **'developmental vulnerability hypothesis'** certainly provides a useful starting point, prompting a variety of questions that need to be addressed through empirical research. For example, which developmental factors increase vulnerability and why? How do the various risk factors interact with each other? Are different risk factors associated with different types of sexual offence? To what extent can risk factors be alleviated through preventative intervention? The research required to provide answers to these questions, especially the use of longitudinal studies, is extraordinarily complex and expensive.

Conclusions

In common with many other areas of applied social and psychological practice, the development of theory has lagged behind practice. To some extent this is inevitable: practitioners cannot always wait for advances in understanding. There are particularly strong moral and ethical arguments supporting the treatment of sex offenders in an effort to protect the potential victims of sexual offending. The work of practitioners has also been instrumental in focusing public and academic attention on the problem of sexual offending, and has contributed enormously to theoretical developments in this area.

However, it seems that a watershed has now been reached. The rapid expansion in programme development has given rise to a period of reflection and a search for theories to guide future practice. There is now a general consensus that juvenile (and adult) sexual offending has multiple determinants and seems to involve a combination of factors, some of which predispose an individual to sexually deviant, aggressive behaviour, and others that trigger the behaviour in specific situations. Further, there seem to be different 'types' of sexual offender, each associated with different clusters of individual, family and social characteristics. There is unlikely ever to be a single theory, which can satisfactorily account for all juvenile sexual offences. Rather, different theories may be needed for the various types of offender, which together

recognise the complexity of sexual offending behaviour. Empirical, data-driven research is essential to the development of theory and practice in this field of work. Particular priority should be given to research looking at the most useful way to classify and categorise the various types of juvenile sex offender and to the search for developmental variables that increase vulnerability to specific types of sexual offending.

One theme that is consistent throughout the theoretical literature on juvenile sexual offending is that of **learning**. Some learning experiences seem to enhance vulnerability to the acquisition of sexually deviant, aggressive, or abusive behaviours. All the theoretical models described in this chapter are ultimately concerned with learning and the factors which either hinder or enhance the learning of appropriate, responsible sexual behaviour and self-control. Intellectual limitations; temperamental difficulties; behavioural and conduct problems; psychological defense mechanisms; dysfunctional thought processes; rigid belief systems; psychological trauma arising from abuse; peer pressure; poor parenting; exposure to inappropriate experiences, often supported by the ideas and images conveyed in the media and in social, cultural and political structures, all serve to distort or hinder learning. These factors also serve as obstacles to personal change. Regardless of theoretical persuasion, the purpose of treatment is to help the offender to learn new ways to think and behave in an effort to reduce the risk of re-offending. Personal change, however, is never easy, especially when the behaviour is underpinned by deeply entrenched attitudes, beliefs, thought processes, and fantasies that are common-place in society. The roots of the problem do not lie entirely within the offender or within the family. It is therefore unrealistic to expect treatment programmes alone to provide the solution to this complex social problem. A great deal more attention should be devoted to identifying and changing the social and cultural factors that support and perpetuate the development of sexual offending behaviour in children and young people.

References

Abel, G.G., Osborn, C.A., and Twigg, D.A. (1993). Sexual Assault Through the Life Span: Adult Offenders with Juvenile Histories. In Barbaree, H.E., Marshall, W.L., and Hudson, S.M. (Eds.). *The Juvenile Sex Offender*. London: Guilford Press.

Ageton, S.S. (1983). *Sexual Assault Among Adolescents*. Lexington MA: Lexington Books.

American Psychiatric Association (1994). *Diagnostic and Statistical Manual of Mental Disorders*. Fourth edition (revised) (DSM-IV). Washington DC: American Psychiatric Association.

Atcheson, J.D., and Williams, D.C. (1954). A Study of Juvenile Sex Offenders. *American Journal of Psychiatry*, 111: 366–370.

Awad, G.A., and Saunders, E.B. (1989). Adolescent Child Molesters: Clinical Observations. *Child Psychiatry and Human Development*, 19: 195–206.

Awad, G.A., and Saunders, E.B. (1991). Male Adolescent Sexual Assaulters: Clinical Observations. *Journal of Interpersonal Violence*, 6: 446–460.

Bala, N., and Schwartz, I. (1993). Legal Responses to the Juvenile Sex Offender. In Barbaree, H.E., Marshall, W.L., and Hudson, S.M. (Eds.). *The Juvenile Sex Offender*. London: Guilford Press.

Bandura, A. (1977). *Social Learning Theory*. Englewood Cliffs, NJ: Prentice-Hall.

Bandura, A. (1986). *Social Foundations of Thought and Action: A Social-cognitive Theory*. Englewood Cliffs, NJ: Prentice-Hall.

Barbaree, H.E., Marshall, W.L., and Hudson, S.M. (Eds.) (1993). *The Juvenile Sex Offender*. London: Guilford Press.

Beck, A.T. (1976). *Cognitive Therapy and the Emotional Disorders*. New York: University of Pennsylvania Press.

Becker, J.V. (1988). Adolescent Sex Offenders. *Behaviour Therapist*, 11: 185–187.

Becker, J.V., Johnson, B.R., and Hunter, J.A. (1996). Adolescent Sex Offenders. In Hollin, C.R., and Howells, K. (Eds.). *Clinical Approaches to Working with Young Offenders*. Chichester: Wiley.

Becker, J.V., and Kaplan, M. (1988). The Assessment of Adolescent Sex Offenders. *Advances in Behavioural Assessment of Children and Families*, 4: 97–118.

Becker, J.V., and Kaplan, M. (1993). Cognitive Behavioural Treatment of the Juvenile Sex Offender. In Barbaree, H.E., Marshall, W.L. and Hudson, S.M. (Eds.). *The Juvenile Sex Offender*. London: Guilford Press.

Brownmiller, S. (1975). *Against Our Will: Men, Women and Rape*. New York: Simon and Schuster.

Burkhart, B., and Bohmer, C. (1990). Hidden Rape and the Legal Crucible: Analysis and Implications of Epidemiological, Social, and Legal Factors. *The Expert Witness, the Trial Lawyer, the Trial Judge*, 5: 3–6.

Canter, D. (1994). *Criminal Shadows: Inside the Mind of the Serial Killer*. London: Harper Collins.

Chodorow, N. (1978). *The Reproduction of Mothering*. Berkeley: University of California Press.

Coltrane, S. (1988). Father-child Relationships and the Status of Women: A Cross-cultural Study. *American Journal of Sociology*, 93: 1060–1095.

Coltrane, S. (1992). The Micropolitics of Gender in Non-industrial Societies. *Gender and Society*, 6: 86–107.

Conte, J.R., and Berliner, L. (1988). The Impact of Sexual Abuse on Children: Clinical Findings. In Walker, L. (Ed.). *Handbook on Sexual Abuse of Children: Assessment and Treatment Issues*. New York: Springer.

Day, K. (1993). Crime and Mental Retardation: A Review. In Howells, K., and Hollin, C.R. (Eds.). *Clinical Approaches to the Mentally Disordered Offender*. Chichester: Wiley.

Dolan, M., Holloway, J., Bailey, S., and Kroll, L. (1996). The Psychosocial Characteristics of Juvenile Sexual Offenders Referred to an Adolescent Forensic Service in the UK. *Medicine, Science and the Law*, 36: 343–352.

Epps, K.J. (1996a). Sex Offenders. In Hollin, C.R. (Ed.). *Working with Offenders: Psychological Practice in Offender Rehabilitation*. Chichester: Wiley.

Epps, K.J. (1996b). Sexually Abusive Behaviour in an Adolescent Boy with the 48, XXYY Syndrome: A Case Study. *Criminal Behaviour and Mental Health*, 6: 17–26.

Farrington, D.P. (1995). The Development of Offending and Antisocial Behaviour from Childhood: Key Findings from the Cambridge Study in Delinquent Development. *Journal of Child Psychology and Psychiatry*, 36: 929–964.

Farrington, D.P. (1996). Individual, Family and Peer Factors in the Development of Delinquency. In Hollin, C.R. and Howells, K. (Eds.). *Clinical Approaches to Working with Young Offenders*. Chichester: Wiley.

Fehrenbach, P.A., Smith, W., Monastersky, C., and Deisher, R.W. (1986). Adolescent Sexual Offenders: Offender and Offence Characteristics. *American Journal of Orthopsychiatry*, 56: 225–233.

Finkelhor, D. (1984). Four Preconditions: A Model. In Finkelhor, D. (Ed.). *Child Sexual Abuse: New Theory and Research*. New York: Free Press.

Finkelhor, D., and Browne, A. (1986). Sexual Abuse: Initial and Long-term Effects: A Conceptual Framework. In Finkelhor, D. (Ed.). *A Sourcebook on Child Sexual Abuse*. Beverly Hills, CA: Sage.

Fisher, D. (1994). Adult Sex Offenders: Who are They? Why and How do They do it? In Morrison, T., Erooga, M., and Beckett, R.C. (Eds.). *Sexual Offending Against Children: Assessment and Treatment of Male Abusers*. London: Routledge.

Freud, S. (1953). Three Essays on the Theory of Sexuality. In *The Complete Psychological Works of Sigmund Freud* (vol. 7). London: Hogarth Press.

Frude, N. (1991). *Understanding Family Problems: A Psychological Approach*. Chichester: Wiley.

Groth, A.N. (1977). The Adolescent Sexual Offender and his Prey. *Journal of Offender Therapy and Comparative Criminology*, 21: 249–254.

Groth, A.N. (1979). *Men Who Rape: The Psychology of the Offender*. New York: Plenum Press.

Groth, A.N., Burgess, A.W., and Holstrom, L.L. (1977). Rape: Power, Anger and Sexuality. *American Journal of Psychiatry*, 134: 1239–1243.

Groth, A.N., Hobson, W.F., and Gary, T.S. (1982). The Child Molester: Clinical Observations. In Conte J., and Shore, D.A. (Eds.). *Social Work and Child Sexual Abuse*. New York: Haworth.

Hawkes, C., Jenkins, J.A., and Vizard, E. (1997). Roots of Sexual Violence in Children and Adolescents. In Varma, V.P. (Ed.). *Violence in Children and Adolescents*. London: Jessica Kingsley.

Hodges, J., Lanyado, M., and Andreou, C. (1994). Sexuality and Violence: Preliminary Clinical Hypotheses from Psychotherapeutic Assessments in a Research Programme on Young Sexual Offenders. *Journal of Child Psychotherapy*, 20: 283–308.

Hoghughi, M., and Richardson, G. (1997). Theories of Adolescent Sexual Abuse. In Hoghughi, M.S., Bhate, R., and Graham, F. (Eds.). *Working with Sexually Abusive Adolescents*. London: Sage.

Hollin, C.R. (1990). *Cognitive-behavioural Interventions with Young Offenders*. Oxford: Pergamon Press.

Hollin, C.R. (1992). *Criminal Behaviour: A Psychological Approach to Explanation and Prevention*. London: Falmer Press.

James, A.C., and Neil, P. (1996). Juvenile Sexual Offending: One-year Period Prevalence Study within Oxfordshire. *Child Abuse and Neglect*, 20: 477–485.

Johnson, R.E. (1987). Mother's Versus Father's Role in Causing Delinquency. *Adolescence*, 22: 305–315.

Kendall, P.C. (1991). Guiding Theory for Therapy with Children and Adolescents. In Kendall, P.C. (Ed.). *Child and Adolescent Therapy: Cognitive-behavioural Procedures*. London: Guilford Press.

Knight, R.A., and Prentky, R.A. (1993). Exploring Characteristics for Classifying Juvenile Sex Offenders. In Barbaree, H.E. Marshall, W.L., and Hudson, S.M. (Eds.). *The Juvenile Sex Offender*. London: Guilford Press.

Knight, R., Rosenberg, R., and Schneider, B. (1985). Classification of Sexual Offenders: Perspectives, Methods and Validation. In Burgess, A. (Ed.). *Rape and Sexual Assault: A Research Handbook*. New York: Garland.

Knopp, F.H. (1982). *Remedial Intervention in Adolescent Sex Offenses: Nine Program Descriptions*. Orwell, Vermont: Safer Society Press.

Koss, M.P. (1988). Hidden Rape: Sexual Aggression and Victimization in a National Sample in Higher Education. In Burgess, A.W. (Ed.), *Rape and Sexual Assault*, (Vol. 2). New York: Garland.

Koss, M.P., and Dinero, T.E. (1988). Predictors of Sexual Aggression Among a National Sample of Male College Students. In Prentky, R.A. and Quinsey, V.L. (Eds.). *Human Sexual Aggression: Current Perspectives*. New York: New York Academy of Sciences.

Koss, M.P., Dinero, T.E., Siebel, C.A., and Cox, S.L. (1988). Stranger and Acquaintance Rape: Are There Differences in the Victim's Experience? *Psychology of Women Quarterly*, 12: 1–24.

Koss, M.P., and Leonard, K.E. (1984). Sexually Aggressive Men: Empirical Findings and Theoretical Implications. In Malamuth, N. and Donnerstein, E. (Eds.). *Pornography and Sexual Aggression*. New York: Academic Press.

Lamb, M.E. (Ed.), (1997). *The Role of the Father in Child Development*. Chichester: Wiley.

Lane, S., and Zamora, P.A. (1985). A Method for Treating the Adolescent Sex Offender. In Mathias, R.A., Demuro, P., and Allinson, R. (Eds.). *Sourcebook for Treatment of the Violent Juvenile Offender*. San Francisco: National Council on Crime and Delinquency.

Lanyado, M., Hodges, J., Bentovim, A., Andreou, C., and Williams, B. (1995). Understanding Boys who Sexually Abuse Other Children: A Clinical Illustration. *Psychoanalytic Psychotherapy*, 9: 231–242.

Lanyon, R.I. (1991). Theories of Sex Offending. In Hollin, C.R., and Howells, K. (Eds.). *Clinical Approaches to Sex Offenders and their Victims*. Chichester: Wiley.

LeDoux, J.E. (1994). Emotion, Memory and the Brain. *Scientific American*, June: 50–57.

Lipsey, M.W. (1991). Juvenile Delinquency Treatment: A Meta-analytic Inquiry into the Variability of Effects. In Wachter, K.W., and Straf, M.L. (Eds.). *Meta-analysis for Explanation: A Casebook*. New York: Russell Sage Foundation.

Lipsey, M.W. (1995). What do we Learn from 400 Research Studies on the Effectiveness of Treatment with Juvenile Delinquents? In McGuire, J. (Ed.). *What Works: Reducing Reoffending: Guidelines from Research and Practice*. Chichester: Wiley.

Lisak, D. (1991). Sexual Aggression, Masculinity and Fathers. *Signs. Journal of Women in Culture and Society*, 16: 238–262.

Lisak, D., and Roth, S. (1990). Motives and Psychodynamics of Self-reported, Unincarcerated Rapists. *American Journal of Orthopsychiatry*, 60: 268–280.

Losel, F. (1996). Working with Young Offenders: The Impact of Meta-analysis. In Hollin, C.R., and Howells, K. (Eds.). *Clinical Approaches to Working with Young Offenders*. Chichester: Wiley.

Malamuth, N. (1984). Aggression Against Women: Cultural and Individual Causes. In Malamuth, N.M., and Donnerstein, E. (Eds.). *Pornography and Sexual Aggression*. San Diego: Academic Press.

Markley, O.B. (1950). A Study of Aggressive Sex Misbehaviour in Adolescents Brought to Juvenile Court. *American Journal of Orthopsychiatry*, 20: 719–731.

Marshall, W.L. (1989). Intimacy, Loneliness and Sexual Offenders. *Behaviour Research and Therapy*, 27: 491–503.

Marshall, W.L., and Barbaree, H.E. (1989). Sexual Violence. In Howells, K., and Hollin C.R. (Eds.). *Clinical Approaches to Violence*. Chichester: Wiley.

Marshall, W.L., and Eccles, A. (1993). Pavlovian Conditioning Processes in Adolescent Sex

Offenders. In Barbaree, H.E., Marshall, W.L., and Hudson S.M. (Eds.). *The Juvenile Sex Offender*. London: Guilford Press.

Marshall, W.L., Hudson, S.M., and Hodkinson, S. (1993). The Importance of Attachment Bonds in the Development of Juvenile Sexual Offending. In Barbaree, H.E., Marshall, W.L., and Hudson S.M. (Eds.). *The Juvenile Sex Offender*. London: Guilford Press.

Marshall, W.L., Hudson, S.M., and Ward, T. (1992). Sexual Deviance. In Wilson, P.H. (Ed.). *Principles and Practice of Relapse Prevention*. London: Guilford Press.

Mazur, (1983). Physiology, Dominance, and Aggression in Humans. In Goldstein, A.P. (Ed.). *Prevention and Control of Aggression*. New York: Pergamon.

McGuire, R.J., Carlisle, J.M., and Young, B.G. (1965). Sexual Deviations as Conditioned Behaviour: A Hypothesis. *Behaviour Research and Therapy*, 2: 185–190.

Mohr, J.W., Turner, R.E., and Jerry, M.B. (1964). *Pedophilia and Exhibitionism: A Handbook*. Toronto: University of Toronto Press.

Moore, S., and Rosenthal, D. (1993). *Sexuality in Adolescence*. London: Routledge.

Muehlenhard, C.L., and Linton, M.A. (1987). Date Rape and Sexual Aggression in Dating Situations: Incidence and Risk Factors. *Journal of Counselling Psychology*, 34: 186–196.

O'Brien, M.J., and Bera, W. (1986). Adolescent Sexual Offenders: A Descriptive Typology. *A Newsletter of the National Family Life Education Network*, 1: 1–5.

Perry, B.D. (1994). Neurobiological Sequelae of Childhood Trauma: PTSD in Children. In Murray, M. (Ed.). *Catecholamines in Post-traumatic Stress Disorder: Emerging Concepts*. Washington DC: American Psychiatric Press.

Phares, V. (1996). *Fathers and Developmental Psychopathology*. Chichester: Wiley.

Pynoos, R.S., and Nader, K. (1993). Issues in the Treatment of Post-traumatic Stress in Children and Adolescents. In Wilson, J.P., and Raphael, B. (Eds.). *International Handbook of Traumatic Stress Syndromes*. New York: Plenum Press.

Quinsey, V.L., Rice, M.E., Harris, G.T., and Reid, K.S. (1993). The Phylogenetic and Ontogenetic Development of Sexual Age Preferences in Males: Conceptual and Measurement Issues. In Barbaree, H.E., Marshall, W.L., and Hudson, S.M. (Eds.). *The Juvenile Sex Offender*. London: Guilford Press.

Rada, R.T., Laws, D.R., and Kellner, R. (1976). Plasma Testosterone Levels in the Rapist. *Psychosomatic Medicine*, 38: 257–268.

Rescorla, R. (1988). Pavlovian Conditioning: It's not What you Think it is. *American Psychologist*, 43: 151–160.

Richardson, G., Graham, F., Bhate, S.R., and Kelly, T.P. (1995). A British Sample of Sexually Abusive Adolescents: Abuser and Abuse Characteristics. *Criminal Behaviour and Mental Health*, 5: 187–208.

Rotter, J.B. (1954). *Social Learning and Clinical Psychology*. Englewood Cliffs, NJ: Prentice-Hall.

Russell, D.E.H. (1984). *Sexual Exploitation: Rape, Child Sexual Abuse, and Workplace Harassment*. Beverly Hills, CA: Sage.

Ryan, G. (1991). Historical Response to Juvenile Sexual Offences. In Ryan, G.D., and Lane, S.L. (Eds.). *Juvenile Sexual Offending: Causes, Consequences and Correction*. Massachusetts: Lexington Books.

Schwartz, M.D., and DeKeseredy, W.S. (1997). *Sexual Assault on the College Campus: The Role of Male Peer Support*. London: Sage.

Van Ness, S.R. (1984). Rape as Instrumental Violence: A Study of Youth Offenders. *Journal of Offender Counselling, Services, and Rehabilitation*, 9: 161–170.

Vinogradov, S., Dishotsky, N.I., Doty, A.K., and Tinklenberg, J.R. (1988). Patterns of Behaviour in Adolescent Rape. *American Journal of Orthopsychiatry*, 58: 179–187.

Vizard, E., Monck, E., and Misch, P. (1995). Child and Adolescent Sex Abuse Perpetrators: A Review of the Research Literature. *Journal of Child Psychology and Psychiatry*, 36: 731–756.

Vizard, E., Wynick, S., Hawkes, C., Woods, J., and Jenkins, J. (1996). Juvenile Sex Offenders: Assessment Issues. *British Journal of Psychiatry*, 165: 259–262.

Wasserman, J., and Kappel, S. (1985). *Adolescent Sex Offenders in Vermont*. Burlington: Vermont Department of Health.

Weis, K., and Borges, S.S. (1973). Victimology and Rape: The Case of the Legitimate Victim. *Issues in Criminology*, 8: 71–115.

White, J.W., and Koss, M.P. (1993). Adolescent Sexual Aggression within Heterosexual Relationships: Prevalence, Characteristics and Causes. In Barbaree, H.E. Marshall, W.L., and Hudson, S.M. (Eds.). *The Juvenile Sex Offender*. London: Guilford Press.

Whiting, B. (1965). Sex Identity Conflict and Physical Violence: A Comparative Study. *American Anthropologist*, 67:, 123–140.

Williams, B., and New, M. (1996). Developmental Perspectives on Adolescent Boys who Sexually Abuse other Children. *Child Psychology and Psychiatry Review*, 1: 122–129.

Wolf, S.C. (1985). A Mutli-factor Model of Deviant Sexuality. *Victimology: An International Journal*, 10: 359–374

Woods, J. (1997). Breaking the Cycle of Abuse and Abusing: Individual Psychotherapy for Juvenile Sex Offenders. *Clinical Child Psychology and Psychiatry*, 2:, 379–392.

World Health Organization. (1992). *The ICD-10 Classification of Mental and Behaviour Disorders, Clinical Descriptions and Diagnostic Guidelines*. Geneva: WHO.

Yule, W. (1993). Children as Victims and Survivors. In Taylor, P.J. (Ed.). *Violence in Society*. London: Royal College of Physicians.

Zinbarg, R.E. (1990). Animal Research and Behaviour Therapy: Part 1. Behaviour Therapy is not What you Think it is. *Behaviour Therapist*, 13: 171–175.

Chapter Two

The Case for Paraphilic Personality Disorder:

Detection, Diagnosis and Treatment

Frank J. MacHovec Ph.D.

The Case for Paraphilic Personality Disorder: Detection, Diagnosis and Treatment

Introduction

Sex is a basic and universal drive, a major part of human development and social-interpersonal relations. It has been so across history. However, when sexual behaviour significantly deviates from societal and legal norms, offenders find themselves along two paths: first, in the hands of law enforcement, court, and corrections, and second, in rehabilitative psychotherapy. The question for both courts and therapists is when sexual behaviour passes beyond 'normal' to 'abnormal' and/or 'criminal,' when sex is no longer *agreed* but *a greed* of the offender and clearly excessive. While violent sex crimes leave no doubt as to their criminality, consensual though technically unlawful sexual behaviour and that of minors are often more difficult to assess. Courts and mental health professionals are asked to identify, diagnose, then correct deviant or criminal sexual behaviour.

The concept of a paraphilic personality disorder would meet these needs and also satisfy current diagnostic criteria for personality disorder (ICD-10, 1992; DSM-IV, 1994). Using this model would simplify and expedite communication among those involved when sexual behaviour becomes a public problem — when police, courts, corrections, therapists, clergy, teachers, and news media are involved. It would also improve early detection, clarify diagnostic criteria, and better facilitate meaningful treatment planning and parole-probation guidelines.

The concept of a paraphilic personality disorder is consistent and compatible with earlier and current clinical and research data. It applies to all long-term patterns of deviant or excessive sexual behaviour, by male or female offenders, juvenile or adult. Existing sex offender typologies do not take into account the versatility of sex offending, that a voyeur, fetishist, or exhibitionist can become a rapist or child molester. A sex offender personality disorder encompasses all sexual acting out as well as its progressive development such as from fantasy to passive acting out (e.g. voyeurism, fetishism) to overt inappropriate behaviour, on a continuum of seriousness, and preconceived notions (e.g. women are sex objects) into false beliefs (cognitive distortion).

Clinical literature has moved slowly from anecdotal reports of specific sexual deviance and crime to various typologies for specific sex offences. Groth (1979) described three rapist and two child molester types. Lanning (1986) described four rapist and four molester types. Knight and Prentky (1990) described ten types of child molesters and nine types of rapists. Mathews, Mulhern, and Speltz (1989) described four types of female sex offenders. Carnes (1983, 1989) described sex addicts, those with a seemingly uncontrollable compulsion to act out sexually. As the types of sex offenders grew there was increasing awareness that deviant sexual behaviour is far more complex than has been assumed (MacHovec, 1993a; Youngstrom, 1992). Typologies specific for one type of sex offence have expanded but do not include crossover across several types of offences (Knight and Prentky, 1990). Offender psychodynamics can be highly individualised, more complex than typologies suggest, and current diagnostic criteria for paraphilics are incomplete (ICD-10, 1992; DSM-IV, 1994).

Personality disorder is defined as 'an enduring pattern of inner experience and behaviour that deviates markedly from the expectations of the individual's culture' (DSM-IV, 1994, p 629). Clinical case studies and court reports support the hypothesis that using and abusing others sexually can become an enduring pattern and a significant deviation from socio-cultural norms. While personality disorders fall in the mainstream of adult mental disorders, antecedents are evident in childhood and adolescence, especially with overt sexual behaviour (ibid, 632). Court and therapy records confirm an early onset of a pattern of sex offending.

There are three kinds of psychopathy. It is interesting to note that all three contain sexual pathology:

1. sexual psychopath, with predominantly sexual symptoms with some degree of ego disorder

2. benign psychopath, incapacity to conform to societal sexual standards

3. antisocial psychopathy, where there is delinquency and criminality.

Cleckley (1941) continued to develop the concept of psychopathy as a separate entity and a psychosis with distinguishing features of absence of affect, reframing the world by acting out so the environment not she or he suffers, and chronic externalisation of blame (Hinsie and Campbell, 1973). Millon (1981) observed that personality disorders have historically been 'tangential' and 'diagnostically never achieved significant recognition.' Becoming 'central to the diagnostic schema' by achieving Axis II status in the DSM-III (1980) was according to Millon a 'significant breakthrough.' Until then they were 'a melange of miscellaneous and essentially secondary syndromes.' Millon defines personality disorders as an 'enduring pattern' of 'pervasive features.' It is a lifelong style of relating, coping, behaving, thinking, and feeling, all that is personality, and these traits and features enable therapists to 'see into more florid and distinct psychopathology' (Millon, 1981, p 3).

Psychopaths can be differentiated from paraphilics by the scope, frequency, and depth of their behaviours. Not all psychopaths exhibit inappropriate sexual behaviour and when they do it is often to vent their power-dominance need or narcissism. For paraphilics sexuality is a major driving force manifested in a pattern of inappropriate or unlawful acts exclusively or predominantly sexual. Extremes of inappropriate sexual acting can combine psychopathy and paraphilia and are then sexopathic.

Evidence of psychopathic tendencies in childhood are inability to establish and maintain close relationships, fire setting, teasing or torturing animals, and disregard for the rights of others (Hare, 1987; Meloy, 1988). Inappropriate sexuality in paraphilic personality disorder is usually of early onset. It can be learned and conditioned by the offender's own victimisation, most frequently as a victim of child sexual abuse. It is very much a historical disorder, rooted in the past, with both acute and chronic features. Deviant or bizarre erotic fantasy contribute to sexual acting out, often progressing from passive to active sexual acting out. When repeated and reinforced it can escalate into rape, incest, or molestation. The offender's own victimisation, real, feared, fantasised, or perceived as real by an inept therapist, can intensify the eroticisation of otherwise normal cognition and affect.

A paraphilic pathology loop can develop in childhood. From deviant fantasy, a love object is imagined, leading to unrealistic expectations and cognitive distortion. This is a distinguishing feature of paraphilia. Fantasies acted out with inappropriate sexual behaviour, if untreated, are reinforced and embedded in the personality more deeply over time. Societal norms and values fade, yielding to the individual's own deviant belief system. This leads to inappropriate or eccentric behaviour and can deteriorate further into depression, delusion, dissociation, or bizarre sex crimes. The denial and minimisation typical of confronted or challenged paraphilics is a defence of what has become a basic belief and value system. Others *are* sex objects and abusing them is *normal* according to paraphilic logic. This belief system is well fortified, defies reason and reality, and is a classic example of Festinger's cognitive dissonance theory (1957).

The length of treatment for sex offenders is typical of other established personality disorders: long-term and tedious. Most daily residential treatment programs for youthful sex offenders take at least a year. If untreated, paraphilics commit a variety of offences. This increases the difficulty in treating them because the sex drive, already deviant, can generalise into other sexual and non-sexual offences. It is like treating only one habituated behaviour without addressing the root cause, such as stopping smoking, then overeating or drinking excessively. The use or threat of force, physical or psychological, is a frequent concomitant to paraphilic personality disorder. The benchmark for differentiating normal from pathological is 'the reasonable person rule' of Common Law, that a reasonable person would consider coercion to be beyond normal limits and inappropriate or criminal.

Distinguishing Features

When sex offenders and offences are integrated into a single clinical entity it is possible to standardise treatment reporting and risk assessment. Treatment progress and risk factors can be assessed by 20 factors, the first 16 relevant to treatment and these plus four others for risk assessment. Each factor can be quantified on a rating scale, 0 if no evidence for the factor, 1 for some but mild to moderate prevalence, and 2 for strong and definite evidence.

1. History
There is a history of similar or various inappropriate sexual behaviour, usually over a period of years, often beginning in childhood, often escalating in seriousness. The best predictor of future risk is the nature, frequency, and severity of previous offences. As a risk factor, score 1 for one reported or confided offence, 2 for more than one.

2. Secrecy
The more concealed or secret the sexual misbehaviour, the more entrenched the psychopathology, and treatment is more difficult. Score 1 if the behaviour has been concealed for two years or less, 2 if two or more years.

3. Offence Cycle
Paraphilia follows a distinctive pattern, usually progressing from pleasurable sensing into a perception of target victim, fantasy of contact, hypersensitivity to trigger situations, and strategy and tactics to complete the cycle and achieve gratification. In these ways deviant sexuality is learned, conditioned, and reinforced. Score 1 for weak cycle, 2 if clearly established.

4. Deviant Fantasy
Paraphilic fantasy differs from normal variations by its recurrence, intensity, and effect on behaviour such as masturbation excessive by frequency or force, recurrent dreams, daydreams, obsessions, or erotomania. Score 1 if there is significant pre-occupation with deviant fantasy, 2 if it is intense (daily and nightly).

5. Deviant Behaviour
The victim is sexually inappropriate according to ethical, legal, or social standards, or there is ritualistic or eccentric behaviour (e.g. fetishism, touching, smelling, exhibitionism, cross-dressing, obscene phone calls, collecting pornography or objects identified with sex). The sex drive is deviant by thought (obsession, fantasy, pre-occupation) or action (inappropriate sexual behaviour). Often there is a history of non-conformity or poor adaptive coping (e.g. violating school, job, or home rules, parole or probation). Score 1 if there is some but limited conformity to social standards, 2 if deviant behaviour is extensive or varied (more than one type of sexually deviant behaviour).

6. Cognitive Distortion/Dissonance
Paraphilics develop irrational or illogical assumptions about their sexuality and that of others in the form of generalisation, oversimplification, stereotyped thinking, unrealistic expectations, and preconceived notions. Score 1 for personal but clearly wrong beliefs about sexuality (distortion) and 2 if they are entrenched (dissonant or delusional).

7. Denial and Minimisation
Avoidance and resistance, from total denial, defiance, or hostility to formidable defences of rationalisation, isolation, circumstantiality, or externalising blame. A common rationalisation of youthful sex offenders is 'she really wanted it.' Together with distortion and dissonance, the extent and depth of denial and minimisation are rough prognostic signs — the deeper they are, the longer the therapy and more guarded the prognosis. Score 1 if there is any denial, 2 if entrenched.

8. High or Precocious Sex Drive
Carnes (1983, 1989) considers some people to be **sex addicts**. DeSalvo, the Boston Strangler, claimed he needed to have sex several times a day. This may be a genetic trait or the result of a sustained high testosterone level. Paraphilics who report being 'oversexed' and whose sexual behaviour confirms frequent outlet (more than once a day) score 2; score 1 if sexual outlet is less frequent than once daily.

9. Impulsivity
There is a low threshold to trigger stimuli and provocative situations. Disinhibition by alcohol

or drugs, mental disorder, or mental retardation is a common contributing factor but not the sole cause of sexual misconduct. Paraphilics are unable or unwilling to conform to school, job, family, or societal controls. They know but do not comply with legal, social, or ethical standards. Score 1 if controls are less than the average person, 2 if impulse control is very weak.

10. Affectivity
Paraphilics lack normative social awareness, what the commentator Walter Lippmann called a 'public conscience.' Score 1 if controls are less than the average person, 2 if impulse control is very weak.

11. Insensitivity
This trait is marked by a lack of empathy and/or use of direct physical force, threat of it, or psychological manipulation by coercion, deception, or bribery, to satisfy a sexual need. There is little or no remorse or guilt, empathy or sympathy for victims. Paraphilics often feign emotions but as a means to the end of satisfying their own needs. Paraphilics demean and de-humanise others, using them only as sex objects, and are insensitive to them as persons. Score 1 if there is some but limited empathy, 2 if there is a total lack of sensitivity.

12. Low Stress Threshold
Stress, as 'intrapsychic noise' from the demands of work, school, home, significant loss, or other external factors, can disinhibit social controls and contribute to sexual acting out. Score 1 if there is evidence of mild to moderate stressors, 2 if stressors are severe.

13. Asocialisation
Paraphilics are poorly socialised, evidenced by their inappropriate sexual behaviour. Most are *under*socialised but some, whose behaviours are bizarre or violent, are *un*socialised. Many paraphilics describe themselves as 'loners' and they lead a nomadic lifestyle. Others are socially isolated or socially inept. Even those who feign appropriate social skills have difficulty maintaining long-term socio-sexual relationships. Some are active sexually but mostly 'one night stands.' Social withdrawal distances paraphilics from others and from societal values. Score 1 if there is some socialisation though less than most 'normals,' 2 if socialisation is poor.

14. Weak Self Concept
The paraphilic self is underdeveloped, personal identity unclear, and there is a lack of insight as compared to non-paraphilics. Schizoid (loner) and schizotypal (deviant thoughts and feelings) traits are common. What seems to be strong character (macho male or Prince Charming; witch or Wonder Woman), is not authentic and does not withstand scrutiny or the test of time and is often immature and narcissistic. Score 1 if the self concept is less than most 'normals,' 2 if much less.

15. Victimisation
Being sexually victimised increases the likelihood of becoming a victimiser. The earlier the trauma, the greater the impact on healthy adaptive coping (Erikson, 1950; Freud, 1965). Score 1 if there has been one such incident, 2 if more than one.

16. Family Dysfunction
Disruptive home life interferes with and can confuse appropriate, healthy interaction with others and development of self-esteem. Score 1 if there is any form of family dysfunction (e.g. alcoholism, drug abuse, absentee parent, separation or divorce, etc.), 2 if extensive.

17. Demographics
Male sex offenders in criminal databases tend to be in their 30s, full scale intelligence around 85, with three or more sexual assaults, and a history of juvenile delinquency (Norton, 1988). Other negatives: family dysfunction, poverty, substance abuse, juvenile crime, job/personal loss, mental illness or retardation. Scoring here is based on comparing the offender with crime statistics for offence type. Score 1 if weakly correlated, 2 if the correlation is strong.

18. Victim Access
When fantasy-ideal targets are available to paraphilics it is only a matter of time before they will be victimised. Availability and easy access to victims and the relative number of opportune situations increases risk of sexual acting out. Score 1 if there is some but limited target access, 2 if there is relatively free access.

19. Opportunity and Means
Accessibility of an opportune secluded place, away from surveillance by police or the public and the means to act out sexually, increases

risk. Score 1 if there is moderate opportunity and/or means, 2 if more so.

20. Progress/Prognosis
Is the paraphilic actively participating in treatment and showing progress toward meeting treatment goals? Score 0 if this is so without any doubt whatever, 1 if there is little or slow progress, 2 if no substantive progress at all.

From these data, a paraphilic personality disorder can emerge in childhood into adolescence, separate and distinct from otherwise normal personality development or from other mental disorders. The personality disorder construct parsimoniously describes male and female, juvenile and adult sex offenders who violate reasonably expected or societal standards of sexual behaviour. It satisfies current diagnostic criteria (DSM-IV, 1994, p 633, paraphrased):

For six months or more there has been:
A. An enduring pattern of inner experience and behaviour that deviates markedly from the expectations of the individual's culture, manifested in two or more of the following areas:

  – **cognition** (perceiving and interpreting self, others, and events);

  – **affectivity** (range, intensity, lability, and appropriateness of emotional responses);

  – **interpersonal functioning;**

  – **impulse control.**

B. The enduring pattern is inflexible and pervasive across a broad range of personal and social situations.

C. It leads to clinically significant distress or impairment in social, occupational, or other important areas of functioning.

D. The pattern is stable, of long duration, and onset can be traced back at least to adolescence or early adulthood.

E. It is not better accounted for as a manifestation or consequence of another mental disorder.

F. It is not due to the direct physiological effects of a street drug, medication, or a medical condition.

There are ten personality disorders listed in ICD-10 (1992) and the DSM-IV (1994), in three 'clusters' (A, B, and C) based on 'descriptive similarities' (DSM-IV, 1994, p 629). Cluster A includes odd or eccentric behaviours (paranoid, schizoid, and schizotypal personalities). Cluster B disorders often appear dramatic, emotional, or erratic (antisocial, borderline, histrionic, and narcissistic personalities). Cluster C disorders appear anxious or fearful (avoidant, dependent, and obsessive-compulsive personalities). Traits from two or more personality disorders can occur in the same individual (DSM-IV, 1994, pp 629-630). While paraphilic personality disorder might be considered a Cluster B disorder because of the antisocial, self-centred nature of sex offences, the underlying psychodynamics are more relevant to Cluster A features. Distrust of others, beginning with mothers and transferred to females who reject or resist advances (Erikson's trust versus distrust first life stage), suggests a more deeply rooted paranoia than antisocial acting out. Erotic fantasy, a common factor in sex offenders leading to and reinforcing cognitive distortion, is a schizotypal trait. Social isolation is schizoid. Some child molesters have more Cluster C than B traits. Though many sex offenders have some Cluster B or C traits, the predominant features of Cluster A are more inclusive.

Classification.

Can all sex offenders, male and female, juvenile and adult, be classified in one comprehensive system? As we have seen, current typologies are narrowly defined, mostly male offenders who rape or molest children. One unified classification system would eliminate duplication and confusion and focus on the specifics of the offender and the sexual behaviour involved.

MacHovec and Wieckowski (1992) have proposed a 10-factor system to classify male and female sex offenders and their offences by type, victim, and underlying dynamics. Each factor is rated on a 5-point scale from 0 (no clinical significance) to 5 (extreme severity):

  1. Physical aggression (PAG): offender's history of non-sexual violence, from 0 (none) to 5 (extremely violent, severe injury, torture, or death even after victim submits).

2. Sexual aggression (SAG), aggression specific to sex offending, rated 0 (totally consensual) to 5 (extremely violent sexual attack event after victim submits; severe injury, torture, or death).

3. Asocialisation (SOC), ability to conform to socio-sexual norms, 0 (socially appropriate in all situations) to 5 (poor socialisation, all situations).

4. Fantasy (FAN), fantasy about deviant sexual behaviour, 0 (none) to 5 (fantasy-dominated to delusional extreme).

5. Sexual arousal (SAR), deviation in what is sexually arousing, 0 (conforms to societal standards, no clinical significance) to 5 (aroused only by inappropriate or deviant sexual stimuli or fantasy).

6. Offence cycle (CYC), awareness of and ability to interrupt the cycle and pattern of sex offending, thoughts, feelings and events before, during, and after offence, their own victimisation, family dysfunction, substance abuse if significant, 0 (fully aware, understands, likely to stop cycle every time), to 5 (no awareness or understanding, not likely to stop cycle any time).

7. Cognitive distortion (COG), recognising cognitive distortions or unrealistic expectations, thinking that distorts reality, blocks responsibility for offending behaviour, knowledge of sex and sexuality, aware of knowledge and skills deficits that contribute to offences, relapse prevention, rated 0 (none) to 5 (severe distortion).

8. Denial-minimisation (DEN), offender's use of denial and minimisation and conversely self-disclosure, 0 (no denial, accepts full responsibility) to 5 (total denial; 'it didn't happen').

9. Remorse-empathy (REM), social sensitivity, adaptive and coping skills, 0 (heavily affect-laden verbally and non-verbally, 5 (no remorse, victims are objects, targets, prey).

10. Prognosis (PRO), readiness and potential for therapy, 0 (excellent), 5 (poor).

Victim gender (SXV) and age (AGV) are included by acronym: Victim gender (SXV), M male victims, F females only, Mf mostly male some females, Fm mostly females some male, MF or FM males and females equally; victim age (AGV), AGV/4-6 victims 4-6 years old; AGV/A only adults; specific sex offences by type, Mol (molestation); Ped (paedophilia); Rap (rape); Inc (incest); by nature of contact, Vag (vaginal, Vag/p for penile penetration, Vag/o by object or other); Anl (anal, Anl/p if penile, Anl/o by object or other); Fel (fellatio); Cun (cunnilingus); Fro (frottage); other deviant behaviour, Acc (accessory, instigator, covert assistance); Add (sex addict); Bst (bestiality); Cop (coprophilia); Exh (exhibitionist); Fet (fetishist), Rit (ritual abuse) and so on. Offender behaviour can further described by + if active (perpetrated the offence), - if passive (recipient of a sex act), or 0 if the offender watched, photographed, videotaped, or recorded; other treatment factors, DSM (DSM mental disorder); Fam (family dysfunction), and so on.

Using this system, a sex offender can be classified and described in a 2-line formula:

PAG/0 SAG/0 SOC/0 FAN/3 SXV/F AGV/4-6 Cun
SAR/4 CYC/4 COG/3 DEN/2 REM/2 PRO/2 Vic

This profile describes an otherwise well socialised (SOC/0) female offender with a moderate degree of fantasy (FAN/3) who does not use physical force (PAG/0 SAG/0), victimises girls four to six years old (SXV/F AGV/4–6 Cun) by performing oral sex on them. She shows little awareness of her arousal cycle (SAR/4 CYC/4) and was sexually abused herself (Vic). There is significant cognitive distortion (COG/3), some denial (DEN/2) but she shows appropriate remorse and empathy (REM/2). Prognosis is good (PRO/2).

Using the 10FC system detailed information can be contained in two lines, the central focus being on the individual and the specific offence, and valuable information about the offender's personality dynamics. This would be especially helpful in treating repeat offenders since the formula includes a detailed assessment at the time of a previous offence. An added advantage of the 10FC system is that it can graphically show a paraphilic profile. Viewed on its horizontal axis 'peaks' of treatment need and 'valleys' of more appropriate function are clearly visible. A rating of 0 to 1 presents a flat landscape of essentially normal behaviour. Scores above 1 deviate from normative behaviour.

The 10FC Classification Profile is as follows:

Classification factor	Deviance from Sociosexual Norms					
	None	Mild	Moderate		Severe	
	0	1	2	3	4	5
1. Physical aggression (PAG)	—	—	—	—	—	—
2. Sexual aggression (SAG)	—	—	—	—	—	—
3. Asocialisation (SOC)	—	—	—	—	—	—
4. Fantasy (FAN)	—	—	—	—	—	—
5. Sexual arousal (SAR)	—	—	—	—	—	—
6. Offence cycle (CYC)	—	—	—	—	—	—
7. Cognitive distortion (COG)	—	—	—	—	—	—
8. Denial-minimisation (DEN)	—	—	—	—	—	—
9. Remorse-empathy (REM)	—	—	—	—	—	—
10. Prognosis/progress (PRO)	—	—	—	—	—	—

Sex offence(s):

Victim sex:

Victim age(s):

Fifty consecutively committed Virginia juvenile sex offenders yielded this profile: N=50   (Ages 11–17; mean 13.8)

10 FC factor	Mean score
1. Physical aggression	2.1
2. Sexual aggression	2.6
3. Asocialisation	3.1
4. Aberrant fantasy	1.5
5. Sexual arousal	2.0
6. Offence cycle	2.8
7. Cognitive distortion	2.3
8. Denial-minimisation	2.6
9. Lacks remorse-empathy	3.2
10. Prognosis-progress	2.9

Adult sex offenders, institutionalised and seen in private practice in the community, score an average of one point above juveniles across the ten factors. This cross-validation suggests the system is valid and reliable. If adopted in the criminal justice system, police and protective services could consistently identify offenders and courts sentence offenders to the most appropriate treatment. Therapists could quickly focus on treatment needs. It would be especially useful in treating repeat offenders and maintaining longitudinal data.

Risk Assessment

Police, protective services, courts, and therapists are called upon to assess risk of re-offending, despite the generally acknowledged difficulty in doing so. Eighteen risk factors emerged from a review of relevant clinical and research literature (Abel *et al.*, 1977, 1986; Berlin and Krout, 1986; Finkelhor, 1986; Groth and Birnbaum, 1978; Norton, 1988; Smith, 1985). They are formatted on a 5-point rating scale consistent with classification and treatment criteria previously described in this chapter:

Risk Factor	Relative Risk					
	0	1	2	3	4	5
1 History of violence The best predictor of future violence is past violence	—	—	—	—	—	—
2. Progressive offence pattern Problem sexual behaviour is repeated, reinforced, and becomes entrenched	—	—	—	—	—	—
3. Precipitating events Impulsivity, effect of trigger stimuli and provocative situations	—	—	—	—	—	—
4. Environmental controls Control effect of school or job rules, family values, public scrutiny	—	—	—	—	—	—
5. Offender demographics Sex offender base rates; Norton (1988) found highest risk to be males 35, IQ 84, 3+ assaults, family dysfunction, juvenile crime, job/personal loss	—	—	—	—	—	—
6. Drive state High, unvented sex drive with anger/power	—	—	—	—	—	—
7. Stress 'noise' level High stress and high anxiety disinhibit, increase impulsivity	—	—	—	—	—	—

8. **Cognitive distortion**
   Muddled/muddled illogical
   thinking, preconceived notions,
   myths

   — — — — — —

9. **Affectivity**
   Insufficient control of
   anger and frustration

   — — — — — —

10. **Adaptive coping**
    History of difficulties adapting
    to societal standards

    — — — — — —

11. **Mental state/personality dynamics**
    Effect of any underlying
    mental disorders; Norton
    (1988) found schizophrenia
    common

    — — — — — —

12. **Opportunity/victim access**
    Available victim plus
    opportunity and impulse

    — — — — — —

13. **Method, means**
    Secluded place, vehicle,
    situation, weapon, etc.

    — — — — — —

14. **Remorse-empathy**
    Compassion, sympathy, guilt,
    over the offence

    — — — — — —

15. **Baseline conduct**
    Day-to-day adaptation
    to societal values

    — — — — — —

16. **Socialisation**
    Appropriate social skills

    — — — — — —

17. **Substance abuse**
    Disinhibits sex drive

    — — — — — —

18. **Self concept**
    Relative stability,
    self esteem, spiritual
    values (AA 12 steps)

    — — — — — —

Therapist Preparation

Therapists who treat sex offenders are an emerging speciality in an unpopular and controversial area of practice. It is a difficult and unpopular clientele to treat and rehabilitate. While recidivism is reduced with therapy it is never completely eliminated. Yet, sex offenders need therapy to protect society and restore their normal personality development. Treatment of sex offenders is as important as treatment of victims because it is in society's interest to reduce the numbers of both victims and offenders, heal the victim's wounds, and eliminate the offender's sociopathy. Unless the number of offenders decrease sex crimes will continue.

Sex offender therapists should be qualified mental health professionals with appropriate education, training, and experience. Paraprofessionals should have specialised training in this area. Equally important are objectivity and critical judgement without which treatment is more likely to fail. Many sex offenders have highly developed social skills and can manipulate the most experienced therapists. Because of this, and also to ensure a consistent standard of care, a conscious degree of healthy scepticism is needed. A self-rating caring-critical grid has been helpful in training, case consultation, and clinical supervision:

```
┌─────────────────────────────────────────┐
│           Caring/Critical grid           │
│          5 __                            │
│          4 __  __                        │
│  More    3 __  __  __                    │
│  caring  2 __  __  __  __                │
│          1 __  __  __  __  __            │
│          0 __  __  __  __  __  __        │
│                                          │
│            0   1   2   3   4   5         │
│                                          │
│              More critical               │
└─────────────────────────────────────────┘
```

Highly caring therapists place in the upper left quadrant. Sceptical, critical therapists are in the lower right quadrant. Experienced sex offender therapists agree the most effective approach is to be more confrontive and critical than accepting and caring (Carnes, 1989, pp 236-240; Ingersoll and Patton, 1990, pp 31 and 84; Hollin and Howell, 1991, pp 170-171; Prendergast, 1991, pp

106-114). In terms of the C-C graph, recommended therapist orientation is minimally a 2-4 blend of mild caring with moderate criticality. Traditional therapy is at least a 3-3 caring-critical balance and a 4-2 or more caring emphasis is **not** effective in treating sex offenders.

A sceptical, slightly biased critical approach is more conducive to overcoming denial and minimisation typical of sex offenders. Such a treatment climate has been called 'the tough love' approach. Caring, uncritical therapists are more easily manipulated and more susceptible to becoming emotionally involved in defence of offenders, lose their objectivity, and diminish treatment effectiveness. The down side of a highly critical approach is the increased probability of negativism and a more punitive attitude. There is a need for balance with a slight tilt toward scepticism to maintain objectivity and maximal therapeutic effect.

Once therapists achieve and maintain an appropriate degree of objectivity they should be aware of ten obstacles cited by Meloy (1988):

1. Endogenous factors, a therapist's own personal mental unfinished business or unconscious bias.

2. Reactivation or re-enacting the offender's early parenting and thus reinforcing dysfunctional behaviour.

3. Nihilism, the belief offenders cannot be treated or rehabilitated, that therapy is useless.

4. Illusory alliance believing there is a treatment contract when there isn't.

5. Fear of assault or reprisal by the offender.

6. Denial of the above fear by the therapist.

7. Guilt or feelings of helplessness from the lack of perceived or observed treatment progress.

8. Therapist devaluation by 'continuous narcissistic wounding' by the offender during therapy sessions.

9. Anger or hostility similar to the offender's conscious or unconscious attempts to destroy goodness, Freud's 'swallowing the monster.'

10. Wrong assumption that normal intelligence means normal ego function or potential.

Doren (1987) cautions against five 'therapist traps':

1. Battling to win
2. Becoming an advocate
3. Believing what you're told
4. Fearing or denying being manipulated
5. Becoming fascinated or entertained

There are two basic treatment goals needed for all sex offenders regardless of age or gender: normalisation and re-socialisation.

Normalisation is intra-personal, an internal process within the self, based on the major premise that there is awareness and thorough understanding of societal, community, and family values, what is and is not considered normal or appropriate sexually and as defined by law. It requires a significant level of self-realisation and includes self-esteem, and self, sexual, and role identity and sexual self-esteem. The goal is to restore the offender to socially appropriate behaviour and restore personality dynamics to normal function and continued development.

Re-socialisation is interpersonal, achieved through normative interaction with others and requires sensitising offenders to societal, community, and family expectations and standards, how best to conform to these standards, interact appropriately with others, and practice and apply them daily.

Treatment objectives for sex offenders are also similar regardless of the nature and seriousness of inappropriate sexual behaviour and the age and gender of the offender. Certain of them can be emphasised to meet individual needs. These ten treatment objectives emerge from a review of clinical and research literature (Becker, 1990; Burgess *et al.*, 1978; Carnes, 1983, 1989; Finkelhor, 1984, 1986; Groth, 1979; Ingersoll and Patton, 1990; Knopp, 1984; Laws, 1989; Loss and Ross, 1988; Marsh *et al.*, 1988; Marshall *et al.*, 1990; Mayer, 1988; Salter, 1988; Sgroi, 1982; Watts and Courtois, 1981).

Sex offender treatment needs assessment and progress summary

Treatment factor	Poor	Low	Avg	Avg	Good	Very Good
1. Responsibility Assumes without denial, minimisation or blaming	—	—	—	—	—	—
2. Readiness-amenability Open to analysing thoughts, feelings, behaviours, fantasies, and lack of awareness, knowledge, skills	—	—	—	—	—	—
3. Cognitive distortion Overcomes denial, fantasy, and avoidance	—	—	—	—	—	—
4. Processes own victimisation Loss, rejection, abandonment, or family dysfunction	—	—	—	—	—	—
5. Offence cycle Understood how to interrupt/ control it, their sexual arousal pattern, how and when to get help	—	—	—	—	—	—
6. Impulse control Anger, power need, frustration, helplessness; improved coping skills	—	—	—	—	—	—
7. Remorse/empathy For victim, the victim's family, offender's family, friends, society	—	—	—	—	—	—
8. Resocialisation Appropriate social and interpersonal skills appropriately expressed	—	—	—	—	—	—
9. Normalisation Understands what appropriate sexual outlets, what is and is NOT considered normal, lawful behaviour	—	—	—	—	—	—
10. Self concept Sexual identity, self-esteem	—	—	—	—	—	—

Successful/Recommended treatment interventions:

Unsuccessful/Not recommended treatment interventions:

Using this form provides a quick description of current treatment progress specific to sex offenders, helpful in pre-post evaluations and to assess treatment progress. When compared to previous reports it is a historical record of relative progress over time. Lack of progress is immediately obvious. Current and previous successful and unsuccessful therapy helps focus and individualise treatment and ensures continuity of care by future therapists. Routine use of standardised progress reports will help refine treatment techniques. Program evaluation would be enhanced with the ability to isolate and assess program objectives and treatment goals ensuring cost-effective services.

Psychoanalytic therapy is noticeably absent from sex offender treatment programs despite a substantial body of data that suggests it would be helpful. 'Analysis has been considered the best treatment for certain sexual disorders,' according to Freedman *et al.* (1972). These same authors succinctly describe the psycho-dynamic treatment plan of 'assessing analysability' then an 'analytic pact' to progressively deeper processing, 'internal change through increasing self-awareness' to 'tolerate frustration of impulses without serious acting out or shifting from one pathological pattern to another'. Existing treatment programs rely on cognitive-behavioural methods to frustrate impulses but do little to probe and systematically process underlying dynamics. This increases the risk of generalising into other equally deviant sexual behaviour in the future.

Initial Offender Assessment

Before any treatment is provided it is necessary to have a detailed history of the offender prior to the offence and the exact nature of the offence itself. This preliminary workup includes mental state (baseline and at time of offence), intelligence, personality development, family dynamics and significant early and present stressors, current lifestyle, first and subsequent sexual experience, sexual preference (sex, age, behaviour), nature and intensity of sex fantasies, offender's own victimisation, behavioural and emotional controls, defence mechanisms, coping skills, prior offences (sexual and non-sexual), and any

substance abuse history. Sgroi (1982) described a variety of dysfunctional family dynamics that can contribute to sex offending: poor communications; blurred boundaries; inadequate controls or failure to set limits to protect victims; emotional deprivation or neediness; lack of empathy and understanding; isolation; denial; magical expectations; fear of external interference; and abuse of power.

Court records and offender statements are often of limited use because of vague terms and reduced charges by plea bargaining. Rape can be reduced to carnal knowledge or sexual battery, not clearly describing what happened. These reinforce offender denial and minimisation. Police reports, photos of victims, and victim statements provide needed details. Important factors: nude or clothed; manual or oral, anal or genital contact; active (only offender to victim) or passive (victim to offender); penetration by finger, penis, or object; place, time, and frequency; with or without force, extent of coercion and psychological or physical injury.

ICD-10 (1992) and the DSM-IV (1994) are of little use because the list of paraphilias is too limited. In cases of repeated serious sex crimes and to better assess future risk therapists should be aware of the criteria for psychopathy (Cleckley, 1941; Meloy, 1988). Some, not all, sex offenders are psychopaths. The Hare Psychopathy Checklist, Revised (1991) is an empirically derived, fieldtested screening and evaluation instrument of 20 items scored 0, 1, or 2 with a maximum score 40. Meloy (1988) interprets a 10 to 19 score as mild, 20 to 29 moderate, and over 30, severe or 'primary psychopathy.' Though developed from research on adults, by definition a psychopathic personality is a lifelong pattern and the 20 items should prove helpful in its early detection:

1. Glib superficial charm
2. Grandiose self worth
3. High stimulation need, prone to boredom
4. Pathological liar
5. Cunning and manipulative
6. Lacks remorse or guilt
7. Shallow affection
8. Callous, lacks empathy
9. Parasitic lifestyle

10. Poor behavioural controls

11. Sexually promiscuous

12. Early behaviour problems (fire setting common)

13. Lacks realistic long-term goals

14. Spontaneous impulsivity (7-year-old level)

15. Irresponsible (no duty-loyalty)

16. Fails to accept personal responsibility (externalises blame, projects, discounts, devaluates)

17. Many short-term marital or sexual relationships

18. Juvenile delinquency (below age 17)

19. Violates parole or probation

20. Criminal versatility (more than one kind of crime)

Most sex offenders reflect psychopathic traits and it is recommended they be screened with the Hare checklist to confirm or rule out pure or primary psychopathy. Clinical and research data from Cleckley (1941) to Hare (1987) give the impression psychopaths are totally inaccessible to treatment. Suedfeld and Landon (1979) reported 'no demonstrably effective treatment' for psychopathy (p 347). Doren (1987) disagrees observing 'the situation is not hopeless, just difficult' and a major obstacle to effective treatment is a 'therapist's counterproductive reactions' (p 244). 'The client,' Doren maintains, 'does not need to *want* to be in therapy for it to have effect' (p 159). He recommends control theory, which focuses on five target behaviours:

1. Preoccupation with perceived challenge and control.
   He recommends therapists deliberately setting themselves up to be manipulated, similar to Freud's admonition to 'use the transference.'

2. Limited behavioural repertoire.
   Under-socialised or un-socialised unrealistic expectations of self and others, poor judgement, impaired reality testing of social relationships.

3. Typically acting out when frustrated.
   Treatment approaches: B-mod ignoring attention-getting behaviours to extinguish them; increase awareness of consequences that will hurt them (lengthy incarceration, execution).

4. Attention deficit, easily bored.
   Doren recommends letting them win fairly regularly to maintain their interest in what they see as the therapy 'game.'

5. Perception people are objects, obstacles, or targets.
   A psychopath cannot be taught to have empathy or guilt, to have a superego where there is none. But they can be taught 'as if,' as Shakespeare put it 'to assume a virtue though you have it not and by practice make it so.'

Doren reports that psychopathic personalities exhibit typical defences and 'gamey' manipulation such as: verbal intimidation and testing limits, negative comparison (previous therapist or treatment was better), throwing guilt ('what would you have done?'), demanding trust ('see it my way'), 'yes but' rationalisations, (twisting truth by reframing, misinterpretation, exaggeration), 'poor me' sympathy appeal, avoidance through flattery, telling you what you want to hear, or just laughing it off (pp 179–227).

Yochelson and Samenow (1977) provide a checklist to assess therapeutic change of criminal conduct. Adapted to sex offenders, six factors emerge:

1. Disclosure and amenability.
   Full disclosure; receptive self-criticism without denial, minimisation, blaming, excuses, or an 'I can't' attitude.

2. Responsibility.
   Self-generated responsible effort, attitude without complacency; realistic expectations and initiatives; sound, reasonable decision making; ingrained fear and respect for consequences.

3. Affect.
   Unselfish empathy appropriately expressed; firm commitment not to hurt self or others; an aware interdependence; trusting and trustworthy; re-channelled energy; effective anger control.

4. Cognition.
   No criminal thinking, tactics, or motives (anger, power, selfish gratification); socially appropriate, responsible management of money and career.

5. Self concept.
   Self respect and excellence but with genuine, sustained self disgust for offences rather than criminal pride.

6. Sexuality.
   Changed sexual pattern and responsivity with deterrents implemented.

Most juvenile residential sex offender treatment programs blend psychodynamic, behaviourist, and humanist interventions to meet therapy needs. This includes the following objectives, easily adapted to treatment planning in community programs and private practice:

1. Overcoming denial, minimisation, blaming, excuses.
   Evaluating defence mechanisms to avoid responsibility for and justify offences. This objective should be addressed early and continually using a more critical than caring approach.

2. Autobiography.
   The offender details their own life history, used to confront denial, overcome minimisation, and facilitate insight.

3. Complete disclosure.
   This is the offence history, used also to discover, explore, and document the offence cycle.

4. Individualised treatment objectives.
   Specific to the offender and offences.

5. Overcoming cognitive distortion.
   Faulty thinking relating to sexual and social behaviours and realistic expectations of everyday life, monitored, assessed, confronted, and changed.

6. Fantasies and arousal.
   Acknowledged and examined, their role and degree, eliminating extremes and exaggeration that contribute to increased risk of re-offending.

7. Appropriate affect management.
   Offender's poor controls of anger, irritation, or frustration, power need, and their tactics to manipulate and dominate others.

8. Victim empathy.
   The effect of the offence on the victim, present and future, and on his or her family.

9. Personal victimisation of the offender, to identify, explore, and integrate the past into the present and neutralise it as a future precipitating factor.

10. Dysfunctional family dynamics that may have contributed to sex offending, identified and processed.

11. Offence cycle.
    Awareness and understanding of trigger situations, preferred victim and setting, motive and opportunity, identified, discussed, and charted.

12. Daily log, journal, or diary, where offender writes thoughts, feelings, fantasies, used to detect and correct cognitive distortion.

13. Relapse prevention.
    Awareness, understanding, and prevention of trigger situations and precautions to reduce re-offending.

14. Role modelling.
    Help offenders identify role models in the therapy setting (peers, therapists) and in the community, to develop personal autonomy, mutual support, positive relationships, bolster self esteem, and reward and reinforce socially appropriate behaviours.

15. Bibliotherapy. Selected readings and study materials, processed in individual and group sessions.

Character and Values

Because individual and group therapies do not completely eliminate recidivism there is a trend to augment therapy with self-help groups and post-therapy personal guidelines similar to Alcoholics Anonymous. The primary focus is on character building and developing a 'non-denominational spirituality' of personal values which in time and continued development replaces the immaturity, impulsivity, and self-interest of the past. There are 'Anonymous' groups for a variety of excessive behaviours such as debtors, gamblers, narcotics users, smokers, overeaters, anorexics, child abusers, incest survivors, workaholics, and shoplifters. Carnes (1989) recommends including the AA 12-step recovery process in sex offender treatment. He sees steps 1–5 as intervention to stop 'self-destructive behaviours,' steps 6–9 as facilitating renewal and restoration, and steps 10–12 as 'systems maintenance.' Here is the 12-step AA program adapted to sex offenders:

1. *Admit* there is a problem that has been and is beyond control.

2. *Need* for a higher power, outside and beyond yourself, to control it, change, and prevent recurrence. This higher power can be a real or imagined role model, in religion, history, literature, or current events. It need not be God or a religious figure.

3. *Firm Decision* and contract to be open to whatever is needed to change.

4. *Detailed Self-inventory* of yourself.

5. *Freely Admitting* wrongdoing and weakness.

6. *Open and Receptive* to therapy and help.

7. *Active Search* for truth to overcome weaknesses.

8. *List* of all who have been harmed, directly and indirectly, willing to make amends if possible and appropriate.

9. *Make Amends* unless doing so is harmful in any way. Genuine apology — but don't expect forgiveness.

10. *Continued Personal Growth*, correcting errors as they are made aware or become evident.

11. *Continued Reliance on Higher Power* for good and to phase out lower, evil power and impulses.

12. *Pass It On.* Help others do the same.

Eastern philosophies such as Buddhism are also a rich source of easily understood, universally applied character steps (Theras, 1979). Buddha's four noble truths and 8-fold path address the same core ideas of the 12-step AA program, easily adapted to individual and group therapies.

Buddha's first noble truth is 'the wheel': realisation that 'to live is to know pain', that wherever there is life there will be problems and conflict. Signs of this truth are birth, hunger, thirst, pain, injury, disease, ageing, and death. Psychological aspects are anger, hate, fear, frustration, dissatisfaction, separation, aversion, and unpleasantness. Buddha taught that pleasure brings pain because it is brief, seldom enough, and we crave more and feel deprived and frustrated when we cannot have it.

The second noble truth is 'the wheel's hub': much pain is self inflicted, exaggerated by illusion and materialism. A major negative aspect is ignorance which Buddha described as darkness or clouding. From three defilements (greed, blaming-aversion, and insensitivity-delusion) others develop such as jealousy, ambition, lethargy, and arrogance, growing from these basic three.

The third noble truth is 'the promise': it need not be so. There is a way out. This introduces hope and offers enlightenment.

The fourth noble truth is 'the way,' the 8-fold path, 'middle way' or 'message from the heart.'

Buddha's first and second noble truths are pessimistic, reflecting the dark side of human nature. Taoism, contemporary with Buddhism, symbolised this negative aspect in the yin half of the yin-yang symbol, an S-curve in a circle, used in martial arts programs and on the flag of Korea.

These last two noble truths bring light to the darkness, the yang force in the yin-yang symbol. This dualistic approach of positive from the negative is a basic principle in Buddhist psychology applicable and relevant to psychotherapy.

The 8-fold path is the Buddhist treatment plan, interrelated steps Buddha described as interwoven strands of rope that tie to the enlightened self. They are co-existent, need not be achieved sequentially as the 12 AA steps, and blend together in a gestalt of a self greater than the sum of its parts. They are:

1. *Attitude* (right view), a positive basic orientation to life and living. This requires understanding of self and others, truth and evil and their roots, realities of suffering in thought and feeling, of peace and the 8-fold path. Buddha considered no single factor as responsible for suffering as wrong view and none as powerful in promoting good as right view (Bodhi, 1984, p16).

2. *Intent-motive* (right wisdom) direction, purpose, intent, by self control, free of negative influences such as selfishness, anger, hate, rudeness, or cruelty, 'pure as a gentle breeze.' This step is achieved three ways: renounce and avoid sources of suffering by understanding them; develop and apply caring and compassion to all; and do no harm. Changing harmful to harmless can be achieved by the polarity principle, substituting positive for negative words and actions.

3. *Speech and silence* (right speech), to state truth simply or in silence, kindly, to simplify and unify not to complicate and divide, and without lies, gossip, or exaggeration. Wrongful speech hurts, makes enemies, and causes bitterness. Good speech heals, makes friends, and enhances wisdom. Wrongful speech is rooted in anger, intended to hurt. Without control 'lies stretch, multiply, and connect until they lock us into a cage of falsehoods and subjective illusion' (Bodhi, 1984, p 51). This step requires honesty and truth in describing reality not illusion or a respectful silence, to say the right thing at the right time in the right way.

4. *Action-reaction* (right action), to let every action weaken a fault or evil intent, to love life in all its forms, accepted and appreciated, without craving or indulging, stealing or killing. The three categories of wrong actions: killing and mistreatment; stealing; and wrongful sex. The counterbalance to killing is compassion. Stealing is taking what is not yours, directly or deceitfully. Counterbalances are honesty, respect, generosity, sharing, and being content with what you have. Wrongful sex is with an inappropriate person (adultery, rape, incest, child abuse) by deception or force which physically or psychologically hurts. The counterbalance is love and mutual respect between consenting equals.

5. *Livelihood* (right livelihood), to revive and restore yourself, to realise life can be a mission not just a career, that living is giving, and you keep only what you give away, in work and people enjoyed, every day an opportunity lived to be lived as the last because some day it will be. Wrongful livelihood is the pursuit of power or profit by wrongdoing, directly or indirectly, or an illegal, unethical, or harmful occupation. It is better to co-operate than compete, to render service to others without deception or misrepresentation.

6. *Attention* (right effort), to attend to whatever you're doing wherever you are and to awaken, maintain, and continue to develop your mind. The 'seven enlightenment factors' apply: mindful insight, study of states and consequences, enthusiastic energy, reverie and rapture, tranquil contemplation, 1-pointed concentration, and equanimity between stimulus and response (no knower or known). Humphreys (1951) described it as consciousness where the pendulum of opposites comes to rest, where both sides of the coin are equally valued and immediately seen.

7. *Contemplation* (right mindfulness), meditative awareness that 'sees with the third eye' and 'hears with the third ear,' a blank screen of unbiased sensitivity, impartial objectivity, serene detachment, without preconceived notions or interpretation, the mind in repose, quiet, open, in the unhurried, uncluttered here and now, reflecting on function and not fiction. 'Four fundamentals' of contemplation are: the body; sensation; mind; and inner thoughts and feelings. They are further explored as body-in-body, feelings-in-feelings, mind state-in-mind state, and phenomena-in-phenomena. The body is studied in breathing, walking, standing, sitting, lying down, feelings as craving, undecided, and satisfied. This step is sometimes referred to as 'cemetery meditation' because it involves life's transience and ultimate truth.

8. *Concentration* (right concentration) or 1-pointed mind realises a higher or cosmic consciousness from the journey along the 8-fold path. There is focused attention to an object or concept that results in a tranquil mind. The mind is then free of external and internal influences, no longer deluded or distracted. This requires discipline, instruction and supervision, and practice on suitable objects of meditation. This step can be reached from two directions: the 'serenity path' as an end by itself; and the 'insight path' indirectly by achieving all eight steps.

Issues

Sex offender therapy is a relatively new speciality and there are several issues to be resolved: Do we *really* know what a sex offender is? There's no doubt when a victim is forcibly sexually attacked. But laws defining sexual offences vary from one jurisdiction to another or are imprecise. Serious offences are sometimes plea bargained to lower offences to ensure conviction. Some courts are inconsistent or lax in requiring therapy.

Without clear operational definitions, statistics can be inconsistent, even contradictory. Interview and self-report data can be flawed if there is no way to validate them, the usual situation. Inept or leading questions can miss important information. Sex offenders are generally unreliable reporters, often denying, minimising, or externalising blame. Descriptions of sex offenders are often based on individual case studies or limited research data. They are psychological snapshots of offenders with selective, often incomplete detail to support a hypothesis.

We have no really strong psychological tests to assess sex offender personality dynamics, validated on that specific population. An item on the original (1943) and latest (1989) MMPI is 'I have never indulged in any unusual sex practice'. What's an unusual sex practice? In successive diagnostic manuals being homosexual has been diagnosed a perversion, then a disorder, and now is a matter of sexual preference. Was it more 'unusual' then than now? Existing tests do little to qualify or quantify the dynamics specific to sex offences.

It is difficult to correct abnormal behaviour without a clear understanding of what is normal. 'Normal' is a reflection of current societal values. It is whatever society says it is, in a specific culture at a specified time. It is not an international, universal standard except for the most violent sex crimes. Date and spouse rape and sexual harassment can be grey areas far more obscure.

How can we know sex offender treatment is effective? We need longitudinal studies and comparative evaluations of different modalities and techniques before we can accept any one of them as the benchmark standard. Group methods are preferred to individual therapy, another choice lacking a clear empirical basis at this time. If sex offending is a characterological problem why is therapy mainly cognitive-behavioural? That method is goal-oriented and more easily researched. Psychodynamic and experiential therapies focus more deeply on characterological and affective factors and are under-represented in current treatment. The most effective sex offender therapy, according to research studies, is in full-time residential programs. They are expensive in terms of buildings, staff, and operating costs. It seems likely that therapy services for most sex offenders will be lifelong. Would an intensive residential program for a few months followed by one-to-one outpatient therapy be as effective? An intensive wholly outpatient programme?

Can any mental health professional be a sex offender therapist? Based on current practice, the answer is yes. The clinical and research literature is virtually unanimous that 'traditional therapies' are *not* effective with sex offenders. A more direct 'tough love' approach is recommended. Traditional therapists tend to believe what they're told and are more easily manipulated by avoidant sex offenders. Some therapists have a personal bias against sex offenders, which may be unconscious and adversely affect therapy.

Can intrusive methods not acceptable in everyday practice be imposed on sex offenders? Are we free to impose involuntary treatment of sex offenders, like the plethysmograph, biofeedback, or more intrusive psychological tests beyond a standard screening battery? Should sex offenders have the same right to informed consent as non-offenders or does a cost-benefit analysis of offender rights versus public safety justify the use of intrusive instruments and tests?

Despite these questions we cannot wait for unequivocal data. Most sex offences *are* clearly antisocial and offenders are in need of therapy. Society demands something be done whether mental health professionals and community services are ready or not. Current treatment has evolved from the best clinical judgement at a time of need years ago. It is time now to standardise definitions, diagnoses, and treatment. Treatment should be based on empirical evidence and comparative analysis of what kind of therapy works best. It should be both cognitive and affective and include developing a non-denominational spirituality to develop insight and a socially appropriate personal value system. Psychopathy should be routinely screened and if present to a significant degree, treated specifically. Screening should include organicity and a research database for it should be maintained. Certain realities remain constant:

1. The map is not the territory.
   Sex offences exceed the limits of current data. Everything an individual needs in may not be in the structured treatment program.

2. Technique is not the process.
   There is far more to sex offender therapy than simple cognitive-behavioural or other techniques. A 'busy' treatment program does not necessarily mean there is treatment progress.

3. When the apple is ripe, it drops from the tree of its own weight (Zen proverb).
   You can't teach or force insight, victim empathy, remorse, or personal responsibility. The good news is, as gestaltist Fritz Perls said: 'All roads lead inside.' An effective therapist can lead any conversation toward treatment goals. Effective therapy is, as it has always been, using the right approach at the right time. We must find more 'right' ways to do it.

References

Abel, G.C., Blanchard, D.H., and Gould, D. (1977). The Components of a Rapist's Sexual Arousal. *Archives of General Psychiatry* 34, 895–903.

Abel, G.C., Rouleau, J., and Cunningham-Rathner, J. (1986). Sexually Aggressive Behavior. In Curran, W.A., McGarry, L., and Shah, A. *Modern Legal Psychiatry and Psychology*. Philadelphia PA: F.A. Davis.

American Psychiatric Association (1994). *Diagnostic and Statistical Manual of Mental Disorders (DSM-IV)*. Washington DC: American Psychiatric Press.

Becker, J. (1990). Treating Adolescent Sex Offenders. *Professional Psychology: Research and Practice*, 21, 362–365.

Berlin, F.S., and Krout, E. (1986). Pedophilia: Diagnostic Concepts, Treatment, and Ethical Considerations. *American Journal of Forensic Psychology*, 8.

Bodhi, B. (1984). *The Noble Eightfold Path*. Kandy, Sri Lanka: Buddhist Publication Society.

Burgess, A.W., Groth, A.N., and Holstrom, L.L., (1978). *Sexual Assault of Children and Adolescents*. Lexington MA: Lexington Books.

Carnes, P. (1983). *Out of the Shadows: Understanding Addiction*. Minneapolis MN: CompCare.

Carnes, P. (1989). *Contrary to Love*. Minneapolis MN: CompCare.

Cleckley, H. (1941). *The Mask of Sanity*. St. Louis MO: Mosby.

Doren, D.M. (1987). *Understanding and Treating the Psychopath*. New York: Wiley.

Erikson, E. (1950). *Childhood and Society*. New York: Norton.

Festinger, L. (1957). *A Theory of Cognitive Dissonance*. Stanford, CA: Stanford University Press.

Finkelhor, D. (1984). *Child Sexual Abuse: New Theory and Research*. New York: Free Press.

Finkelhor, D. (1986). *A Sourcebook on Child Sexual Abuse*. Beverly Hills, CA: Sage.

Freedman, A.M., Kaplan, H.I., and Sadock, B.J. (1972). *Modern Synopsis of Comprehensive Textbook of Psychiatry*. Baltimore, MD: Williams and Wilkins.

Freud, S. (1965). *Normality and Pathology in Childhood*. New York: International Universities Press.

Groth, A.N. (1979). *Men Who Rape: The Psychology of the Offender*. New York: Plenum Press.

Groth, A.N., and Birnbaum, H.J. (1978). Adult Sexual Orientation and Attraction to Underage Persons. *Archives of Sexual Behavior*, 7, 175–181.

Hare, R.D. (1987). Psychopathy and Violence. In Hays, J.R., Roberts, T.K., and Solway, K.S. (Eds.), *Violence and the Violent Individual*. New York: Spectrum.

Hare, R.D. (1991). *The Hare Psychotherapy Checklist* (Revised).

Hinsie, L., and Campbell, R.J. (1973). *Psychiatric Dictionary*. 4th edition. New York: Oxford University Press.

Hollin, C.R., and Howell, S.K. (Eds.) (1991). *Clinical Approaches to Sex Offenders and their Victims*. New York: Wiley

Humphreys, C. (1951). *The Wisdom of Buddhism*. New York: Random House.

Ingersoll, S.L., and Patton, S.O. (1990). *Treating Perpetrators of Sexual Abuse*. Lexington MA: Lexington Books.

Knight, R.A., and Prentky, R.A. (1990). Classifying Sexual Offenders. In Marshall, W.L. Laws, D.R., and Barbaree, H.E. (Eds.). *Handbook of Sexual Assault*. New York: Plenum Press.

Knopp, F.H. (1984). Retraining Adult Sex Offenders: Methods and Models. Syracuse NY: Safer Society Press.

Lanning, K.V. (1986). *Child Molesters: A Behavioral Analysis for Law Enforcement Officers Investigating Cases of Child Sexual Exploitation*. 2nd edition. Washington DC: National Center for Missing and Exploited Children.

Laws, D.R. (Ed.) (1989). *Relapse Prevention with Sex Offenders*. New York: Guilford Press.

Loss, P., and Ross, J.E. (1988). *Risk Assessment: Interviewing Protocol for Adolescent Sex Offenders*. Mount Pleasant, SC: Authors.

MacHovec, F.J. (1993a): Treatment and Rehabilitation of Sex Offenders. *Treating Abuse Today*, 3, 2, 5–12.

MacHovec, F.J. (1993b): Is There a Paraphilic Personality Disorder? *Treating Abuse Today*, 3, 6, 5–10.

MacHovec, F.J., and Wieckowski, A. The 10FC Ten Factor Continua of Classification and Treatment Criteria for Male and Female Sex Offenders. *Medical Psychotherapy*, 5: 53–63.

Marsh, L.F., Connell, P., and Olson, E. (1988). *Breaking the Cycle: Adolescent Sexual Treatment Manual*. Beaverton, OR: St. Mary's Home for Boys.

Marshall, W.L., Laws, D.R., and Barbaree, H.E. (Eds.) (1990). *Handbook of Sexual Assault: Issues, Theories, and Treatment of the Offender*. New York: Plenum Press.

Mathews, R., Mulhern, J.K., and Speltz, K. (1989). *Female Sex Offenders: An Exploratory Study*. Orwell, VT: Safer Society Press.

Mayer, A. (1988). *Sex Offenders: Approaches to Understanding and Management*. Holmes Beach, FL: Learning Publications.

Meloy, J.R. (1988). *The Psychopathic Mind*. New York: Jacob Aronson.

Millon, T. (1981). *Disorders of Personality*. New York: Wiley.

Norton, S.C. (1988). Predictor Variables of Violent Behaviour. *American Journal of Forensic Psychology*, 6, 53–65.

Prendergast, W.E. (1991). *Treating Sex Offenders in Corrective Institutions and Outpatient Clinics*. Binghampton, NY: Haworth Press.

Salter, A.C. (1988). *Treating Child Sex Offenders and Victims*. Newbury Park, CA: Sage.

Sgroi, S.M. (1982). *Handbook of Clinical Intervention in Child Sexual Abuse*. Lexington, MA: D.C. Heath.

Smith, T. (1985). Developing a Theoretical Framework for Evaluating Offenders. *Sexual Violence Quarterly*, 1, 4–5.

Suedfeld, P., and Landon, P.B. (1979). Approaches to Treatment. In Hare, R.D., and Schalling, D. (Eds.), *Psychopathic Behaviour: Approaches to Research*. New York: Wiley.

Theras, P. (1979). *The Buddha's Ancient Path*. Kandy, Sri Lanka: Buddhist Publication Society.

Watts, D.L., and Courtois, C.A. (1981). Trends in the Treatment of Men who Commit Violence Against Women. *Personnel and Guidance Journal*, 60, 246–249.

Yochelson, S., and Samenow, S.E. (1977). *The Criminal Personality*. New York: Jacob Aronson.

Youngstrom, N. (1992). Rapist Studies Reveal Complex Mental Map. *APA Monitor*, July 1992. Washington DC: Am Psychol Assoc.

Chapter Three

CASPARS:

Clinical Assessment Instruments that Measure Strengths and Risks in Children and Families

Jane F. Gilgun Ph.D.

CASPARS: Clinical Assessment Instruments that Measure Strengths and Risks in Children and Families

Introduction

Clinical instruments that identify client strengths are of high interest to practitioners. Some practitioners value strengths more than risks as a foundation for practice (Kwang and Cowger, 1998). Strengths-based practice not only promotes more comprehensive, balanced, and optimistic views of clients and their situations than deficit-based treatment, but such a positive emphasis also is one of several factors associated with treatment effectiveness (Miller, Duncan, and Hubble, 1997). Strengths-based practice also builds upon the observation that persons can overcome even substantial risks if they are able to mobilise resources that help them cope with, adapt to, or overcome the risks.

The Clinical Assessment Package for Client Risks and Strengths (CASPARS) brings strength perspectives to practice. Not only do these instruments direct attention to positives, but they also contribute to treatment plans, help estimate progress in treatment, and provide measures of outcome. Short, easy to administer and score, and based on research and theory on risk and resilience, the CASPARS are ecological in scope. They cover five domains that are central to child and family well-being. These domains are emotional expressiveness, sexuality, peer relationships, family relationships, and family embeddedness in the community.

Tested on children and families where the children have a range of adjustment problems including sexually acting out, the instruments have excellent reliabilities and validities. The purpose of this chapter is to demonstrate the conceptual basis of the instruments and their use with children and their families where the children have experienced adversities that are interfering with their development and quality of life.

The Concepts on which the CASPARS are Based

The CASPARS grew out of my decade-long life history research on adults who have experienced child and adolescent adversities, such as child abuse and neglect, abandonment, and parental chemical dependency. These factors are commonly found among persons who act out in violent ways, as well as among those who do not. Most of my informants were convicted of violent felonies, while about one quarter had no involvement in legal systems. Early in my research, I focused on the differences between men who had committed child sexual abuse and their non-offending wives (Gilgun, 1991). In an effort to isolate what specifically characterises perpetrators of child sexual abuse, I gradually added other persons to my sample, such as men and women with risks and who turned out well, rapists, perpetrators of physical violence, murderers, and armed robbers (Gilgun, 1990, 1992; 1996b).

Confidant relationships. During the first phases of my study, I found having a confidant differentiated incest perpetrators and child molesters from their non-offending wives (Gilgun, 1990; Gilgun and Connor, 1990). I later replicated this finding when I compared the incest perpetrators and child molesters to men who had risks for such offences but did not commit them. Again, I found that having confidant relationships was a differentiating factor (Gilgun, 1990). Over and over, with a range of informants and a variety of outcomes, I consistently found that the presence of a confidant—that is, a person with whom the informant had a long-term relationship of trust that involved the exchange of sensitive, personal information—differentiated those who turned out well from those who did not.

Confidants could be peers or adults and of either gender. What appeared to be essential was for the confidant to convey an understanding of informants and informants' situations. In turn, informants had to experience themselves as understood and accepted. The confidants also espoused and modelled pro-social values and behaviours and frequently not only encouraged informants to develop new skills but actively taught them these skills (Gilgun, 1992; 1996b). Reciprocally, informants sought to emulate their confidants. I gradually called the ability to share personal issues 'emotional expressiveness,' a term gaining some visibility in child development research (Boyum and Parke, 1995; Cassidy *et al.*, 1995; Roberts and Strayer, 1996).

Peer relationships. The quality of peer relationships was also a differentiating factor. Early on in my research, I had a poor understanding of peer relationships. I assumed that having friends is good and not having friends is bad. Then I listened to the life history of a man who as an adolescent was part of a group of team-mates from the school ice hockey team. He felt a deep sense of belonging to this group. These boys had parties where they got girls drunk in order to have sex with them. Sometimes the girls had passed out. They sometimes 'pulled a train;' that is, had gang rapes. The boys called themselves 'The Cherry Club.' From then on, I knew that quality of peer relationships differentiated good outcomes from bad in high risk individuals. Subsequent case studies confirmed this observation.

Other aspects of peer relationships were important. How informants saw themselves in relationship to peers—as having similar abilities, as being able to develop friendships, and being able to stand up for themselves in pro-social ways—also distinguished pro-social outcomes from anti-social.

Family relationships. Quality of family relationships became significant in my findings. Confidants could be family members, but sometimes children were isolated and neglected within their families but sought and found acceptance and understanding in extra-familial relationships with peers and unrelated adults. Other aspects of family life, such as how parents got along, how parents treated other children in the family, and how siblings treated informants seemed to have an influence in the outcomes informants experienced.

Finally, parents' recognition of children's accomplishments and affirmation of their pro-social behaviours, as well as modelling them, are factors in children turning out well under adverse circumstances.

Family embeddedness. Family's relationships in communities also had an effect on outcome for informants. Families whose members gave and received emotional and material support to persons outside of their families and who had warm connections within churches, schools, and other social institutions were less likely to have children with problematic outcomes. Public libraries, playgrounds and recreational opportunities in communities that informants used also were associated with overcoming adversities. Feeling part of communities and being affirmed for abilities and personal qualities are components of positive extra-familial relationships.

Sexuality. Finally, sexuality is an obvious major issue for sex offenders. What was different about the sexuality of sex offenders as compared to other groups? In my life history research, male sex offenders differed from women non-offenders in their patterns of masturbation and in the amount of time they spent 1) thinking about sexuality, 2) seeking sexual arousal, 3) and fantasising about and planning for sexual encounters, usually of the unlawful and harmful type, such as rape, child molestation, peeping, and flashing. They, then, of course, acted on their sexual fantasies. For child molesters in particular, these sexual patterns developed early, often before age 10. Rapists, who had patterns similar to child molesters, usually developed their patterns a bit later, unless they also molested children. In those cases, they often had these patterns before age 10. I did not find rapists who focused exclusively on adults fantasising about molesting children.

Some men and women were similar to sex offenders in their patterns of masturbation, their seeking of sexual arousal (Gilgun, 1990) and in some instances of peeping and flashing (e.g. voyeurism and exhibitionism). Some even had brief fantasies of sex with children, but they immediately set those thoughts aside. If the thoughts were about specific children, they avoided situations where they could act out, and they sought treatment. Somehow, they had developed patterns of thought that put brakes on desires that would harm themselves or others. These patterns served protective functions.

Summary. Emotional expressiveness in a range of domains is a major factor in overcoming adversities and appears to be a major factor in overcoming risks for violent behaviours. Other factors that also are significant in this regard are opportunities to develop a sense of self-efficacy, to be well-regarded by others, and to have pro-social behaviours modelled and affirmed within a broad range of domains.

Other relevant research

As I was developing these findings in my case study research, I read child psychology research and theory on risk and resilience (Cicchetti, 1987; Cicchetti *et al.*, 1993). Garmezy and Masten, 1994; Masten, 1994; Werner, 1992). Research on resilience seeks to identify factors that moderate the effects of risks. When individuals are able to mobilise their resources and cope with, adapt to, or overcome risks, they are said to be resilient (Gilgun, 1996a; Masten, Best, and Garmezy, 1991; Rutter, 1987). Resilience researchers have investigated the effects of such adversities as homelessness, child maltreatment, poverty, foster home placement, and parental mental illness. They showed that resources within individuals, families, and systems external to families are associated with resilience, or good outcomes under adverse conditions.

Definition of key concepts

This body of research and theory provided definitions of two key concepts on which the CASPARS are based: Risks and Assets. Both are probabilistic concepts. Risks predict that a proportion of at-risk groups will have the associated outcomes but they cannot predict that any one individual will have that outcome. Thus, for example, individuals who have been maltreated in childhood have a risk for maltreating their own children, but other factors could moderate the effects of that risk. Empirical research has shown that this is so (Egeland *et al.*, 1988; Gilgun, 1990, 1991, 1992, 1996b; Kaufman and Zigler, 1987). This

research provides further evidence that moderating factors exist.

Examples of risks include a history of childhood and adolescent abuse and neglect, homelessness, family disruptions, separations and losses, loss of jobs, dangerous neighbourhoods, poverty, racial and ethnic discrimination, and genetic risks predisposing individuals to particular types of physiological reactivity (Cicchetti, 1987; Rende and Plomin, 1993; Richters and Martinez, 1993; Werner and Smith, 1992).

Assets, too, are probabilistic concepts and can only predict to groups and not to individuals. Examples of assets are above average IQ, physical appeal, verbal ability, caring parents, resources within neighbourhoods, adequate income, and good schools (Cicchetti, 1987; Garmezy and Masten, 1994; Masten *et al.*, 1991; Richters and Martinez, 1993; Rutter, 1987; Werner and Smith, 1992). Some individuals with assets have poor outcomes. They are not able to use their assets to moderate risks, and sometimes their risks overwhelm the assets they have (Masten, 1994; Masten *et al.*, 1991; Rutter, 1987). Assets are protective factors when they are associated with overcoming risks (Gilgun, 1996a; Masten, 1994).

Some persons experience cumulative risks; that is, a series of risks that may interact and overwhelm whatever resources an individual can marshal, while in other cases persons appear to have sufficient resources to cope. This idea helps to explain why there is such a wide variation in outcomes among persons who have experienced a single known risk, such as child sexual abuse. Those who have relatively mild outcomes not only have fewer risks, but they also have turned assets into protective factors. Those who have more serious outcomes probably have many interacting risks and fewer assets on which to draw, or do not use well whatever assets their environments offer.

The significance of assets in models of risk

The CASPARS are based on the principle that assets are significant in models of risk. I can demonstrate this principle through survey research and case study research. In a survey that compared Minnesota prison inmates with an adult and an adolescent non-inmate samples (Gilgun, Klein, and Pranis, 1998a), my colleagues and I demonstrated through logistic regression analyses that the addition of assets significantly improved risk models. When assets were entered into the model first, they correctly classified inmates and non-inmates 74 per cent of the time, as compared to an 84 per cent correct classification rate when risks were entered first. We had this outcome despite the fact that our measures of risk were much more thorough than our measures of assets. Any classification above 50 per cent is better than chance.

Case study research provides additional insight into assets as moderators of risks. The case of Rob (not his real name) provides an example. Rob, in his late twenties, married, and the father of two sons, had major risks in his childhood and adolescence (from Gilgun, 1996b). These risks included an alcoholic father who sexually abused him from age 8 to 13, who physically abused him, who had tantrums and threw objects in the family home, and who called Rob names such as 'dumbfucker,' 'faggot,' 'stupid little shit,' and 'jackass.' His parents fought verbally on a continual basis. His mother meted out punitive discipline and was non-responsive to his requests for emotional support. Rob experienced no trust in his family. He confided in his sister once, and she told her parents. Rob was punished. Rob said, 'We never talked. We never hugged.'

Rob responded to these family issues by withdrawing from them. During adolescence he attempted suicide twice, and he became homophobic. He didn't join the school chess team because he was afraid other teens would think he was gay. Rob vowed never to be like his father.

On the basis of Rob's risks and his responses to them, it is logical to think that he did not turn out well. His risk profile, however, gives an incomplete picture. The following are some of Rob's individual, family, extended family, and community assets. His parents had a good, steady income. His mother was a well-organised household manager. When his father hit Rob, his mother would stand between them and insist the father stop. His father did not physically abuse Rob's mother. Rob lived with his family in same home from kindergarten until he left home in his late teens. The neighbourhood was pleasant and residential, with abundant recreational opportunities and excellent schools. Rob's race, ethnicity, and religion were congruent with other persons in the neighbourhood.

No one in Rob's extended family were alcoholics, and he had two uncles who were well-known public figures. Rob had frequent contact with these uncles and other members of the extended family, and these experiences were affirming to him. For example, he and his sisters spent several summers with his aunt and uncle on their farm, where he learned to operate farm machinery and take care of animals. His aunt and uncle told him frequently how much they appreciated and admired his abilities.

Rob had many personal assets. He was bright, creative, physically active, industrious. At risk for alcoholism because of his father's alcoholism, he didn't like the taste of alcohol and what it did to him. He rarely drank. He took no pleasure in the sexual abuse, and he therefore was not confused by it. He did not doubt that his parents often were abusive and tended not to blame himself for their behaviours.

Rob had a life-long best friend named Pete, and he was a second son in Pete's family. Pete had been at Rob's many times when his father came home drunk and he also had helped Rob retrieve his father from a neighbourhood bar. Rob also was close to Pete's parents, eating dinner with them frequently and going on outings to a local lake. When Rob was a young teenager, Pete's father helped Rob pick out a snowblower and encouraged him to start a snow clearing business, which became successful. Rob and Pete frequently talked about their families with Rob wishing his family was more like Pete's.

Rob kept a diary he named Sam, and in it he wrote his intimate thoughts and feelings. After family fights, he frequently cried himself to sleep at night. He had a degree of privacy in his own bedroom, where he also had stereo equipment. He often consoled himself with music. He wrote stories and one of them was published in a well-known U.S. magazine.

He often dreamed of a better life, and he did not masturbate to soothe himself. He enjoyed the ejaculations he had during wet dreams, and he was not sexually aggressive toward other teenage girls. He once protected a young woman from a rape at a party and ordered the perpetrator out of the home. The perpetrator was giving the party in his family home. Rob went out of his way to please others, and he wanted to be a nice kid. He consciously told himself that he didn't want to be the 'little shit' his father said he was.

Looking at both assets and risks gives a comprehensive picture of Rob. He is emotionally expressive, he developed long-term confidant relationships, he functioned well sexually, and he consciously wanted to be a nice person.

How did Rob turn out? He put himself through trade school. He became the youngest foreman in his shop. He married Ann, whom he loved and who loved him. Ann had strong ties to her family of origin, and they welcomed Rob like a son. Rob felt part of his Ann's family. Yet, early in his marriage, he was verbally abusive and physically intimidating to his wife and physically abusive to his infant son. When he became abusive, Ann would take the children and go to her parents' home. She urged him to go into therapy. He told her she was crazy, and he wasn't.

One day, Rob had a tantrum, and Ann left with the children. He saw that he had broken his son's toy train. It was then he had an epiphany. The broken toy triggered memories of how his father got into rages and broke his toys. He cried for a long time, and then called Ann to say he wanted therapy. Within a few weeks of couple counselling, he remembered his own sexual abuse, a trauma he had repressed. He then went into treatment for his sexual abuse. Gradually, he saw that he indeed was an abusive parent, and he joined Parents Anonymous (PA), a support group for parents who want to change abusive behaviours toward their children. Rob told the executive director that he was in my research. The executive director told me that Rob has taken a major leadership role in PA.

Rob did not emerge unscathed from a troubled childhood and adolescence, but he turned his assets into protective factors that not only helped him see the consequences of his behaviours, but also gave him motivation to pursue a series of therapeutic experiences that helped him let go of his abusiveness.

On the basis of 65 case studies, the survey, a review of risk and resilience research and theory, and a commitment to social work's strengths perspectives, I was ready to develop instruments that I hoped would measure the concepts I had discovered in my case study research. I saw for my   self tha

many risks for adverse outcomes can cope with, adapt to, and overcome risks and lead satisfying lives. I had identified many factors associated with resilience. To me, this approach is optimistic and humane, and it shows much more promise than deficit-based approaches.

I wrote the instruments as part of a consultancy I did for a family service agency that was developing a program for children who were acting out sexually against others. My job was to develop the program's evaluation tools. The program never got off the ground, but by the time that became evident I had already created the instruments but had not yet tested them for reliability and validity. So, I applied for and received funding through the Allina Foundation, which was created by a health maintenance organisation and is located in Minneapolis, Minnesota, USA.

Sources of Items for the CASPARS

My case study research was the primary source of items for the CASPARS. In addition, research on risk and resilience provided concepts and ideas for the instruments and also assured me that my research had taken a viable direction. Social work's strengths' perspectives also supported the conceptualisation of the instruments. Strengths' perspectives emphasise the importance of mobilising resources to facilitate change in client systems (Saleebey, 1992, 1996). In addition, social work researchers have pointed out the debilitating effects of the stigmatisation that deficit-based thinking has on clients (Kwang and Cowger, 1998).

Once I had a draft of the five CASPARS instruments, two clinical social workers and two clinical psychologists subjected them to a rigorous critique. They suggested rewording of some items, additional items, and the discarding of some items. The two social work clinicians then piloted the instruments. We continued to pilot modify them until there seemed to be no need for further changes.

Testing the Instruments

Upon completion of the piloting, I did reliability and validity studies on a sample of 146 boys and girls and their families. (See Gilgun, 1998, for details on testing.) The children were between the ages of 5 and 13, with an average age of 9. Fifty-one percent were girls, and 51% were European-American in descent, 12 % were African-Americans, almost 8 % were American Indians, 6% were of mixed racial backgrounds, and about 3% were of Latino/Hispanic heritage. The race of 18% of the sample was not known. More than half the sample had been in out-home care at least once in their lives. Most of the sample had experienced childhood abuse and neglect, parental abandonment, and had a variety of behavioural and neurological issues. Many had sexual issues, such as being abuse reactive and in acting out sexually against others. A large portion of the sample had been in therapeutic foster homes and in individual, group, and family therapy. Professionals such as social workers, child care workers, therapeutic foster parents, and psychologists filled out the instruments on the children.

The CASPARS Instruments

The CASPARS are clinical rating scales; that is, they are filled out by practitioners and not by clients. From that point of view, the CASPARS

Figure 1: Sample items from the Emotional Expressiveness Instrument

Assets				**Risks**		

1. Child shows a range of feelings; not only a few, such as happiness, anger or sadness

Child does not show a range of feelings; only a few, such as happiness, anger or sadness

| 3 | 2 | 1 | 0 | 1 | 2 | 3 |

2. Child puts own feelings into words

Child does not put own feelings into words

| 3 | 2 | 1 | 0 | 1 | 2 | 3 |

3. Child's expression of feelings is appropriate to situations

Child's expression of feelings is not appropriate to situations

| 3 | 2 | 1 | 0 | 1 | 2 | 3 |

4. Child's feelings and reactions are linked to the events that precipitated them

Child's feelings and reactions are not linked to the events that precipitated them

| 3 | 2 | 1 | 0 | 1 | 2 | 3 |

5. Child can identify a wide range of feelings others

Child cannot identify a wide range of in feelings in others

| 3 | 2 | 1 | 0 | 1 | 2 | 3 |

6. Child sympathises with other people's feelings

Child does not sympathise with other people's feelings

| 3 | 2 | 1 | 0 | 1 | 2 | 3 |

7. Child appears to respect the feelings of others; does not mock, tease, or use others

Child does not appear to have respect for the feelings of others; mocks, teases or uses others

| 3 | 2 | 1 | 0 | 1 | 2 | 3 |

8. Child has a person in family and/or community who facilitates appropriate expression of feelings

Child has few or no persons in family community who facilitate appropriate expression of feelings

| 3 | 2 | 1 | 0 | 1 | 2 | 3 |

are intended to extend and document clinician's assessments and evaluations. As stated earlier, the five CASPARS instruments are emotional expressiveness, peer relationships, family relationships, family's embeddedness in community, and sexuality. Number of items range from 13 to 20 and coefficient alphas, which are an index of reliability, ranged from .90 to .97, highly satisfactory for clinical instruments. Item- total correlations were high, suggesting a unity among the items. Construct validity with instruments thought to measure similar concepts ranged from .46 to .81 which are in the highly acceptable range. (See Gilgun, 1998 for details on reliability and validity.) The instruments have good face validity, as four experienced clinicians contributed to their development.

Scoring. Each item has a risk side and an asset side. I used the term asset instead of strengths because asset is the term used in research on risk and resilience, the source of my definitions of risk and assets, as discussed earlier. To score the instruments, clinicians first decide whether or not an item represents an asset or a risk. After making that decision, clinicians then

decide whether the client is high (3 points), medium (2 points), or low (1 point) on the asset or high (3 points), medium (2 points), or low (1 point) on the risk. Scores are computed by summing the columns. Figure 1 shows items form the Emotional Expressiveness Scale.

With two scores, children can be classified according to their mix of assets and risks as shown in Figure 2 below. The ideal is to move children into a high asset/low risk classification. Two scores helps clinicians and clients identify and work with both assets and risks.

Figure 2: A Classification by Assets and Risks

	Low Risks	High Risks
High Assets	Group 1	Group 2
Low Assets	Group 3	Group 4

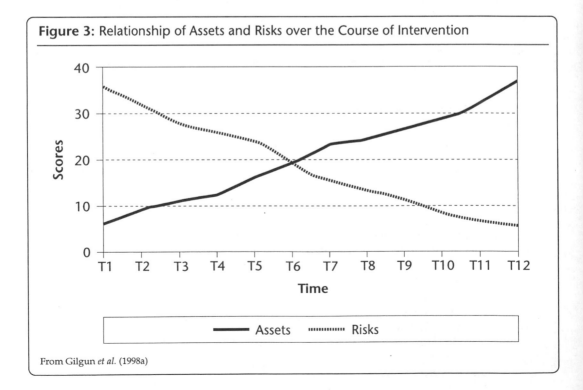

Figure 3: Relationship of Assets and Risks over the Course of Intervention

From Gilgun *et al.* (1998a)

The results of administering the CASPARS over the course of treatment can be graphed. Most clients begin treatment high in risks and low in assets, at least on the issues that brought them into treatment in the first place. The goal of treatment is to reduce risks and increase assets. Figure 3 shows the graph of a successful course of treatment. Using graphs to assess the effects of treatment has many benefits. They are a visual representation of progress or lack of progress in treatment. Clients can see for themselves how they are responding to treatment. Such easy-to-interpret information can spark discussions and insights about what is working and not working in treatment in a variety of settings. That is, clinicians can talk to clients directly about their progress, or clinicians can discuss the case in group and peer supervision. Finally, having scores and graphs documents the effects of treatment. Such documentation is important to funders and to the general public, as well as to clinicians, clients, and their agencies.

Discussion

The CASPARS are a set of five instruments that are designed to give equal consideration to client strengths and risks. Developed from case study research, research and theory on risk and resilience, and in consultation with social workers and psychologists, they were tested on a sample of 146 children and their families, where the children had a range of adversities and were at risk for poor outcomes. The CASPARS have high reliabilities and validities. The instruments yield a risk and an asset score and the items are written so they can account for changes over time. Thus they can be used for both assessment and evaluation of the effects of intervention. As clinical rating scales, the instruments are filled out by practitioners and not by clients. Based on both theory and practice, they are an adjunct to treatment and put into words how practitioners see clients and how clients change over time. Clients usually begin treatment high on risks and low on assets and the goal of treatment is to reduce risks and increase assets.

The CASPARS were developed and tested for use in work with children and families where the children have experienced adversities that put them at risk for poor outcomes. Their solid grounding in both research and practice make them good models for the construction of other strengths-based instruments. Practitioners can modify the items of the CASPARS and develop new ones to customise the instruments to their own treatment settings. As Kwang and Cowger (1998) found, practitioners want to work with client strengths. Some view strengths as more important than risk, but they lack the tools that support their strengths-based perspectives. The CASPARS and instruments modelled after the CASPARS meet the expressed wishes of practitioners.

The CASPARS have a commonsense structure that guide clinicians to identify both strengths and risks. They provide a down-to-earth approach that appeals to practitioners. In addition, there is a great need to document the effects of practice. Instruments that are grounded in clients' experiences and that draw upon the insights that practitioners develop over time not only meet clinician's demands for relevance but also meet funders' demands for documentation of the effects of treatment.

The CASPARS are a potentially useful tool in work with young people who sexually abuse, as descriptions of this group rarely mention their strengths. Given that many abusers are raised in dysfunctional families, the simultaneous emphasis on identifying and working with the strengths of their parents is essential if they are to support the necessary work. I have described elsewhere (Gilgun *et al.*, 1998b) a community-based treatment programme for children aged 5 to 13 years who have sexually inappropriate behaviours, abusive-reactive behaviours and molestation of other children. The challenge is to now utilise and test the usefulness of these instruments with young people who sexually abuse.

Note. Copies of the CASPARS (and feedback on their use)can be obtained from the Center for Advanced Studies in Child Welfare, School of Social Work. Send all correspondence to School of Social Work, University of Minnesota, 224 Church St., SE, Minneapolis MN 55455 USA. Or email Jane Gilgun at jgilgun@che2.che.umn.edu.

References

Boyum, L.A., and Parke, R.D. (1995). The Role of Family Emotional Expressiveness in the Development of Children's Social Competence. *Journal of Marriage and the Family*, 57: 593–608.

Cassidy J., and Asher, S.R. (1992). Loneliness and Peer Relations in Young Children. *Child Development*, 63: 350–365.

Cicchetti, D. (1987). Developmental Psychopathology in Infancy: Illustrations from the Study of Maltreated Youngsters. *Journal of Consulting and Clinical Psychology*, 55: 837–845.

Cicchetti, D., Rogosch, F.A., Lynch, M., and Holt, K.D. (1993). Resilience in Maltreated Children: Processes Leading to Adaptive Outcomes. *Development and Psychopathology*, 5: 629–647.

Cowger, C.D. (1994). Assessing Client Strengths. Clinical Assessment for Client Empowerment. *Social Work*, 39: 262–268.

Egeland, B., Jacobvitz, D., and Sroufe, L.A. (1988). Breaking the Cycle of Abuse. *Child Development*, 59: 1080–1088.

Garmezy, N., and Masten, A.S. (1994). Chronic Adversities. In Rutter, M., Taylor, E., and Hersov, L. (Eds.). *Child and Adolescent Psychiatry*. Oxford: Blackwell.

Gilgun, J.F. (1998). CASPARS: New Tools for Assessing Client Risks and Strengths. Manuscript submitted for publication.

Gilgun, J.F. (1996a). Human Development and Adversity in Ecological Perspective: Part 1: A Conceptual Framework. *Families in Society*, 77: 395–402.

Gilgun, J.F. (1996b). Human Development and Adversity in Ecological Perspective: Part 2: Three Patterns. *Families in Society*, 77: 459–576.

Gilgun, J.F. (1992). Hypothesis Generation in Social Work Research. *Journal of Social Service Research*, 15: 113–135.

Gilgun, J.F. (1991). Resilience and the Intergenerational Transmission of Child Sexual Abuse. In Patton, M.Q. (Ed.). *Family Sexual Abuse: Frontline Research and Evaluation* (pp 93–105). Newbury Park, CA: Sage.

Gilgun, J.F. (1990). Factors Mediating the Effects of Childhood Maltreatment. In Hunter, M. (Ed.). *The Sexually Abused Male: Prevalence, Impact, and Treatment* (pp 177–190). Lexington, MA: Lexington Books.

Gilgun, J.F., and Connor, T.M. (1990). Isolation and the Adult Male Perpetrator of Child Sexual Abuse. In

Horton, A.L., Johnson, B.L., Roundy, L.M., and Williams, D. (Eds.). *The Incest Perpetrator: The Family Member No One Wants to Treat* (pp 74–87). Newbury Park, CA: Sage.

Gilgun, J.F., Klein, C., and Pranis, K. (1998a). The Significance of Strengths in Models of Risks. Manuscript submitted for publication.

Gilgun, J.F., Keskinen, S., Jones Marti, D., and Rice, K. (1998b). Clinical Applications of the CASPARS Instruments: Boys who Act out Sexually. Manuscript submitted for publication.

Kaufman, J., and Zigler, E. (1987). Do Abused Children Become Abusive Parents? *American Journal of Orthopsychiatry*, 57: 186–192.

Kwang, S., and Cowger, C.D. (1998). Utilizing Strengths in Assessment. *Families in Society*, 79: 25–31.

Masten, A.S. (1994). Resilience in Individual Development: Successful Adaptation Despite Risk and Adversity. In Wang, M.C., and Gordon, E.W. (Eds.). *Educational Resilience in Inner-city America: Challenges and Prospects* (pp 3–23). Hillsdale, NJ: Erlbaum.

Masten, A.S., Best, K.M., and Garmezy, N. (1991). Resilience and Development: Contributions from the Study of Children who Overcome Adversity. *Development and Psychopathology*, 2: 425–444.

Miller, S.D., Duncan, B.L., and Hubble, M.A. (1997). *Escape from Babel: Toward a Unifying Language for Psychotherapy Practice*. New York: W.W. Norton.

Rende, R., and Plomin, R. (1993). Families at Risk for Psychopathology: Who Becomes Affected and Why? *Development and Psychopathology*, 5: 529–540.

Richters, J.E., and Martinez, P.E. (1993). Violent Communities, Family Choices, and Children's Chances: An Algorithm for Improving the Odds. *Development and Psychopathology*, 5: 609–627.

Roberts, W., and Strayer, J. (1996). Empathy, Emotional Expressiveness, and Pro-social Behavior. *Child Development*, 67: 449–470.

Rutter, M. (1987). Psychosocial Resilience and Protective Mechanisms. *American Journal of Orthopsychiatry*, 57: 316–331.

Saleebey, D. (1996). The Strengths Perspective in Social Work Practice: Extensions and Cautions. *Social Work*, 41: 241–336.

Saleebey, D. (Ed.) (1992). *The Strengths Perspective in Social Work Practice*. New York: Longman.

Werner, E.E., and Smith, R.S. (1992). *Overcoming the Odds: High Risk Children from Birth to Adulthood*. Ithaca, NY: Cornell University Press.

Chapter Four

Recovery Assessments with Young People who Sexually Abuse

Mark S. Carich Ph.D. and Matthew C. Lampley B.S.

Recovery Assessments with Young People who Sexually Abuse

Introduction

The issue of 'recovery' is often controversial when applied to sex offenders. Many professionals seem to ignore it totally. The field of sex offender treatment is rapidly evolving and developing. As part of that development, the concept of recovery can no longer be ignored. Over the last 8 years it has been defined and applied to adult and older adolescent offenders. It has not been applied to the youthful offender, i.e. child reactors and adolescent offenders. The purposes of this chapter is to:

- provide a concise definition of recovery
- provide multi-level criteria to evaluate recovery
- apply the 15 recovery factors to the youthful offender

Recovery is defined as:

> the capability of an offender to maintain abstinence from offending (Carich, 1997a). It is based on the belief that there is not an acceptable cure or absolute permanent abstinence from offending (ATSA, 1997; Carich, 1997 a, 1997 b. 1997 c, 1998, 1991 a, b; 1996 Laws, 1989; Carich and Metzger, 1998 a,b). However, offenders can learn to significantly reduce their deviant arousal and rearrange their behaviour.

The above definition of recovery is based on several common assumptions. These include:

1. There is no cure for sex offenders.
2. Offending is a series of learned choices at all levels of awareness.
3. Recovery is a lifelong process.
4. Offenders can learn to reduce their deviant arousal significantly and manage their deviant behaviour.
5. Offending is a learned complex set of behaviours from different exponential domains.
6. Offenders may have new types of offences.

Different Types of Assessment:

There are four proposed differentiated types of assessments which include the following:

- basic data collection assessments
- treatment progress assessments
- risk assessments
- recovery assessments
    (Carich and Metzger, 1998 a,b).

The first type of assessment is simply basic data collection (Carich and Adkerson, 1995; McGrath, 1990; Salter, 1988; Stickrod-Gray and Wallace, 1993). Historical and non-historical information is collected from the offender in order to make a case disposition and problem/needs assessment. This is done before planning and defining the characteristics or profile of the offender.

The second type of assessment is treatment progress evaluation (Metzger and Carich, 1997). In this situation, treatment plans are compared to the offender's behavioural progress within the program. The offender either accomplishes various objectives or does not.

The third type of assessment is risk assessment (Carich and Adkerson 1995; Hanson and Bussiere, 1996; McGrath 1991, 1992). In this type of assessment, the offender is evaluated in terms of predicting the probability of re-offending. The offender is evaluated in terms of both static (historical or non-changeable) and actuarial (statistically significant) risk predictors, (Hanson R.K., October 1998, personal communication to Carich, M.).

The fourth and final type of assessment is whether the offender has the capability to maintain abstinence. This should correlate with any risk assessment prediction. Historically, recovery was measured by the dynamic variables of progress in treatment. This wouldn't necessarily apply to those offenders not in treatment. Currently, many professionals use risk assessments to evaluate 'recovery'. However, problems arise because of the static and actuarial predators that may contaminate the evaluation. Risk assessment terminology of recovery is based on dynamic predictors, some of which may be statistically significant (House, 1998, personal communication to Carich, M.).

What is Recovery?

Recovery can be analysed in a number of ways. Several authors have provided a list of characteristics of recovering sex offenders. Roys (1995) developed an 'exit exam' to re-evaluate recovery, whilst Carich, (1997b; 1998) constructed a list of general characteristics of what a recovering sex offender looks like:

- More honest.
- Less frequency of deviant behaviour.
- Consistently appears less crooked.
- Consistently appears less entitled.
- Consistently appears less narcissistic.
- Takes responsibility in general.
- Takes responsibility for one's offending.
- Expresses/experiences victim empathy.
- Capable of explaining dynamics of (their) offending without blaming.
- Motivating (core) issues seem to be less intense.
- Know one's cycle.
- Know one's cues.
- Know one's triggers.
- Refutes cognitive distortions.
- Uses anger controls and interventions.
- Has a variety of coping strategies.
- Works on long-term goals.
- Proud of accomplishments.
- Positive self-esteem.
- Upkeep of personal hygiene.
- Admit they need treatment for life.
- Good support system.
- Know and stick to structure.
- Consistency in behaviour.
- Stable support system.

- Sense of independence.
- Able to confront self and others.
- Empathy in general.
- Sense of spiritualism.
- Doesn't keep secrets.
- Knows ones non offending adaptive lifestyle.
- Isn't hostile.
- Expresses feelings appropriately.

Below is a similar list of characteristics provided by Freeman-Longo and Blanchard (1998):

- The abuser accepts full responsibility (p 171).
- The abuser acts differently. He doesn't promise he will never do it again. He is humble and educated enough to acknowledge that he is always at risk to return to a former way of life. Consequently, his everyday behaviours and his entire lifestyle, rather than just words, reflect this change away from power seeking, manipulation, and control (p 171).
- The abuser is less selfish and self-absorbed. He shows more concern and empathy for others. (p 171).
- The abuser stays in touch with other recovering men...Humility is ever present (p 171).
- The abuser knows his high-risk situations...His insights are quickly translated into a corrective plan (p 172).
- The abuser doesn't use sex or alcohol abusively (p 172).
- The abuser's thinking is no longer distorted...He is less confused...more honest (p 172)
- The abuser may be more spiritual...he shows sensitivity for others...(and) adheres to values...(p 172).
- The abuser's time is well spent...purpose in life...job is satisfying...(p 172).
- The abuser's self-esteem has improved. He no longer berates himself or needs to berate others...confidence is up. He is at peace with himself.
- The abuser's sex life is more serene...He

has learned to enjoy a quieter and more satisfying sex life. Intensity has been replaced with intimacy (p 172).

- The abuser is more assertive, but less aggressive. (p 172)
- The abuser's need to control is reduced... Compromise is a part of his life (p 173).
- The abuser's anger has diminished. Now the ability is there to express a wide range of emotions other than just anger. He can identify an appropriately ventilate the emotions that previously led to angry outbursts...(p 173).
- The abuser's social skills have improved... He is not afraid to meet new people. Listening skills are better. Relationships are less competitive. People are less threatening. He trusts more. Loneliness has diminished (p 173).
- The abuser handles family problems with greater ease. Not everything is crisis...He seeks consensus (p 173).
- The abuser is less jealous and level of insecurity has lessened (p 173).
- The abuser has reassessed old friends... dangerous people/environments are avoided.
- The abuser's anxiety is diminished...He can enjoy the moment (p 173).
- The abuser is no longer depressed...more of a positive quality (p 173).
- The abuser understands his cycle and uses interventions...(p174).
- The abuser demonstrates empathy... identify with feelings of others (p 174).
- The abuser thinks about the impact of his actions on himself and others (p 174).

These characteristics of recovery imply and correspond to the 15 factor criteria of recovery discussed in the next section. From both lists, the following characteristics appear to apply to the youthful offender:

1. Accepts full responsibility for offence specific behaviour and global behaviour.
2. Less self-centred and has developed humility.
3. Doesn't use alcohol and/or drugs.
4. Thinking is no longer distorted.

5. Developed social skills and appropriate patterns of attachment.
6. Reduced anger and appropriate expression of affect.
7. Appears to trust more and has less authority issues.
8. Has less interpersonal issues of jealousy, insecurity, possessiveness, etc.
9. Identifies and applies the assault cycle.
10. Has developed a positive peer group.
11. Reduced core issues derived from personally perceived trauma, victimisation or neglect.
12. Developed victim empathy and remorse.
13. Adheres to structure.
14. Utilises relapse intervention skills or appropriate coping skills.
15. Doesn't keep secrets.
16. Appropriate personal hygiene.
17. Improved self-concept, worth, esteem, etc. based on appropriate behaviour.
18. Seems to be more spiritual in the sense of developed values, empathy, care and concern for others, belief in a higher power.
19. Seems to have developed a purpose and direction in life.

From a combination of these lists, clinical observations, treatment goals/plans and risk factors, etc., the following 15 factors were extracted to help professionals determine whether recovery has been achieved. They apply at different levels to the youthful offender.

The 15 Recovery Factors

1. Motivation towards recovery.
2. Commitment towards treatment.
3. Personal responsibility.
4. Social interest (i.e. victim empathy, remorse).
5. Social (interpersonal) dimension.
6. Insight into the offending or assault cycle.
7. Lifestyle behaviours (i.e. antisocial, narcissistic).

8. Insight into developmental/motivational dynamics.

9. Resolution of developmental/motivational dynamics.

10. Sexual identity issues.

11. Control/management of deviant arousal.

12. Type of psychopathology.

13. Level of disowning behaviours.

14. Relapse intervention skills.

15. Self-structure.

Each factor is briefly defined below. For more detailed discussions of these factors, the reader is referred to Carich (1997a, 1997b).

Factor 1 Motivation Towards Recovery.
Motivation refers to the drive to succeed in maintaining abstinence. For adults, we hope it is an internal drive 'I don't want to hurt anyone anymore' versus external 'I don't want to go to jail or get into trouble.' If the offender is in treatment, the following are reviewed; actual behaviour in relation to others, program attendance and participation, task assignment completion, etc. In some form the youthful offender has to make a decision not to sexually violate others. This is followed up by a commitment to that decision.

Factor 2 Commitment Towards Change.
Commitment in this context is defined as a pledge, an agreement or compliance towards the primary goal of *no more victims*. In terms of treatment the offender is expected to be compliant and co-operative while working towards treatment goals. For non-treatment participants, the offender needs to demonstrate the commitment of maintaining change or a state of abstinence.

Factor 3 Personal Responsibility. Personal responsibility is the placement of control of one's own behaviour. This encompasses both assuming full responsibility and accountability for both offence specific behaviours and global behaviours. In other words, the offender assumes full ownership of behaviour, without defences, cognitive distortions, etc.

Factor 4 Social Interest. Social interest is the general care and concern for others. This includes victim empathy and remorse at both cognitive and emotional levels; and empathy for others in general. Offenders are expected to demonstrate empathy for victims in general and one's specific victims. Victim empathy is defined as the compassionate understanding of the victim's painful experiences. Remorse is the painful regret or guilt for violating another person. For the youthful offender, they understand the hurt or 'bad' feelings the victim has because of his behaviour. They should feel guilt for violating others.

Factor 5 Social Dimension. The social dimension involves the interpersonal skills and dynamics. More specifically, it refers to basic social skills (i.e. eye contact, 'I' messages, respect, conversational skills, active listening, etc.). The latter includes interpersonal issues i.e. jealousy, possessiveness, dependency, enmeshed boundaries, isolation, alienation, disengaged, etc. The offender's interpersonal network needs to be appropriate, positive and healthy. Negative peers and family relationships need to be appropriate, functional and healthy.

Factor 6 The Assault Cycle. The offender needs to know his pre-assaultive, assaultive behaviours and post-assaultive (i.e. aftermath) behaviours. It is important that the offender is able to understand and conceptualise his assault cycle.

Factor 7 Lifestyle Behaviours. This highly controversial element refers to chronic patterns of behaviour that tend to cluster around the personality disorders of antisocial, narcissistic, schizoid, and borderline. For specific details, see (APA, 1994, Carich, 1997a,b; Carich and Adkerson, 1995). This element will not usually apply to the youthful offender, unless these patterns begin to emerge or perhaps to those offenders who have conduct disorders. In the latter case, these behaviours need to be addressed and evaluated. A detailed lifestyle cognitive-behavioural inventory (Carich and Steckel, 1992), designed to measure an individual's level of thought and behaviour on specific personality categories is reproduced in Calder (1999).

Factor 8 Insight into Developmental/ Motivational Dynamics. Insight into developmental and motivational dynamics refers to the aetiologically and teleological elements of offending. In terms of treatment of the youthful offender, it is considered important to address these issues, since they can be reality accessed. These dynamics are broken down into developmental perceptions and residual problems stemming from those developmental perceptions (interpretations) which are commonly 'care issues'. Early contributing factors include feelings of abandonment; rejection; issues of authority; trust; and resentments, etc.

Factor 9 Resolution of Developmental and Motivational Dynamics. Identification of developmental and motivational dynamics are important in maintaining recovery, but resolution to a lower degree is continued. Insight is nice, but action is necessary for change. All the insight in the world is useless without resolution. Care issues need to be resolved, or at least addressed. It is also critical that the offender does not play the 'abuse excuse' or 'blame game' for his offending. Resolution includes taking full responsibility for their behaviour, instead blaming a negative environment or trauma suffered over the years. They need to access and resolve traumatic and resulting core issues without self-pity.

Factor 10 Sexual Identity. Sexual identity issues or problems involve confusion in sexual roles and preferences. Many youthful offenders usually have degrees of sexual identity issues. For example, they may question their 'manhood' or perhaps 'womanhood' (for female offenders). In addition they may feel unsure of their sexual preferences. To maintain recovery, it helps if the offender has clear notions of sexual identity, and sexual preference.

Factor 11 Deviant Arousal Control. This factor is one of the primary goals in sex offender treatment. Deviant arousal control is a critical aspect of maintaining recovery. This factor addresses the level of deviant arousal and appropriate arousal. High levels of deviant arousal need to be significantly reduced and replaced with appropriate arousal. This includes learning specific ways to reduce and manage deviant fantasies, urges, cravings and other forms of arousal. High levels of deviant arousal do not exclusively mean that an

offender will re-offend, However research does indicate it is a significant dynamic risk predictor (Hanson and Bussiere, 1996).

Factor 12 Psychopathology. Psychopathology refers to any other mental disorder or emotional problems besides the offending behaviour. This may include any personality disorders (see factor 7); Paraphillas (See factor 11); affective disorders; psychotic disorders; behavioural disorders, etc. Psychopathology directly relates the therapist and client approached treatment.

Factor 13 Disowning Behaviour. Disowning behaviours refers to any way that an offender avoids or evades responsibility and/or behaviours that enable offending. This includes: offence specific cognitive distortions, offence specific defences or maladaptive coping strategies and global defences and/or maladaptive coping responses or patterns. For a detailed review of disowning behaviours, please refer to Carich, Michael and Stone (1992) and Carich (1993).

Factor 14 Relapse Interventions. Relapse prevention (RP) approaches have dominated the offender treatment approaches for the last 15 years (Laws, 1989). RP is a combination of cognitive-behavioural methods for learning self-management and control in order to maintain abstinence. Relapse Intervention is a variation of the RP based on an active approach to maintain abstinence or recovery (Carich and Stone, 1992; 1997b). In this approach, offenders are continuously intervening and utilising coping strategies. Offenders need to know their cycle behaviours, risk factors/situations, triggers and appropriate coping responses (interventions). This is one of the cornerstones of maintaining abstinence.

Factor 15 Self-structure. Self-structure is summarised by one's self-concept. This includes one's worldview, perceptions and beliefs of self and others. It has to do with how and what one feels about self. This element is evaluated in terms of the offender's self-worth, self-esteem, self-confidence, self-image, etc. without narcissism, inferiority/superiority beliefs. In recent years, Bill Marshall *et al.* (1996) has been emphasising the importance of self-esteem, image and worth in the treatment of sex offenders. For a detailed review of the literature in relation to self-esteem and sexual offending, please refer to Marshall *et al.* (1996).

Supporting Data

Recently, the members of ATSA (Association of the Treatment of Sexual Abuse) and the Wisconsin Sex Offender Network were surveyed in order to gather professional opinions concerning the 15 factors of recovery. The estimated percentage of agreements are found in table 1. The results are highlighted below. Eight factors ranged from 90–99% agreement as significant factors indicating recovery. Another six factors ranged form 80–85% agreement, while only three factors received 73–78% agreement. Only one factor had 69% agreement. It is suggested that further research needs to be conducted.

Applications of the 15 recovery factors to the youthful offender

One of the best documents with specific guidelines, published on adolescent offenders and child reactive or the youthful offender is the National Task Force on Juvenile Sex Offending (1993).

The application of the 15 recovery factors are based on the task force document. This document was originally published in 1988 and revised in 1993. It was developed by some of the best minds in the field. Several areas of this document were compared or paralleled with the 15 recovery factors. These included (1) issues in treatment; (2) indicators of progress in treatment; and (3) issues with abusive children (for details see tables 2, 3, and 4). The Task Force outlined 22 specific issues addressed in treatment. They state 'Certain definable issues have been identified as a result of clinical experience and should be addressed in the treatment process of every sexually abusive youth' (p43). For details see Table 2.

Table 1: Percentage agreement

Over 90%		80–90%		Under 80%	
RP Skills	99%	Aetiological/Insight	85%	Schizoid	69%
Responsibility	99%	Disowning/Behaviour	85%	Sexual Identity	73%
Motivation	98%	Psychopatholiqical	84%	Narcissistic	76%
Social Skills	98%	Antisocial	83%	Borderline	78%
Empathy/Remorse	97%	Resolution/Aetiology	81%		
Cycle/Arousal	97%	Commitment	80%		
Control	96%				
Self	96%				

Table 2: Task Force (1993) Treatment Issues

1. Acceptance of responsibility for behaviour without minimisation or externalising blame (Factors 3,4).
2. Identification of pattern or cycles of abusive behaviour (Factor 6).
3. Interruption of cycle before abusive behaviour occurs and control of behaviour (Factor 6).
4. Resolution of victimisation in the history of the abusive youth (i.e. sexual abuse, sexual trauma, physical abuse, emotional abuse, abandonment, rejection, loss, etc.) (Factors 8,9,10).
5. Development of victim awareness/empathy to a point where potential victims are seen as people rather than objects (Factor 4).
6. Development of internal sense of mastery and control (Factors 3, 13,15).
7. Understanding of the role of sexual arousal in sexually abusive behaviour, reduction of deviant sexual arousal: definition and formation of non-abusive sexual fantasy (Factor 11).
8. Development of a positive sexual identity (Factor 10).
9. Understanding the consequences of offending behaviour for self, the victim, and their families in addition to developing victim empathy (Factor 4).
10. Identification (and re-mediation to the extent possible) of family issues or dysfunction which support or trigger offending (Factors 8 , 9).
11. Identification of cognitive distortions, irrational thinking or 'thinking errors' which support or trigger offending (Factors 3, 12).
12. Identification and expression of feelings (Factor 5).
13. Development of pro-social relationship skills with peers (Factor 5).
14. Development of realistic levels of trust in relating to adults (Factor 9).
15. Management of addictive/compulsive qualities contributing to reinforcement of deviancy (Factors 12,14).
16. Re-mediation of development delays/development of competent psychological health skills (Factors 15,12).
17. Indications of substance abuse, or gang involvement (Factors 15, 12).
18. Reconciliation of cross-cultural issues (Factor 4).
19. Management of concurrent psychiatric disorders (Factor 12).
20. Re-mediation of skill deficits which interfere with successful functioning (Factor 12).
21. Development of relapse prevention strategies (Factors 14, 6).
22. Restitution/reparation to victims and community. (p 44) (Factor 4).

Progress was defined by the Task Force (1993) as being 'determined by accomplishment of specific measurable goals and objectives, their co-operation in treatment, maintenance of control and self-responsibility, changes in thinking, and observable changes in behaviour over time' (p 52). For details see table 3.

The issues and goals with specialised treatment or sexually abusive children were addressed by the Task Force (1993, p 44) and are reproduced in table 4.

Table 3: Indicators of progress

- Acknowledgement of responsibility for offences without denial, minimisation, or projection of blame (Factors 3 or 12).
- Behavioural indications of work towards treatment goals (Factors 1, 2).
- Ability to consider contributing factors to offending cycle (Factors 6, 8, 14).
- Positive changes in or resolution of contributing factors to sexually abusive behaviour (Factor 9).
- Capacity for victim empathy/demonstration of empathic thinking (Factor 4).
- Ability to manage stress and modulate negative feelings (Factor 15).
- Improvement in self-esteem (Factor 15).
- Increases in positive sexuality (Factor 10).
- Pro-social interactions: and involvement with pro-social peers (Factors 4, 5).
- Positive family interactions (Factor 9).
- Openness in examining thoughts, fantasies and behaviours (Factors 1, 2, 3).
- Ability to reduce and maintain control of deviant sexual arousal (Factor 11).
- Reduction of deviant fantasies and concurrent increases in healthy, non-abusive, pro-social sexual fantasies (Factor 11).
- Ability to counter irrational thinking/thinking errors (Factor 13).
- Ability to interrupt cycle and seek help when destructive or risk behaviour pattern begins (Factor 5).
- Assertiveness and communication (Factor 5).
- Resolution of personal victimisation or loss issues (Factors 8, 9).
- Ability to experience pleasure in normal activities (Factors 1, 5).
- Ability to communicate and understand behaviour patterns in the treatment milieu and correlate them to behaviour in the home/community (Factor 5).
- Family's ability to recognise the risk factors (in the youth's cycle) and to help the adolescent manage differently and/or to seek help (Factor 5).

Table 4: Issues with Abusive Sexual Children

- Definition of abuse (Factors 1, 2).
- Control of abusive behaviour (Factor 12).
- Reduction of sexual confusion, fears, preoccupation, misinformation (Factor 10).
- Improving communication, especially labelling and verbalising feelings (Factor 5).
- Fostering empathy skills (Factor 14).
- Promoting healthy sexuality, expression of affection (Factor 10).
- Managing sexual and aggressive impulses (Factor 4).
- Develop healthy sexual fantasies and arousal (Factor 11).
- Decreasing sexualisation of interactions and relationships (Factor 10).
- Identifying precursors in patterns of abusive behaviour (Factor 6, 14).
- Balancing external/internal boundaries (Factors 8,9).
- Increasing internal inhibitors (Factors 11, 14).
- Decreasing manipulative/externally controlling behaviour (Factors 7, 13).
- Challenging beliefs about sexual roles and behaviours (Factors 3, 13).
- Holding children accountable for abusive behaviour, increasing responsibility (Factors 3, 13).
- Engaging, educating, and supporting non-abusive parents to (1) provide primary sex education, (2) create a therapeutic environment, and (3) support relapse prevention (Factor 14).
- Relevant, adjunct treatment issues may include: social skills, self esteem, assertiveness, anger management, problem solving, attachment disorders, boundary problems, victimisation and trauma issues, (Factors 5, 8, 9, 10) (p 66).

Conclusions

The goal of any sex offender treatment programs and clinical criminal justice systems centres on the prevention of sexual assault in all groups. The slogan is *'no more victims'*.

The National Task Force on Juvenile Sex Offending (1993, p 35) provided an excellent brief summary of treatment goals:
'The goals of specialised offence-specific treatment are (1) to stop all sexually abusive behaviour, (2) to protect members of society from further sexual victimisation, (3) to prevent other aggressive or abusive behaviours which the youth may manifest, and (4) to assist the youth in developing more functional relationship skills.'

The concept of recovery applies to both the adult and youthful offender. The concept of recovery is applicable both to those in treatment as well as those who are not in treatment. This is an effort to explore the dynamic variables of treatment. Recovery evaluation parallels the dynamic changeable risk factors or predictors (Hanson, Oct. 1998, personal communication to M. Carich.). These are reasons or at least variables as to why some offenders re-offend and others do not. Further research in this area will help professionals discover the dynamic factors of why some offenders with and without treatment re-offend versus those who don't. Even though some static or historical risk factors are considered statistically significant, the dynamic 15 Recovery Factors outlined in this chapter are also considered significant in determining recovery for both adults and the youthful offender.

References

American Psychiatric Association (1994). *Diagnostic and Statistical Manual: Vol. 4* Washington DC

ATSA (Association of Treatment of Sexual Abusers) (1997). *Ethical Standards and Principles for the Arraignment Of Sexual Abusers*. Beaverton, Oregon: ATSA

Carich, M.S. (1991a). The Recovery of Sex Offenders: Some Basic Elements. *INMAS Newsletter*, 4(4): 3–6.

Carich, M.S. (1991b). Definitions of the Sex Offender Recovery Scale and Inventory. *INMAS Newsletter*, 4(4): 7–9.

Carich, M.S. (1992). Notes on Sex Offender Recovery. *INMAS Newsletter*, 5(3): 9–10.

Carich, M.S. (1993). A list of Disowning Behaviours. *INMAS Newsletter*, 6(1): 9–11.

Carich, M.S. (1994). List of Risk Factors Used in Risk Assessment, *INMAS Newsletter*, 7(2): 9.

Carich, M.S. (1996b). *Identifying Risk Behaviour of Sex Offenders*. Springfield, IL: Illinois Department of Corrections.

Carich, M.S. (1997a). *Evaluating Sex Offender Recovery: A Booklet for Professionals*. Unpublished manuscript.

Carich, M.S. (Ed.) (1997b). *Sex Offender Treatment and Overview: Training for the Mental Health Professional*. Springfield, IL: Illinois Department of Corrections.

Carich, M.S. (1997c). Towards the Concept of Recovery in Sex Offenders. *The Forum*, 9(2): 10–11.

Carich, M.S. (Oct. 15, 1998). *Towards the Validation of the 15 Factor Recovery Criteria*, Poster Session Presented at the 17th Annual ATSA Conference (Vancouver, Canada).

Carich, M.S., and Adkerson, D. (1995). *The Adult Sexual Offender Assessment Packet*, Brandon, VT: Safer Society Press.

Carich, M.S., and Metzger, M.S. (1998a). *Types of Assessments in Sex Offender Treatment*. Submitted to The Forum.

Carich, M.S., and Metzger, M.S. (1998b). *Another Look at Sex Offender Recovery*. Submitted to The Forum.

Carich, M.S., Michael, D.M., and Stone, M. (1992). Categories of Disowning Behaviours. *INMAS Newsletter*, 5(3): 2–13.

Carich, M.S., and Steckel, S.R. (1992). Sex Offender Lifestyle Cognitive-Behavioural Inventory. In Calder, M.C. (1999). *Assessing Risk in Adult Males who Sexually Abuse Children: A Practitioner's Guide*. Dorset: Russell House Publishing.

Carich, M.S., and Stone, M. (1996a). *Sex Offender Relapse Intervention Workbook*. Chicago: Adler School of Professional Psychology.

Freeman-Longo, R., and Blanchard, G.T. (1998). *Sexual Abuse In America: Epidemic of the 21st Century*. Brandon, VT: The Safer Society Press.

Freeman-Longo, R.E., Bird, S.L., Stevenson, W.F., and Fiske, J.A. (1994). *The 1994 Nationwide Survey*. Brandon, VT: The Safer Society Press.

Hanson, R.K., and Bussiere, T. (1996). *Predictors of Sexual Offender Recidivism: A Meta-analysis*. User report No. 1996-04. Ottawa: Department of the Solicitor General of Canada.

Knopp, F.H., Freeman-Congo, R., and Stevenson, W. (1992). *The 1992 Nationwide Survey on Juvenile and Adult Sex-offender Treatment Programs*. Brandon, VT: The Safer Society Press.

Knopp, H.F. (1984). *Retraining Adult Sex Offenders: Methods and Models*. Brandon, VT. The Safer Society Press.

Laws, D.R. (Ed.) (1989). *Relapse Prevention with Sex Offenders*. NY: Guilford Press.

Marshall, W.L., Anderson, D., and Champagne, F. (1996). Self-esteem and its Relationship to Sexual Offending. *Psychology, Crime and Law*, 3: 81–106.

Marshall, W.L., Laws, D.R., and Barbara, H.E. (Eds.) (1990). *Handbook of Sexual Assault: Issues, Theories and Treatment of the Offender*. New York: Plenum Press.

Marshall, W.L., Anderson, D., and Champayne, F. (1996). Self-esteem and its Relationship to Sexual Offending. *Psychology, Crime and Law*, 3: 81–106.

McGrath, R. (1990). Assessment of Sexual Aggressors. *Journal of Interpersonal Violence*, 5(4): 507–519.

McGrath, R. (1991). Sex Offender Risk Assessment and Disposition of Planning: A Review of Empirical and Clinical Findings. *International Journal of Offender Therapy and Comparative Criminology*, 35(4): 328–350.

McGrath, R. (1992). Assessing Sex Offender Risk. *American Probation and Parole Association Perspectives*, 16(3):, 6–9.

Metzger, C., and Carich, M.S. (1997). Eleven Point Comprehensive Offender Treatment Plan. In Calder, M.C. (1999). *Assessing Risk in Adult Males Who Sexually Abuse Children*. Dorset: Russell House Publishing.

National Task Force on Juvenile Sex Offending. (1993). The Revised Report from the *Juvenile and Family Court Journal*, 44(4): 1–121.

Roys, D.T. (1995). Exit Examination for Sexual Offenders. *Sexual Abuse: A Journal of Research and Treatment*, 7(1): 85–106.

Ryan, G., and Lane, S. (Eds.) (1993). *Juvenile Sexual Offending: Causes, Consequences and Correction* (2nd Ed.) San Francisco: Jossey-Bass

Salter, A. (1988). *Treating Child Sex Offenders and Victims*. Newbury Park, CA: Sage.

Schwartz, B.K., and Cellini, H. (Eds.) (1997). *The Sex Offender: New Insights, Treatment Innovations and Legal Developments*. Volume II, Kingston, NJ: Civic Research Institute, Inc.

Schwartz, D.K., and Cellini, H. (Eds.) (1995). *The Sex Offender: Corrections, Treatment and Legal Practice*. Kingston, NJ: Civic Research Institute, Inc.

Stickrod-Grey, A., and Wallace, R.C. (1992). *Adolescent Sexual Offender Assessment Packet*. VT: The Safer Society Press.

Chapter Five

Attachment and Intimacy in Young People who Sexually Abuse

Spencer Santry and Gerard McCarthy

Attachment and Intimacy in Young People who Sexually Abuse

Introduction

The main aim of this article is to outline some ways in which the concepts of attachment and intimacy can be used to throw light on the development of young people who sexually abuse. While the experience of love and emotional safety characterise both parent-child attachments and later intimate relationships, the main difference between these two types of close relationship is that intimate adult relationships are typically reciprocal with both partners providing and receiving care and commitment, whereas in parent-child attachment relationships the adult is expected to be the principal care-giver (Morris, 1983). Intimacy can be understood as being an enduring motive that reflects an individual's preference or readiness to experience emotional closeness, warmth and mutual regulation in close relationships (Ward, McCormack, and Hudson, 1997). High levels of this motive result in more intimacy enhancing behaviours such as self disclosure, displays of affection, and support (McAdams, 1980). The concept of intimacy with its emphasis on mutuality, commitment, vulnerability and knowledge of the self and other (Morris, 1983) is not seen as being appropriate to describe the abilities of a child and it is from adolescence onwards that the desire for intimacy is thought to become an increasingly important aspect of human behaviour. Having said this, the capacity for intimacy and the skills necessary to attain it develop through attachment relationships during childhood (Marshall, 1989). Intimacy can also be conceptualised as an outcome of interpersonal skills and experiences, developing from attachment styles that arise from important attachment related experiences (Ward et al., 1997). This outcome can be seen as a continuum with high intimacy at one end, and emotional loneliness and intimacy failure at the other.

In a series of publications Marshall and his colleagues have outlined a general theory of sexual offending in males. In this model insecure childhood attachment relationships and the capacity for intimacy are seen as essential links in the chain of development underlying the emergence of an inappropriate sexual disposition.

Marshall's (1989, 1993) proposed framework argues that childhood attachment difficulties and the failure to achieve intimacy are crucial factors in the aetiology and maintenance of sexual offending. Marshall's model can be divided into two dimensions, the development of 'vulnerability', and 'priming' that sexualises vulnerability.

Vulnerability

Through an insecure attachment relationship with the primary care-giver, children are thought to experience difficulties in learning the interpersonal skills necessary to attain intimacy, such as developing appropriate empathic capacities. The initial attachment relationship allows an affective/cognitive representation or internal working model to develop that holds concepts for how loveable the child is and how available others are in times of emotional need (Bowlby, 1969; Bretherton, 1985). Failure to establish a secure attachment with parents is therefore thought to often lead to low levels of self-esteem. The failure to develop intimate relations during adolescence and early adulthood may lead to emotional loneliness and the experience of alienation. Individuals who are emotionally lonely may have many superficial relationships, however these relationships often remain emotionally unfulfilling. Emotional loneliness is known to be related to hostile attitudes and interpersonally aggressive behaviour (Diamant and Windholz, 1981), and the acceptance of violence and hostility toward women (Check, Perlman and Malamuth, 1985). This developmental pattern can lead to the state of 'vulnerability'.

Vulnerability is not exclusive to sexual abuse. Marshall (1989) originally argued that it was not specific to sexual abuse but to a risk state which could lead to other problems, such as non-sexual offences. Research has found that sexual offenders do have intimacy deficits (Garlick *et al.*, 1996), but these deficits are found in men who have committed non-sexual offences (Ward *et al.*, 1997). The concept accounts for the sexualised nature of vulnerability.

Priming

The 'priming' dimension is not made so clear in the model. It accounts for the sexualised nature of 'vulnerability' often found in men who commit sexual offences. If the individual is 'pre-primed' to view situations in sexual terms, then the fusion of intimacy and sex may result in him seeking to gain intimacy through inappropriate sexual behaviour. The fusion can lead to persistent promiscuity and increasing sexual deviancy as attempts to meet intimacy escalate (Ward *et al.*, 1995). Social and cultural factors are also thought to be important in the development of priming. Media images may convey inappropriate messages to vulnerable young men (Ward *et al.*, 1996; Marshall, 1989). Brownmiller (1975) has presented a case for the association between rape and power in patriarchal societies. Anthropological evidence has been provided by Sanday (1981) to suggest that some societies are 'rape prone', while others are 'rape free'. Gender roles and power relations are likely to influence the development of individuals within a society. It would be useful to explore these avenues further in an attempt to examine the association between intimacy and sex, as well as providing more of understanding of the attitudes and cognitive distortions often held by young people who sexually abuse.

In the following sections we will aim to look in more detail at some of the processes by which adverse parent-child attachment experiences and later difficulties in establishing intimate relationships may increase the risk of developing abusive sexual behaviour.

The Development of Sexually Abusive Behaviour

The development of psychosocial disorders

As children develop they face a range of age and stage-related developmental tasks/issues (e.g. establishing a secure attachment,

developing a positive sense of self, effective entry into the peer group) and failure to achieve competent adaptation at one developmental period makes adaptation at the next more difficult (Cicchetti, 1993; Sroufe, 1997; Sroufe and Rutter, 1984). Psychopathology can therefore be conceptualised in terms of developmental deviation, reflecting repeated failure of adaptation with respect to these issues (Sroufe, 1997). Particular failure at any point in time is best viewed as placing an individual on a pathway potentially leading to disorder. In our opinion, as well as failing to establish secure attachment relationships, children who go on to exhibit sexually abusive behaviour in adolescence are also likely to have experienced significant difficulties in relation to a number of other important developmental issues. Despite early deviation, a change in context, for example an improvement in the quality of parenting a child receives, may lead individuals back to a more positive pathway. However, the longer a maladaptive pathway has been followed the more difficult it appears to be for the person to bring about positive change. From this point of view development is seen as involving a series of structural reorganisations within and between biological, psychological, and social systems. While we will focus here on a number of psychological factors, it seems likely that genetic and wider social and cultural factors are also involved in the development of sexually abusive behaviour in adolescence. A more detailed examination of the role of genetic, biological, and social factors in the aetiology of sexually abusive behaviour in adolescence is beyond the scope of this chapter. Readers may wish to refer to Laws and O'Donohue (1997) for a comprehensive overview of these issues.

The development of attachment relationships in childhood and adolescence: implications for the development of sex offending in adolescence

Attachment in infancy

The concept of attachment as proposed by John Bowlby, the founder of attachment theory, is not synonymous with the term parent-child relationship (Bowlby, 1969). The function of the attachment behavioural system is to provide protection to the infant by promoting parent-child proximity in times of danger and stress. From an internal perspective the system is thought to provide the child with a sense of security. In this way the attachment system is thought to have evolved to maximise the child's likelihood of survival. In human infants specific attachments appear by the third quarter of the first year of life and they are thought to be based on social interactions. These interactions do not need to be positive and infants become attached to insensitive or maltreating parents. A reciprocal parental care giving system is also hypothesised to have evolved to monitor infant attachment behaviours and to optimise the child's experience of safety and security. According to Bowlby's theory, children develop cognitive-affective representations or internal working models of their experiences in attachment relationships. These are thought to be used by the child to guide subsequent relationships with peers and adults (Bretherton, 1985). Parents' internal working models of childhood attachment experiences are also thought to determine in part the quality of parenting a child receives (Main, 1991). Parents who have insecure internal working models are thought to block or distort their infant's attachment-related signals because they find these signals threatening to their current state of mind with respect to attachment.

Over the past twenty years, a body of research on the development of secure and insecure infant-parent attachment relationships has developed. This has largely been based on an assessment procedure established by Ainsworth and her colleagues known as 'the Strange Situation' (Ainsworth, Blehar, Waters, and Wall, 1978). This procedure consists of a series of separations and reunions of the infant and care-giver and is designed to activate the infant's attachment system so that the organisation of this system in relation to the care-giver can be revealed. Infants classified as *secure (Group B)* typically use the mother as a secure base to explore, become distressed by her absence, greet her positively on her return, are easily soothed and soon return to exploration. This pattern is associated with a history of responsive care. Secure in the knowledge of being able to effectively elicit care from the parent these infants are thought

to develop a generally positive view of others and themselves. Infants classified as *insecure/avoidant (Group A)* tend to explore with minimal reference to the mother, show little distress on separation and avoid or ignore the mother on reunion. This pattern is associated with a history of rejection of the infant's attachment behaviour and also with low levels of tenderness in holding and touching and with high levels of insensitive intrusiveness (Ainsworth, *et al.*, 1978; Isabella, 1993). This strategy is hypothesised to have developed to distract the child from cues that might stimulate the desire to seek comfort from a parent who is likely to reject them in their time of need. These infants tend to deal with attachment-related issues by restricting the communication of distress and anger and displacing their attention on to the inanimate environment. Infants classified as being *insecure ambivalent/preoccupied (Group C)* are highly distressed on separation, are difficult to settle on reunion, and often display high levels of anger. The pattern is associated with a history of inconsistent care or neglect and this is thought to leave the infant uncertain regarding the care-giver's availability and their own effectiveness and in a state of hyper-arousal and hyper-vigilance (Cassidy and Berlin, 1994). More recently, a further pattern known as *insecure disorganised/disorientated or A/C (Avoidant/Ambivalent)* has been identified (Crittenden, 1988; Main and Soloman, 1986,1990). On reunion with the caregiver (following a short separation in the Strange Situation), these infants show a mixture of bizarre, contradictory and inappropriate behaviours. In contrast to the three other organised patterns, the disorganised strategy refers to the lack of, or collapse of, a consistent and coherent strategy for organising attachment behaviour in times of low felt security. This attachment pattern is thought to reflect confusion about, or fear of, caregivers who have behaved in confusing or frightening ways. Having a care-giver who is often both the source of alarm and the biologically expected source of safety and protection is thought to place the infant in a unresolvable position (Main and Soloman, 1990; Sroufe, 1997). Very high levels of disorganised/disoriented attachment have been found in infants who have been abused or neglected (Carlson, Cicchetti, Barnett, and

Braunwald, 1989), in children growing up in multiple problem families, and in families where a parent has serious psychiatric difficulties (Lyons-Ruth, Repacholi, McLeod, and Silva, 1991).

Importantly, research on adolescents with sexually abusive behaviour has revealed that many have experienced maltreatment in childhood and it seems likely that many will have experienced very insecure attachment relationships. Problems in the parental context are often reported for adolescents who commit sexual offences. Inconsistent parenting has been suggested as a risk factor (Ryan *et al.*, 1987), as well as parental loss. Research on the families of intra-familial abusers has found the parents to be distant and inaccessible, and often a very maladaptive sexual climate appears to exist in the home (Smith and Israel, 1987). Another study found that all abusers felt isolated within the family (O'Callaghan and Print, 1994). Poor relationships with parents and dysfunctional family homes set the developmental context for many young people who sexually abuse. When compared to a low violence group, a combined sexually abusive group reported greater exposure to serious physical abuse and to domestic violence involving weapons, attitudes more accepting of sexual and physical aggression, and more aggressive role seeking in response to stress (Spaccarelli, Bowden, Coatsworth and Kim, 1997). Other research reports marital discord, parental rejection, physical discipline, negative family atmosphere, dissatisfaction with family relationships, childhood sexual abuse, victimisation, and the presence of a younger child in the family (Becker and Kaplan, 1988; Worling, 1995). Within such contexts it is very unlikely that secure attachment relationships can develop. Children who go on to exhibit sexually abusive behaviour in adolescence are likely to have developed internal working models of close relationships that are characterised by fear, indifference and exploitation. They are also likely to have developed a very negative view of themselves and other people.

Attachment beyond infancy and into adolescence

Once an attachment develops it continues to undergo transformations and re-integrations with subsequent developmental accomplishments. For example in the second and third years the development of expressive language and more sophisticated representational capacities have an impact on the organisation of attachment relationships (Cicchetti, Cummings, Greenberg, and Marvin, 1990). During the pre-school years the primary care-givers are expected to be engaged in building what is termed a 'goal-corrected partnership' in which it is possible to negotiate goals and plans and where the parent also labels the child's emotional states (Greenberg and Speltz, 1988). The toddler becomes an active negotiator in the attachment relationship and the quality of communication and co-operation become paramount. Parents of young people who sexually abuse may well have experienced difficulty in establishing a 'goal corrected partnership' where the child was able to learn, among other things, to take the perspective of another, effective communication, the ability to tolerate and share negative feelings and the ability to empathise with others' distress. Rather these children may learn a pattern of relating where their own needs are rejected and neglected and where they learn to resort to coercion and intimidation to get what they want. The development of a positive and autonomous sense of self is another important developmental issue that affects the organisation of attachment relationships in the early years (Cicchetti, 1990). Towards the end of the second year children begin to develop a sense of self-awareness and over time they come to develop thoughts and feelings about various aspects of themselves (Kagan, 1982; Stern 1985). The development of an ongoing sense of self allows children to begin to own various aspects of their inner experiences including their desires, feelings and needs (Pine, 1985). It is likely that children who go on to exhibit sexually abusive behaviour in adolescence develop a negative sense of themselves and fail to develop a strong sense of self which allows them to own and think about various aspects of their psychological experiences.

The development of linguistic and symbolic capacities during the school years and into adolescence continues to have an impact on attachment relationships. In particular the ability to think about and reflect upon attachment-related thoughts, feelings, and beliefs comes increasingly to the fore (Fonagy, Steele, Steele, Moran, and Higgitt, 1991; Main, 1991). According to Fonagy and his colleagues, the quality of security children experience in their attachment relationships becomes increasingly reflected in the child's relationship with it's own mental world. That is, children who have had their attachment-related needs appropriately reflected upon and accurately responded to by their care-givers come to feel secure in relation to their mental world and come to feel safe exploring the internal world of feelings, desires and intentions. Similarly, children who have been poorly parented and who have not had their attachment-related needs accurately responded to or reflected upon are thought to establish a poor capacity to reflect upon mental functioning in oneself and others. Furthermore, Fonagy suggests that children who have been abused by care-givers may find thinking about the contents of the abusers mind unbearable and, as a result, they may be forced to inhibit their capacity to think about the mental worlds of others (Fonagy, 1991). While this may provide them with some sense of security in very frightening and uncontrollable situations it may also leave these children with a very impoverished understanding of human relationships and very poor empathic capacities. Often these children appear to lack a sense of concern for others and may show few signs of guilt or remorse in response to hurting those around them and they may be at risk of developing abusive relationships in the future.

It has generally been accepted by clinicians that people who sexually abuse suffer from empathy deficits (Abel, Becker and Skinner, 1983; Marshall and Barbaree, 1990; Salter, 1988; Williams and Finkelhor, 1990). A lack of empathy is reported to be one of the most common features of men who rape (Marshall, Hudson, Jones and Fernandez, 1985), and that a failure to empathise with children predisposes sexual abuse (Finkelhor and Lewis, 1988). A relationship has been found between empathy and attachment pattern in children. Research has indicated that securely attached children demonstrate more empathic skills at the age of three years than insecurely attached children during story telling exercises. Securely attached children were found to be more 'emotionally open' at the age of six and

were able to give more competent representations of their families (Cassidy, 1988). Hanson (1994) has also demonstrated that convicted sex offenders score worse on the Hanson empathy for women measure than unconvicted individuals, and that those who report sexual aggression toward adult women among unconvicted individuals also score worse (Thornton *et al.*, 1996). Though this research has been conducted with adults, Hudson and Ward have demonstrated that such factors are likely to be mediated by attachment styles (Hudson and Ward, 1997). Adolescents who exhibit sexually abusive behaviour are also reported to lack empathic capacities and have often been exposed to experiences of aggression, intimidation, and domination (Ryan *et al.*, 1987).

Children who have experienced maltreatment are also thought to be at risk of developing 'multiple models' of attachment figures and the self. This term was devised by Bowlby (1973) and refers to a tendency he observed in some troubled individuals to develop multiple and inherently contradictory models of something which ought to have a singular model. For example, children growing up in families where the parents deny or distort the existence of abusive events that the child has actually observed, are likely to develop two contradictory memories or images of the events, while being under pressure to remember only the version put forward by the parents (Bowlby, 1973; Main, 1991). Children who have lost touch with their own memories of abusive emotional experiences and who tend to identify with the perspective of the perpetrator are thought to be at an increased risk of behaving abusively in later intimate relationships (Fraiberg, Adelson, and Shapiro, 1975).

In adolescence, teenagers begin to develop attachment figures amongst their peers in preparation for establishing adult attachments (Weiss, 1982). Weiss has argued that in adolescence teenagers redirect their attachment behaviour towards peers and away from parents and begin to become emotionally autonomous (Douvan and Adelson, 1966). However other authors have argued that this detachment does not facilitate individuation in adolescence, and that attachment to parents permits optimal autonomy in the context of emotional support (Bretherton, 1987). Indeed research suggests that emotional autonomy is associated with a negative self-concept, and a greater expectation of rejection (Ryan and Lynch, 1989). Further evidence of the importance of family relationships is demonstrated by the fact that quality of parent rather than peer relationships moderated the effects of life stress (Greenberg *et al.*, 1983; Nada Raja *et al.*, 1992). Parents are rated higher than peers in interpersonal significance throughout the adolescent years (Rosenberg, 1979), and poor attachment to parents is not compensated for by high quality attachment to peers (Nada Raja *et al.*, 1992). Adolescents utilise their parents even when they perceive their relationship with them to be unsatisfying (Greenberg *et al.*, 1983). Adolescents with secure attachments to parents score higher on self-esteem than those with insecure attachments to parents (Armsden and Greenberg, 1987). Low perceived attachment to parents by adolescents was associated with greater problems of conduct, inattention, depression and frequent experience of negative life events (Nada Raja *et al.*, 1992). Support for individuation is missing from many adolescent sex offenders' lives. Some receive little or no support from parents, whereas for others they may be required to take on a parental role in relation to their own care-givers (Marshall, 1989).

Studies on adolescent attachment have discovered a gender bias in the attainment of intimacy. Adolescent females score higher than males on different aspects of attachment behaviour to both parents and peers (Armsden and Greenberg, 1987; Nada Raja *et al.*, 1992). Female adolescents also score higher on measures of communication and trust (Lapsley *et al.*, 1990). This suggests a gender bias in the development of interpersonal skills necessary for intimacy. Nada Raja *et al.* (1992) argue that females find it easier to form intimate relationships, giving the explanation that women are more orientated towards attachment to others, whereas men are orientated towards separateness towards others (Colby and Damon, 1983). This may relate to a gender bias in Western culture that places males as more susceptible to Marshall's vulnerability.

Intimate relationships in adulthood

As suggested in the introduction, intimacy can be thought of as an enduring motive that reflects an individual's readiness or preference to experience warmth, emotional closeness, and mutual communication in close relationships. People experience different degrees of intimacy, from romantic partners to acquaintances (Davis, 1973; Wong, 1981). Intimacy is thought to be both dispositional and a function of interaction (Marshall, 1993), and it is conceived as a continuous dimension, from intimacy to emotional alienation. The composition of intimacy has been argued to consist of three continua: 1) closeness and interdependence of partners, 2) mutual self-disclosure, and 3) warmth and affection for one another (Perlman and Fehr, 1987). Weiss (1974) has described six factors that affect the nature of intimate relationships: 1) the provision of a sense of security and feelings of emotional comfort, 2) companionship and a sense of shared experience, 3) the chance to provide nurturance to another person which gives meaning to life, 4) reassurance of personal worth and self competence, 5) guidance and support when facing adversity, 6) a sense of kinship that assures the continuation of the relationship.

The capacity to form intimate relationships is seen as dependent on early infant and childhood experiences (Weiss, 1982). Parents play a vital role in providing warm supportive attachment figures, instilling self-confidence as the transition to adult intimacy is facilitated, as well as providing the skills necessary to act effectively upon the need for intimacy. Intimacy and loneliness in adulthood are manifestations of a lifelong need to establish enduring affection bonds with others. The experience of loneliness has been described as 'separation distress without an object' (Weiss, 1982). It is described as a pervasive feeling of emptiness. Weiss (1973) distinguished between two types of loneliness: social and emotional loneliness. The difference lies in that social loneliness arises from an impoverished social network, such as someone moving to a new area will have to make new friends and acquaintances, whereas emotional loneliness results from the absence of intimacy in personal relationships (Cutrona, 1982; Jones; 1982). Marshall (1989,1993) identifies emotional loneliness for importance in the development of sexually abusive behaviour, as it reflects a failure in intimacy.

Intimacy motivation greatly varies, and high intimacy motivation has been found to positively correlate with attributes relating to pro-social behaviour (McAdams, 1980). McAdams (1980) found that high scorers in intimacy motivation were viewed as warm, sincere and less self-centred than low scorers, and their behaviours were found to match these judgements. The thoughts of high scorers were found to be orientated towards others, and such individuals were found to hold relationships to be important. High intimacy scores have been correlated with resilient behaviour in the face of adversity (Perlman and Fehr, 1987), with a strong sense of personal well-being (Klinger, 1977), better physical health (Fehr and Perlman, 1985), and being more resistant to depression (Brown and Harris, 1978) and less likely to seek psychiatric help (Horowitz, 1979). Failure in intimacy can result in loneliness and profound dissatisfaction with quality of life (Ward, McCormack and Hudson, 1997).

Many researchers have commented on the lack of intimate relationships and the experience of loneliness in both young people and adults who sexually abuse (Fehrenbach *et al.*, 1986; Langevin, Paitich and Russon, 1984). Loneliness is reported in adult sex offenders to such a degree that enables differentiation between men who perpetrate sexual offences and men who perpetrate non-sexual offences (Bumby and Hansen, 1997; Garlick *et al.*, 1996). Loneliness has been associated with both aggression and hostility, and negative attributions towards women, which have also been identified as characteristics of young people who sexually abuse (Check *et al.*, 1985). Even research with student populations has shown results indicating a relationship between loneliness and negative attitudes towards women. The experience of loneliness is thought to increase during adolescence. Separation from parents, acceptance of more personal responsibility, and the struggle for personal autonomy and individualisation are all thought to lead to more intense feelings of loneliness. The development of new close relationships to ameliorate feelings of loneliness can be impaired by inadequate social skills, excessive experience of failure, adult ambivalence

regarding adolescent independence, and the lack of challenging and meaningful age-related tasks.

Other Related Issues in the Aetiology of Sexually Abusive Behaviour in Young People

The pattern of adaptation children achieve in relation to attachment is thought to affect the way they deal with a number of other developmental issues, each of which have important implications for understanding the development of sexually abusive behaviour in adolescence. In our opinion, as well as experiencing major difficulties in the domain of attachment relationships, children who go on to sexually abuse in adolescence also experience severe difficulties in relation to a number of other developmental issues. We will focus here on two salient developmental issues that have implications for understanding the development of sexually abusive behaviour in young people. These are peer relationships and psychosexual issues. However, we will aim to show that these issues are also mediated by attachment issues. Attachment patterns seem to influence the development of other factors during the life course, factors that have been identified for importance in the development of a general state of 'vulnerability'.

Peer relationships, social competence and interpersonal skills

The establishment of peer relationships is thought to be an important developmental issue during the pre-school and early school age period, although like other stage-salient issues, peer relationships continue to be an important issue throughout the lifespan (Asher, Erdley, and Gabriel, 1994). Many important issues of emotional and social development are learnt by children in their interactions with peers and consequently poor peer relationships are associated with a range of negative outcomes in adolescence (Rutter and Giller, 1983). Psychological health is associated with social networks and number of friendships in adolescence (Nada Raja *et al.*, 1992). Research on adult intimacy and psychological health has produced similar findings (Miller and Lefcourt, 1982)

Children who have been maltreated and children with insecure attachment relationships have been found to experience difficulties in establishing harmonious relationships with peers (Cicchetti and Toth, 1995). In particular they tend to show heightened levels of physical and verbal aggression in their interactions with their peers, and researchers have also found high levels of withdrawal from, and avoidance of, peer interactions in maltreated children. In this way early experiences of abuse and neglect can lead children along a pathway to peer rejection, isolation and loneliness. Increased levels of anger are also known to be associated with loneliness. Research indicates that attachment patterns held by children act as a mediator for peer acceptance and the development of friendships. There is considerable evidence for a relationship between attachment classifications in infancy and social competence in peer settings from pre-school to school age (LaFreniere and Sroufe, 1985; Youngblade and Belsky, 1992). Insecure attachments have been associated with more difficult peer relations and less self-regulatory ability in school related activities (LaFreniere and Sroufe, 1985). There is evidence that securely attached children were found to have given further evidence of the relationships between social competence and attachment by showing that securely attached children were found to play and resolve interpersonal problems more competently than insecure peers. Thus insecure attachment patterns with primary care-givers do not appear to give children the interpersonal skills necessary to achieve some form of intimacy with peers. Therefore even at an early age maltreated and very insecure children appear to be already more 'vulnerable' as Marshall (1989, 1993) defines the term. Marshall argues that due to insecure attachment patterns with the primary care-giver, interpersonal skills do not sufficiently develop, thus predisposing individuals to intimacy failure (Marshall, 1989). Poor interpersonal skills and the experience of isolation have been noted in young people who sexually abuse (Becker and Abel, 1985). In fact the fear of rejection has also been reported as a common characteristic among adolescents who exhibit sexually abusive behaviour (Becker and Abel, 1985). Ryan *et al.* (1987) commented on adolescents who exhibit sexually abusive

behaviour lacking trusting relationships. Other studies have reported higher levels of withdrawal and social anxiety for young people who abuse than for young people who perpetrated non-sexual offences (O'Callaghan and Print, 1994). Research also suggests that young people who sexually abuse experience lower levels of intimacy in their romantic relationships. This same study reported that fewer adolescents who exhibit sexually abusive behaviour had girlfriends and fewer had regular sexual intercourse. Young people in the study who sexually abused felt that they were less successful with girls than their peers.

Interpersonal skill deficits appear to hinder attempts to achieve romantic intimacy, and these deficits are thought to be linked to negative internal working models that may suggest others to be inaccessible, the self to be unlovable, or both. According to Bowlby, the internal working model becomes more resistant to change during development, and even when they are no longer appropriate these representational models often continue to guide behaviour in pathological ways (Bowlby, 1980). Poor social skills (Groth and Burgess, 1977; Becker and Abel, 1985) have been reported in young people who sexually abuse. Social skills deficits can be used to differentiate between different types of sexual offenders, as child molesters have been found to exhibit significantly more isolation than adults who commit assaults or rapes (Awad and Saunders, 1991). Social skill deficits can also be used to differentiate between young people who sexually abuse and those who commit non-sexual offences. Young people who have sexually abusive behaviour are reported to exhibit higher levels of withdrawal and social anxiety than non-sexual offenders (O'Callaghan and Print, 1994). In this sample, twice the amount of young people who had sexually abusive behaviour reported being bullied at school and many felt they had few social contacts.

As already presented, attachment research has generated results to suggests a gender bias in the field of intimacy (Nada Raja *et al.*, 1992). Young males are more likely to develop less intimate friendships than young females, and are less likely to have a close intimate friend. Such trends in gender roles may render males more 'vulnerable' if rejected by peers.

Psychosexual issues

Another important task during childhood and adolescence occurs in relation to psychosexual development (Rutter, 1980). Research suggests that the development of sexual and social behaviour are closely linked and that sexual competence, far from being an innate mechanism, has to be learned. Monkeys who have been deprived of the opportunity to develop normal attachments show deviant sexual behaviour in adulthood (Harlow and Harlow, 1969). It seems likely in humans that early learning about sexuality has an important impact on sexual functioning in adulthood. In fact, there is clear evidence that children are interested in sexual matters from an early age (Rutter, 1980; Yates, 1991). Infants soon begin to touch and rub their genitals and they soon learn that genital stimulation may be pleasant. Between the ages of two and five interest in the genital organs appears to increase and games involving undressing and sexual exploration are common, and sexual activities and interests appear to be common and widespread between 5 or 6 years and puberty. During and after adolescence there is a marked upsurge in sexual activity in both sexes. In adolescence, there is a sharp increase in gonadal hormone production stimulated by gonadotropins from the anterior pituitary gland (Yates, 1991). Higher levels of androgens in males produce an increase in erotic interests. Pubertal girls appear to experience less intense sexual desire, although research suggests that they seem to spend a good deal of their free time talking or thinking about boys (Yates, 1991).

Children who have experienced disturbed early attachment relationships may be at increased risk of experiencing difficulties in their psychosexual development. Lack of emotional and phy   sical comf intellectual stimulation may encourage children who are deprived of these basic psychological requirements to seek them through masturbation or premature involvement in other sexual activities. Early attachment difficulties may also give rise to an internal confusion between attachment-related feelings and sexual feelings. Some children may have difficulty in discriminating between the feelings and desires associated with these two distinct behavioural sy   st children may attempt to deal with their

feelings of loneliness and insecurity through sex. In adolescence, children who have experienced abuse and neglect may have difficulty in dealing with the upsurge of sexual feelings and this may lead to increased sexual deviancy and promiscuity as they attempt to deal with the need for security and safety through sexual contact. In particular, attachment problems in some instances may give rise to the premature activation of the sexual mating sy   stem. T activation of the sexual sy   stem m following sexual abuse or through exposure to sexual materials or the observation of adult sexual activities.

Factors in the family environment that may lead to sexualised behaviour have been addressed by Smith and Israel (1987) who commented on the parents of adolescents who exhibit sexually abusive behaviour stimulating sexual climates within the home. Ryan *et al.* (1987) have also commented on the non-normative sexual environments in which adolescents who sexually abuse often develop. Research also suggests that traumatic early sexual experiences may adversely effect the development of major physiological systems and that this appears to have implications for later patterns of biological maturation (Putman and Trickett, 1993).

The failure to achieve intimacy does not directly account for the way in which social behaviour becomes sexualised. Marshall (1989) argues that priming also operates on a cultural level. Men who report higher loneliness levels have been found to be more likely to accept hostile attitudes towards women. Thus men who are vulnerable may be more susceptible to the priming factors in both personal and cultural environment. Marshall gives the example of media images that may greatly influence adolescent males who are particularly vulnerable. Sex and intimacy become confused, and sex is then employed almost as a tool for acquiring the satisfaction of intimacy.

Research on Attachment and Intimacy with Adult Sex Offenders

Research by Ward and his colleagues suggests that Marshall's model is limited in a number of important ways (Ward *et al.*, 1995). In particular the model makes no differentiation between offender types. Ward *et al.* (1995) argue that different types of offender are likely to experience different types of intimacy problems.

Ward and Hudson *et al.* (1995, 1996, 1997) have aimed to address the limitations of Marshall's framework by utilising Bartholomew's model of attachment (Bartholomew and Horowitz, 1991; Horowitz, Rosenberg and Bartholomew, 1993). Bartholomew has argued that attachment styles are defined by two underlying dimensions. These are models of the self and models of others. The self-model refers to the level of emotional dependence people have on others for self-validation (Bartholomew, 1997). A positive view reflects an internalised sense of self worth that does not rely on ongoing external validation, whereas the negative view is associated with anxiety regarding acceptance and rejection in close relationships. The other dimension reflects perceptions of others' availability and supportiveness. People at the positive end of the dimension tend to seek intimacy in close relationships, whereas people at the negative end tend to avoid intimacy. These dimensions give rise to four possible attachment styles: secure (positive model of self and others); preoccupied (negative model of self and positive model of others); dismissing (positive model of self and negative model of others); and fearful (negative model of self and others). This conceptualisation differs from earlier work by differentiating the tendency to avoid becoming intimate with others into a fearful avoidant pattern and a dismissing avoidant pattern. The secure prototype is characterised by a positive image of self and others. Secure prototypes consist of high autonomy and intimacy and it is believed that reliable and sensitive care in childhood facilitates the development of this attachment style. The preoccupied prototype is characterised by a negative self-model and a positive other model. This prototype involves preoccupation with attachment needs and active attempts to fulfil these needs in close relationships. The result is a dependent style of interaction, where self-validation is derived from others' acceptance and approval. Inconsistent parenting in which children believe they are to blame for the lack of care they experience from their parents is thought to generate this style of attachment. The fearful

prototype is characterised by the belief that others are uncaring and inaccessible, and that they themselves are unlovable. They desire intimate relationships and the acceptance of others, but avoid becoming too close out of the expectation of rejection. This contrasts with the dismissing prototype, which is characterised by positive self concept through distancing themselves from others and developing a self reliant model invulnerable to the rejection of others. It is argued that both avoidant patterns develop from a history of unresponsive attachment figures. More recently, fearful avoidant attachment style has been found to be related to a number of high risk environments such as having had problem drinking parents (Brennan, Shaver, and Tobey, 1991), and being the victim of incestuous abuse (Alexander, 1993).

The three insecure attachment styles of the model are thought to reflect different interpersonal goals and strategies, and therefore different types of intimacy deficits and relationship problems (Ward *et al.*, 1995). Ward and his colleagues argue that different types of insecure attachment styles are likely to predispose individuals to certain styles of offences and they have used Bartholomew's model to investigate intimacy deficits in sexual offenders. For example, in relation to the preoccupied attachment style, the authors propose that the combination of a negative self concept and a positive model of others will lead individuals who sexually abuse to desire intimacy but also to be anxious about relationships. Ward and his colleagues suggest that individuals who sexually abuse who have a preoccupied attachment style will try to select people who will be approving of the person and may therefore look to children for emotional intimacy. The authors argue that this style is likely to lead to a relationship that is victim or mutually focused. Very little or no coercion is used and the child is likely to be known to the offender. The fearful avoidant attachment style consists of an internal working model with low self/low other concept. It is proposed that individuals with this style also desire intimacy but are fearful of rejection. As with the preoccupied style, this style is characterised as non-hostile but also uncaring. These individuals tend to seek non-rejecting intimacy figures in relationships that are devoid of closeness and they are thought to be self focused and aim to avoid emotional contacts. The authors suggest that patterns of non-hostile impersonal sex are likely to arise. Suggested offence types are passive exhibition, secretive peeping, and sexual offences against an unknown child using instrumental coercion. Finally the dismissing avoidant attachment style is proposed to result in the desire for autonomy and independence, along with hostility. The style is characterised by a tendency to be dismissive of close relationships and it is suggested that such individuals will look for contacts that are devoid of emotional closeness and that are self-focused. Patterns of hostile impersonal sex are therefore seen as being likely to emerge. For example, exhibition would tend to be aggressive, and peeping would tend to be non-secretive. The authors suggest that individuals who sexually abuse who have a dismissing avoidant attachment style will tend to commit offences against children or adults, and that coercion will be expressive rather than instrumental, and possibly sadistic.

Initial research has indicated that adult sexual offenders are insecurely attached (Ward et al., 1996). However this was also the case with other criminal comparison groups. This is consistent with Marshall's theory that many offenders have experienced abusive or neglectful childhoods (Marshall, 1989). Violent offenders and rapists were found to hold 'dismissing' attachment styles, which are characterised by high levels of aggression in their interactions with other people (Bartholomew and Horowitz, 1991). Child molesters were found to have fearful or preoccupied attachment styles, which correlates well with reports of social anxiety and poor social skills in child molesters (McFall,1990). Child molesters have also been found to be more fearful of intimacy than rapists (Bumby and Marshall, 1994).

Differentiating between different types of offenders failed when using the loneliness construct (Hudson and Ward, 1997). When attachment style was used to differentiate between groups, it was found that the secure and dismissing groups of offenders reported the lowest loneliness scores. Fearful and dismissing offenders were more likely to be avoidant in their intimate relationships. Fearful and dismissing styles were associated with higher levels of interpersonal hostility, and

reported greater anger suppression. Rape myth attitudes could also be differentiated using attachment style, secure offenders reported the lowest hostility to women, and the fearful offenders reported the highest hostility to women. Dismissing offenders were found to be most accepting of rape myths and preoccupied offenders were found to be least accepting of rape myths.

There are dangers of applying research findings from adult samples to young people, but the authors believe that these issues are very relevant to young people who sexually abuse. Marshall (1989) originally identified the adolescent period to be of importance. Not all adults who commit sexual offences begin during the adolescent period, and the nature of the offences or the intentions behind them can change over time. However, attachment and intimacy behaviour is a continuous process, and allows an understanding of the development of a person. The next section will propose how attachment and intimacy theory may be used with young people who sexually abuse.

Clinical Implications of Attachment Theory for Working with Young People Who Sexually Abuse

The research reviewed above suggests that issues to do with attachment, intimacy, and loneliness should feature heavily in treatment programmes for young people who sexually abuse (Marshall, 1989). The importance of understanding the close relationship between emotions, behaviours and intimate relationships has also been emphasised (Ward et al., 1995). Attachment style and the associated beliefs and interpersonal strategies need to be taken into account when assessing intimacy deficits (Bumby and Hansen, 1997; Ward et al., 1996). The authors argue that these factors provide the context for intimacy difficulties. If they are not considered, social skill-based interventions may not be optimally effective. Programmes encouraging skills necessary for intimacy should be included in treatment, such as interpersonal skills (Marshall, 1989). Empathic capacities need to be improved and components enhancing reciprocity in relationships would increase the chances of offenders developing effective intimate and supportive relationships. Even though working models are thought to be resistant to change they are not thought to be fixed.

The factors that have been identified as leading to vulnerability, such as emotional loneliness and poor social skills have been examined via attachment style rather than the nature of the offence (Hudson and Ward, 1997). Hudson and Ward argue that attachment is a crucial piece in the aetiological puzzle of sexual offending. The relationship between attachment and problems such as fear of intimacy, affective deregulation, and negative attitudes towards women seem to be more fundamental than offender type. The experience of loneliness differs according to attachment styles held by offenders. The authors found that secure and dismissing types reported the lowest loneliness scores, while preoccupied and fearfully attached men reported significantly higher levels of loneliness. These results are thought to reflect the self and other concepts held in the internal working model and the associated attitudes and beliefs require challenging during treatment. Attachment and intimacy can be used to provide a framework to approach the loneliness experienced by young people who sexually abuse, and allow professionals some awareness of the 'self' and 'other' concepts held by them.

Attachment has been found to be associated to regulation of affect in adults who commit sexual abuse (Alexander, 1992; Hudson and Ward, 1997). Adults who sexually abuse with secure or preoccupied attachment styles reported lower anger expression scores. The avoidant attachment styles were more strongly associated with felt anger towards others. This related to the negative view of others thought to be held in the internal working model. Interpersonal skills training and practice of personal disclosure may facilitate the building of trusting relationships for these adolescents. Treatment also needs to consider the relationship between emotions and representations of attachment relationships (Collins and Read, 1993). A primary function of the internal working model is to regulate emotions (Kobak and Sceery, 1988). Past attachment relationships and their associated affects will be activated by those relationships in which people are currently engaged. These emotions will influence information processing

and strategies adopted for the situation. Attachment style has also been found to be related to rape myths. Securely attached men reported the lowest hostility towards women and those with fearful attachment styles reported the highest levels. This again relates to the internal working models held by these men. A fearful attachment style reflects the expectancy of rejection, due to the low selfconcept, and a distrust of others, due to the low other concept. Preoccupied styles were least accepting of rape myths, and dismissing styles were most accepting of rape myths. This again reflects the concept of 'other' held in the internal working model. Empathy and conflict resolution skills could be used to address these difficulties, enabling adolescents to develop sufficient communication skills to build trusting relationships.

Therapy implementation needs to be modified according to the attachment style. Someone with a fearful attachment style engaged in the treatment process will interpret ambiguous comments in personally demeaning ways. Therapists must take this into account and use the opportunity to discount maladaptive beliefs and self-defeating behaviours (Safran and Segal, 1990). Treatment programs should include cognitive based interventions which challenge specific attitudes and beliefs that are related to intimacy avoidance, such as the fear of intimacy, vulnerability and rejection (Bumby and Hansen, 1997; Marshall, 1993; Ward et al., 1995).

It is important to have a clear idea of the particular processes that are contributing to the difficulties young people who sexually abuse are experiencing in their close relationships. Any assessment of a young person who sexually abuses should include a full account of their attachment history and of any maltreatment or traumatic events experienced in childhood. It is also important to try to make a clinical assessment of the adolescent's internal working model of attachment. This would involve attempting to build up a detailed view of the child's model of close relationships and the way they have learnt to deal with attachment-related issues. In addition it is important to have profiles of the pattern of adaptation they have achieved in relation to the other developmental issues discussed above: emotional regulation, self-system, peer relationships, and psychosexual development. It is also helpful to have detailed information about the adolescent's intellectual functioning, perspective-taking skills, empathic abilities and self-reflective capacities. Constructing a full picture in relation to these issues enables professionals to devise an individual treatment plan that is specifically tailored to the psychological needs of the adolescent. Indeed, treatment programs currently being run do address many of the issues outlined in this chapter. Interpersonal skills (Lakey, 1995), history of abuse, sexual knowledge, heterosexual skills, self-esteem and anger control (Epps, 1991).

When working with young people whether as in-patients or in the community, attachment theory and developmental theories of psychopathology can provide useful models to guide both direct work with individuals and with the planning and overall organisation of therapeutic environments and treatment approaches. It is important that, through their relationships with members of staff, the adolescents have the opportunity to learn more adaptive ways of relating with others. In particular it is important that they are encouraged to confide in others in times of need and that they are given the opportunity to develop trusting relationships. It also gives the professionals involved with the adolescents the opportunity to model important interpersonal skills such as effective communicating, perspective taking, and adaptive ways of dealing with feelings. It is likely that young people who sexually abuse have had very few opportunities to develop secure relationships in the past. Individual and group psychological therapies are likely to be required to help these adolescents begin to explore and review their ideas about sexual relationships and to begin to develop new interpersonal skills. For some young people helping them to understand the links between their own childhood attachment experiences and their current difficulties can help them begin to understand the origins of their deviant behaviour and this in turn can help them start to develop more adaptive ways of relating to others. Group-based work may be particularly useful in helping children develop new relational skills and helping them to develop psychological insight into the meaning of their own and other people's behaviour. It is important that attempts are made to assess and where possible improve the quality of the adolescents' close relationships and social support in their natural environment. This may involve helping parents, care-givers or other people closely involved with the individual to be able to provide more sensitive and responsive care. This in turn may involve attempting to provide emotional and practical support to these adults many of whom may be experiencing their own psychosocial difficulties. Research suggests that if the parents of these young people feel more supported then this may enable them to be more emotionally available to their children (Belsky, 1984). Young people who sexually abuse are also likely to need assistance with their education and would benefit from any input that helps them to increase their self-esteem, such as developing age-appropriate hobbies and interests. It has been reported that adolescents who sexually abuse experience difficulties in the educational system, often presenting as low achievers or having learning difficulties (Fehrenbach *et al.*, 1986; Saunders and Awad, 1988). Other studies have found adolescent sex offenders' intelligence levels were similar to that of the non-sexual offenders, though they were more likely to perceive themselves as having a learning disability (O'Callaghan and Print, 1994). It could be argued that this is a reflection of the poor self-concept held in the internal working model. Finally, these young people may benefit from educational programs focused around the topic of close relationships. On a practical level this may help to provide them with basic information on family life and sexual relationships and may help to correct some of the distorted ideas they have acquired about intimate human relationships.

References

Abel, G., and Becker, J.V. (1985). Sexual Interest Card Sort. In Salter, A. (Ed.) (1988) *Treating Child Sex Offenders and Victims — A Practical Guide.* Beverley Hills, CA: Sage.

Abel, G., Becker, J.V., and Skinner, L. (1983). Behavioural Approaches to Treatment of the Violent Sex Offender. In Roth, L. (Ed.) *Clinical Treatment of the Violent Person.* Washington, DC: NIMH Monograph Series.

Ainsworth, M.D.S., Blehar, M.C., Waters, E., and Wall, S. (1978). *Patterns of Attachment.* Hillsdale, NJ: Erlbaum

Alexander, P. (1992). Application of Attachment Theory

to the Study of Sexual Abuse. *Journal of Consulting and Clinical Psychology*, 60(2): 185–195.

Alexander, P. (1993). The Differential Effects of Abuse Characteristics and Attachment in the Prediction of Long-term Effect of Sexual Abuse. *Journal of Interpersonal Violence*, 8: 346–362.

American Academy of Pediatrics, Committee on Adolescence. Rape and the Adolescent. *Pediatrics*, 81(4): 595–597.

Armsden, G., and Greenberg, M. (1987). The Inventory of Parent and Peer Attachment: Individual Differences and their Relationship to Psychological Well-being in Adolescence. *Journal of Youth and Adolescence*, 16(5): 427–454.

Bartholomew, K., and Horowitz, L.M. (1991). Attachment Styles Among Adults: A Test of a Four Category Model. *Journal of Personality and Social Psychology*, 61: 226–244.

Bartholomew, K. (1990). Avoidance of Intimacy: An Attachment Perspective. *Journal of Social and Personal Relationships*, 7: 147–178.

Bartholomew, K. (1997). Adult Attachment Processes: Individual and Couple Perspectives. *British Journal of Medical Psychology*, 70: 249–263.

Becker, J.V., and Abel, G.G. (1985). Methodological and Ethical Issues in Evaluating and Treating Sex Offenders. In Otey, E.M. and Ryan G.O. (Eds.). *Adolescent Sex Offenders: Issues in Research and Treatment*, 109–129. Rockville, MD. US Dept. of Health and Human Services.

Becker, J.V., and Kaplan, M. (1988). The Assessment of Adolescent Sex Offenders. *Advances in Behavioural Assessment of Children and Families*, 4: 97–118.

Belsky, J. (1984). The Determinants of Parenting: A Process Model. *Child Development*, 55: 83–96.

Bowlby, J. (1969). *Attachment and Loss: Vol. 1 Attachment*. New York: Basic Books.

Bowlby, J. (1973). *Attachment and Loss, Vol 2: Separation*. New York: Basic Books.

Bowlby, J. (1980). *Attachment and Loss, Vol. 3: Loss, Sadness and Depression* New York: Basic Books.

Brennan, K., and Morris, K. (1997). Attachment Styles, Self-esteem, and Patterns of Seeking Feedback from Romantic Partners. *Personality and Social Psychology Bulletin*, 23(1): 23–31.

Brennan, K.A., Shaver, P., and Tobey, A. (1991). Attachment Styles, Gender, and Parental Problem Drinking. *Journal of Social and Personal Relationships*, 8: 451–461.

Bretherton, I. (1985). Attachment Theory: Retrospect and Prospect. In Bretherton, I., and Waters, E. (Eds.). *Growing Points of Attachment Theory and Research. Monographs of the Society for Research in Child Development*, 50 (Serial No. 5–38).

Bretherton, I. (1987). New Perspectives on Attachment Relations: Security, Communication and Internal Working Models. In Osofsky, J. (Ed.). *Handbook of Infant Development*. New York.: Wile.,

Brown, G.W., and Harris, T. (1978). *Social Origins of Depression: A Study of Psychiatric Disorder in Women*. New York: Free Press.

Brownmiller, S. (1975). *Against Our Will: Men, Women, and Rape*. New York: Simon & Schuster.

Bumby, K.M., and Hansen, D.J. (1997). Intimacy Deficits, Fear of Intimacy, and Loneliness Among Sexual Offenders. *Criminal Justice and Behaviour*, 24(3): 315–331.

Bumby, K.M., and Marshall, W.L. (1994). *Loneliness and Intimacy Deficits Among Rapists and Child Molesters*. Paper to 13th Annual Conference of Association for Treatment of Sexual Abusers. San Francisco, October 1994.

Carlson, V., Cicchetti, D., Barnett, D., and Braunwald, K. (1989). Disorganized/Disoriented Attachment Relationships in Maltreated Infants. *Developmental Psychology*, 25: 525–531

Cassidy, J., and Berlin, L. (1994). The Insecure/Ambivalent Pattern of Attachment: Theory and Research. *Child Development*, 65: 971–991.

Cassidy, J. (1988). Child-mother Attachment and the Self in Six-year-olds. *Child Development*, 59: 121–134.

Cassidy, J., Kirsh, S.J., Scolton, K.L., and Parke, R.D. (1996). Attachment and Representations of Peer Relationships. *Developmental Psychology*, 32(5). 892–904.

Check, J.V.P., Perlman, D., and Malamuth, N.M. (1985). Loneliness and Aggressive Behaviour. *Journal of Social and Personal Relationships*, 2: 243–252.

Cicchetti, D. (1990). The Organisation and Coherence of Socioemotional, Cognitive, and Representational Development: Illustrations Through a Developmental Psychopathology Perspective on Downs Syndrome and Child Maltreatment. *Nebraska Symposium on Motivation*, 36: 259–366.

Cicchetti, D. (1993). Developmental Psychopathology: Reactions, Reflections, Projections. *Developmental Review*, 13: 571–602.

Cicchetti, D., Cummings, M., Greengerg, M., and Marvin, R. (1990). Attachment Beyond Infancy. In Greenberg, M., Cicchetti, D., and Cummings, E.M. (Eds.) *Attachment During the Preschool Years* (pp 3–49). Chicago: University of Chicago Press.

Colby, A., and Damon, W. (1983). Listening to a Different Voice: A Review of Gilligan's in a Different Voice. *Merrill-Palmer Quart.*, 29: 473–481.

Collins, N.L., and Read, S.J. (1993). Cognitive Representations of Attachment: The Structure and Function of Working Models. In Perlman, D., and Bartholomew, K. (Eds.). Advances in Personal Relationships, Vol. 5. *Attachment Processes in Adulthood*. London: Jessica Kingsley.

Cornell, D. (1990). Prior Adjustment of Violent Juvenile Offenders. *Law and Human Behaviour*, 14: 569–577.

Crittenden, P.M. (1988). Distorted Patterns of Relationship in Maltreating Families: The Role of Internal Representational Models. *Journal of Reproductive and Infant Psychology*, 6:, 183–199.

Cutrona, C.E. (1982). Transition to College: Loneliness and the Process of Social Adjustment. In Peplau, L.A., and Perlman, D. (Eds.) *Loneliness: A Sourcebook of Current Theory, Research, and Therapy*. New York: Wiley.

Davis, G., and Leitenberg, H. (1987). Adolescent Sex Offenders. *Psychological Bulletin*, 101: 417–427.

Davis, M.S. (1973). *Intimate Relations*. New York: Free Press.

Diamant, L., and Windholz, G. (1981). Loneliness in College Students: Some Theoretical, Empirical and Therapeutic Considerations. *J. Coll. Stud. Person.*, 22: 515–522.

Douvan, E., and Adelson, J. (1966). *The Adolescent Experience*. New York: Wiley.

Epps, K. (1991). The Residential Treatment of Adolescent Sex Offenders. *Issues in Criminological and Legal Psychology*, 1: 58–67.

Fehr, B., and Perlman, D. (1985). The Family as a Social Network and Support System. In L'Abate, L. (Ed.). *Handbook of Family Psychology and Therapy Vol. 1.* IL: Dow.

Fehrenbach, P.A., Smith, N., Monastersky, C., and Deisher, R.W. (1986). Adolescent Sexual Offenders: Offenders and Offense Characteristics. *American Journal of Psychiatry*, 56(2): 225–233.

Fisher, D., and Howells, K. (1993). Social Relationships in Sexual Offenders. *Sexual and Marital Therapy*, 8(2): 123–136.

Fonagy, P. (1991). Thinking About Thinking: Some Clinical and Theoretical Considerations in the Treatment of the Borderline Patient. *International Journal of Psychoanalysis*, 72: 639–656.

Fonagy, P., Steele, M., Steele, H., Moran, G.S., and Higgit, A.C. (1991). The Capacity for Understanding Mental States: The Reflective Self in Parent and Child and its Significance for Security of Attachment . *Infant Mental Journal*, 13: 200–217.

Fraiberg, S.H., Adelson, E., and Shapiro, V. (1975). Ghosts in the Nursery: A Psychoanalytic Approach to the Problem of the Impaired Infant-mother Relationship. *Journal of the American Academy of Child Psychiatry*, 14: 387–422.

Garlick, Y., Marshall, W., and Thornton, D. (1996). Intimacy Deficits and Attribution of Blame Among Sexual Offenders. *Legal and Criminological Psychology*, 1: 251–258.

Greenberg, M.T., and Speltz, M.L. (1988). Attachment and the Ontegeny of Conduct Problems. In Belsky, J., and Nezworski, T. (Eds.) *Clinical Implications of Attachment*, p 177–218. Hillsdale, NJ: Erlbaum.

Greenberg, M.T., Seigel, J.M., and Leitch, C.J. (1983). The Nature and Importance of Attachment Relationships to Parents and Peers During Adolescence. *Journal of Youth and Adolescence*, 12(5): 373–386.

Groth, A.N., and Burgess, A.W. (1977). Motivational Intent in the Sexual Assault of Children. *Criminal Justice and Behaviour*, 4: 253–264.

Hanson, K. (1994). *Assessing Sex Offenders' Capacity for Empathy*. Paper presented at the International Conference on the Treatment of Sex Offenders at Coventry.

Harlow, H.F., and Harlow, M.K. (1969). Effects of Various Mother-infant Relationships on Rhesus Monkey Behaviours. In Foss, B.M. (Ed.). *Determinants of Infant Behaviour Vol 4*. London: Metheun.

Horne, L., Glasgow, D., Cox, A., and Calam, R. (1991). Sexual Abuse of Children by Children. *The Journal of Child Law*, Sept–Dec.

Horowitz, L. (1979). On the Cognitive Structure of Interpersonal Problems Treated in Psychotherapy. *Journal of Consulting and Clinical Psychology*, 47: 5–15.

Horowitz, L.M., Rosenberg, S.E., and Bartholomew, K. (1993). Interpersonal Problems, Attachment Styles, and Outcomes in Brief Dynamic Psychotherapy. *Journal of Consulting and Clinical Psychology*, 61: 549–560.

Hudson, S., and Ward, T. (1997). Intimacy, Loneliness and Attachment Style in Sexual Offenders. *Journal of Interpersonal Violence*, 12(3): 323–339.

Isabella, R.A. (1993). Origins of Attachment: Maternal Interactive Behaviour Across the First Year. *Child Development*, 64: 605–621.

Jones, W.H. (1982). Loneliness and Social Behaviour. In Peplau, L.A., and Perlman, D. (Eds.). *Loneliness: A Sourcebook of Current Theory, Research, and Therapy*. New York: Wiley.

Kagan, J. (1982). The Emergence of Self. *Journal of Child Psychology and Psychiatry*, 23: 1–19.

Kenny, M. (1987). The Extent and Function of Parental Attachment Among First-year College Students. *Journal of Youth and Adolescence*, 16(1): 17–29.

Klinger, E. (1977). *Meaning and Void: Inner Experience and the Incentives in Peoples' Lives*. Minneapolis: University of Minnesota Press.

Kobak, R.R., and Sceery, A. (1988). Attachment in Late Adolescence: Working Models, Affect Regulation, and Representations of Self and Others. *Child Development*, 59: 135–146.

LaFreniere, P.J., and Sroufe, L.A. (1985). Profiles of Peer Competence in the Preschool: Interrelations Between Measures, Influence of Social Ecology, and Relation to Attachment History. *Developmental Psychology*, 21: 56–69.

Lakey, J.F. (1995). The Profile and Treatment of Male Adolescent Sex Offenders. *International Journal of Adolescence and Youth*, 6:, 67–74.

Langevin, R., Paitich, D., and Russon, A. (1984). Are Rapists Sexually Anomalous, Aggressive, or Both? In Langevin, R. (Ed.). *Erotic Preference, Gender Identity, and Aggression in Men: New Research Studies*. New York: Erlbaum.

Lapsley, D.K., Rice, K.G., and Fitzgerald, D.P. (1990). Adolescent Attachment, Identity, and Adjustment to College: Implications for the Continuity of Adaptation Hypothesis. *Journal Counsel. Develop.*, 68: 561–565.

Laws, D., and O'Donohue, W. (Eds.) (1997). *Sexual Deviance. Theory, Assessment, and Treatment*. The Guilford Press.

Lyons-Ruth, K., Repacholi, B., McLeod, S., and Silva, E. (1991). Disorganized Attachment Behaviour in Infancy: Short-term Stability, Maternal and Infant Correlates, and Risk-related Sub-types. *Developmental Psychopathology*, 3: 397–412.

Main, M., and Cassidy, J. (1988). Categories of Response

to Reunion with the Parent at Age 6: Predictable from Infant Attachment Classifications and Stable over 1-month Period. *Developmental Psychology*, 24: 415–442

Main, M., and Hesse, E. (1990). Parents' Unresolved Traumatic Experiences are Related to Infant Disorganized Attachment Status: Is Frightened and/or Frightening Parental Behavior the Linking Mechanism? In Greenberg, M.T., Cicchetti, D., and Cummings, E.M. (Eds.). *Attachment in the Preschool Years*, 161–182. Chicago: University of Chicago.

Main, M., and Soloman, J. (1990). Procedures for Identifying Infants as Disorganized/Disoriented During the Ainsworth Strange Situation. In Greenberg M.T., Cicchetti, D., and Cummings, E.M. (Eds.). *Attachment in the Preschool Years: Theory, Research and Interventions*, 121–160. Chicago: University of Chicago Press.

Main, M., and Solomon, J. (1986). Discovery of an Insecure-disorganised/Disoriented Attachment Pattern. In Brazelton, T.B., and Yogman M. (Eds.). *Affective Development in Infancy*, 95–124. Norwood, NH: Ablex.

Main, M. (1991). Metacognitive Knowledge, Metacognitive Monitoring and Singular (Coherent) Versus Multiple (Incoherent) Models of Attachment: Findings and Directions for Future Research. In, Parkes, C.M., Stevenson-Hinde, J., and Marris, P. (Eds.). *Attachment Across the Life Cycle*, 127–159. London: Routledge.

Main, M., Kaplan, N., and Cassidy, J. (1985). Security in Infancy, Childhood and Adulthood: A Move to the Level of Representation. In Bretherton, I., and Waters, E. (Eds.) *Growing Points of Attachment Theory and Research. Monographs of the Society for Research in Child Development*, 50: 66–104.

Marshall, W.L., and Barbaree, H.E. (1990). An Integrated Theory of the Etiology of Sexual Offending. In Marshall, W.L., Laws, D.R., and Barbaree, H.E. (Eds.). *Handbook of Sexual Assault: Issues, Theories, and Treatment of the Offender*. New York: Plenum Press.

Marshall, W.L. (1989). Invited Essay: Intimacy, Loneliness, and Sexual Offenders. *Behaviour Research and Therapy*, 27: 491–503.

Marshall, W.L. (1993). The Role of Attachments, Intimacy, and Loneliness in the Etiology and Maintenance of Sexual Offending. *Sexual and Marital Therapy*, 8: 109–121.

Marshall W.L., Hudson, S.M., Jones, R., and Fernandez, Y.M. (1995). Empathy in Sex Offenders. *Clinical Psychology Review*, 15(2): 99–113.

McAdams, D.P. (1980). A Thematic Coding Scheme for the Intimacy Motive. *Journal Res. Person.*, 14: 413–432.

McCormick, C., and Kennedy, J. (1994). Parent-child Attachment Working Models and Self-esteem in Adolescence. *Journal of Youth and Adolescence*, 23(1): 1–18.

McFall, R.M. (1990). The Enhancement of Social Skills: An Information Processing Analysis. In Marshall, W.L., and Barbaree, H.E. (Eds.). *Handbook of Sexual*

Assault: Issues, Theories, and Treatment of the Offender. New York: Plenum.

Miller, R.S., and Lefcourt, H.M. (1982). The Assessment of Social Intimacy. *Journal of Personality Assessment*, 46: 514–518.

Morris, D. (1983). Attachment and Intimacy. In Stricker G., and Fisher, M.N. (Eds.). *Intimacy*. New York: Plenum Press.

Nada Raja, S., McGee, R., and Stanton, W. (1992). Perceived Attachments to Parents and Peers and Psychological Well-being in Adolescence. *Journal of Youth and Adolescence*, 21(4): 471–485.

O'Callaghan, D., and Print, B. (1994). Adolescent Sexual Abusers. Research, Assessment and Treatment. In Morrison, T., Erooga, M., and Beckett, R. (Eds.). *Sexual Offending Against Children*. Routledge.

Perlman, D., and Fehr, B. (1987). The Development of Intimate Relationships. In Perlman, D., and Duck, S. (Eds.). *Intimate Relationships: Development, Dynamics, and Deterioration*. Newbury Park, CA: Sage.

Pine, F. (1985). *Developmental Theory and Clinical Practice*. New Haven: Yale University Press.

Putman, F.W., and Trickett, P.K. (1993). Child Sexual Abuse: A Model of Chronic Trauma. *Psychiatry*, 56: 82–95.

Rice, K. (1990). Attachment in Adolescence: A Narrative and Meta-analytic Review. *Journal of Youth and Adolescence*, 19(5): 511–538.

Rosenburg, M. (1979). *Society and the Adolescent Self-image*. Middletown, Connecticut: Western University Press.

Rutter, M., and Giller, H. (1983). *Juvenile Delinquency, Trends and Perspectives*. New York: Guilford Press.

Rutter, M. (1980). Psychosexual Development. In *The Scientific Foundations of Developmental Psychiatry*. London: Heineman Medical.

Ryan, G., Lane, S., Davis, J., and Isaacs, C. (1987). Juvenile Sex Offenders: Development and Correction. *Child Abuse and Neglect*, 55: 385–395.

Ryan, R., and Lynch, J. (1989). Emotional Autonomy Versus Detachment: Revisiting the Vicissitudes of Adolescence and Young Adulthood. *Child Development*, 60: 340–356.

Safran, J.D., and Segal, Z.V. (1990). *Interpersonal Processes in Cognitive Therapy* (Chaps. 1–4). New York: Basic Books.

Salter, A. (1988). *Treating Child Sex Offenders and Victims: A Practical Guide*. Beverly Hills, CA: Sage.

Sanday, P.R. (1981). The Socio-cultural Context of Rape: A Cross-cultural Study. *Journal of Social Issues*, 37(4): 5–27.

Saunders, D.G., and Awad, G.A. (1988). Assessment, Management and Treatment Planning for Male Adolescent Sexual Offenders. *American Journal of Orthopsychiatry*, 54(4).

Smith, H., and Israel, E. (1987). Sibling Incest: A Study of the Dynamics of 25 Cases. *Child Abuse and Neglect*, 2.

Spaccarelli, J., Bowden, B., Coatsworth, J.D., and Kim, S. (1997). Psychosocial Correlates of Male Sexual Aggression in a Chronic Delinquent Sample. *Criminal Justice and Behaviour*, 24: 71–97.

Sroufe, L.A., and Rutter, M. (1984). The Domain of Developmental Psychopathology. *Child Development*, 55: 17–29.

Sroufe, L.A. (1997). Psychopathology as an Outcome of Development. *Development and Psychopathology*, 9: 251–268.

Stern, D. (1985). *The Interpersonal World of the Infant*. New York: Basic Books.

Stevenson, H., and Wimberley, R. (1990). Assessment of Treatment Impact of Sexually Aggressive Youth. *Journal of Offender Counselling, Services and Rehabilitation*, 15(2): 55–65.

Thornton, S., Todd, B., and Thornton, D. (1996). Empathy and the Recognition of Abuse. *Legal and Criminological Psychology*, 1: 147–153.

Ward, T., Hudson, S.M., and Marshall, W.L. (1996). Attachment Style in Sex Offenders: A Preliminary Study. *The Journal of Sex Research*, 33: 17–26.

Ward, T., Hudson, S.M., Marshall, W.L., and Siegert, R. (1995). Attachment Style and Intimacy Deficits in Sexual Offenders: A Theoretical Framework. *Sexual Abuse: A Journal of Research and Treatment*, 7: 317–335.

Ward, T., McCormack, J., and Hudson, S.M. (1997). Sexual Offenders' Perceptions of their Intimate Relationships. *Sexual Abuse: A Journal of Treatment and Research*, 9: 57–74.

Weiss, R.S (1982). Attachment in Adult Life. In Parkes, C.M., and Stevenson-Hinde, J. (Eds.). *The Place of Attachment in Human Behaviour*. New York: Basic Books.

Weiss, R.S. (1973). *Loneliness: The Experience of Emotional and Social Isolation*. Cambridge, MA: MIT Press.

Weiss, R.S. (1974). The Provisions of Social Relationships. In Rubin, Z. (Ed.). *Doing Unto Others*. Englewood Cliffs, NJ: Prentice-Hall.

Williams, L.M. and Finkelhor, D. (1990). The Characteristics of Incestuous Fathers: A Review of Recent Studies. In Marshall, W.L., Laws, D.R. *et al.* (Eds.). *Handbook of Sexual Assault: Issues, Theories, and Treatment of the Offender*. Applied Clinical Psychology. New York: Plenum Press.

Woike, B., Osier, T., and Candela, K. (1996). Attachment Styles and Violent Imagery in Thematic Stories About Relationships. *Personality and Social Psychology Bulletin*, 22(10): 1030–1034.

Wong, H. (1981). Typologies of Intimacy. *Psychol. Women Q.*, 5: 435–443.

Worling, J.R. (1995). Adolescent Sibling-incest Offenders: Differences in Family and Individual Functioning When Compared to Adolescent Nonsibling Offenders. *Child Abuse and Neglect*, 19: 633–643.

Yates, A. (1991). Childhood Sexuality. In Lewis, M. (Ed.). *Child and Adolescent Psychiatry*, Baltimore: Williams.

Youngblade, L., and Belsky, J. (1992). Parent-child Antecedents of Five-year-olds' Close Friendships: A Longitudinal Analysis. *Developmental Psychology*, 28: 700–713.

Zussman, R. (1989). Forensic Evaluation of the Adolescent Sex Offender. *Forensic Reports*, 2: 25–45.

Chapter Six

A Framework for a Multi-agency Approach to Working with Young Abusers:

A Management Perspective

Jacqui McGarvey and Lynne Peyton

A Framework for a Multi-agency Approach to Working with Young Abusers: A Management Perspective

Introduction

The Juvenile Perpetrators Project was established by the Southern Area Child Protection Committee (SACPC) in Northern Ireland in 1995, as a multi-disciplinary, inter-agency specialist project working with young people who sexually abuse between the ages of 10 and 18 years. The project offers a standard risk assessment followed by individual treatment and, when appropriate, group work with young abusers. Increasingly, parents are also offered group work support. Its success has depended on explicit commitments by each agency to adhere to the project's policy and procedures.

Nationally and internationally the co-ordinated management of work with young abusers is in its infancy. This chapter illustrates the pioneering work of the Southern Area Child Protection Committee and its member agencies in Northern Ireland, in commissioning and developing in a systematic and paced way, an effective inter-disciplinary and inter-agency approach to working with young abusers. In looking retrospectively at experiences of setting up and overseeing the Juvenile Perpetrators Project, we identified 9 key factors, which are crucial to success:

- Agencies' commitment to a partnership approach.
- Clear accountability arrangements.
- Identified core workers in each discipline.
- Common philosophy and agreed model of intervention.
- Standard assessment and treatment.
- Information collection and analysis.
- Evaluation.
- Communication and public relations strategy.
- Funding arrangements.

It also describes a framework, which will be of benefit to other ACPCs or their equivalents outside the United Kingdom, for use when developing multi-agency projects for young abusers. Calder (1997a) argued that

> A systematic approach must be developed with agencies defining their specific responsibilities and developing policy statements and child protection procedures. Sexually abusive behaviours require a multi-disciplinary, multi-model, multi-system, multi-theory combination of interventions. Whilst we have to create an infrastructure for the operational work I would argue that further accessible information, training and co-ordinated research and using good examples of best practice is the best way forward rather than further central guidance.

We support this view and in describing the development of the Juvenile Perpetrators Project seek to test out how far we have achieved these objectives.

Strategic Context

While both the National Children's Homes (NCH) and Department of Health Reports of 1992 recommended that the work be tackled on an inter-agency basis under the auspices of Area Child Protection Committees (ACPCs), Masson (1996) reported that only 17 per cent of 106 ACPCs had drawn up inter-agency procedures for this work. Morrison (1997), while welcoming policy development by some ACPCs, was pessimistic about their capacity as non-operational bodies to secure agencies' rather than individuals' commitment to young abusers' projects.

A number of recent developments are bringing renewed impetus to the issue. 'Childhood Matters' (1996), the Report of the National Commission of Enquiry into the Prevention of Child Abuse, questions the effectiveness of current legislation in Northern Ireland, Scotland as well as England and Wales in providing a framework for closer collaboration between child protection, criminal justice and welfare agencies. Given the evidence in, for example, the work of Schram, Molloy and Rowe (1991), that early intervention with young abusers can modify behaviour and reduce risk, the Commission's implementation initiative calls for a separate strategy to deal with young people who sexually abuse to be included in Children's Services Plans. These plans must be developed by local authorities/Health and Social Services Boards (N.I.) to cover all aspects of services for children through close collaboration between child protection, criminal justice, health, education and welfare agencies. Inclusion of a strategy to provide adequate identification, assessment, treatment and supervision for this client group on a cross-agency basis is essential.

The DoH's consultation paper 'Working Together to Safeguard Children', (DoH, 1998) while acknowledging the need to address in guidance the inter-agency dilemmas, leaves juvenile sexual abuse firmly within ACPC procedures. It is hoped that the process of consultation on 'Working Together' can be used as a mechanism to both endorse the legitimacy of ACPCs' role in facilitating collaboration at local level, while at the same time, calling for a strong national context which reconciles existing legislation and policy across different government departments. The lack of a coherent national approach is also stressed in 'Exercising Constant Vigilance. The Role of The Probation Service in Protecting the Public from Sex Offenders' (Home Office, 1998). The report challenged the lack of

provision for young people who sexually offend and argued that responsibilities did not lie solely with the Probation Service. It fell short of recommending how this situation might be tackled.

Official guidance in Northern Ireland still tends to minimise the complexities of achieving this inter-agency collaboration and falls far short of the in-depth consideration of issues contained in the 1993 United States National Task Force Report on juvenile sex offending. This report argues that none of the agencies that typically intervene in these cases can effectively control or intervene single handedly. It recommends that inter-agency co-ordination should govern all phases of intervention including reporting, investigation and prosecution; assessment, evaluation and placement; treatment; after care; and monitoring and research.

Morrison (1994) advocates both a UK Task Force and a systematic approach by ACPCs in which a series of organisational building blocks provide a framework for a corporate response (see figure 1).

The SACPC Young Abusers' Project reflects the US model in that it has tackled and addressed inter-agency issues at all stages of intervention and developed appropriate policy, procedures and protocols. It also compares favourably with Morrison's organisational framework, in particular reflecting his additional emphasis on the need for a mandate to work with young sex offenders; the need for a common philosophy of intervention; and an acknowledgement of the impact of this work

---

Figure 1: Organisational building blocks (Morrison, 1992)

Evaluation of practice

Staff care policy and provision

Supervision and consultation

Resources and prioritisation of service delivery

Training for managers and practitioners

Policy and practice guidance

Philosophy of intervention

Structures for policy and practice development plus leadership

Mandate and legitimisation for work with sex offenders

Recognition of the need to work with sex offenders

on the staff involved. For a discussion of the risks inherent in dysfunctional inter-agency working practice the reader is referred to Calder (1999) and Chapter 7, this volume.

Historical Context

Within Northern Ireland, acknowledgement of the need to include work with perpetrators of abuse in any multi-dimensional strategic approach to protecting children, was formally acknowledged in 'Co-operating to Protect Children' (DoH, 1989). This guidance, which represented the Northern Ireland equivalent to 'Working Together' (DoH, 1991), noted the need for an inter-disciplinary approach and at a conference in April 1991 professionals from a range of disciplines set the problem in a provincial context and offered feedback and examples of best practice on their early attempts at working with different classifications of offenders which included those with significant learning difficulties and young people who sexually abuse. McCune and Scott (1994) examined a group treatment programme for adolescent offenders, run jointly by the NSPCC and child psychiatry department in Craigavon, and paved the way for an area wide inter-agency approach to working with young sex offenders. As in many other situations, a few dedicated professionals led the way and offered a group treatment approach based on the model developed by Smets and Cebula (1987). This model is outlined and developed further by O'Boyle and her colleagues in Chapter 11.

Organisational Arrangements

The reader will need to have some understanding of the organisational structures within Northern Ireland, if they are to fully appreciate how agencies tackled and overcame boundary issues. We will set out the key agencies below and provide a summary of each.

Statutory social services

Since 1973 social work services have been provided by four integrated Health and Social Services Boards, which are agents of the Department of Health and Social Services. The 1994 Health and Social Services Order delegated statutory authority for the provision of services to self-governing trusts, each with an Executive Director of Social Work. The primary responsibility of these Health and Social Services Area Boards became the strategic planning and commissioning of high quality services based on the assessed needs of the resident population. Within their statutory responsibilities for children, the Boards retained a leadership role in Area Child Protection Committees, chaired by the Directors of Social Services and more recently have been given responsibility for developing inter-agency Children's Services Plans.

Police

The Royal Ulster Constabulary (RUC) polices the entire province. In an effort to ensure prompt and appropriate support for the victims of child abuse and of rape, they set up pilot Child Abuse and Rape Enquiry Units (C.A.R.E) in the mid 1980s. Three C.A.R.E. units were established in Belfast, Londonderry and Craigavon each led by an Inspector and each with both male and female officers. Close relationships with local childcare teams paved the way for joint investigations and the policy and procedures for these were formulated on a regional basis in the Protocol for Joint Investigation by Social Workers and Police Officers of Alleged and Suspected Cases of Child Abuse and Neglect (1991). A revised edition of the Protocol in 1996 takes into account the implementation of the Children's Evidence (NI) Order 1995 and the associated Memorandum of Good Practice. Following their successful evaluation, C.A.R.E. units have now been established throughout the province and have increasingly taken over responsibility for handling more of the criminal investigation and prosecution of abuse cases.

Since the implementation of the Sex Offender Act (1997) C.A.R.E. units have assumed an increased responsibility for convening risk assessment meetings on all young people who have either been cautioned or convicted of a sexual offence. They also maintain the Sex Offender Register.

Probation

The Probation Board for Northern Ireland has a number of area managers reporting to the

Chief Probation Officer who is in turn accountable to a Board. Probation officers have a statutory responsibility to supervise young people on probation orders mandated by the court. In cases where the offence is a sexual offence against a child the court has the option of mandating attendance at the Juvenile Perpetrators Project as an additional requirement of the probation order. They undertake offence-focused work in order to help the young person develop strategies to prevent re-offending.

Local authorities

The twenty six district councils in Northern Ireland made up of elected representatives have much more limited responsibilities than their counterparts in other parts of the UK and look after mainly local environmental health services, leisure services - including outside play areas and building control functions. While the five district councils within the Southern Board area have not taken any direct role in child protection issues, and are not represented on SACPC they have always co-operated in launches and public educational initiatives. Opportunities to work more closely with both statutory and voluntary childcare agencies were created by the European Union Peace and Reconciliation Programme for Northern Ireland and the Border Counties of Ireland. This initiative aimed to promote economic regeneration and promote social inclusion through broad ranging community development measures.

Education

Five Education and Library Boards provide the entire range of all education services and youth services within their geographical area.

Obviously this fragmented and overly bureaucratic infrastructure for a population of 1.6 million (of whom approximately half a million are children), poses major challenges to inter-agency work (Peyton 1997). Elected representatives on district councils have no explicit responsibility for child protection issues - Education and Health Boards have difficult geographical boundaries and while there is an advantage in having one police force and probation service they find it difficult to serve four ACPCs and eleven Trust Child Protection Panels.

While each Board is represented on appropriate ACPCs the Southern Education and Library Board is unique in having its own formal Child Protection Committee.

Fortunately, there were a number of services and developments in place within the area which facilitated a joint approach to work with young people who sexually abuse, and included:

- A pilot police C.A.R.E. unit.
- An NSPCC Child Protection Team.
- A multi-disciplinary Child and Adolescent Psychiatry Team.
- An independent family therapist, specialising in child sexual abuse.
- A probation team with close links to the regional adult sex offender project.
- Close working relationships among front line workers in different agencies all with an interest in child sexual abuse.
- A sympathetic resident magistrate and county court judge.
- A strong multi-agency ACPC, led by the Director of Social Services.
- Growing evidence and interest in the extent of sexual abuse by young people.

Assessing the Need

For a thorough discussion of the statistics that have accelerated the response to this problem, the reader is referred to Calder (1997;1997b). The Northern Ireland Research Team (1991) uncovered some startling facts when they were commissioned by the DHSS (Northern Ireland) to estimate prospectively the number of children who were reported to be abused during 1987, the nature of the abuse and the circumstances surrounding it. A staggering one third of the sexually abused children were abused by perpetrators under the age of 20 years and almost 20 per cent by abusers under 16 years of age. Kennedy and Maxwell (1990) reported that this correlated with other studies within the UK (such as Glasgow *et al.*, 1994) and internationally (such as Davis and Leitenberg, 1987). Other salient features from the Northern Ireland study (1991) was that 77 per cent of the victims of adolescent sex abusers were under 16, with 51% in the 6–11 age range. The abuser was known to the majority of children and there was no significant difference between boys and girls regarding the relationship of the abuser. Approximately one third of girls and boys were abused by a relative while about half of the children were abused by a person known to the child, often a friend or a neighbour who was trusted by the family. 25% of the adolescent sex abusers were already known to have committed sexual abuse against children, highlighting the dangers of not tackling their behaviour at an earlier stage (see Calder, 1997 for a review of the need for early intervention with this group). Worryingly, adolescent sexual abusers were responsible for the highest rate of penetrative sexual abuse in both boys and girls. This included vaginal, anal or oral intercourse. Sequelae on the part of the victims included pervasive sadness, over sexualised behaviour, relationship difficulties, inability to mix with peers and generalised fear of men. The researchers concluded that given the level and complexity of abuse by young people, an adolescent treatment centre for young sexual offenders was an urgent priority for the province, and, given that most offenders minimise the seriousness of their offences, urged close liaison between the courts and probation service to ensure compliance with treatment. Nevertheless, for many professionals within Northern Ireland at this time there was a great deal of scepticism that the extent of abuse by young people could be of this proportion. This is the basis of the arguments put forward by Leheup and Myers in Chapter 9, and by Myers (1998).

Seven years later in Northern Ireland there is no regional adolescent treatment centre for young people who sexually abuse. Approaches to the work vary from area to area and despite good liaison between interested workers on the ground, across Northern Ireland and with colleagues in the Republic there is, as yet, no standardised approach to this work. The reader is referred to Calder and Horwath (1999) and Calder (Chapter 7) for a discussion on how to develop a framework for ACPCs to respond to the void of central guidance and associated resources.

There is no mechanism for collating information on the number of young people who allegedly sexually offend and official police figures probably only represent the tip

of the iceberg. Table 1 illustrates the number of prosecutions only, and is not reflective of the number of reports and investigations completed by the statutory agencies and C.A.R.E. units.

Table 1: Official Police Statistics on Young Abusers under 21 Years		
	Proceeded Against	Convicted
1995	55	31
1996	52	27

The Southern Area Child Protection Committee were persuaded to adopt a strategic, integrated, coherent, and evaluated approach, to the growing identified population of young abusers. Despite resource limitations, the child psychiatry service had already joined forces with the NSPCC to set up a group work approach to treat these young people, to complement individual therapeutic interventions. Justification for a group-led approach can be found in Chapter 11. This chapter proposes to detail the process whereby the work of two teams became recognised, endorsed and subsequently sponsored by all of the relevant agencies under the auspices of SACPC.

The Juvenile Perpetrators Project

While the term young abusers is now commonly used to refer to this client group the project has traditionally been known as the Juvenile Perpetrators Project and the literature marketing the scheme bears this title. Increasingly workers refer to young abusers and are sensitive to the importance of terminology for both the young people themselves and their parents. The project's name will inevitably change at an appropriate time.

The Southern Area Juvenile Perpetrators Project is an assessment and treatment project for young people aged 10–18 years who have sexually abused. While the majority have offended against younger children, a small number have offended against peers, women or animals. The project offers individual work, group work for young abusers (see Chapter 11 for further details) when appropriate and increasingly educational sessions and/or group work with parents (see Chapter 10).

In recognition of the need for early intervention, the project accepts young people who appear to be at risk of abusing, as well as those who have actually committed offences. Therefore criteria for inclusion in the project include:

- Young people who have been cautioned/convicted of a sexual offence.

- Young people who have allegedly committed an offence but where there is unlikely to be a court hearing.

- Young people who have been subject to a child protection case conference and deemed to have offended/be at risk of offending.

The project has recently extended its catchment to embrace referrals from any agency where there is concern about the possibility of offending even if the young person is not subject to criminal prosecution or child protection procedures. This extension was necessary to respond to incidents of abuse not followed up.

Policy guidelines produced by SACPC in December 1994 outlined the rationale for working with young abusers, identified relevant research and set out the strategic context for the work. It went on to set out the procedures for inter-agency working, for interfacing with the legal system and setting out the treatment approach. Referral to the project is mandatory for staff in all nine participating agencies which include the NSPCC, Southern Health and Social Services Board, Newry and Mourne, Armagh/Dungannon, Craigavon/Banbridge Trusts, Child and Family Clinic (Child and Adolescent Psychiatry Service), the RUC, Probation Board for Northern Ireland and an independent family therapist.

In practice, adherence to this requirement is monitored by the Inter-agency Steering Group who cross-reference referrals to the project with anonomysed data on young abusers investigated by the C.A.R.E. unit. Discrepancies are raised with the relevant agency and in most instances agreement has been reached as to the need for referral.

The team has only one full time worker, a social worker employed by the NSPCC. The other workers are four social workers, one psychologist, one family therapist, one psychiatrist, one probation officer and the co-ordinator all being seconded for the equivalent of one day a week to the project.

The pilot project which ran from January 1995 to December 1997 dealt with 59 young abusers. At the time of the evaluation in early 1998, 41 of the 59 cases were closed, while 18 young people were receiving an ongoing service. The majority of young people were male with only two girls in the pilot. 42 of the young people (70%) attended the project voluntarily, 6 (14%) attended voluntarily while awaiting a court mandate, whilst the remaining 11 (16%) refused to attend the project.

The project was evaluated in a number of ways. Information on the young people and their families was collated on the database, questionnaires were sent to all the 59 young people, and semi-structured interviews were conducted with 6 young people. Questionnaires were also sent to all the referring agencies to obtain feedback on the responsiveness and relevance of the service offered by the project. The evaluation was mainly completed internally, with the steering group monitoring the process and the NSPCC National Practice Development Unit analysing the findings. The interviews with young people were conducted by an independent researcher. The evaluation demonstrated strong evidence of the project's impact on helping young people exercise controls over and hence reduce their abusive behaviour.

Self-reporting by the young people combined with agency reports indicated that only 1 young abuser is known to have re-offended post treatment. Obviously the follow-up period was short and other studies have referred to recidivism rates being lower within the first five years followed by a rapid rise (Debelle *et al.*, 1993). In both the questionnaires and semi-structured interviews, many of the young people referred to their dependence on the project for help both during and after treatment. As a consequence of these findings the project has secured longer-term funding to sustain and further develop its activities by offering additional programmes to address specific needs. For example, a group for young abusers with learning difficulties (see

O'Callaghan, Chapter 12 for a proposed groupwork programme), the development of community education programmes, and support groups for those who have completed treatment.

Key factors

In reviewing the process of establishing, funding, maintaining and evaluating the project a number of factors were critical to success. These are discussed below:

Agencies' commitment to a partnership approach

Prior to the formal establishment of the Juvenile Perpetrators Project in 1995, many of the agencies who were working with young abusers recognised the complexity of the work, and started to develop informal partnerships. At this time, the Southern Area Child Protection Committee provided the appropriate and essential forum whereby agencies such as probation, child psychiatry, NSPCC and the child and family care teams who were working together informally with young abusers, could report and reflect on their experiences. Good practice developments, such as treatment groups for young abusers, run jointly by the Child Psychiatry Service and the NSPCC were evaluated and emphasised the need for a co-ordinated, systematic, assessment and intervention package. The Probation Service was keen to assess the relative benefits of treatment; of comparing custodial and non-custodial approaches and in determining the relevance of legal sanctions. Close liaison with the police and courts was critical and gradually the groundrules for working with young people and for working together were established.

In order to formalise the work, middle managers made a recommendation to SACPC that a specific multi-agency project be established, with identified members of staff, clear inter-agency commitments, and an agreed philosophy and model of work. This was embraced in an agreed policy and procedure.

All nine agencies recognised the inherent stresses in working with this client group and

the need to complement each other's contributions. Immediate issues to be resolved included the need for the project to be staffed and managed on an inter-agency basis; clear accountability structures; an agreed model of intervention; access to supervision and appropriate consultation; funding, communication and liaison arrangements; monitoring and evaluation. These areas are explored later in this chapter.

Accountability arrangements

The establishing of a steering group, accountable corporately to SACPC, and individually to their own member agencies provided the appropriate mechanism for both development and accountability. Both the steering group and SACPC had a role in monitoring adherence to procedures and in overcoming non-compliance.

The commitment required by staff and managers at all levels of each organisation cannot be over-emphasised. There have been occasions when changes of staff or external pressures have weakened an agency's commitment. These lapses must be challenged, and resolved, if projects of this nature are to be sustained.

The accountability structure outlined in Figure 2 has demonstrated that it can deal effectively with upwards and downwards communication, while responding to issues on an inter-agency basis at all levels in the process. The steering group is chaired by a childcare manager from one of the H and SS Trusts and comprises middle managers from probation, NSPCC and the RUC, as well as a clinical psychologist. To ensure the group had a good understanding of the issues involved in working with young people who sexually abuse, and the models used in other projects, they visited the Young Abusers Project in London and individual members availed of relevant courses and learning opportunities. Managers, as well as practitioners, must be cognisant with theory and good practice if they are to be effective in their role.

The steering group corporately brought resolved advice to SACPC and obtained a mandate from SACPC to take the work forward. Their initial recommendations included an evaluated two-year pilot project comprising:

Figure 2: Accountability structure of the JPP Team

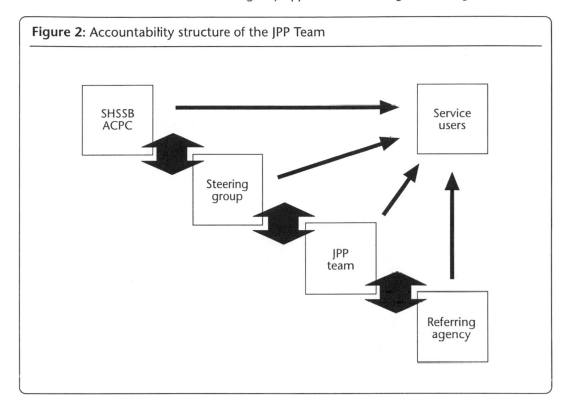

- A common approach throughout the Board's area, based on an agreed philosophy and utilising an agreed model of intervention and assessment.

- Identified key workers in each agency for whom involvement in the project would be a recognised element of their caseload.

- A computerised database to collate comprehensive information on the young people and their families. It specifically built on the NI Research Team's findings and sought to establish information on the number of incidents in the area and how these were spread geographically; the nature of the abuse in terms of the type of offence committed; where the abuse occurred; who else was present; the age of the victim and of the offender; the relationship of victim and offender; and the number of victims per abuser. It was felt this information would add to the knowledge base on young abusers and inform the project's development in respect of the resources required.

- A specialist worker devoted to the project who would act as co-ordinator and administrator and who would also be custodian of the database.

- Appropriate supervision and consultation arrangements for individual workers in the multi-disciplinary inter-agency project team. Supervision was to be provided by line managers, case allocation and co-ordination by the NSPCC team manager, while consultation was available, on request, from the child psychiatrist.

The steering group is essential and is the key mechanism for:

- Moulding inter-agency provisions of services.

- Clarifying single agency responsibility.

- Ensuring agency understanding and ownership by both front line staff and senior management.

- Agreeing and providing a common approach. The steering group ensured the multi-disciplinary team trained together regularly to develop an integrated approach to the assessment and treatment for young people referred to the project.

- Negotiating resources and funding.
- Setting and monitoring standards such as ensuring that all the young abusers and their families received a comprehensive and responsive service in each trust area.
- Recommending and reviewing policy and procedures. For example, pressure was placed on the project to continue to work with high-risk young people beyond the age of 18 years as adult services were extremely limited. Although it was a difficult decision the steering group agreed to keep the age limit to 10–18 year olds as the project could not cope with extending the age range without extra funding and staffing.
- Assessing the extent of inter-agency co-operation. The steering group met with each of the relevant agencies within a year of developing the project to review the agency perspective and try to identify and resolve any issues.
- The Area Child Protection Committee also kept the project as a standing agenda item at its bi-monthly meetings. Co-operation between agencies was generally good except for the issue of replacing core workers immediately, if, for example, a worker moved to a new job. Sometimes several months elapsed before a replacement was identified and this issue illustrated the need for negotiation and good will as there are no real consequences for non-adherence.

Behind the scenes, individual agency representatives have significant responsibilities in communicating the project to their organisation; consulting on policy and procedures; securing resources and commitment from senior staff; and supporting those workers who are directly involved. While all of the agencies were committed to the project, in practice most needed to be constantly reminded of their responsibilities and undertakings. The project would not have succeeded without the steering group members' commitment.

Identified core workers in each discipline

Earlier attempts to work across disciplines with young abusers demonstrated that while staff were individually committed, they were often struggling to address competing demands and their work with young abusers was not always officially recognised (Morrison, 1997).

The structure and composition of the team was largely a pragmatic response which gave official recognition and a mandate for this work to those workers in each agency who had already developed expertise and experience with young abusers.

The project is 'housed' within the NSPCC Children's Centre and is supervised by the NSPCC Team Manager who acts as co-ordinator, allocates referrals, chairs team meetings, consults on cases and oversees the collation and analysis of the database. While the need for one full-time worker was clear, the decision to second the rest of the staff was based on a number of factors.

Figure 3: Multi-disciplinary/Inter-agency Project Team

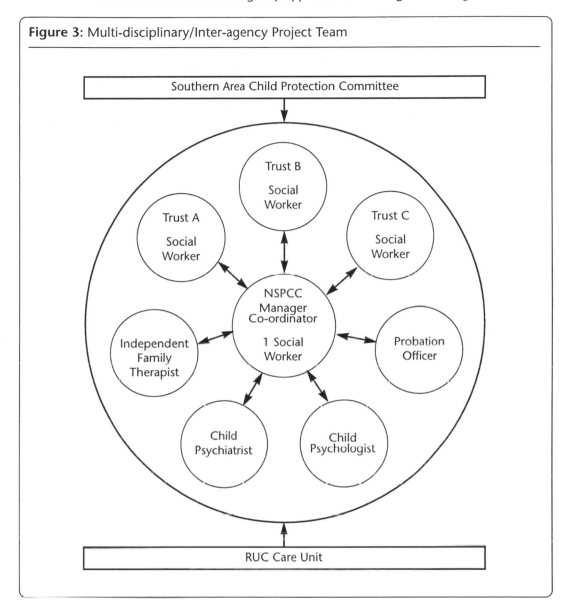

All the agencies in the circle are seconded staff and one full-time member of the project. The CARE UNIT is situated outside the circle as it contacts and liases on all referrals. The ACPC role is to monitor the service offered. The estimated referral rate would only have justified at most one full-time staff.

A desire to procure clinical involvement in the project by all individual agencies. As seconded staff are based within their own agencies they are well placed to act as a link person between the agency and the project and secure agency

identification with the project. They are perceived as a resource person within their agency. Recognition of the need for co-working cases with referring agencies and hence ensuring their ongoing commitment to the young person. The project worker deals exclusively with the sexual offending and associated behaviours and not general child care issues. This is clearly negotiated at the referral stage as the project team resources are limited to the offending focused work.

Example

> *A 14-year old male young abuser has sexually abused his two younger female siblings and is referred to the project by the Social Services Department. The Juvenile Perpetrators Project Worker is contracted to work with the young person and his parents on his sexually abusive behaviour and how to minimise the rise of re-occurrence. The social worker from the referring agency continues to have responsibility for treatment services for the victim, issues relating to parenting, and to their protection. Close liaison is also needed between the project worker and the social worker and joint sessions with the adolescent and/or his parents may be indicated.*

Secondment to the team for a period of not less than 2 years helps to develop skills and expertise in this area of work and allows for a reasonably consistent team. Inevitably, some of the initial workers move on and criteria for selection of new workers for the team was subsequently agreed as follows:

- Self-selection. Workers must elect to become engaged with this client group.
- Experienced staff within their own profession.
- Evidence of appropriate knowledge and experience of working with sexual abuse victims and offenders.
- Ability to work as part of a multi-disciplinary team.
- A willingness to learn new approaches and develop intervention methods.
- Agreement from the agency to be released to serve the project.
- Line Manager's support for secondment to the project team.

Each worker's commitment to the project must be reflected in an appropriate reduction in their agency workload. Where this is not the case, an inevitable tension results in unnecessary stress for the worker and potentially a reduced commitment to the team. This remains a crucial issue as the number of referrals to the project has greatly exceeded expectations and the work is often relatively long-term. While this arrangement has worked, to date it does require considerable investment in team maintenance to overcome the potential for disparate approaches (see Baxter and Print, 1999 for a discussion of group issues in multi-agency small group forums).

Regular meetings, systems for communications and feedback, and common training all help to create a sense of belonging. The team meets on average every month to provide peer review on cases and share ideas and issues. Initial meetings focused on: developing knowledge and skills with the team; understanding the role and responsibility of a project worker; selecting appropriate models of interventions, and joint training.

The psychiatrist and psychologist provide consultation on very high-risk cases and provide an immediate response by seeing any young person with serious mental health problems and those who are a suicide risk. Although supervision for each team member is provided by their individual agencies, the co-ordinator reviews cases within both the team meetings and during informal/formal child protection case discussions.

Team training is provided and funded by the project and staff benefit from team maintenance days twice a year, as this facilitates a review of existing practice and often shapes new models of service delivery. One example is the extension of group work sessions to whole days as this had been seen to be more effective than shorter sessions. As external training courses for this client group are limited the project has brought in external consultants and trainers (such as Judith Becker in May 1997). Additionally, the team meet with a consortium of 12 projects from Southern and Northern Ireland every 6 months, to share experiences and skills in working with young abusers. Staff care issues need to be formally addressed as the project team have not to date looked at the pressures of this type of work on staff nor the implications on their personal lives. The project needs to prioritise time out to look at these issues.

Common Philosophy and Agreed Model of Intervention

A project with such diverse and dispersed workers could only be successful if there was clear policy and procedures, built on sound principles as well as an agreed methodology for intervention.

As existing SACPC policy and procedures did not address working with young abusers, a representative working group chaired by the consultant psychiatrist drafted and consulted on appropriate guidance which was endorsed by SACPC in 1994 (see Appendix One). More detailed guidance covered the referral process and a format for assessment and treatment was agreed. In order to establish a database, which would provide information on the extent of offending, the age of offenders and victims, the nature of abuse and the impact of the project, it was critical that all member agencies made referrals to the project mandatory. In order to establish the validity of the project all teams and agencies received the SACPC policy and procedures for working with young people who sexually abuse and were visited by team members to discuss and clarify the nature of the work. Although time-consuming, this proved beneficial in securing support and referrals. It also allowed concerns and issues to be addressed and relationships to be formed for future co-working.

The flow diagram in Figure 4 illustrates the referral and assessment process.

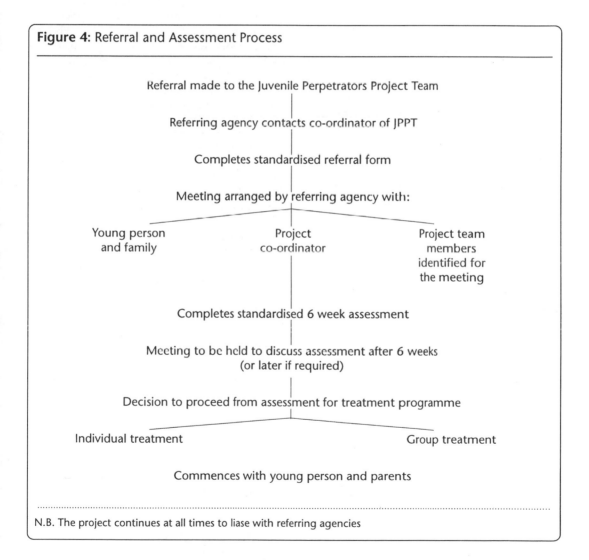

Figure 4: Referral and Assessment Process

Referral made to the Juvenile Perpetrators Project Team

Referring agency contacts co-ordinator of JPPT

Completes standardised referral form

Meeting arranged by referring agency with:

| Young person and family | Project co-ordinator | Project team members identified for the meeting |

Completes standardised 6 week assessment

Meeting to be held to discuss assessment after 6 weeks (or later if required)

Decision to proceed from assessment for treatment programme

Individual treatment   Group treatment

Commences with young person and parents

N.B. The project continues at all times to liase with referring agencies

The referring agencies are aware of the need to advise the co-ordinator of the project immediately to ensure early intervention and enable project team members to be identified to work with the young person after the investigative interview and prior to case conference or case planning meetings. A detailed standardised referral form was specifically developed for the project to obtain relevant information prior to the referral meeting. In practice this is rarely used by the referring agency as they often have no previous contact with these families, so little information is known at the referral stage.

Standard Assessment and Treatment

Ford and Lunney (1995) stressed that work with juveniles who are sexually abusive has developed from a 'one size fits all' treatment model to recognition of the heterogeneous nature of this population. Hence, in developing the assessment and treatment models for the team, agencies agreed on the need for a range of responses. Referrals ranged from 'high risk' individuals requiring intensive programmes of work as a result of sexually abusing a number of children to 'low risk' young people who are on the periphery of abusing and receive very specific input in relation to sex education, boundaries and consent. An example of a high-risk case involves one young abuser who from the age of 10 abused three young children of mixed gender in his neighbourhood. The children were aged from 5–7 years old, and the abuse included penetration over a 2-year period.

The initial assessment model was developed by the Consultant Psychiatrist for the project. Regardless of the referring agency or the discipline of the worker to whom a case is allocated, the young person and his family undergoes a standardised 6 week assessment process covering agreed aspects of the young person's circumstances. The assessment can sometimes take longer than 6 weeks if constraints such as denial, or learning difficulties arise. This initial assessment is discussed at a case review and a plan constructed as to how best to proceed. For many young people engagement is difficult and time consuming and a further period of assessment may be indicated. A retrospective analysis of 59 cases (1998) revealed periods of minimum involvement of one month to 34 months (maximum). The Ross and Loss risk assessment model (1991), used for the pilot, has been successfully evaluated and endorsed for continued use. This format of assessment meets the needs of the formal child protection systems and informs the case conference/case planning meeting.

Decisions regarding the nature of treatment and how it is to be managed are taken jointly by the project co-ordinator, the referring agency and any other involved agencies such as education and probation. The treatment programme includes either individual work or group work or both, depending on which method is more appropriate for the young abuser. The group work programme follows an adaptation of the Smets and Cebula (1987) model, which is described in detail in Chapter 11.

It is essential that all work with this client group is informed, reviewed and documented. 'All agencies within a service delivery system should adopt a common treatment philosophy and practice which enables treatment to continue as the juvenile changes placement or moves into more or less restrictive or intensive shapes of treatment' (Juvenile and Family Court Journal, 1993).

A common approach not only facilitates co-working across agencies but also ensures a consistent approach, which is capable of being evaluated.

Recording policy/procedures

In developing the project it was important to have clear recording procedures. Although case files are used within each agency and comply with agency internal recording systems, a master file for each young abuser is kept by the co-ordinating agency and on closure a copy of all relevant information is placed in the centralised master file in the NSPCC. The NSPCC open access policy is complied with by all agencies in the project. The project team are currently developing a standardised work agreement with the young person and their carers. This will be a formal record, which can be reviewed on a regular basis, normally every 3–4 months.

The collection of reliable information which aided SACPCs understanding of the needs of this client group and their victims was a priority. Additional monies were identified to provide appropriate hardware and software to support a computerised information system. SPSS was chosen because it facilitated analysis of a wide range of valuables as well as producing standard reports: details were obtained on the number of young abusers, the nature, extent and frequency of their abusive behaviour, the time intervals within which abuse is more likely to take place, the age and relationship of victims. This is all critical information to effective inter-agency planning of services for both young abusers and victims of abuse. Data inputting is undertaken by the project worker to ensure reliability. Standard reports have added much to our understanding but we have not yet had the capacity or expertise to make full use of the system. Data is being analysed for a further report to enable future planning of services for young abusers. Information about victims of abuse will help to develop more effective prevention strategies including appropriate education programmes.

Evaluation

SACPC emphasised the importance of evaluating both the inter-agency working arrangements and the efficacy of treatment. Project members struggled to develop an appropriate database and seriously underestimated the time and skills needed. More expertise will be needed to fully analyse the information collected this far. The statistical data was complemented by information gathered through a range of evaluative techniques:

- Questionnaires completed by referring agencies reflect a high level of satisfaction regarding the responsiveness and quality of the service offered by the project. They did request information leaflets which have since been disseminated.

- Anonymous postal questionnaires, completed by young abusers, provide evidence of their dependence on parents and social workers, their anxiety about re-abusing and a self report as to whether they have committed further acts of abuse.

- Semi-structured interviews with young people indicated that they had previously been denied an opportunity to address their offending behaviour.

- Psychological questionnaires completed by young people and their parents will be analysed in early 1999.

The success of the project can really only be measured in terms of the decrease in offending behaviour or in the risk of offending. Significantly only 3 of the 59 young people referred to the project are known, (either by their own admission or through coming to the attention of any of the agencies), to have re-abused. The evaluation has been crucial in further developing the model, services and support for the future, as acknowledged by the Juvenile and Family Court Journal (1993): 'Clinicians in this field are eager for research to support this work and will modify current treatment assumptions if new developments provide evidence of more effective methods for treatment.'

Communications and public relations

Many inter-agency projects fail to be sustained because their work is not continually promoted and reported on to those people in agencies on whom their continuing success is dependent. Communication about this project has taken many forms and has been time consuming for the project co-ordinator, steering group and team members. Communications has taken many forms. For example, a high profile conference in 1994 organised jointly by SACPC, NSPCC and Orana House, a children's residential project, was a timely mechanism for raising awareness of the need for work with young abusers, of demonstrating the work already ongoing throughout Northern Ireland and for gaining the commitment of agency chief executives; Professor Judith Becker, as keynote speaker, left no-one in any doubt of the necessity for the complex work to be undertaken by skilled practitioners on an inter-agency basis. A further international symposium the following year and an interim conference and seminar kept the focus on this client group. The project has been presented at a number of major conferences, such as BASPCAN (1994, 1997), ISPCAN (1996), as well as publications in Child Abuse Review

(1996) and in the Child Care Journal (N.I.) (1994).

Initially team members visited all referring agencies to explain the service and the referral process and to build up working relationships. Steering group members made regular presentations at SACPC and at Trust child protection panels as well as providing feedback to individual sponsoring agencies.

Information leaflets for professionals, for young people and for parents have all been developed and made available through appropriate outlets. Of equally crucial importance is the feedback on individual young abusers to referring agencies, to parents and to the young people themselves.

Community awareness and education is an issue which also needs to be addressed and the steering group plan to tackle this in the future. Negative public reaction to adult offenders, resulting in vigilante-style responses, have been a worrying feature within Northern Ireland. Punishment beatings of young people engaged in 'anti-social' activities are also a common occurrence. Educating the community and enlisting their support for work with young sex offenders as part of a child protection strategy will have to be tackled in a sensitive, timely and appropriate manner. Lessons will hopefully be learned from a Belfast-based project, which is using parents as peer educators within a community.

Funding arrangements

Securing revenue funding is obviously a pre-requisite to any service development. The attraction of this partnership was that many agencies were able to contribute in kind. Funding for the set up costs, one full-time worker, administrative support, IT equipment and management for the two year pilot project was £70,000 and was funded on a 75:25 per cent basis by the Health and Social Services Board and NSPCC. As indicated earlier, member agencies resource the project by seconding staff, providing consultation and by facilitating access to or funding residential and other outings during the life of the project. This obviously keeps costs down. It is hoped that long term funding can be secured from the three statutory agencies, police, probation and social services. This requires relatively radical

departures from traditional expenditure patterns for some agencies like the RUC, and it is particularly encouraging that on the back of the evaluation the Policy Authority for Northern Ireland has agreed to £20,000 per year for three years. Restructuring within the Probation Service to reflect new emphasis on adjudicated offenders has frustrated negotiations, but this emphasis along with the critical findings of the Home Office Report should hopefully bring results. Joint funding is tangible and demonstrable evidence of agencies' commitment.

Conclusion

While the project has been successfully evaluated, the evaluation process revealed many tensions and resource issues, which resulted in a series of recommendations to SACPC. The findings included:

- The number of referrals was significantly underestimated. The project anticipated 18 referrals per year for two years and received 59.

- Referrals to the project fluctuate from day to day, week to week, with obvious implications for case allocation to the project team members.

- One area has had significantly lower rates of referrals compared to the other two areas. We need to determine whether the threshold for referral is lower than the other two areas or the reporting of young people abusing is lower in this area, or the extent of the offending behaviour is lower in this area.

- In underestimating the referrals resources for the team were insufficient to meet demand. All agencies were placed under pressure and it has now been clarified that seconded workers to the team need to set aside approximately one day per week.

- Replacement workers must be found immediately if seconded project team workers are no longer available for the team.

- In the evaluation process of the project the time to develop the database, analyse the physiological questionnaires, load on the information collated on the database and analyse this information in a coherent report to all the partners was extremely underestimated, and in doing so put undue pressure on the team

- The project team recommended in some cases that the young people needed to be assessed in appropriate residential accommodation due to the nature of their high risk offending behaviour. Unfortunately, in some instances, there were no appropriate facilities, or family placements. This issue needs to be further considered and options for providing placements developed.

- The needs of young people under threat from paramilitary factions needs to be addressed.

- The needs of young abusers with learning difficulties suggest the need for ongoing involvement up to say 21 years.

Reflecting on Calder's theory (1997), we believe that the Juvenile Perpertrators Project has achieved a systematic multi-agency approach of interventions with young people who sexually abuse and through its evaluations, continues to demonstrate and develop good practice. This took almost ten years to develop and seems set to continue with a more secure funding base and the potential to make it more generally available in Northern Ireland.

References.

Baxter, E., and Print, B. (1999). Groupwork Processes and the Impact of Working Together in Core Groups. In Calder, M.C., and Horwarth, J. (1999). *Working for Children on the Child Protection Register: An Inter-agency Practice Guide.* Aldershot: Arena

Calder, M.C. (1997). *Juveniles and Children who Sexually Abuse: A Guide to Risk Assessment.* Dorset: Russell House Publishing.

Calder, M.C. (1997b). *Young People who Sexually Abuse: Towards International Consensus. Social Work in Europe* 4: 36–39.

Calder, M.C. (1999). *Assessing Risk in Adult Males who Sexually Abuse Children: A Practitioner's Guide.* Dorset: Russell House Publishing.

Calder, M.C., and Horwarth, J. (1999). *Working for Children on the Child Protection Register: An Inter-agency Practice Guide.* Aldershot: Arena

Davis, G.E., and Leitenberg, H. (1987). Adolescent Sex Offenders. *Psychological Bulletin* 101(3): 417–427

Debelle, G.D., Ward, M.R., Burnham, J.B., Jamieson, R., and Ginty, M. (1993). Evaluation of Intervention Programmes for Juvenile Sex Offenders: Questions and Dilemmas. *Child Abuse Review,* 2: 75–85.

DHSS (1989). N.I. *'Co-operation to Protect Children'*

DoH (1991). *Working Together: A Guide to Arrangements for Inter-agency Co-operation for the Protection of Children from Abuse.* London: HMSO.

DoH (1995). *Child Protection: Messages from Research — Studies in Child Protection.* London: HMSO.

DoH (1998). *Working Together to Safeguard Children: New Government Proposals for Inter-agency Co-operation.* Consultation Paper. London: HMSO.

Ford, M.E., and Linney, J.A. (1995). Comparative Analysis of Juvenile Sexual Offenders, Violent Non-sexual Offenders, and Status Offenders. *Journal of Interpersonal Violence* 10 (1): 56–70.

Glasgow, D., Horne, L., Calam, R., and Cox, A. (1994). Evidence, Incidence, Gender and Age in Sexual Abuse of Children Perpetrated by Children: Towards a Developmental Analysis of Child Sexual Abuse. *Child Abuse Review* 3: 196–210.

H.M. Inspection of Probation (1998). *Exercising Constant Vigilance: The Role of the Probation Service in Protecting the Public from Sex Offenders. Report of a Thematic Inspection.* London: HMSO.

Kennedy, M.T., Maxwell, M.K.C., MacKenzie, G., Blaney, R., Chivers, A.T., Hay, I., and Vincent, O.E. (1990). *Child Sexual Abuse in Northern Ireland: A Research Study of Evidence.* Belfast: Greystone Books.

Masson, H. (1996). *Children and Adolescents who Sexually Abuse Other Children: An Emerging Problem, Second Interim Report April 1996.* Huddersfield: University School of Human and Health Sciences.

McCune, N., and Scott, F. (1994). Group Treatment Programme For Adolescents Sex Offenders. *Child Care In Practice* 1(2): 1–9.

McGarvey, J., and Lenaghan, M. (1996). A Structured Group Approach With Adolescent Perpetrators. *Child Abuse Review* 5: 203–213.

Morrison, T. (1992). Managing Sex Offenders: The Challenge for Managers. *Probation Journal* 39(3): 122–128.

Morrison, T. (1997). Where Have We Come From: Where Are We Going? Managing Adolescents Who Sexually Abuse Others. *N.O.T.A. News,* 21: 15–27.

Morrison, T., and Print, B. (1995). *Adolescent Sexual Abusers: An Overview.* Hull: Bluemoon Corporate Services/NOTA.

Morrison, T., Erooga, M., and Beckett, R. (Eds.) (1994). *Assessment and Treatment of Male Abusers.* London: Routledge.

Myers, S. (1998) Young People who Sexually Abuse: Is Consensus Possible or Desirable? *Social Work in Europe* 5(1): 53–56.

National Childrens' Homes (1992). *Report of the Committee of Enquiry into Children and Young People who Sexually Abuse Other Children.* London: NCH.

National Commission of Enquiry into the Prevention of Child Abuse (1996) *Childhood Matters* (Vols. 1 and 2). London: HMSO.

Northern Ireland Protocol for Joint Investigation by Social Workers and Police Officers of Alleged and Suspected Cases of Child Abuse. March 1996.

Peyton, L. (1997) Re-Organisation Trends and Issues in Northern Ireland. In Cohen, B. and Hagen, U. (Ed.) *Children's Services: Shaping up for the Millennium.* Edinburgh: The Stationery Office.

Ross, J., and Loss, P. (1991). Assessment of the Juvenile Sex Offender. In Ryan, G.D., and Lane, S.L. (Eds.). *Juvenile Sex Offenders: Causes, Consequences and Corrections,* 199–251. Lexington, MA: Lexington books.

Schram, D.D., Malloy, C.D., and Rowe, W.E. (1991).

Juvenile Sex Offenders: A Follow-up Study of Re-offence Behaviour. Washington: Urban Policy Research.

Smets, A.C., and Cebula, C.M. (1987). A Group Treatment Programme For Adolescent Sex Offenders: Five Steps Toward Resolution. *Child Abuse and Neglect,* 11: 247–254.

Southern Area Child Protection Committee Policy and Procedure for Working with Young People who Sexually Abuse. December 1994.

The Revised Report From The National Task Force on Juvenile Sex Offending (1993). *Juvenile and Family Court Journal* 44(4).

Appendix One

Policy and Procedures
for
Working with Young People
who
Sexually Abuse

DECEMBER 1994

SOUTHERN AREA CHILD PROTECTION COMMITTEE

Policy and Procedures for Working with Young People who Sexually Abuse

1.0 Introduction

1.1 Incidence

There is increasing evidence that a significant number of young people engage in sexual offences involving other children and young people. In the Northern Ireland Child Sexual Abuse Study of 1989, 36% of all cases of abuse involved a juvenile perpetrator. Other studies have reported similar rates of approximately one-third of all child sexual abuse incidents committed by young people.

1.2 Nature of Abuse

The nature of the sexually abusive behaviour ranges from non-contact offences such as indecent exposure and obscene telephone calls, to sexual offences that involve physical assaults and sadistic behaviour. In some instances there is evidence of sophisticated planning both to gain access to victims and to exercise control over victims to avoid discovery.

1.3 Research Studies

Research studies indicate that the frequency of sexual victimisation is higher in young people who abuse than in the general population of young people. However the majority of studies put this figure at less than 50%. It appears therefore that over half of young abusers have not themselves experienced sexual victimisation. Most abuse appears to be carried out by young males and often young perpetrators will have abused a number of victims prior to being apprehended.

2.0 Strategic Context

The inter-departmental group on child sexual abuse in its document 'A Strategic Statement on Working with Abusers' highlighted the need to:

● formulate a coherent policy for the management and treatment of abusers and evaluate and review policy at regular intervals.

● build up a better understanding of characteristics of abusers and the context in which abuse takes place

- view sexual abuse as a problem which requires assessment and treatment for the abuser as well as the abused and help abusers learn ways of minimizing the risks of re-offending

- promote an inter-disciplinary and inter-agency approach to the planning, delivery and review of programmes for managing and treating abusers and others involved

- encourage the development of local and national resource networks for staff working with abusers in recognition of the high demands of their work

- educate professional staff about the nature and approach to sexual abuse

3.0 Policy

The Southern Area Child Protection Committee is committed to providing appropriate services for young people who abuse others in order to prevent the young person re-offending as well as providing protection for children. While it is likely that the majority of young abusers are adolescents, it is recognised that sexual abuse can be perpetrated by pre-adolescents as well. The terms 'young perpetrator' or 'young abuser' will therefore be used throughout, to avoid confusion and applies to anyone under the age of 18 years.

4.0 Principles

The following principles underpin effective child protection activity in respect of young abusers:

4.1 In any intervention, the welfare of the child victim must always be paramount, this overrides all other considerations.

4.2 Children and young people who abuse others are in need of help and are entitled to appropriate services. Intervention and treatment should occur as soon as possible.

4.3 Intervention should not deal with the child/young person in isolation but in the context of their family situation.

4.4 Whenever possible young people who abuse have a right to be consulted and involved in all matters and decisions which may affect their lives. Their parents have a right to information, respect and participation in matters which concern their family.

4.5 The criminal dimension of the offending behaviour must be addressed and young people must be held accountable for their actions. Whenever possible there should be a formal mandate for intervention and treatment.

4.6 There should be effective communication between all agencies involved with young abusers.

4.7   There should be appropriate communication between those professionals working with the victim and those working with the abuser. The wishes of the victim and their family should be acknowledged in determining which information is shared.

5.0 Inter-Agency Child Protection Procedures

5.1 Investigation

Southern Area Child Protection Procedures are instigated in respect of any young person up to 17 years of age who allegedly abuses another child. (SACPC Procedures Page 9)

These cases normally come to the attention of social services or the RUC through a referral that a child/young person is being abused or is potentially at risk of abuse and the Joint Investigation Protocol will be implemented.

These procedures deal only with the young abuser and should be read in conjunction with other relevant sections of the Southern Area Child Protection Procedures.

5.2 Case Conference

The young abuser should also be the subject of a multi-disciplinary child protection case conference which will take account of both legal and treatment issues and formulate plans with firm recommendations on the young person's management. Some young abusers may themselves have been victims of abuse. Where the criteria for registration are met, the young abuser should be included on the child protection register. The criteria for registration are:

1.   The child/young person has been or is suspected of being abused

2.   There is need for a multi-disciplinary child protection plan

5.3 Assessment/Case Review

A full multi-disciplinary assessment must be carried out in respect of all suspected abusers. A standardised assessment procedure which considers the developmental, behavioural and cognitive aspects of the young person should be used.

6.0 Legal Process

Allegations against the young abuser will be investigated by the police and social services in accordance with the Joint Protocol. The decision on prosecution is a matter for the Director of Public Prosecutions (DPP) acting on information collated from a variety of sources, by the RUC. Research shows that work with perpetrators is more successful when imposed by legal sanctions and some way of mandating treatment is essential. The RUC report for the DPP should have regard to the seriousness of the offence and the wishes and feelings of the victim and may advocate one of the following treatment options:

a) prosecution followed by a sentence in the form of a probation order with a condition attached mandating treatment

b) deferment of a decision to prosecute for a limited period, conditional on voluntary admission to an evaluated treatment programme. A further report should be sent to the DPP detailing progress or otherwise, which may then be taken into account when a decision on prosecution is being reached.

NB: Sometimes victims and their families may not wish the offender to be prosecuted. They should be helped to recognise the potential risk to other children if the perpetrator is not treated and advised that there is a high drop out rate from voluntary treatment programmes. Therefore, while they may not wish prosecution to proceed they should accept that the possibility of prosecution must be retained as an option if co-operation with treatment is withdrawn.

7.0 Treatment

Treatment programmes for young abusers should include the following components:

a) Individual psychotherapy

b) Group psychotherapy sessions for young abusers

c) Parallel group sessions for parents of abusers

d) Family therapy and/or focused casework with parents

Both the individual and group psychotherapy with young abusers should include specific therapeutic techniques aimed at increasing victim awareness and empathy; social skills training; assertiveness training; sex education incorporating attitudes towards sexuality and gender; cognitive therapy addressing arousal patterns and masturbatory fantasies; and relapse prevention strategies.

There should be a formal review of the young person's behaviour, attitudes and disposition when the full treatment programme has been completed.

All treatment programmes should be fully evaluated with regard to outcomes.

8.0 Information Leaflets

Information leaflets should be given to parents whose child/young person has been accused of abusing another child. The chance of reducing the risk of re-offending is enhanced when young abusers have parental support and involvement throughout the treatment process. It is recommended that these leaflets are provided for parents during the early stages of investigation.

Appendix Two

INFORMATION LEAFLET

GENERAL INTRODUCTION

This short leaflet has been written for parents whose child has sexually abused another child. A child is anyone under the age of 18. The leaflet gives brief information to help parents understand why young people sexually abuse others and how parents can help their own child and indeed themselves through what is a very difficult, stressful, painful and confusing time for all.

WHAT IS SEXUAL ABUSE?

The sexual abuse of a child occurs whenever any person persuades, forces, tricks or threatens a child in order to have sexual contact with him or her. Sexual contact can include touching the child's genitals and can progress to more extreme forms of sexual behaviour. Sometimes there is no direct physical contact, but the child/young person is shown pornographic materials (including photographs and books or films).

In all cases of child sexual abuse the child is being used as an object to satisfy the adolescent/adult's sexual needs or desires.

EFFECTS ON THE VICTIM

A child victim is damaged by their experiences, even if no force was used. The victim frequently suffers emotional disturbance such as:

- embarrassment, fear, confusion

- guilt, anxiety, sense of rejection

- distrust of adults and strangers

Some of these effects may be long lasting, and some of these symptoms of emotional harm may not be evident for years, often not until some time in adulthood.

Help for the victim can alleviate these effects.

HOW PARENTS FEEL

The first reaction of most parents when they learn that their child has abused is one of disbelief. The news of what a child has done comes as a great shock and parents will find themselves with many difficult thoughts, questions and mixed up emotions.

Parents may find themselves defending their child with other explanations for what has happened especially when the child denies what he has done, because he too is feeling ashamed, embarrassed and afraid.

It is important that parents do not simply accept that their child could not have abused. Although it will be very difficult it is essential that parents stand by and support their child during this difficult time and help their child to talk about what they have done.

One of the best ways to do this is to use the help that is available for the child and for parents.

Family members have an important part to play in giving support and ensuring that their child receives the help which is necessary. It is important for everyone to look honestly at how the abuse happened and to try to help one another, to work with others, to correct the situation.

Parents can make a vital contribution by working closely and in co-operation with the professionals who provide counselling and treatment.

Parents will also need some time for themselves so that they have the chance to talk about their own thoughts and feelings, to try and find some answers to the many questions they may have.

This time and help is available for parents.

WHY CONCERN?

Sexual abuse by young people is unfortunately not uncommon. It is of growing concern to everyone who works with children, both with children who have been victims of abuse and also with those who abuse.

There are many reasons for this concern, some of which are given below:

1.   We know that many adults who sexually abuse begin offending in their teenage years and even earlier. This early abuse often goes undetected or is dismissed as of no real concern. Help is not then given. Unfortunately many of these young people then continue to abuse into adulthood, when the abuse is exceedingly more difficult to stop.

2.   Sexual abusing is caused by problems in the way the young person thinks and feels about himself and others. These problems are not often obvious or easy to see. If they are not understood and help is not given then these problems will lead to more abuse.

3.   Sexual abuse has a damaging effect on the person who is abused. Almost always the young person who abuses is not aware of this and as a result they go on abusing.

4.   Sexual abuse very quickly becomes an addictive behaviour and one which the young person finds difficult to control and stop, even when caught.

Many parents question the need for their child to have help. Concerned parents may fear that dwelling on the matter will make things worse, that things are better 'left alone'. As a result they may resist the idea of help for their child.

Without fully exploring the problem with the possibility of help for the young person the risk of more abuse is great. The danger is that the young person will find the behaviour beyond his control so that control by others is needed.

Assessment, which aims to understand the underlying problems that led to the abuse and treatment/intervention to provide help with these problems are essential.

Assessment and treatment is available from a number of people and agencies working with young people who have sexually abused.

CONFIDENTIALITY

The information made available by any young person and his or her family during exploration of the problem and treatment will be shared among those people directly involved in taking decisions about the young person.

An exception to this may be in the event of a young person disclosing information such as further sexual abuse which would need to be shared with other agencies, namely social services and/or police, in order to protect that young person themselves or others who may be at risk.

Chapter Seven

A Conceptual Framework for Managing Young People who Sexually Abuse:

Towards a Consortium Approach

Martin C. Calder

A Conceptual Framework for Managing Young People who Sexually Abuse: Towards a Consortium Approach

Introduction

This chapter aims to explore the advantages and barriers of working together, both within and across agencies/boundaries — in general terms, then in relation to child sexual abuse, and latterly in relation to young people who sexually abuse. In doing so, it will identify the issues which need to be embraced by the Area Child Protection Committee (ACPC) if a local response is to be formulated to compensate for the lack of central government guidance. A conceptual framework is provided for this purpose. The need for a broader, cross ACPC approach to achieve some effective management of young people who sexually abuse is suggested, and this is termed 'the consortium approach'. I will argue that the organisational fragmentation of services, the acute shortfall in resources and the lack of any consensus approach to the management of this group can be partially offset by harnessing the resources, knowledge and skills of different individuals, agencies and localities. In turn, the developing responses can be utilised to promote good practice within the UK (and beyond), so as to avoid any unnecessary duplication.

The Case for Working Together

The call for multi-disciplinary working and inter-agency working has had a long and distinguished history, despite the serious limitations uncovered in practice by a succession of child abuse inquiries into child deaths (see DHSS, 1982 and DoH, 1991a for a review).

The ongoing focus on working together is based on a belief that it has the potential for achieving more than the sum of the collaborating parts operating individually. The central goal of working together is the achievement of some degree of consensus by a group of individuals about a plan of action and its execution. It usually includes an interpersonal process in which members of a group contribute, each from their knowledge and skill, to the accomplishment of a task, yet are responsible as a group for the outcome. A process of cross-fertilisation of ideas is presumed to occur that encourages new perspectives and reformulations of difficult problems and solutions that exceed the boundaries of separate disciplines. The more generalised the task and the more the individual professional is dependant on the co-operation of others in its accomplishment, the greater their motivation will be for collaborative activity (Mailick and Ashley, 1989).

In light of this belief, central guidance has been repeatedly issued, becoming more prescriptive in nature, in order to achieve this desired outcome. The DoH guidance accompanying the Act itself (DoH, 1991b) stated that: 'The authority cannot expect to be the sole repository of knowledge and wisdom about particular cases. Full inter-agency co-operation including sharing information and participating in decision-making is essential' (Vol. 1, para 3.10, p 22).

Margetts (1998) set out clearly the benefits of working together in sexual abuse cases:

- Shared information: allowing the different information on a particular person to be pooled, providing a better knowledge base for an assessment (of risk).

- Shared responsibility: is important, particularly in very difficult and dangerous cases where agencies working together and agreeing a plan of work do not expose themselves to be singled out in the event of a disaster. Although professionals may choose to work together, no theory exists to define the obligations of a group of individuals involved in a shared task. Calder and Horwath (1999) highlighted three models of collective responsibility which need to be explored if working together is to be accompanied by a clarity of roles, responsibilities and accountability. The models are:

The Identification model: which holds the group and all its members responsible for the acts of individual members simply because of their identification as members of the group.

The Participatory model: which attributes to an individual the full responsibility for the acts or omissions of the group as a whole and all its members just because an individual is a participant in a situation at a particular time and place. When responsible action by any individual would have helped, the whole aggregate is held collectively responsible.

The Authorisation model: where the single act of authorisation on the part of the individual serves to signify membership in the collective. It bonds people to those who operate within the same-governed framework (Newton, 1982).

- Services are not duplicated: if agencies work in isolation from each other, it is increasingly likely that they will either duplicate resources or not be prepared to recognise the value of each other's work.

- Deploying services according to need rather than referral route: The service a sexual abuser receives often seems to depend upon the point of referral, rather than through an assessment of their needs and the risk they pose. Sexual abusers may be treated in the medical, criminal justice or child protection systems without reference to resources deployed in other fields.

- Development of effective practice: specialists in this work often feel isolated and can benefit from links to other professionals and the ability to share knowledge and skills.

- Shared intelligence and public safety concerns: this will become a growing responsibility for all agencies concerned with sexual abusers.

- All agencies stand to be able to use resources more efficiently and increasing their effectiveness (p 34–5).

Hallett and Birchall (1992) provided us with an excellent summary of the extensive literature on collaboration between different professionals and agencies. Within this, they point out that three commonly used terms — co-ordination, collaboration and co-operation — are used interchangeably and synonymously, yet there is a clear differentiating factor: the degree of formalisation involved in the arrangements. Co-ordination is the most formalised, involving agreement between organisations at the highest level and the use of specifically allocated co-ordinative machinery. Collaboration is characterised by looser, lower-level agreements, whilst co-operation is the least formalised arrangement of the three. This is significant in as much as the government's choice to guide the child protection framework has been 'Working Together Under the Children Act 1989 - A guide to Arrangements for Inter-agency **Co-operation** for the Protection of Children Against Abuse' (DoH, 1991c). This makes a local response essential.

The collaborative process is useful for social workers as it encourages a structure for co-operation; a culture for consultation; the development of consensus among professionals; promoting a policy of inclusion of the inter-professional group; offering a support mechanism and building coalitions. It also elevates them to equal terms with other groups that command far greater public esteem, e.g. police and doctors (Jenkins, 1992, p202).

Barriers to Working Together

In general terms

Child protection is not the exclusive province of any one agency. Unfortunately, different constituent agencies of the child protection system are guided by different legislation and government guidance, and these, at times, seem to pull in different directions (Margetts, 1998, p 28). Working together among different professionals and between different agencies is also not a uniform activity. It can range from the face to face contact between a doctor and a health visitor concerned about a shared patient, to a network of professionals employed by different agencies to meet the needs of a particular client group (Loxley, 1997, p 42).

There is ample evidence in the child protection arena that individuals and agencies have found it most difficult to co-operate. This goes beyond individual personality conflict and professional incompetence. It is rooted in a variety of differences in values, practices, perspectives, and professional ethos, arising out of a range of social, cultural and historical processes. I will use an extended and adapted version of Charles and Stevenson (1990) and Stevenson (1989) to explore some of the explanations why working together often runs into difficulties.

1.   **Differences in background and training:** professionals bring a range of personal and professional experiences combined with extensive differences in temperament and views of life and society. They will differ greatly in their educational experiences, particularly their professional training, which has a profound socialising effect upon them. Their expectations of training will also differ. For social workers, they will have experienced training which encourages the development of self-awareness and is based on abstract values like self-determination. This mirrors the complex and uncertain situations, which they will face in practice. Other professionals will have experienced more decisive and directive training and may be frustrated by the lack of definitive answers to child protection problems.

2.   **Varied attitudes to family life:** individual attitudes to family life are shaped by personal experiences, ethnic origin, culture and social class combining with the effects of professional socialisation. It follows, therefore, that attitudes will vary over issues such as what constitutes good/ bad family life, 'normal' behaviour, etc.

3.   **Stereotypes and prejudices:** are a pervasive feature held by us in relation to disciplines which we rarely encounter, and have the potential to damage trust and create stress and confusion about what skills and responsibilities they actually have to offer. The different approaches necessarily adopted by professional groups may give rise to stereotypical 'cardboard' images of each other. Such stereotyping can be dangerous

when it allows us to distance ourselves from others, and to fail to see the individual through the distorting lens of our own prejudices. It can be used defensively to convince ourselves we do not need to take their ideas, understandings and values seriously, and to reinforce our own superior knowledge.

4.   **Role identification and socialisation:** each professional will have been socialised into their particular role, and will have a value system and language unique to their particular profession. These value systems are constant sources of potential conflict, which affect how professionals view each other's work and the level of risk acceptable to the respective professions. This has a profound effect on how they see each other, on the nature of their interaction and on their perceptions of specific family situations and the action taken. Stevenson (1989) has reminded us that we should not overlook the effect of role definition upon the attitudes and feelings of the workers involved. Roles have emotional as well as intellectual dimensions. There can be consequences for staff within their own agencies of subscribing to their role in the child protection system, e.g. they are pilloried and may have their career prospects affected.

5.   **Differences within and between professionals:** no individual is the same, whether they are from the same agency or from a different one. Subsystems exist each with different aims and values, relating to personal and social characteristics (such as class and gender). Not all individuals hold the same interests, beliefs or expertise.

6.   **Status and power:** differences in contracts of employment, the different types and standards of professional training, occupational status and prestige, gender, race, class, language, and public image all contribute to the real and felt power differentials within the inter-agency network. Working together means contact between different emotional realities, different systems of meaning and different types of bias. At its most acute, the statutory responsibility of social

services for the protection of abused children is at odds with its low status, salary and less certain identity. Professionals working together require significant personal investments, inducing a sense of vulnerability, such as exposing practice to peer scrutiny and with it the prospect of being assessed as being incompetent. Such anxieties can become infectious and compound the presenting problems. One profession may regard another as hostile or inferior to their own and shape their attitudes accordingly. Status affects performance: those who perceive themselves of low status may offer no contributions or feel unable to question information or comments made by those of seeming high status or power. Hallett (1995) developed a hierarchy of professionals involved in the child protection system:

Level 1: Keyworker and core profession (social services).

Level 2: Other core professionals (police, paediatricians).

Level 3: Frontline professionals (health visitors, teachers and general practitioners).

Level 4: Peripheral contact professionals (education welfare officers and school nurses).

Level 5: Case-specific professionals (lawyers, psychologists, psychiatrists).

This system echoes the 'inner' and 'outer' circles of professionals found by Hallett and Stephenson (1980). Calder (1991) used the term 'conference cabals' to describe the small group of senior representatives from agencies who monopolise the child protection conference and expect others to align their views with their own in order to achieve some 'consensus'. Stevenson (1994) has argued that we must consider the amount of time agencies spend on child protection work when constructing procedures and there should be a mechanism through which those agencies in the outer circles (peripheral, periodically involved) can have the complexities explained to them (p 176).

7. **Professional and organisational priorities:** the nature of the work undertaken by the various agencies varies greatly. Those with statutory and lead procedural responsibilities will spend much of their time doing child protection work, compared to other agencies where it plays one part of a much more generic caseload. For example, Hallett (1995) found that teachers only spent half a day a month on child protection and thus remain detached from the system. The importance of staff training will be given different emphasis by the various agencies (varying from essential to being seen as a 'luxury').

8. **Structures, systems and administration:** the variety of structures, and the systems within them, of the different agencies create difficulties and make co-ordination difficult. Agencies hold different powers and duties, and some do not have coterminous geographical boundaries. Accountability and authority is fragmented, with individuals having differing degrees of authority with which to speak for their agencies. All these differences affect co-operation and inhibit the transfer of information between agencies. Each agency has a different job to do, a different area of activity, and different interests and concerns. Some have a focused role at a particular stage whilst others have a more diffuse role that spans all the stages. Similarly, within any stage, different agencies may need to focus on different aspects (Stainton-Rogers, 1989, p 88–9). Charles and Stevenson (1990) have argued that we must all have some appreciation of the diversity of employing agencies, with their differing structures, nature and functions. They noted that many of the professionals involved in child protection work belong to agencies featuring strict hierarchical structures, e.g. the police, whilst local authority departments are ultimately accountable to committees of elected representatives, who delegate powers and duties through senior officers to teachers and social workers. GPs and consultants, although immediately accountable to their relevant professional bodies, are less directly influenced or constrained in their day-to-day actions by a professional hierarchy. Other doctors,

such as hospital and community paediatricians, have clear lines of accountability from basic staff through more senior staff to lead workers. As such, the agency structure inevitably poses limits to the degree of professional autonomy exercised by the various disciplines. For those whose freedom of action is constrained by agency structures, a certain tension exists between the exercise of individual professional judgement and what is agency permissible. This tension is easily compounded by the attitudes of other professionals, who may express frustrations about delays in decision making, being unaware of the processes needing to be gone through. Organisational structures affect the availability of staff, e.g. surgery hours, shift systems, daily patterns of working and duty rotas all influence the nature of inter-professional co-operation (p 86–88).

9. **Different roles and responsibilities:** the issue of role clarity is important, particularly when their blurring can relieve staff of knowing who is doing what and why, and who should be held accountable in the event of failure. Hallett (1995) found some confusion about the roles of various professionals in the system, partially supported by the research of Calder and Barratt (1997) in the core group. Here, the authors found a discrepancy between what health visitors, teachers and social workers conceptualised as their own roles and those of others with what was found in practice. They concluded that roles had to be grounded in what was realistic rather than being overtly idealistic. There appears to be a shift towards acceptance that whilst there is an expectation of collective responsibility, the reality is that social services have the lead responsibility and any offers of support will be gratefully received. Yet unless this is agreed and understood formally and locally, there will be confusion and a culture of blame will prevail. There is also a need to acknowledge that child protection is dirty work and it can lead to social workers defining their own role and that of others in such a way as to enable

them to ditch the dirty work on to others (Blyth and Milner, 1990, p 197). Social services have a broad role in the management of child abuse, ranging from partnership and rehabilitation to investigation and removal. The police have a duty to prosecute (punitive), whilst probation have a crime prevention role, plus working with those convicted of sexual offences. For a detailed discussion about the roles of different agencies in child sexual abuse work, please refer to Margetts (1998). Morrison (1998b) pointed out that, for the police and probation, the concept of risk is overwhelmingly a negative association, e.g. the risk of danger. This is in stark contrast to debates in the child protection field in which the risk of potential danger is continually weighed against risk of potential benefit (p 4).

10. **Lines of authority and decision-making:** social services are the lead agency in child protection, joined by the police and others. Only recently has the law required key agencies to co-operate with social services in the investigation of child abuse. The problem with such mandated working together is that people and agencies will not necessarily collaborate just because someone tells them to do so. This is most acute when seen in the context that few professionals would choose to work together given a choice. Different agencies and individuals may have varying degrees of acceptance of, or commitment to, co-operate and differing capacities to resist. The recommendations of a child protection conference are not binding and agencies can, and do, act independently of them (especially when they did not sign up to them originally). Within agencies, the aims and approaches of people at different levels are often at odds, e.g. 'managerial safety' versus practitioner option for risk.

11. **Different perspectives:** professionals define and explain child abuse in different and sometimes conflicting ways and adopt quite different stances about the way work should be undertaken. Different theories often emerge from particular disciplines and are maintained

without reference to, or acknowledgement of, parallel theories. This blinkered approach to problem definition affects our ability to provide a problem resolution strategy (see Calder, 1999a for an overview of theory relating to sexual abuse and offending). Some of the conflicts that emerge are associated with particular ideologies, e.g. family dysfunction theorists and feminists clash over the issue of offender responsibility for their behaviour.

12. **Complexity and co-ordination:** Rai (1994) defined complexity as the degree of structural differentiation or internal segmentation, as reflected by the number of divisions, number of hierarchical levels, and the number of geographical locations of the organisation (p 90). He found a very clear negative relationship between complexity and co-ordination in child welfare agencies, particularly relating to communication.

13. **Communication:** information is power and sharing it symbolises some ceding of autonomy. Disagreements exist both as to the content of what is to be shared and about the actual value of talking together at all. What seems essential to communicate for one may seem a breach of confidentiality or peripheral to another. Professionals from different fields are used to working within their own particular culture and organisational structure with their established rules on issues such as confidentiality. The very differences in language and traditions can lead to a breakdown in communication, especially when dominated by technical terms and/or jargon. The differences in status, position and hierarchy inhibit communications among members of an organisation, particularly inter-level.

14. **'Underlapping service provision':** is a tactic employed by agencies where they choose the narrowest possible view of their duties and then they discharge them in as perfunctory a way as possible. Once one agency has taken this view, others may do so to avoid 'dumping', thus depriving the client of any service rather than a complementary inter-agency response (Margetts, 1998).

15. **Changes in philosophy:** is a pervasive feature of current child protection work. Following the Children Act (1989) and the introduction of parental responsibility and partnership (see Calder, 1995); and the report 'Messages from Research' (DoH, 1995), which recommended that we review the balance between family support and child protection approaches, there has been conflict between agencies on how to respond to these concepts. This is important, as we cannot separate partnership with families from partnership practice between and within agencies (Morrison, 1996a). If there are deficits in collaboration between agencies, then it undermines the experience of partnership for the families: 'If partnership is to become a reality, it must be ingrained and modelled within organisational structures, cultures, and working relationships which seek to reward collaboration rather than competition' (Morrison, 1996a, p 135).

16. **Organisational restructuring:** reorganisations in key agencies have taken place in the context of tight financial constraints on local government. There has been a major shift in the balance of power from local to central government as local authority expenditure and taxation has been brought firmly under central control. As Morrison (1998a) has noted 'The past seven years have seen an escalation in both the extent and rate of organisational change across the public sector. No agency or discipline has been left unaffected... Reforming legislation has occurred in social services, health, education, and criminal justice sectors, in pursuit of greater efficiency and effectiveness with the introduction of market principles against a backcloth of fiscal retrenchment...' (p 122–3). This has led to agencies redefining their core business and basing collaboration on fiscal as opposed to inter-professional arrangements. The result is that 'collaboration is currently dangerously over-dependent on the commitment and skills of individuals, rather than organisations, and thus too easily disrupted by their departure.

Unfortunately, this means that whilst the quality of response may be very good if it involves individuals committed to collaboration, it cannot guarantee it maintains that response across populations or over time.' Morrison also notes that the organisational context has therefore become less predictable, less stable and more conflictual in the short-term, as the competition for resources becomes even more acute. Whilst the emphasis on contractual, accountable and targeted services may in the longer-term result in strategic inter-agency partnerships for the planning, commissioning and evaluating of child protection services, in the short-term at least, 'partnerships' across agencies are under severe strain (p 125). Morrison (1997) concluded that these cumulative forces have 'placed an almost intolerable strain on inter-agency work and the ethos of collaboration which has been the heart of modern child protection work. Given that, even under reasonable conditions, multi-agency work is not easy, current conditions mean that its sternest test since its importance was first recognised in the early 1970s (p 196). These changes may spell the end of specialist knowledge and the need to train and support more, but smaller, teams of staff. Morrison (1996a) also pointed out that the fragmentation of central structures means that it is no longer possible for senior managers to guarantee a response to child protection throughout their agency. The result is that a culture of 'survivalism' has developed, in which individual energies are directed towards self-protection, with little spare energy left to engage with the external world of other agencies. For an excellent article reviewing the impact of a market forces approach on the organisation of child protection services, the reader is

referred to Barker (1996); and for a review of the implications of the purchaser-provider separation for service delivery, the reader is referred to Hood (1997). To conclude, Corby (1995) has argued that 'the assumption that co-ordination is inevitably the best way to achieve goals is questionable. Indeed, there is a distinct possibility that co-ordinative action can be misused as a substitute for shortage of resources' (p 212).

17. **Anxiety and child protection:** Morrison (1995) has argued that anxiety runs like a vein throughout the child protection process. This can relate both to the work as well as the struggle to survive in the current external climate of change. If it is not contained, learning cannot take place. Failures at an organisational level to appropriately contain anxiety can permeate all aspects of the agency's work, as well as affecting its relations with the outside world and other agencies. This is demonstrated in the dysfunctional learning cycle described by Vince and Martin (1993) — see figure 1. In this environment, anxiety is seen as unprofessional, a sign of weakness and not coping. As a result, uncertainty is suppressed through fight and flight mechanisms. The absence of forums where feelings and doubts can be safely expressed leads to defensiveness, and a resistance to share and reflect on practice. It also undermines confidence to experiment with new practice. Emotional defensiveness then deepens into cognitive distortion whereby the principal reality is warded off via denial of dissonant information and attitudes, offering a temporary but false sense of security. If this process worsens with more wilful and sustained ignorance, it may lead eventually to total disengagement.

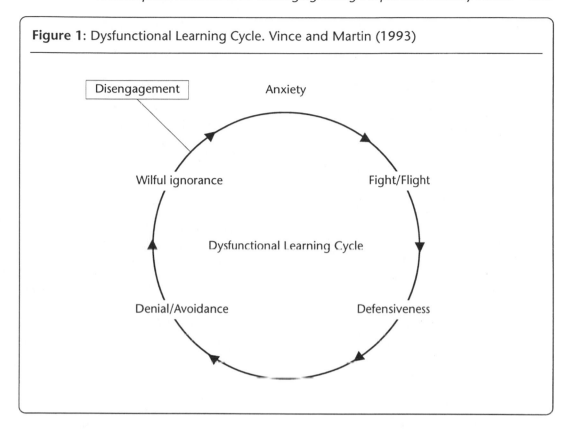

Figure 1: Dysfunctional Learning Cycle. Vince and Martin (1993)

Disengagement

Anxiety

Wilful ignorance

Fight/Flight

Dysfunctional Learning Cycle

Denial/Avoidance

Defensiveness

In relation to child sexual abuse

1. **Anxiety and child sexual abuse:**
   Woodhouse and Pengally (1991) explored in detail the relationship between anxiety and working together. They noted that there is a heightened anxiety relating to child sexual abuse — both in society as well as in the helping services. This often results in splitting — undermining collaboration precisely when it is most needed. The Cleveland inquiry (Butler-Sloss, 1988) catalogued clearly the defence responses to task-related anxiety. As Kraemer (1988) noted, 'the price paid for (such) protection is a kind of stupidity in which only half the mind is able to work at a time'. In the interplay of agencies, with only 'half minds' at work, departmental policies, priorities and interests tend to be protected at the expense of the shared task. In addition, conflict is likely to arise and dispute be uncompromisingly pursued when the defence of splitting is the protective mechanism, and to the extent that the largely unconsciously determined institutional defences embodied in agency practices are not of mutual emotional value (p 234).

   A dimension is added both to anxieties and to defences by child sexual abuse. In a field so characterised by uncertainty, the implications of 'not knowing' become too fearful to contemplate. Integrity and autonomy, institutional as much as personal or professional, can be threatened by uncertainties which in reality should be seen as relevant and inescapable. Meanwhile, preoccupation with the rules and such less concrete issues as professional status serve to obviate the need to think the unthinkable: sexual abuse with its compulsive and repulsive aspects. Tony Morrison (1994) set out several defence systems used by workers and agencies to contain their anxieties:

- Depersonalisation: as victims cease to be individuals and become statistics.

- Detachment and denial: of feelings as the language of intervention becomes bureaucratised, talking less about relationships than packages, less about change than throughput, and less about process than child protection plans.

- Ritual task performance: in which procedures dominate practice.

- Reducing the weight of decision-making: by constant counter-checking, as we assess and re-assess, delaying decisions, and avoiding the question of how treatment will be resourced.

- Redistributing responsibility by projection: and blaming of individuals or other agencies.

- Re-framing and minimising: the true nature of concern.

- Avoiding change and clinging to the familiar: even when it has ceased to be functional, making plans we know cannot work.

Tony Morrison (1992) has set out the following (inter) agency problems with child sexual abuse work:

2. **Lack of agency ownership:** reflected via the lack of agency policies for this area of work. In this vacuum of policy and management leadership, services develop in the absence of the necessary debate as to their place within agencies' overall policies and strategic planning. Individual staff commitment is not indefinite and resources may only be available whilst committed staff remain in the agency. This is because the commitment is based on the agency's support of the individual as opposed to the commitment by the agency to the work.

3. **Clashes of philosophy:** these clashes or conflicts may occur either within the agency between staff and management or across agencies at a senior level. The fact that practitioners know more about sex offenders than their managers serves to fuel such problems. Most developments in this area are practitioner led. Tensions can exist within the probation service as

they struggle to weigh their duties to the offender and the victim. Their response to sex offenders is often at odds with their response to the rest of their clients, by being tougher, more invasive and less concerned with the rights of the sex offender than with his responsibilities. Tensions exist between agencies regarding whether to help or punish sex offenders. There needs to be a clear and coherent philosophy of intervention within or between agencies.

4. **Absence of professional guidance or standards:** this makes it difficult for agencies to exercise accountability and leaves staff uncertain and vulnerable. Complaints are not easily resolved as agencies, staff and clients are 'at risk' in this environment. There is also an absence of a gauge to determine the value of the work important when agencies have to assess how to allocate resources against competing demands.

5. **Inadequate supervision:** can result in inappropriate staff self-selection and lack of access to appropriate supervision for staff. As many managers are male, emotional and practical support for workers may not be available and insensitive or uninformed supervision can leave staff vulnerable. Pearce (1991) found that extra support is needed for workers in the field of sexual abuse. This may be available in part from within the team and informal groups, yet it needs to be organised and not ad hoc, and it is easier to achieve this 'in-house' than across agencies.

6. **Alienation from colleagues:** can result from a lack of management support and policy and ignorance on the motivation of the worker and the aim of their work. It is of concern where workers become isolated as the lack of support can induce professional dangerousness and mirror the families with whom they are working. The combination of the volume of the work and the emotiveness of the issues combine to make this draining and debilitating work, with an associated elevated risk of 'burnout'.

7. **Abstraction from other crime:** this is where we negate our previous experience

gathered in our work with abusive parents and this can lead to de-skilling of staff and tensions about how work with sex offenders fits with the rest of our practice. We should never re-conceptualise problems just for the sake of it: we need to look at how we can adapt and transfer our skills and knowledge across work settings.

8. **Inter-agency factors:** all the above can be replicated in a more complex way on an inter-agency basis, particularly where there is no inter-agency forum at a senior level to oversee and support the work. Inter-agency programmes/initiatives are vulnerable to conflicts, poor rates of referral and even premature closure occurs without management support. This can also lead to serious problems in decision-making over cases.

Fargason *et al.* (1994) set out several underlying sources of conflict that impairs inter-organisational functioning in the management of child sexual abuse. These included:

1. **Socialisation:** raising conflicts over the boundaries of confidentiality, as related to their professions standing and the individuals place in the inter-agency 'pecking order'.

2. **Goal incompatibility:** whilst service providers from individual agencies want to provide the best possible services, they also have to answer to a series of sub-goals that may be at odds with the overriding goal of providing co-ordinated care.

3. **Interdependence:** the exchange of information is a necessary prerequisite for the delivery of an optimal service. When information needed for decision-making is not available from another agency, or when information traverses inter-agency channels in a form that is not understood by members of the receiving agency, stress is increased, as is the likelihood of conflict.

4. **Performance expectations:** these are best exemplified by the time conflicts that arise when individuals from different organisations attempt to co-ordinate activities. For example, when police surgeons or teachers are required to attend court or conferences and this disrupts their schedule, more so if it involves financial loss.

5. **Resource limitations:** given the extent of sexual abuse, its impact, and societal interest in controlling expenditures, resource limitations will continue to accentuate conflicts over performance expectations in the sexual abuse field, as well as heighten conflicts in other domains (p 860–1).

Pearce (1991) set out several conflicting factors affecting attitudes concerning inter-professional collaboration in sexual abuse work:

1. **Punishment and therapy:** sexual abuse is perceived by many to be a more serious crime, different to other forms of abuse, and which crosses some assumed moral boundary. It is more likely to involve the police, with the aim of prosecuting the offender. Yet the legal process is only effective for the small minority of men who are successfully prosecuted for their behaviour.

2. **Interests of the child and interests of the offender:** to prosecute the offender, the child has to be subjected to interview and examination: both have the potential to harm them further. By intervening in the family, the child may be held, or hold themselves accountable for the multiple consequences which follow their disclosure. The harm of intervention might outweigh the experience of the abuse itself, and the effect on the offender of imprisonment is debatable.

3. **Role of agencies with statutory duties and those without:** risks are associated with the process of decision-making in the early stages of an investigation where they have to act quickly and form judgements which, though considered and shared, have of necessity to be based on assumptions rather than 'hard' evidence. The risks are always present whatever course is taken. Moreover, the outcome more often than not arouses anger, resentment, withdrawal and even violence in the family affected. It is hardly surprising then to find tensions between those agencies who *have* to be involved and those who can *choose*.

4. **Agency as servant and surveyor of the community:** this relates to a conflict between a service traditionally offering help that has been instigated by the client, and carried out with their voluntary approval and co-operation, and one which has a duty and authority to investigate, monitor and, if necessary, attempt to change the functioning of a family, where a child is thought to be in danger of abuse without necessarily having that approval. The voluntary or involuntary nature of the work must shape both the perception of the client for the professional, the professional for the client and professionals for each other. This can be played out as the professionals reflect their own inadequacy by playing power games between themselves, similar to the power between adult and child. The management of sexual abuse involves a complicated mixture of voluntary and involuntary clients, a mixture of professionals acting as carers and custodians and sometimes a choice between the use of a legal mandate or not. There is a negative side to collaboration where a professional may be only too willing to offload responsibility on to another person.

5. **'Criminality' factor:** most professionals apply a greater degree of 'criminality' with sexual abuse for two reasons. Firstly, they accept the perceived differences in the dynamics of sexual abuse and the severity of the effects on the child (see Beitchman *et al.* 1991; 1992 for a review of these). Secondly, the sense of heightened criminality is the emotional response of horror, disgust and bewilderment.

6. **Personality factor:** Collaboration in all fields of work can be a breeding ground for problems associated with *personal* as well as *professional* factors. Dealing with sexual abuse can pose additional difficulties concerning the sensitive and volatile issues of gender, sexuality and power. The other aspect of 'personality' affecting communication is how colleagues see each other in terms of professional credibility.

7. **The media contribution:** there is increasing evidence that some members of the press abuse their responsibility to alert the public conscience and concern and so hinder public servants in the execution of their responsibility to deal with the object of concern (see Atmore, 1996; Franklin, 1998; and Franklin and Parton, 1991).

8. **Complexity:** part of the problem are the above outlined conflicts, although this is aggravated by the greater number of agencies which are necessarily involved; and a very real issue is evidence, or how to proceed in the absence of corroborative evidence, particularly as the threshold for civil proceedings are become more like those in criminal proceedings. These 'grey areas' cause differences in opinion among professionals about what actually happened, and about relevant roles and responsibilities. The nature of the relationships between family members is frequently fragile, volatile, and changeable. Different professionals may be given contradictory 'faces' of the same family. This may result in disagreement among professionals about how to act.

Morrison (1994a) reviewed the state of inter-agency management of sexual abuse in the UK. He set out some additional constraints and deficits, which inhibit the ability to work and learn together. These included:

1. **Societal attitudes:** there is no societal consensus as to how sexual abuse in any form should be managed. This ambivalence permeates governmental, judicial and professional responses, undermining professionals' confidence and their mandate to intervene. Professionals are unclear about what society wants them to do about sexual abuse.

2. **Legislation:** there are philosophical tensions within both of the acts (The Children Act 1989 and the Criminal Justice Act 1991) which provide professionals with their framework for intervention. This debate is summarised by Calder (1995). The outcome is that there are very different views on if, and how, partnership with sexual offenders can be achieved.

3. **The role of the courts:** considerable concerns remain about the experiences of

children in both civil and criminal courts. This is aggravated by the reduced rate of prosecuting the offender, and the disposal often does not match the crime. There remain conflicts of understanding about the nature and effects of sexual abuse between prosecuting authorities, the judiciary, and child protection agencies, which results in a lack of confidence in each other.

4. **The pace of change:** in addition to being faced with diverse and more complex forms of sexual abuse (see Calder, 1999b), the organisational environment has also changed (as described earlier). Whilst these changes are causing fragmentation, the same legislation has also demanded higher standards of inter-agency collaboration. This appears to be left to individuals rather than their agencies, thus allowing the latter to displace their responsibilities and anxieties onto staff (Calder, 1997a).

5. **Resources:** the complexities of managing a growing number of sexual abuse cases is depleting budgets very quickly, whilst still not providing a service to manage the problem effectively. For example, there is an increasing mixture of abusers and victims placed in the same looked after placement; whilst many ACPCs are unable to embrace the government directive to integrate young people who sexually abuse within the existing child protection machinery.

In relation to young people who sexually abuse

Working Together (DoH, 1991c) clearly identified young people who sexually abuse as a child protection issue and stated that official responses and interventions should take place within child protection procedures. It recommended that ACPCs should co-ordinate the development of a strategic plan for dealing with this group, bring them into the child protection system, and devote a annual report to outlining progress. Masson

(1995a) explored the major tension facing ACPCs: how to address and develop a model of good practice in relation to young people who sexually abuse and the assumptions which inform it, are in sharp contrast to the model which has developed more generally in the field of youth justice over the last 15 years.

Calder (1997a) set out the issues relating to the principal tension: the battle between youth justice and child protection for the lead responsibility with this group (see figure 2).

The NCH report (1992) set out several advantages for locating the work within child protection:

*   It broadens the focus for concern from simply dealing with the offender to those who have been abused but not prosecuted, and those who are displaying inappropriate sexual behaviour.

*   It widens the range of options available, e.g. packages of care; and,

*   It reinforces this group of 'abusers' as children 'in need' (p 29).

The criminal justice approach stands at the opposite end of the continuum: they try to adopt a diversionary approach rather than an interventionist approach. They argue that this has worked well with other types of offender, pointing to some 80 per cent cautioned for a first offence that do not go on to re-offend. Official statistics and self-report studies show that most young people stop offending at 16–17 years of age. There is also a good deal of evidence to show that those dealt with on a formal basis by the courts are more likely to re-offend (Brown, 1992). On the basis of these figures, they believe that juveniles who sexually abuse will grow out of, rather than into, a pattern of criminal behaviour. They believe that youth crime is situational. They also believe that the child protection approach is ineffective and will undo a lot of good work with the judiciary, who took some time to be convinced to adopt a diversionary approach. They also point to the many negative, unintended consequences of the criminal justice system, which rendered it an ineffective and risky mechanism of response.

Figure 2: The battle for lead responsibility (Calder, 1997)

	Child Protection	Criminal Justice
Principles	Interventionist Grow into behaviour, which escalates over time. Legal mandate needed for the work to be completed.	Diversionary approach. Grow out of their behaviour. Innocent until proven guilty.
Supporting Positions	'Working Together' (DoH, 1991c). Diversion is collusion, allowing the abuser and their family to minimise their behaviour. Diverted cases are more likely to re-offend.	Practice wisdom (e.g. most young people stop offending at 16–17 years of age). 80% cautioned do not re-offend. Those referred to court most likely to re-offend. Court confusion over change of approach.
Benefits	Broadens the focus of intervention away from only those convicted. Widens the available options. Reinforces this group as children 'in need'.	Allows professional-young person partnership. Prevents stigma and labelling. Diversion avoids mixing delinquent youth together as a peer group.

There are strong feelings that everyone is assumed innocent until proven guilty, and allied to this are concerns over the 'net widening' and 'labelling' that accompany the presumptive child protection approach. Margolin (1984) believes that such labels are aversive to the abuser and will probably induce client resistance. It is also a controversial label to apply given that there is a significant margin for error of mislabelling. The criminal justice approach is designed to ensure that any intervention does not exacerbate the problems, i.e. mixing with, and learning from, other young offenders involved through the court process.

The Children's Society briefing paper (1988) sets out the following advantages and benefits of diversion from court and custody:

- Diversion provides an opportunity to work in partnership with the young person and their family in their own community in an informal way.
- It protects children from stigma, labelling, 'contamination', deviant self-image,

associated with court appearances and custody.

- It acknowledges family, educational, or welfare difficulties, or problems in growing up, and treats them as developmental not criminal issues.

- It recognises that offences are committed in the context of peer groups and community and that attitudes and behaviour on all sides have to be challenged to achieve change.

- It accepts that young people have multiple needs best approached through community-based co-ordination rather than through any one system whether it be child welfare or the penal system.

- It delays entry into the normal legal system and procedures.

The government has repeatedly affirmed the diversionary approach, leading to a significant increase in the numbers cautioned and a significant decline in those prosecuted. The Children Act 1989 also removed the criminal care order as an option (Masson, 1995).

The child protection viewpoint differs significantly and is based on a belief that young people who sexually abuse pose a very real risk and require a programme of early intervention to prevent their behaviour becoming reinforced, ingrained, and even escalating over time. The official line is that 'policies of minimal intervention are not as effective as focused forms of therapeutic intervention which may be under orders of the civil or the criminal courts' (DoH, 1991c, para 5.24.5). They have reinforced this position after finding that many cases are probably not isolated, but more a part of an ingrained pattern known only to the juvenile themselves (DoH, 1992/3, p 28). This approach does not preclude diversion where considered appropriate, and it should always seek to control the situation by adopting the least restrictive option commensurate with the need to undertake a piece of work. Research indicates that juveniles and children are more likely to grow into, rather than out of, a pattern of sexually abusive behaviour, and this can require external sanctions to force them into a position where they have to personally consider their actions and the need for change (Morrison, 1991). Juveniles who sexually abuse are unlike other juvenile offenders in that most of it is carried out alone and rarely boasted about to a peer group. It is likely to involve fantasising and masturbation and to be kept secretive by the young person involved. Because sex is involved the nature and type of offending is very different from most youth crime. As such, diversion and minimal intervention colludes with the offence and can quickly be incorporated into the young person's rationalisation and excuse system for their behaviour. Brown (1992) concludes that there is a need to differentiate between diversion from the court (but with assessment/intervention) and complete diversion from any formal involvement (in the hope that perpetrators will grow out of offending) which some workers still advocate. It is a myth that if the juvenile is apprehended and labelled as a sexual perpetrator, the label itself may predispose them to re-abuse. The assumption that the label will cause lifelong damage to the juvenile is seen as being of greater significance than the risk of sexual recidivism. In reality, the average sex offender will create 380 victims over a lifetime (Abel *et al.*, 1987, 1988). Unless they are identified, they will not receive the necessary help to avoid any repetition of their behaviour. As such, the potential deleterious effects of labelling the juvenile becomes less disturbing (Perry and Orchard, 1992, p 8). As Margolin (1984) pointed out, the label can make it significantly harder for the juvenile to push the assault history to the back of their mind. It is also significant that re-arrest rates are substantially higher among those who escaped being labelled. Brown (1992) has pointed out that 'One of the differences in working with adolescent sex offenders as compared to work with adults, is that adolescents are still developing and maturing. Labelling an adolescent directly as a 'sex offender', without allowing for change and growth could be seen as highly punitive and might also work towards preventing change. It is essential, however, from a child protection perspective, to assess risk and to help the young person find appropriate avenues for change.' Repeat cautions for sexual offences have to be actively discouraged as it suggests that a pattern of offending behaviour is developing.

Whichever of the two positions you choose, there can be little disagreement over the need for a fundamentally different approach to intervention with a burglar and a rapist (Neate, 1990, p 18). For many children and juveniles, sexual abuse may be a one-off experience that will not be repeated, but for others it will be part of a pattern that is already becoming established and which will continue and escalate in seriousness and probably frequency. An apparently isolated incident may well be part of a much more entrenched pattern known only to the young person who abuses. Some will spontaneously self-correct, but we do not know which ones will and which ones will not. Prolonged work will only be needed in some cases, but assessment is needed in them all. It is very difficult to commence an assessment where the abuser is pleading not guilty and the criminal proceedings have not yet been completed. We should be careful not to be drawn into speculation on whether the individual has committed a specific offence beyond any reasonable doubt for the purposes of a criminal prosecution. Only an admission from the abuser will allow us to do so (Becker, 1990, p 363). As Tony Morrison has clearly pointed out, it is not the task of professionals to decide on guilt or otherwise. As such, never say 'I'm sure he won't/hasn't/is not like a young person who sexually offends'.

Masson (1995) in an ongoing study of ACPC annual reports since 1990 and in her own research found that there was a patchy ACPC response, with the result that:

> ...some juvenile sexual abusers are discussed at youth justice panels, a very much smaller number are case conferenced under child protection procedures, and an unknown number of those reported to the police are dealt with without referral through either system (p18).

Masson went on to argue that senior managers need to take responsibility for implementing change as recommended by central government guidance at an ACPC level. She acknowledges that this may be problematic politically, given the inevitable increase in resources required to bring young people who sexually abuse within the child protection system. 'Structures for policy and practice development have to be established with key individuals from the various agencies concerned and given authority to take a lead in the work' (p 19). This

> has to be underpinned by the provision of appropriate resources, including staffing, and community-based and residential facilities, and an infrastructure of training (to address attitudes, definitional problems about...juvenile sexual abuse and to develop professional interventions), supervision and consultation.

The response by ACPCs to young people who sexually abuse has been slow. In a study of English and London Boroughs' ACPC annual reports for 1990–1992, it was noted that only 9.4% of reports mentioned that they had procedures in place while another 16.2% indicated that procedures were being developed (Pont, 1992). Masson's own study of 1992–1993 reports indicated that 17% reported having drawn up procedures and 43% had working parties focusing on this area of work. The increased activity continued, particularly in the northern parts of the country (Masson, 1995b). Masson (1996) reported on the then ACPC response about policy and procedures in relation to young people who sexually abuse. 54% of respondents said that policy and guidance had been developed locally beyond paragraph 5.24 of 'Working Together'. Only 1% were very satisfied with their local area arrangements; 29% were satisfied; 59% were

dissatisfied, and 11% were very dissatisfied. 25% reckoned that Child protection conferences were always held in their area, whilst 60% felt they happened sometimes.

Masson (1995b) identified other difficulties for the inter-agency network: no shared definition of what is normal sexual development and what behaviour is appropriate at different ages; no agreed definition of young people who sexually abuse; no substantial theory to help guide professional interventions; a lack of clarity within the child protection guidance (DoH, 1991c) about the circumstances (if any) when an abusers name can be added to the Child Protection Register; a lack of resources; and societal (and professional) denial that the problem exists, and, if it does, how big a problem it has become. Masson (1997/8) concluded that 'there are many issues and concerns for a majority of the practitioners surveyed' (p 115). She found that the following additional concerns were raised by at least half of the respondents: use of instant cautions and cautioning generally (58%), lack of initial assessment facilities (55%), lack of comprehensive assessment facilities (65%), lack of treatment facilities (77%), dearth of evaluation studies (67%), insufficient training (63%), and a lack of supervision, consultation and support (66%). A further 47% expressed concern about the problems of influencing the Crown Prosecution Service (p 114).

Calder (1997) identified the difficulties of removing abusers from their home, only to provide them with an environment where they could mix with vulnerable children, already the victims of sexual abuse. Epps (1997) and Lindsay (Chapter 15) have looked at how to manage this potentially volatile mix of victims and abusers. However, until we move forward on this issue, there is the potential for in-house and cross-agency differences of opinion on what to do with this group. Since the Sex Offenders Act (1997) came into force, a further conflict is emerging between the police and social services relating to the implications of cautioning and the link to sex offender registration and associated requirements. Brown (1998) has explored the issues relating to young people convicted of a sexual offence. Young people who are either cautioned or convicted of a sexual offence listed in Schedule 1 of the Act need to register with the police in the same way as adult offenders. They are required to provide their current address. There is specified provision in the Act for the duty of notification to be imposed on parents or guardian, and offenders under 18 cannot be imprisoned for failure to notify. Additionally, the registration periods are halved for those under 18. Although this is a diluted system, there is evidence that the police are struggling to accept the need to caution a young person because of the implications of this in statute. This has resulted in disciplinary proceedings being instigated against senior police officers for a failure to apply agreed procedures, and the knock on effect has been to polarise views between the agencies. This has the potential to detract us from the task in hand.

Sanders and Ladwa-Thomas (1997) argued that

> *juveniles who sexually abuse children raise complex issues that challenge traditional agency perspectives and approaches…(yet) very few local authorities have developed a co-ordinated response involving juvenile justice agencies, the police, and social workers. In local authorities, a number of agencies — both statutory and voluntary — have been attempting to come to terms with their roles and responsibilities… (p264).*

They also accept that

> *whenever a new issue arises…agencies again must begin a dialogue on the questions raised and return to sharing perceptions of the issues from their respective agency viewpoints. These agencies need to develop a common value base and have dialogues on priorities to work effectively with young abusers… (p 265).*

Their study involved surveying the perspectives on child sexual abuse and practice issues of working with young people who sexually abuse. 50 practitioners in five different agencies were involved: a specialist child protection team, a non-specialist children and families team, probation officers specialising in work with sex offenders, juvenile justice (diversion from custody projects), and police family support units (specialist child protection teams). Their research explored the theoretical perspectives in child sexual abuse adopted by the five different agencies, and the responses to 10 specific questions considered central to the task of working with young people who sexually abuse.

They found a fair degree of agreement among all agencies other than the police on the theoretical perspectives. The social work

agencies scored high on three perspectives: anti-discriminatory, feminist and children's rights. For the police, only the anti-discriminatory perspective actually scored highly and is the only degree of concordance with other agencies. All the other perspectives were negative. These findings are important given that traditionally the police-social services relationship is among the strongest of the inter-agency relationships.

The researchers predicted that the responses of workers in each agency would reflect their philosophical status and outlooks on treatment or intervention in work with abusers, as well as their general views about sexuality and children. The issue of whether young people who sexually abuse should primarily be seen as victims or abusers produced the greatest diversity of opinion. Child protection specialists felt that they should be seen as victims whereas juvenile justice workers and the police felt that they should be seen as sex offenders. The police were also much less inclined to see young abusers as children in need than child protection workers were. All agencies agreed that treatment was more effective than punishment; yet the police and juvenile justice workers agreed much less so than child protection workers, who endorsed it most strongly. The issue of whether a mandate (either criminal or civil) is needed for work produced the lowest scores and the least divergence between agencies. Only the police thought that children under 10 were responsible for their behaviour. All groups agreed that the younger the child, the more likely they were to grow out of their behaviour. All agencies (apart from child protection workers) felt that professional intervention was needed for children who displayed inappropriate sexualised behaviour. The police were the most strongly in favour of a register of young people who sexually abuse; probation and juvenile justice workers somewhat in favour; and child protection workers and childcare social workers almost equally opposed.

These findings do highlight the conflict between interventionist and diversionary approaches and extend the concerns to the crucial police-social services relationship. Calder (1997b) set out clearly the professional and public barriers to accepting that young people do sexually abuse (see figure 3).

Figure 3: A framework for understanding the barriers to accepting that young people do sexually abuse (Calder, 1997b, p 37)

Societal	Professional
People don't accept that this kind of behaviour exists.	A lack of clarity regarding what actually took place due to either genuine doubt or the abuser's ability to hide their tracks.
Viewing the presenting behaviour as experimentation.	A fear of looking foolish.
A mistaken belief that they will grow out of, rather than into, their behaviour.	A confusion between the victim-victimiser dichotomy, particularly where victims become involved in abusive behaviour themselves.
There is a fear of labelling and stigmatisation.	We are trained to see the best side of the client.
A mistaken view that abuse committed by young people is less serious or harmful than that committed by adults.	A fear that any intervention may make the situation worse.
The relatively low level of reporting (caused by the shame and fear of the victims) and the low level of subsequent convictions feeds the public denial of the problem.	Discomfort with the subject matter.
	A lack of facilities and services.
Deficits in the knowledge bases of the key response agencies.	

(adapted from Knopp, 1982 and Taylor, 1996).

A Conceptual Framework for ACPCs Responding to Young People who Sexually Abuse

There is a need for professionals to overcome their doubts that young people sexually abuse, and then to help the public follow suit. There does appear to have been some movement in the UK in accepting that a problem exists. This has been for four reasons:

1. **The powerful arguments to intervene:**

- Deviant patterns are less deeply ingrained and are thus easier to disrupt.

- Juveniles are still experimenting with a variety of patterns of sexual satisfaction which offer alternatives to consistent deviant patterns.

- Distorted thinking patterns are less deeply entrenched and can be re-directed.

- They are good candidates for learning new and acceptable social skills.

- Public safety is improved by preventing further victimisation, and,

- Fiscal economy is enhanced (Knopp, 1982).

2. **The consequences of failing to respond:**

- It allows the behaviour to continue uninterrupted.

- It limits the perspectives of those investigating child abuse.

- It prevents the development of therapeutic intervention for all children who have been abused.

- It allows agencies not to prioritise inter-agency strategies to respond.

- It fails to prepare staff or support staff for work with these age groups.

- It fails to recognise that young people can be dangerous and need help.

- It fails to protect children in the community, and,

- It allows abusers the opportunity to develop patterns and planning, thus creating a public safety issue. In essence, a failure to respond equates with a failure to protect (adapted from Hollows, 1991, p 71).

3. **More research evidence:**

There are a number of factors, which have combined to influence a professional, if not a societal acceptance of the need to respond. These include:

- An increased awareness of the number of young people committing sexual crimes, e.g. an 834% increase in juvenile sexual crimes between 1983-1992 (Gerdes *et al.*, 1995).

- In the UK, recent estimates suggest that juveniles account for between a quarter (Kelly *et al.*, 1991, p 4) and a third (Northern Ireland Research Team, 1991) of all sexual abuse.

- An uncovering of the fact that 50% of adult sexual perpetrators began their sexually deviant behaviour in their juvenile years (Abel, 1984).

- A recognition that their behaviour escalates over time, with a potential for juveniles to increase their number of victims 55 times if left unchecked (Abel *et al.*, 1993).

- Evidence to dismiss such behaviour as experimentation, e.g. Groth (1977) found that 86% had previous interpersonal sexual experiences prior to their sexually abusive behaviour.

4. **The current central guidance on young people who sexually abuse:**

The 1992 National Children's Homes Enquiry report found:
- No co-ordinated management structure.

- An absence of policy, practice or ethical guidance.

- An uncertainty regarding the legitimacy of the work.

- Clashes of philosophy relating to the minimum intervention with this group.

- A lack of inter-agency co-ordination.

- An inadequate information base and a lack of evaluation.

- A paucity of training.

- Deficits in supervision.

- A shortage of consultation.

It was fortunate, therefore, that the 1991 version of 'Working Together' briefly addressed itself to the issue of abuse carried out by young people (30 lines), and pointed to the need for the appropriate child protection procedures to be followed in respect of both the abuser as well as the victim (DoH, 1991c, para 5.24.1). This is to 'ensure that such behaviour is treated seriously and is always subject to a referral to child protection agencies' (para 5.24.2). It then indicates that a child protection conference in relation to the abuser should be held to consider the current knowledge about the alleged abuser, their family circumstances, the offence committed, their level of understanding they have about it, and the need for further work. This should include consideration of possible arrangements of accommodation, education (where applicable) and supervision in the short-term pending the compilation of a comprehensive assessment (para 5.24.4). The child protection conference, including initial plans, should be as prescribed for the standard conference and should 'reconvene following the completion of the comprehensive assessment, to review the plan in the light of the information obtained and to co-ordinate the interventions designed to dissuade the abuser from committing further abusive acts' (para 5.24.5).

The initial child protection conference on the abuser has the following purposes: to determine whether there are any outstanding child protection issues with regard to any children with whom the alleged abuser is in contact; whether there is any reason to suspect that the alleged abuser has been the victim of abuse and is in need of protection; whether there is any need to provide immediate services to the alleged abuser and their family, and what method of disposal is to be recommended in respect of the alleged abuse.

The need for a local ACPC response

The concept of young people who sexually abuse was very clearly introduced into the child protection system with little central guidance. This left the response systems to evolve in an ad hoc, localised fashion that has thus far defied any consolidation. One of the major problems resulting from sparse central government guidance is that, at best, each ACPC will make its own interpretation and, at worst, each professional (Horwath and Calder, 1998).

This shows us that the void of central guidance has a direct bearing on what is being found in practice. Masson (1995) identified 4 possible models of practice developing in the field:

- In some ACPC areas, special projects have been set up which provide initial assessment reports to both child protection conferences and youth liaison panels, as well as offering full assessments and treatment facilities.

- In some areas, child protection conference reports are available to youth liaison panels in order to assist in decisions about prosecution.

- In other areas the child protection conference follows youth justice panel decisions, and,

- In yet another model, an ACPC mandated multi-disciplinary panel has been established which discusses all cases of youngsters abusing others and makes recommendations to both child protection conferences and youth liaison panels (Masson, 1995, p 5).

The ACPC has a duty to respond to the lack of central guidance and plug the void at a local level. Without this, managers and practitioners have no way of defining what is expected of them, let alone whether they are providing a 'good-enough' service. An enabling local environment is probably the best way of unlocking the potential that different professionals have to bring to this work. Charles and Stevenson (1990) provided us with a framework for developing such a multi-disciplinary learning environment (see figure 4), often used in training.

Figure 4: The development of a multi-disciplinary learning environment (Charles and Stevenson, 1990, p 12)

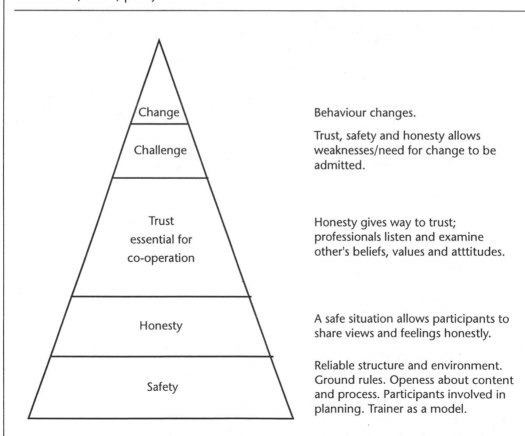

Change	Behaviour changes.
Challenge	Trust, safety and honesty allows weaknesses/need for change to be admitted.
Trust essential for co-operation	Honesty gives way to trust; professionals listen and examine other's beliefs, values and atttitudes.
Honesty	A safe situation allows participants to share views and feelings honestly.
Safety	Reliable structure and environment. Ground rules. Openess about content and process. Participants involved in planning. Trainer as a model.

For effective working together, we need to create a climate, which fosters the trust and mutual respect necessary for different professionals to work together. This can involve an investment in terms of training, focal meeting points, where regular physical and social proximity reduces tensions and stereotyping, and an acknowledgement of the necessity for ongoing maintenance work (to introduce new staff, inform agencies of policy changes, alterations in work pressures, etc.). Where agencies create a safe multi-disciplinary working environment, professionals can share honestly their views and attitudes about each other and begin to develop a sense of mutual trust and respect. Once trust is established, professionals can examine and explore their respective beliefs and be prepared for these to be challenged. Through challenge comes change, and more effective working together for the protection of children (p 12).

Morrison (1995) noted that in a climate of rapid change, organisations and individuals may be forced to relinquish previous certainties, assumptions and practices, in accepting the inevitability of continuous change. For some, this may provide exciting new and creative opportunities: organisational change and fragmentation also mean that many organisational structures are embryonic and immature, and therefore potentially more available to influence, and in need of development. These combined can act as a powerful motivator for learning, as staff seek the opportunity for reflection about the changes, affirmation of existing skills and the acquisition of new ones. Vince and Martins' (1993) functional learning cycle is also relevant here (see figure 5).

In this culture, anxiety is seen as normative, allowing for the expression of healthy uncertainty, and difference, where 'mistakes' are opportunities for learning, not punishment. Risks are taken and innovations are attempted. The unresolvable nature of many issues is openly struggled with, from which unexpected and creative solutions may come. As a result, staff are empowered to tackle further demands. It also means an approach which is more about learning than trouble-shooting.

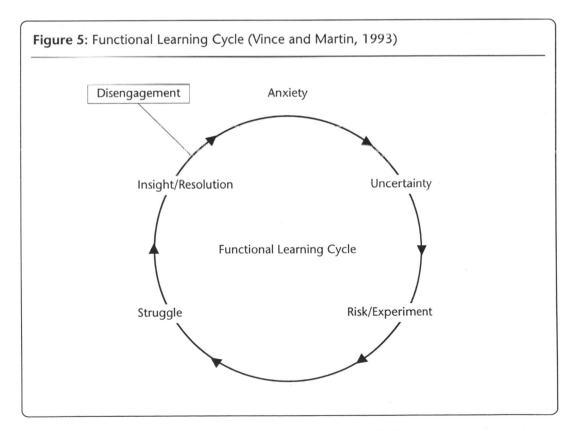

Figure 5: Functional Learning Cycle (Vince and Martin, 1993)

Disengagement

Anxiety

Insight/Resolution

Uncertainty

Functional Learning Cycle

Struggle

Risk/Experiment

Figure 6: Organisational Partnership Model (Morrison, 1998a, p 129)

	Involuntary	Voluntary
No Participation	Strategic	Paternalism
	Us versus the world	You need us
	Adversarial approach	Medical model approach
Participation	Play fair	Developmental
	Involving others	Working and learning together
	Social justice approach	Psychological approach

Morrison (1998a) explored the implications of the partnership ethos for inter-agency collaboration using an organisational partnership model (see figure 6).

This model allows us to look at the differing perceptions of collaboration. In the paternalism position, collaboration is viewed as an activity which is engaged in, as and when the agency deems fit, and only on its own terms. It involves others when it chooses. It sees collaboration as a benefit it confers on other agencies rather than being an obligation. In the strategic/adversarial position, collaboration is approached with considerable wariness and caution, fuelled by the belief that it will involve more losses than gains, that other agencies will exploit the process in order to gain territory or acquire resources at the expense of one's own agency. Territorial behaviours dominate interaction. The result is that collaboration is often conflictual, and endless time is spent on negotiating the terms of engagement. Interaction between agencies is through bureaucratic modes rather than informal or personal communication. In the play fair position, there is a basic belief that clients both need and have an entitlement to an effective multi-disciplinary service. Agencies are therefore concerned to ensure that all are clear about their roles and responsibilities. There is a focus on clarity of mutual expectations, processes of working together and about how clients will be involved in this. An appreciation and respect exists for the different roles played by different agencies/disciplines. In the developmental position, it has a broader vision than that held by the 'fair play' camp. It sees collaboration as providing a dynamic model of positive and developmental processes which are intended to motivate both staff and clients to work for change. There is a place for active informal multi-disciplinary networks (McFarlane and Morrison, 1994), designed to enhance how we work and learn together, and there is a greater focus on outcomes as well as process.

This model is very important when we consider the findings from Sanders, Jackson and Thomas (1997) into the functioning of ACPCs. They noted that, in the earlier work of Evans and Miller (1992), the fact that a two-tier system is emerging was reported, with social services fieldwork staff and the police being in the first tier and the rest of the agencies in the second. Sanders *et al.* argued that there are very clear distinctions between the police and social services roles, and there are variations in the levels of involvement of those in the second tier, which would warrant a further differentiation. They preferred to frame the process in terms of 'ownership', as it shows that representatives can operate at different levels. This is set out in Figure 7:

Figure 7: Three levels of agency involvement in ACPCs (developed from Sanders, Jackson and Thomas, 1997, p 886–7)

Level 1 Full ownership	This is typically only fully exemplified by social services and is characterised by involvement in the full array of subject areas under consideration, regardless of which agency may be most affected. Responsibility is assumed for the planning of the consideration of issues as well as the issues themselves.
Level 2 Significant involvement	This level is typical of agencies whose role cause them to adopt a high profile in the investigative process at a field level. As such, it would encompass the social services as well as the police, but could also include some health agencies. Agencies at this level are very interested in the degree to which other agencies are involved in the process.
Level 3 Peripheral involvement	Representatives in this group consider issues under discussion largely from the perspective of specific relevance to their agencies. Their focus tends to be treatment and prevention, issues that struggle to get on the agenda, or may be given substantially less consideration. This level probably typifies the majority of members of the ACPC, such as probation, education, some health participants, and others.

The ACPC is responsible for creating and shaping child protection policy and procedures; regulating inter-agency working; monitoring practice and outcomes; setting standards for the work; providing training and service development; and establishing the tone and culture of working practice. In order to effectively discharge its responsibilities, each ACPC has to provide an integrated framework which includes clear procedural and practice guidance, an incremental training package and outcome indicators, all influenced by good supervision. Together they provide a framework, enabling managers and practitioners to define aims and objectives, appreciate what this means in terms of practice, and have some idea on how they may be achieved. My suggested conceptual framework for consideration by ACPCs is set out in figure 8. The aim is to look at how professionals and their agencies can effectively collaborate so that there is a plan/strategy for managing young people who sexually abuse, and this can then be used at a higher level to

look at a consortium approach to offset the resource constraints, whilst pooling skills and ideas. There are no certainties that this framework will have the desired result in all cases, although it has the potential to create a multi-disciplinary learning environment, in which anxiety is contained, and where professionals are given the opportunity to reflect, conceptualise and plan together.

Aims and purpose

There has to be a local explicit agreement and a shared understanding between workers and agencies about the aims and purpose of work with young people who sexually abuse. If individuals and agencies are working with different aims, they will interpret their roles and responsibilities in different ways. Morrison (1996a) argued that there has to be an initial recognition of the need to collaborate. This is based on a shared recognition of the problem of sexual abuse, a belief that it cannot be tackled by agencies working alone, and a

Figure 8: A conceptual framework for responding to young people who sexually abuse

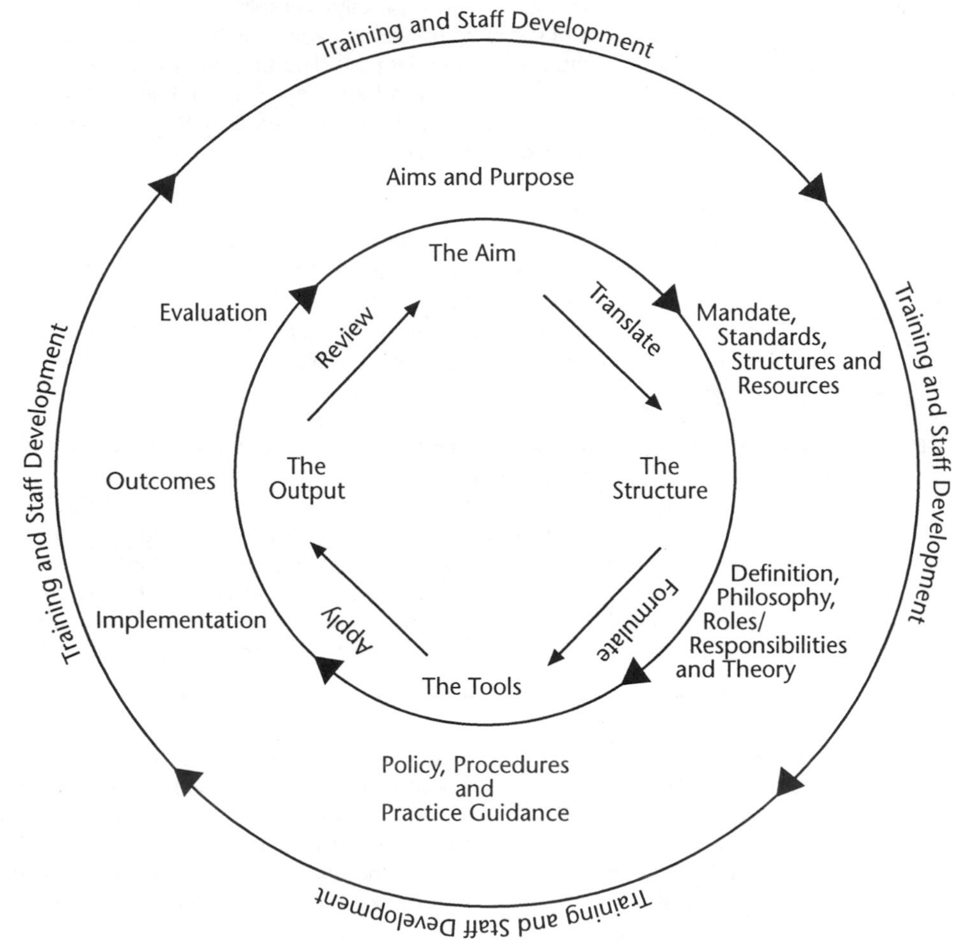

Training and Staff Development

perception that the benefits far outweigh the costs of so doing. There must be detailed consensus between agencies on what constitutes sexual abuse by this group (see Calder, 1997a for detailed guidelines in this area), and we must enter into a process of enhancing public perception and knowledge about sexual abuse. There needs to be agreement reached on the model of organisational partnership to be adopted and which model of collective responsibility is to be adopted by the ACPC.

Mandate, standards, structures and resources

Once a common aim and purpose has been agreed among senior managers, this needs to be enshrined in some local mandate to ensure that each agency cannot deny their roles and responsibilities. There then needs to be a mandate for, and meaning of, collaboration. This means different things to different people in different situations. Collaborative structures and leadership are then needed. This means that ACPCs have to go beyond 'Working

Together' to develop a sense of shared meaning, vision, belonging, and inter-dependence. This can be achieved by developmental work which looks at building confidence, understanding and trust in each other's roles, sharing anxieties and feelings, trouble shooting tensions and conflicts early on, and identifying local needs and resources (McFarlane and Morrison, 1994). ACPCs have to manage and changes any anxieties affecting working together.

Standards offer the baseline for quality assurance, audit and inspection, and provide a benchmark against which both agency and professional performance can be measured. They should be constructed with reference to the available resources and thus have to be both realistic and attainable. Morrison (1992) argued that inter-agency practice standards are needed 'to ensure closer co-ordination between agencies in the exchange of timely, relevant and credible information' (p 127).

In an era of deregulation, practice standards are very unlikely to emerge from government, and there appear to be many advantages in approaching this from a national and multi-disciplinary basis (Morrison, 1996b). He suggests that a National Task Force be established with the aim of consensus building, seeking to identify across the field levels of agreement and difference on what constitutes good practice in terms of knowledge, understanding and skill, which could then be disseminated on a national basis. The areas to explore would include definitions, causation, philosophy of intervention, assessment, intervention goals and methods, evaluation criteria, supervision and training. Such a statement could then act as a national but reviewable benchmark which agencies and the courts could make reference to in determining standards, assessing practice or evaluating reports. A failure to provide such standards ignores the emotional aspects of the job and the impact upon the workers. It also leaves managers 'high and dry' when managing the work as there is no agreed baseline from which to work.

Structures would clearly be needed in all of the agencies that have responsibility for dealing with this problem. Once individual agencies have their own infrastructure in place, the ACPC can use these as the platform from which to construct a corporate framework for responding to this problem. This is crucial since there does not yet appear to be any consensus on who has the lead agency responsibility with this group. For social services, there needs to be some internal agreement on the division of responsibility between the child protection and the youth justice sectors. Fortunately, there does appear to be some reconciliation between the two camps, with a concession from child protectionists that a legal mandate for all young people may not be necessary. Indeed, Calder (1997a) sets out the arguments when a legal mandate should be considered:

- There is not a mandate from the parents supporting the work.
- There is not a supportive helping team.
- When the young person is strongly in denial.
- When the young person's behaviour elsewhere indicates poor impulse control, e.g. non-sexual offending.
- If they do not have a stable base or are not experiencing stable relationships.
- When they are abusive of alcohol or drugs.
- When the offence is of a serious nature and this needs to be reflected by a court appearance.
- When there has been use of force or violence.
- When there are attitudes which continue to justify the use of force or violence, or
- When the young person is not in any agreement to any work.

Whilst legal accountability is important for juveniles in developing self-responsibility, and can sometimes offer an incentive to change, we should remember that:

- Many workers believe that the majority of young people can be worked with on a voluntary basis.
- The type and severity of the abuse are significant indicators of how a case needs to be managed.
- Linkage with the child protection system is helpful, as any controls can be integrated in the child protection plan, e.g. precluding a return home until the necessary work has been completed,

supervised contact with siblings and others, etc. This can reframe the sanctions as incentives, and the assessment can set a series of targets for the abuser.

Workers then need to understand the formal structures of the agencies involved. This includes their geographical boundaries, duties, and the legislation and guidance within which they work. It also requires an understanding of the informal systems operating within them. Agencies working together can operate more or less closely and have links at different layers of their structure (Margetts, 1998).

Resources are a big issue when we don't have many. There is a question mark about how realistic it is to expect ACPCs individually to be in a position to respond to this new problem. Many have set off with the right intention, but have then struggled to translate vision into reality. This is worrying since our current systems have no means of accurately auditing the level of need, and there is a probability that we will uncover a huge unmet need once the structures are in place. An audit to establish the size of the problem may well be needed. It is for this reason that the concept for the future might well be a cross-ACPC boundary 'consortium approach' described later in this paper. This will complement the already existing multi-agency partnerships involving the voluntary and independent sectors (particularly Barnardo's). It is essential that we attract sufficient resources to deal with the abuser and their family; to empower mainstream workers to do the job rather than retaining an over-reliance on specialists; to allow safe substitute care environments to be developed (such as SWAAY)[1]; to set up a priority list about who will be targeted first for services, e.g. highest risk who may be resistant to any work, or lower risk who may engage with the suggested programme of work; and to develop group-work as well as individual programmes of work.

Definition, philosophy, roles and responsibilities, and theory: offering a corporate baseline.

It is essential that we strive to define the philosophical base for what we do, recognising the continuing tensions and confusions (Morrison, 1996b). These principles do need to be congruent with the ACPCs overall approach to sexual abuse work.

Calder (1997a) set out a detailed list of beliefs and philosophical statements underpinning work with young people who sexually abuse:

- Abuse occurs across all groups irrespective of class, race, culture, age or ability.

- All sexual abuse is harmful.

- Sexual abuse is quantitatively different from normal sexual exploration or experimentation and needs to be acknowledged as such.

- All work must recognise the abuser in their total context, particularly in their family.

- All sexual abuse is oppressive. Any effective response must be anti-oppressive.

- Many abusers are themselves in need of help and protection, although they must be held accountable for their actions. Child sexual abuse is always the responsibility of the abuser.

- We should approach the abusers as young people first and not as sex offenders who just happen to be children.

- We have a moral and a statutory duty to work with young people who sexually abuse as well as their victims.

- Sexual abusers are best located within the child protection system and a multi-disciplinary response is essential. The Area Child Protection Committee (ACPC) must take the lead and can be supported by the now compulsory Children's Services plans. Good practice can start, but cannot be sustained, in a fragmented child protection system.

- Clear boundaries are needed for the work and should be expected of anyone using the service.

- We need to target those young people who pose the greatest risk, recognising that we do not currently possess a validated set of factors to guide us in this task.

- Risk assessment, rather than a determination of guilt or innocence, is the basis of all interventions. We do not have sufficiently accurate instruments to know who is guilty or not guilty. It is the task of the court to decide who is guilty.

- Prosecution may in some cases be appropriate to acknowledge the seriousness of the abuse and to ensure that therapeutic programmes can be carried out. Punitive and custodial sentences on their own have not proved effective in changing abusive behaviour and indeed can have the unintended consequence of institutionalising and reinforcing the behaviour.

- Whether a legal mandate is achievable or not, some programme of intervention is necessary if the young person is not to repeat their behaviour.

- The safety of victims and potential victims must be our primary consideration.

- Our next consideration must be to prevent any repetition of the abusive behaviour. The aim is to control the behaviour rather than punish the abuser or expect a 'cure'. Young people are more likely to continue unless challenged.

- All the work is based on the rationale that early intervention is imperative to prevent young people growing into a pattern of behaviour.

- All work needs to balance challenge and respect for the abuser.

- Abusive behaviours rarely occur as an isolated incident and are usually planned in advance.

- Many young people who sexually abuse have themselves been abused — sexually, physically and/or emotionally — and are also 'children in need'.

- All workers involved in this area of work need to be carefully selected and require skilled supervision if we are not to leave workers as well as victims and agencies exposed.

- We must believe that we can help young people and families affect changes in their behaviour, attitudes and thinking.

- Whilst most sexual abuse is carried out by males, we cannot overlook sexual abuse by females and young people with disabilities. We need to challenge the over-representation of young black people who sexually abuse by contextualising their assessment (adapted from O'Callaghan, 1996; Jarman, 1996; and Lewis, 1995).

The definitional debate has been explored by Calder (1997a) in which he provides a comprehensive framework to guide the reader through the individual components: the range of sexual acts, consent, age differences, co-operation and compliance, relationships and coercion. He offered the following definition, which still has merit:

> *Young people (below the age of 18 years) who engage in any form of sexual activity with another individual, that they have powers over by virtue of age, emotional maturity, gender, physical strength, intellect and where the victim in this relationship has suffered a sexual exploitation and betrayal of trust. Sexual activity includes sexual intercourse (oral, anal or vaginal), sexual touching, exposure of sexual organs, showing pornographic material, exhibitionism, voyeurism, obscene communication, frottage, fetishism, and talking in a sexualised way. We should also include any form of sexual activity with an animal, and where a young person sexually abuses an adult (p 11).*

Based on a shared philosophy, each agency next needs to identify its particular roles and responsibilities in relation to this group (Morrison, 1992, p 127).

Theory is an essential foundation upon which practice and procedures are built. We can utilise the very useful ecological approach to help integrate all the uncollated understandings of why young people sexually abuse, to complement the excellent framework provided by Kevin Epps in Chapter 1. Historically, each profession has developed their own theory of child abuse and neglect and adhered rigidly to it regardless of the presenting circumstances of a case. This is blinkered thinking and has led to a failure to offer a holistic framework within which respective theories could be located. The emergence of an ecological framework has offered the potential for conceptual unity across professions and professionals, although it has not explicitly been adopted or recommended to date. A shared knowledge base, which originates from research is essential. Ecology is a science, in which it explores how organisms interact and survive the environment in which they find themselves. It accepts that there are different levels in society where child maltreatment can occur — at an individual, family, community and society level. It allows for the dynamics of child abuse and neglect to be located in a framework which acknowledges that abuse frequently occurs in a socially unhealthy context, with factors such as isolation, poverty, and socially polluted environments acting as crucibles in which latent causal factors are identified (Calder, 1991). The framework integrates rather than abrogates the diversity of theory, as seen in Figure 9 below.

There is also a need to develop further theoretical approaches into inter-organisational and inter-professional behaviour that will help to clarify any common features of the many interfaces between constituent agencies of the child protection supra-structure (Tibbitt, 1982, p 42).

Policies, procedures and practice guidance: plugging the gap

Inter-agency working arrangements need to respond to the existing relationships between agencies. If relationships are bad, or distant, there may be a lot of work to be done to build up understanding and trust. A common mistake of inter-agency work is to assume that an agreement on paper between two small parts of an organisation will change behaviour, attitudes and culture throughout the organisations concerned (Margetts, 1998). The principal challenge for working with this group is clarity coupled with flexibility. The increased level of ACPC activity is encouraging, although there is still a huge gap between aspiration and service delivery. There

appears to be little chance that further central guidance will be issued to elevate this work up the priority list, although the latest consultation paper does suggest it will remain as part of the child protection system, and there may well be more clarity on certain issues such as the circumstances in which a child protection conference could be convened, and when the abusers name could be added to the Child Protection register (DoH, 1998). The issue of whether a local authority could be sued for not disclosing an abusers background to foster carers pre-placement appears to be a greater motivator for ACPCs (see W, and Others v Essex County Council and Another, Court of Appeal, 9, 10 March and 2 April 1998).

Horwath and Calder (1999) argued that policies, procedures and practice guidance together provide a useful framework to guide actions and clarify individual roles and responsibilities. They need to reflect the desired standards for practice. They differentiated between the three terms as follows: policies are the principles or recommended course of action based on the mandate and standards agreed by senior managers. They focus on contextualising the task. Procedures offer the structural framework for practice based on policies. They focus on the process. Practice guidance provides a mechanism for converting the policy and procedures into an operational working tool. This is important when you relate these to the excellent definition of collaboration offered by Challis *et al.* (1988). They argued that collaboration has three elements: the organisational machinery (structures, procedures); the process (sharing, doing things together); and the output (services and benefits).

Clearly defined policies, procedures and practice guidance, supported by senior

---

Figure 9: An ecological framework (Calder and Waters, 1991)

Ecological levels	Levels of analysis/models
Ontogenesis/individual	Psychopathology
Family micro-system	Social-interactional
Community exo-system	Socio-situational
Cultural macro-system	Socio-cultural

representatives of each agency provide front-line practitioners and managers with a clear remit providing a framework to guide action and clarify individual roles and responsibilities. They should be clear, credible, congruent, resourced and monitored, and reflect local conditions (e.g. formal/informal networks and the local collaborative culture) (see Morrison, 1996a).

Inter-agency procedures should always compliment internal agency policies, enabling workers to appreciate not only what is expected of themselves, but of other professionals. Humphreys (1995), argued that good practice should ensure that the ramifications of changed policies in one agency are clearly planned for and negotiated with the other agencies involved (p 808).

Procedures can be a double-edged sword. Firstly, they can help workers by providing a structure for the work, in clarifying professional roles and in resolving any inter-agency difficulties. However, they can constrain practice if they are perceived by workers as an added burden, leading to a rigid and unresponsive service. Many workers tend to utilise procedures as a guide to action so, where none exist, they may hesitate taking any action, fuelled in a belief that the work is of low priority. We should always remember that procedures are no substitute for good practice and, once constructed, are not inviolate. Procedures should never be regarded as set in stone, rather they represent a distillation of what is believed to be best practice at a given point in time. As the knowledge base expands, so it becomes necessary to re-evaluate established policies and practices in order to ensure that they continue to be relevant and appropriate and make best use of available resources (Hampson, 1993). An over-emphasis on procedure can also mask a lack of exploration about philosophy, values and outcomes (Morrison, 1995). Horwath and Calder (1998) also argued that they should be embedded in the real world, with an acknowledgement of the pressures that are being placed on individual agencies and their employees. In this way, they become a benchmark for quality practice rather than a standard against which professionals continually fall short.

Following the research of Sanders and Ladwa-Thomas (1997), it is clear that we need to extend the consensus of the joint investigation between the police and social services to young people who sexually abuse, and in particular, about whether to deal with them as abusers or victims first. Helen Masson's research highlighted that certain key issues need to be addressed in any policy, procedures or practice guidance. She found a range of reasons when a child protection conference on the abuser may be held: including where the abuser was also clearly a victim; where practitioners were aware enough of the need for multi-agency debate; where assessment of the abuser indicated that discussion was needed; when the referral went to social services workers first as opposed to youth justice staff; and when the allegation involved intra-familial abuse (Masson, 1997/8, p 111–2). She also found huge variation regarding the grounds for child protection registration of the abuser: 42% reported they may be registered as an abuser 'in need of services'; 70% indicated that being a victim of abuse might be grounds for child protection registration; whilst 28% mentioned 'other reasons' (such as a separate category to that set out in official guidance).

The failure to develop procedures and policy initiatives in these areas of work can lead to fragmented, sometimes polarised views within the disciplines that should conceptually unite to achieve child protection. Partnerships across agencies need to be driven by managers within the ACPC to ensure that all levels are working towards the same goals. The reality is that multi-disciplinary collaboration often occurs between individuals rather than being supported or sanctioned by management.

Practice guidance is an essential partnership document to policy and procedures, as it attends to the micro-level detail (see Calder, submitted for publication). In the absence of this document, workers tend to end up working in isolation from each other, and practice develops in a fragmented, ad hoc, and unco-ordinated fashion. Good practice can emerge, but cannot be sustained in such an environment.

I reproduce Salford ACPCs procedure for young people who sexually abuse (Appendix 1) as a model of good practice.

Implementation

Whilst careful consideration needs to be given to the choice of workers, it needs to be built on a departmental package of support and procedural guidance. Unfortunately, we can never underestimate the lack of support from managers on the quality of service delivery and ultimately on outcomes. More worrying is that there may well be an open questioning of personal motives and interest in this particular area of work. Such approaches only serve to challenge rather than support workers. Effective supervision needs to look at the triad of feelings, tasks and thinking, and needs to be accompanied by consultation from someone knowledgeable in this area of work. A failure to pair workers together can lead to isolation, stress and secrecy which mirrors the dynamics of the abusers themselves, and leads to unsafe decisions and premature burn-out. Palmer (1995) pointed out that it is important that the work takes place in an environment which supports the sharing of knowledge and responsibility, whilst also prohibiting scapegoating and secrecy. Support of peers, managers and administrative support (procedures for referral, recording, etc.) are all extremely important. 'Normal' supervision is not really adequate for workers who are doing this work and more time is needed to address knowledge and skills, ensuring sensible workloads, monitoring the work, critically analysing the work and providing support and giving praise. 'Live' supervision using CCTV may be one option worth considering. Adequate time is necessary to do the work, which must include time for planning and debriefing. It is important that this time is not eroded and priority is given to it. This is vital if the workers are to stay in control of the sessions and in control of themselves. Co-working is essential to provide protection for the worker, avoidance of collusion and to facilitate better planning, de-briefing, etc. It is important that opt-out mechanisms are in place for workers involved and these may be time-limited or permanent.

Practitioners in each agency need to be provided with structured opportunities to reflect on practice, judgements, feelings and prejudices — either through supervision or consultation — if procedures are not to be used as checklists and families processed through the system without adapting them to the individual circumstances of each case. Senior managers do have a duty to identify ways in which their staff will be provided with opportunities to reflect on and develop their

practice. They also need to promote staff care as staff remain our most valuable resource.

The importance of supervision cannot be over-stated as it is a pervasive feature in the child abuse inquiry reports. Supervision in child protection work is essential as it contains four principal functions: management, education, support and mediation (Morrison, 1993 and Richards and Payne, 1990). In recent years, the concept of supervision has extended beyond social services to health (see Bond and Holland, 1997; Knapman and Morrison, 1998 for a fuller exploration of this point). Flaxington (1995) has provided us with a detailed paper on the supervision of staff working with sex offenders, focusing on the role of the line manager, contracting and the role of consultancy; whilst Morrison (1998c) has provided us with a workbook on consultation in sexual abuse work. These offer us excellent building blocks from which to develop an effective and informed local response.

Outcomes

Outcome measures are important so that workers can become aware of the impact of their actions and decisions on others. There needs to be a very clear differentiation between different kinds of outcome: professionals themselves need to develop outcomes so that they have clear expectations about what they are trying to achieve and also about what change has come about. This replaces the previous emphasis on process. Outcomes for young people are often set and reviewed by adults, and can be as simple as not re-abusing. We need to work with the knowledge that good outcomes to date have been linked primarily with parental commitment and a motivation to plan. Indeed, parental support for the work often provides a better mandate for the work than a legal one.

But we also need to explore the introduction of performance indicators, linked to practice standards. This provides a framework enabling the worker to appreciate exactly what is expected and a measure to determine whether this has been achieved. These should reflect policy and procedures. Quality does protect (DoH, 1998b) and quality assurance mechanisms are imperative if we are to improve our practice and demonstrate this to the media, the public, and central government. We can use the prescribed framework (SSI, 1993) for this purpose, in the hope that we will, in time, become self-regulating.

Evaluation: keeping your eye on the ball

There is a need to set out explicit criteria in terms of methods of evaluation so that the goalposts are not moved, and we begin to get a better feel of what works with young people who sexually abuse. At the present time, there are more unknowns than knowns with this particular group (Morrison, 1994b).

Everitt and Hardiker (1996) have noted that 'evaluation involves processes of dialogue and practice and policy change. The structures and processes through which apparently objective facts and subjective experiences are generated and filtered need to be interrogated. Furthermore, the purpose of evaluation is not merely to provide better or more realistic accounts of phenomena, but to place a value on them and to change situations, practice and people's circumstances accordingly'.

To enable this to take place, the following should be part of the evaluation:

- Do the aims reflect the purpose of practice in light of national guidance and local policies, e.g. children's service plan?

- Are the standards realistic in terms of mandate and resources?

- Do inter-agency policies compliment individual agency policies?

- Is accountability clear?

- What has been achieved in terms of services provided?

- What has been achieved in terms of outcomes?

- What are the opinions of service users regarding policies, procedures and their implementation in practice?

This is a difficult and costly exercise for ACPCs. Gone are the days when a set of procedures could be developed and implemented and the ACPC was able to move on to the next task. Policies, procedures and practice need to be regularly monitored and adjusted to accommodate both local and national changes.

Training and staff development

Training has been defined as 'any organisationally initiated process which is intended to foster learning among organisational members, in a direction contributing to organisational effectiveness' (Hinnicks, 1976). Training may emphasise the need to follow guidelines and procedures but it is ineffective if professionals do not know how to access them or if training is seen as a vehicle to compensate for any lack of procedures. Training is a key for promoting and modelling inter-professional work, desirable inter-professional behaviour and collective responsibility. It also improves attitudes to inter-agency co-operation and enables participants to gain clarity regarding the roles and responsibilities of other professionals. Those who attend inter-agency training often express fewer concerns about occupational rivalries and power struggles (Birchall and Hallett, 1995). We have to do a lot more than bring together a mixed audience in one room, we have to enhance mutual understanding of clarity and of roles and responsibilities (Stevenson, 1994). Effective practice requires a workforce with appropriate knowledge, values (especially around discrimination, perceptions and conflict resolution) and skills. Training is pivotal in developing these areas and in promoting effective working relationships, modelling what is expected in practice.

A strategic approach to training is required that focuses not only on practitioners, but senior front-line managers as well: 'Training should help policy makers and practitioners critically evaluate the developing body of knowledge and implement relevant changes. It should contribute to their knowledge of good policy and practice' (DoH, 1993).

Training is an encompassing structure as it influences every part of the framework. It can become the vehicle whereby senior managers are given an opportunity to consider the aims of core group practice and discuss their mandate and desired standards for practice. Policies and procedures can then follow. Once these are in place, training can help prepare first-line and middle managers to supervise staff involved in this work. These managers need to have knowledge of policy, standards and their role in terms of promoting high quality practice. It is only when these managers have been trained that it is appropriate to train practitioners. This needs to be both intra- as well as inter-agency given the multiplicity of roles and responsibilities they assume in the field of child protection. They need training on the modus operandi of young people who sexually abuse; the content and reasoning behind the assessment frameworks developed for the young person and their family environment (see Calder, 1998); the pros and cons of prosecution and their removal from home (see Calder, 1997a); safe caring (see Rose and Savage, 1999); contact (see Calder, 1999); and criteria for rehabilitating the family. More general training is needed on how to measure change; planning and the process and content of assessment; and specific training on engaging the young person, and how to allocate roles and responsibilities between key professionals.

Although training has an important role in terms of providing opportunities to reflect, develop and evaluate practice, it cannot be undertaken in isolation. Calder and Horwath (1996) found that although it is positive that some training is taking place, questions remain regarding the focus of this training. It appears to be taking place in a vacuum, if, as our study indicates, the use of guidelines and procedures is limited. What framework is being used for the training and what are trainers offering as a measure of good practice? Training cannot be used as the mechanism to compensate for a void in policy and procedure. Training is only effective if it is used as part of a wider strategy to promote and develop practice (Smith, 1993). This broader strategy should include a framework of policies and procedures together with resources and support to enable professionals to work within the framework. Morrison (1995) has argued also that training has a key role to play in the management of change. In a world of fragmenting structures and relationships, training can offer staff a group experience, which is safe and directed at meeting their needs. This can help participants feel a sense of belonging and self-efficacy: both of which are major determinants of successful change and a buffer to burn-out. We can utilise the inter-agency learning environment set out earlier (Charles and Stevenson, 1990) in our training.

A Conceptual Framework for a Cross-ACPC Consortium Approach

Masson (1995) concluded that

> to address chronic problems of insufficient assessment facilities, inappropriate accommodation and a lack of training opportunities, some areas have or are considering the sharing of resources and expertise in order to make best use of what exists (p 19).

In this paper, a consortium is defined as an association or partnership between ACPCs. This approach has the potential to help pool skills and resources across existing geographical and structural boundaries, as well as providing a forum within which to develop corporate strategies, procedures and systems. A regional approach can offer a good strategic overview, direction, and promote harmonious working relationships. This is increasingly important when we consider that the creation of unitary authorities and the reorganisation in the health services, there are more mismatches between health boards, unitary authorities and police forces. There is also a huge potential to lose families when they move between much smaller authorities. A corporate consortium approach represents a very clear proposal to overcome such problems.

The consortium approach has some structural support already. For example the Greater Manchester Police service 10 ACPCs in their catchment area, and the creation of NHS trusts has meant there is often multiple representation by them to a number of different ACPCs. Consortium approaches have evolved already in relation to finding foster placements, and they match many service level agreements between national and local voluntary organisations and local authority partners (Kendrick *et al.*, 1996). In Greater Manchester, there are already four cross-boundary adult male sex offender groupwork programmes being run, with an overarching management group ensuring comparability, consistency of approach, evaluation, etc. This may provide the closest model upon which a consortium for young people who sexually abuse may be constructed.

Fragmentation has evolved systems where the focus could be on duplication, competition, and territorial behaviour, rather than coterminous working together. Each area will have unique characteristics, resources and limitations, so that any attempt to develop consortiums will need to be tailored towards the particular needs of that particular area. Given the huge variations in policy and practice in the UK relating to young people who sexually abuse, this becomes more important. What we do need to promote is a pooling of best practice so that there is a sharing of innovative, yet tried and tested approaches, and this also allows us to avoid reinventing the wheel. This also has the potential to release resources from a management to an operational level.

The principal goal of a consortium approach is to create collaborative advantage, which is achieved when 'something unusually creative is produced — perhaps an objective is met that no organisation could have produced on its own and when each organisation, through the collaboration, is able to achieve its own objectives better than it could alone' (Huxham, 1996, p 14). The key point here is that like Challis the focus is on outputs of collaboration that could not have been achieved except through collaboration. One of the key values of this notion is that it raises the profile of collaboration and legitimises it as an activity worthy of resource investment.

A framework for practice.

Building on the ACPC conceptual framework, which is an essential building block for the consortium model, the following may assist in moving from a local to a more regional response (see figure 10). The reader can access more detailed information on consortium options by referring to Bradford (1993) and Peck, Sheinberg and Akamatsu (1995).

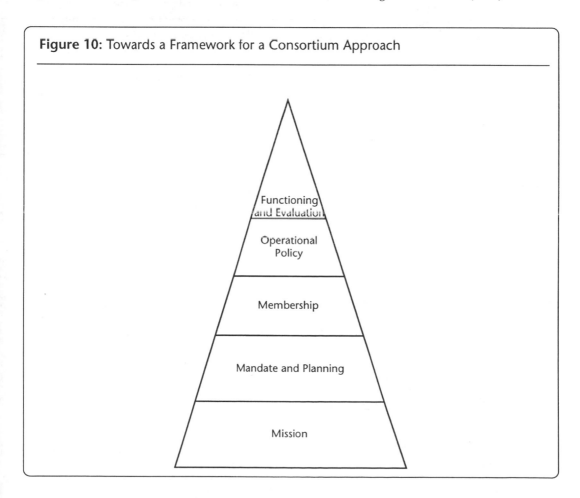

Figure 10: Towards a Framework for a Consortium Approach

Functioning and Evaluation

Operational Policy

Membership

Mandate and Planning

Mission

Mission: To develop a co-operative delivery of service across professional systems and ACPCs. To pool the regional resources and allocate them according to need within an agreed system of priority and risks.

Mandate and Planning: The first task is to get some agreement from agencies and ACPCs that they will support the consortium approach. They need to form a preliminary working group, which can develop proposals for consideration. This working group needs to consider the various options open to them (systems, procedures, etc.) and the potential problems they might encounter (e.g. criminal justice or child protection approach; the numbers involved; respective existing resources; resistance to them being used more regionally, etc.) There needs to be an acceptance that, for managers, they will occasionally inherit decisions that have financial implications for them. This stage should aim to clarify regional roles and responsibilities, agree a baseline definition of the problem, agree on the criteria when a legal mandate may be needed, agree a philosophy of intervention, etc.

Membership: All the key agencies involved in the management of young people who sexually abuse need to be represented in the consortium. This will be led by the social services and be joined by representatives from probation (who assume responsibility for young people over 16 years), NSPCC (possibly for initial and comprehensive assessments and treatment options), the police (as they share the initial responsibility for managing alleged offences), and health (access to psychological time). The social services may need representatives from youth justice, child protection and the residential/fostering section. If we are to internalise the ideas developed, a blend of managers and workers is needed. This is important as it models the varying agendas and different perspectives found in the practice situation.

The overarching consortium should meet quarterly and be chaired by an agreed nominated person of senior management level. Their term of office would be for a year, extendible by agreement. The chair of the consortium could also be involved in any National Task Force to ensure there is a broader consideration of the issues and a continuing exchange of information.

There is the potential for sub-groups to develop which address different issues. For example, staff involved in the work may develop operational materials (such as Calder, 1998); whilst an executive committee can address organisational/ACPC agendas, and look at how to allocate the available resources, how to fund the ongoing work, look at outcomes and mechanisms of evaluating the success of the interventions, etc. They need to meet six-weekly to discharge these responsibilities.

Operational policy: The existing system of child protection is already complex. The goal is for the consortium not to build additional levels of bureaucracy into this; but to utilise the existing systems for managing the problem, such as initial child protection conferences, diversionary panels, and supervision. There needs to be an agreed baseline eligibility criteria for accessing services.

The consortium may choose to employ one worker as a specialist in work with young people who sexually abuse to act with a regional brief on collating the best of practice, theory, and to act as a consultant to those doing the work.

Functioning and evaluation: The consortium approach should be reviewed annually to ensure it is achieving its functions in practice. This should be done by an agreed external auditor. Evaluation criteria might include client satisfaction, referrer satisfaction, an analysis of the impact on service provision, feedback from the courts/conferences, cost effectiveness, etc.

Conclusions

This chapter has covered a lot of ground. There is a detailed review of the obstacles to working together at three levels: generally, in relation to child sexual abuse, and then in relation to young people who sexually abuse. This is important as they combine to make our response to the latter a truly daunting task. Having addressed these difficulties, I moved on to provide a conceptual framework of response at an ACPC level. This is important, as there needs to be a substantial local response from ACPCs to fill the gap left by the void of central government guidance in this area. This paper then goes on to acknowledge that, even where individual ACPCs respond, the resource implications make its operationalisation very difficult. This may signal a need to look beyond ACPC boundaries to a regional cross-boundary/ACPC consortium approach. Whilst this appears to be a logical next step, and it does appear to have worked in relation to adult sex offender group work programmes, nothing has yet evolved in practice in relation to young people who sexually abuse.

The consortium approach may provide the only mechanism by which we can effectively respond to this growing problem in a climate of fragmenting collaborative relationships, limited resources, poor staff morale, and uncollated research and practice wisdom. I will report separately on the details of a consortium approach as we attempt to build such a response in the Greater Manchester area.

[1] SWAAY is a nationally available residential service for adolescent boys who have sexually abused. Their interdisciplinary team offers an integrated service, comprising consultant psychiatric, clinical forensic, cognitive and psychoanalytical therapy, with residential community homes and school, offering a full curriculum. For further information, please contact them at Fox Hill Centre, Pondmoor Road, Bracknell, Berkshire, RG12 7JZ. Tel: 01344 302656, or fax: 01344 302606.

References

Abel, G.G. (1984). *The Outcome of Assessment Treatment at the Sexual Behaviour Clinic and its Relevance to the Need for Treatment Programs for Adolescent Sex Offenders in New York*. Paper presented to a prison research — education-action project. New York: Albany.

Abel, G.G., Becker, J.V., Cunningham-Rathner, J., Mittleman, R.S., and Rouleau, J. (1988). Multiple Paraphiliac Diagnosis Among Sex Offenders. *Bulletin of the American Academy of Psychiatry and the Law*, 16: 153–168.

Abel, G.G., Becker, J.V., Cunningham-Rathner, J., Rouleau, J., and Murphy, W. (1987). Self-reported Crimes of Non-incarcerated Paraphiliacs. *Journal of Interpersonal Violence*, 2: 3–25.

Abel, G.G., Osborne, C.A., and Twigg, D.A. (1993). Sexual Assault Through the Life-span of Adult Offenders with Juvenile Histories. In Barbaree, H.E., Marshall, W.L., and Hudson, S.M. (Eds.). *The Juvenile Sex Offender*. New York: Guilford Press, 104–117.

Atmore, C. (1996). Cross Cultural Mediations: Media Coverage of Two Child Sexual Abuse Controversies in New Zealand/Aotearoa. *Child Abuse Review*, 5: 334–345.

Barker, R.W. (1996). Child Protection, Public Services and the Chimera of Market Force Efficiency. *Children and Society*, 10: 28–39.

Becker, J.V. (1990). Treating Adolescent Sex Offenders. Professional Psychology: *Research and Practice*, 21(5): 362–365.

Beitchman, J.H., Zucker, K.V., Hood, J.E., and Dacosta, J.A. (1991). A Review of the Short-term Effects of Child Sexual Abuse. *Child Abuse and Neglect*, 15: 537–556.

Beitchman, J.H., Zucker, K.V., Hood, J.E., Dacosta, J.A., Ackerman, D., and Cassama, E. (1992). A Review of the Long-term Effects of Child Sexual Abuse. *Child Abuse and Neglect*, 16: 101–118.

Birchall, E., and Hallett, C. (1995). Working Together in Child Protection. London: HMSO.

Blyth, E., and Milner, J. (1990). The Process of Inter-agency Work. In Violence against Children Study Group, *Taking Child Abuse Seriously*, 194–211. London: Unwin Hyman.

Bond, M., and Holland, S. (1997). *Skills of Clinical Supervision for Nurses*. Milton Keynes: Open University Press.

Bradford, R. (1993). Promoting Inter-agency Collaboration in Child Services. *Child: Care, Health and Development*, 19: 355–367.

Brown, A. (1992). Caution Assessments for Adolescent Sexual Offenders — Shropshire Adolescent Sexual Offences Programme. *NOTA News*, 5: 24–36.

Brown, A. (1998). The Sex Offenders Act. Part 1: Issues Relating to Adolescents Convicted of a Sexual Offence. *NOTA News*, 27 (September 1998): 21–27.

Butler-Sloss, E. (1988). *Report of the Inquiry into Child Abuse in Cleveland*. London: HMSO.

Calder, M.C. (1991). Child Protection: Core Groups: Beneficial or Bureaucratic? *Child Abuse Review*, 5(2): 26–29.

Calder, M.C. (1995). Child Protection: Balancing Paternalism and Partnership. *British Journal of Social Work*, 25(6): 749–766.

Calder, M.C. (1997a). *Juveniles and Children who Sexually Abuse: A Guide to Risk Assessment*. Dorset: Russell House Publishing.

Calder, M.C. (1997b). Young People who Sexually Abuse: Towards International Consensus. *Social Work in Europe*, 4(1): 36–39.

Calder, M.C. (1998). *Young People who Sexually Abuse: Assessment and Practice Guidance*. Salford: Salford ACPC.

Calder, M.C. (1999a). *Assessing Risk in Adult Males who Sexually Abuse Children: A Practical Guide*. Lyme Regis, Dorset: Russell House Publishing.

Calder, M.C. (1999b). Managing Allegations of Child Abuse Against Foster Carers. In Wheal, A. (Ed.). *The RHP Companion to Foster Care*, pp 172–182. Lyme Regis, Dorset: Russell House Publishing.

Calder, M.C. (submitted for publication). *Young People who Sexually Abuse: A Framework for Initial Assessment.*

Calder, M.C., and Barratt, M. (1997). Inter-agency Perspectives on Core Group Practice. *Children and Society*, 11: 209–221.

Calder, M.C., and Horwath, J. (1996). *National Core Group Sample: Analysis of Questionnaire Responses.* Salford ACPC/University of Sheffield. Unpublished manuscript.

Calder, M.C., and Horwath, J. (1999). Post-registration Work: A Framework for Collective Responsibility. In Calder, M.C., and Horwath, J. (Eds.). *Working for Children on the Child Protection Register: An Inter-agency Practice Guide*, pp 45–90. Aldershot: Arena.

Calder, M.C., and Waters, J. (1991). *Child Abuse or Child Protection: What's in a Name?* Paper presented to the national conference on Child Abuse of the Association of Psychological Therapies, University of York, 18 June 1991.

Challis, L., Fuller, S., Henwood, M., Klein, R., Plowden, W., Webb, A., Whittingham, P., and Wistow, G. (1988). *Joint Approaches to Social Policy — Rationality and Practice.* Cambridge: Cambridge University Press.

Charles, M., and Stevenson, O. (1990). *Multi-disciplinary is Different!* Nottingham: University of Nottingham.

Children's Society Briefing Paper No. 3 (1988).

Corby, B. (1995). Inter-professional Co-operation and Inter-agency Co-ordination. In Wilson, K., and James, A. (Eds.) *The Child Protection Handbook*, 211–226. London: Bailliere Tindall.

DHSS (1982). *Child Abuse: A Study of Inquiry Reports.* London: HMSO.

DoH (1991a). *Child Abuse: A Study of Inquiry Reports.* London: HMSO.

DoH (1991b). The Children Act 1989 Guidance and Regulations. Volume 1: Court orders. London: HMSO.

DoH (1991c). *Working Together Under the Children Act 1989: A Guide to Arrangements for Inter-agency Co-operation for the Protection of Children from Abuse.* London: HMSO.

DoH (1992–3). *Report of Area Child Protection Committee conferences.* London: HMSO.

DoH (1993). *Working with Child Sexual Abuse: Guidelines for Trainers and Managers.* London: HMSO.

DoH (1995). *Child Protection: Messages from Research.* London: HMSO.

DoH (1998a). *Working Together to Safeguard Children: New Government Proposals for Inter-agency Co-operation.* London: HMSO Consultation Paper.

DoH (1998b). *Quality Protects: Transforming Children's Services.* LAC (98) 28, 11 November 1998.

Epps, K. (1997). *Pointers for Carers.* In Calder, M.C., op cit., 99–109.

Evans, M., and Miller, C. (1992). *Partnership in Child Protection: The Strategic Management Response.* London: National Institute for Social Work/Office for Public Management.

Everitt, A., and Hardiker, P. (1996). *Evaluating for Good Practice.* London: Macmillan.

Fargason, C.A., Barnes, D., Scheider, D., and Galloway, B.W. (1994). Enhancing Multi-agency Collaboration in the Management of Child Sexual Abuse. *Child Abuse and Neglect*, 18(10): 859–869.

Flaxington, F. (1995). *Supervision of Staff Working with Sex Offenders.* Manchester: Greater Manchester Probation Service.

Franklin, B. (1998). Hard Pressed: National Newspaper Reporting of Social Work and Social Services. Sutton, Surrey: *Community Care.*

Franklin, B., and Parton, N. (1991). Media Reporting of Social Work: A Framework for Analysis. In Franklin, B., and Parton, N. (Eds.). *Social Work, the Media and Public Relations*, 1–52. London: Routledge.

Gerdes, K.E., Gourley, M.M., and Cash, M.C. (1995). Assessing Juvenile Sex Offenders to Determine Adequate Levels of Supervision. *Child Abuse and Neglect*, 19(8): 953–961.

Groth, A.N. (1977). The Adolescent Sex Offender and his Prey. *Journal of Offender Therapy and Comparative Criminology*, 21: 249–254.

Hallett, C. (1995). *Inter-agency Co-ordination in Child Protection.* London: HMSO.

Hallett, C., and Birchall, E. (1992). *Co-ordination and Child Protection: A Review of the Literature.* London: HMSO.

Hallett, C., and Stevenson, O. (1980). *Child Abuse: Aspects of Inter-professional Communication.* London: Allen and Unwin.

Hampson, A. (1993). *Annual Report of the Principal Officer — Child Protection.* City of Salford Social Services (Children's Division).

Hinnicks, (1976), as quoted in Morrison (1995).

Hollows, A. (1991). Children as Abusers: What Could we Achieve? In Hollows, A., and Armstrong, H. (Eds.). *Children and Young People as Abusers: An Agenda for Change*, 73– 77. London: National Children's Bureau, .

Hood, S. (1997). The Purchaser/Provider Separation in Child and Family Social Work: Implications for Service Delivery and for the Role of the Social Worker. *Child and Family Social Work*, 2: 25–35.

Horwath, J., and Calder, M.C. (1998). Working Together to Protect Children on the Child Protection Register: Myth or Reality? *British Journal of Social Work*, 28(6): pp 878–895.

Horwath, J., and Calder, M.C. (1999). The Background and Current Context of Post Registration Practice. In Calder, M.C., and Horwath, J. (Eds.). *Working for Children on the Child Protection Register:An Inter-agency Practice Guide.* Aldershot: Aldgate.

Humphreys, C. (1995). Whatever Happened on the Way to Counselling? Hurdles in the Inter-agency Environment. *Child Abuse and Neglect*, 19(7): 801–809.

Huxham, C. (1996). *Creating Collaborative Advantage.* Thousand Oaks, CA: Sage.

Jarman, M. (1996). *Introduction to a One-day Conference on Children and Young People who Sexually Abuse.* Liverpool Town Hall, 14 March 1996.

Jenkins, P. (1992). *Intimate Enemies: Moral Panics in Contemporary Great Britain.* NY: Aldine de Gruyter.

Kelly, L., Regan, L., and Burton, S. (1991). *An Exploratory Study of the Prevalence of Sexual Abuse in a Sample of 16–21 Year Olds.* Child Abuse Studies Unit, Polytechnic of North London.

Kendrick, A., Simpson, A., and Mapstone, E. (1996). *Getting it Together: Changing Services for Children and Young People in Difficulty.* York: Joseph Rowntree Foundation.

Knapman, J., and Morrison, T. (1998). *Making the Most of Supervision in Health and Social Care: A Self Development Manual for Supervisors.* Brighton: Pavilion Publishing.

Knopp, F.H. (1982). *Remedial Intervention in Adolescent Sex Offences: Nine Program Descriptions.* Syracuse, NY: Safer Society Press.

Kraemer, S. (1988). Splitting and Stupidity in Child Sexual Abuse. *Psychoanalytic Psychotherapy,* 3(3): 247–257.

Lewis, D. (1995). *Adolescent Sex Offenders: Proposed Principles.* Greater Manchester and Lancashire Children's Strategy Group, July 1995.

Loxley, A. (1997). *Collaboration in Health and Welfare: Working with Difference.* London: Jessica Kingsley Publishers.

Mailick, M., and Ashley, A.A. (1989). Politics of Interprofessional Collaboration: Challenge of Advocacy. *Social Casework,* 62(3): 131–137.

Margetts, T. (1998). Establishing Multi-agency Working with Sex Offenders: Setting up to Succeed. *NOTA News,* 25: 27–38.

Margolin, L. (1984). Group Therapy as a Means of Learning About the Sexually Assaultive Adolescents. *International Journal of Offender Therapy and Comparative Criminology,* 28: 65–72.

Masson, H. (1995). Juvenile Sexual Abusers: A Challenge to Conventional Wisdom About Juvenile Offending. *Youth and Policy,* 50 (Autumn 1995).

Masson, H. (1995b). *Children and Adolescents who Sexually Abuse Other Children: Responses to an Emerging Problem — An Interim Report.* University of Huddersfield.

Masson, H. (1996). *Children and Young People who Sexually Abuse Other Children: An Emerging Problem.* University of Huddersfield: School of Human and Health Sciences.

Masson, H. (1997/8). Issues in Relation to Children and Young People who Sexually Abuse Other Children: A Survey of Practitioners Views. *The Journal of Sexual Aggression,* 3(2): 101–118.

McFarlane, T., and Morrison, T. (1994). Learning and Change: Outcomes of Inter-agency Training for Child Protection. *Child Care in Practice,* 1(12): 33–44.

Morrison, T. (1991). Change, Control and the Legal Framework. In Adcock, M., White, R., and

Hollows, A. (Eds.). *Significant Harm: Its Management and Outcome* 85–100. London: Significant Publications.

Morrison, T. (1992). Managing Sex Offenders: The Challenge for Managers. *Probation Journal,* 39(3): 122–128.

Morrison, T. (1993). *Staff Supervision in Social Care.* London: Pitman Publishing.

Morrison, T. (1994a). Working Together to Manage Sexual Abuse: Rhetoric or Reality? *The Journal of Sexual Aggression,* 1(1): 29–44.

Morrison, T. (1994b). Context, Constraints and Considerations in Practice. In Morrison, T., Erooga, M., and Beckett, R. (Eds.) *Sexual Offending Against Children: Assessment and Treatment of Male Abusers,* 25–54. London: Routledge.

Morrison, T. (1995). *Learning, Training and Change in Child Protection Organisations.* Keynote presentation to the National Child Protection Trainers Conference, 15 March 1995.

Morrison, T. (1996a). Partnership and Collaboration: Rhetoric and Reality. *Child Abuse and Neglect,* 20(2): 127–140.

Morrison, T. (1996b). *Making an Impact: Where Next with Adolescents who Sexually Abuse?* Keynote presentation to Barnardo's 'Learning to Change' conference, Liverpool Town Hall, 14 March 1996.

Morrison, T. (1997). Emotionally Competent Child Protection Organisations: Fallacy, Fiction or Necessity? In Bates, J., Pugh, R., and Thompson, N. (Eds.) *Protecting Children: Challenges and Change,* 193-211. Aldershot: Arena.

Morrison, T. (1998a). Partnership, Collaboration and Change Under the Children Act. In Adcock, M., and White, R. (Eds.). *Significant Harm: Its Management and Outcome* (2nd edition) 121–147. Croydon, Surrey: Significant Publications.

Morrison, T. (1998b). Managing Risk: Learning Our Lessons. *NOTA News,* 25: 3–17.

Morrison, T. (1998c). *Casework Consultation: A Practical Guide to Work with Sex Offenders and Other High Risk Clients.* Hull: NOTA.

National Children's Homes (1992). *Report of the Committee of Enquiry into Children and Young People who Sexually Abuse Other Children.* London: NCH.

Neate, P. (1990). The Unknown Quantity. *Community Care,* 8.11.90, 17–9.

Newton, L.H. (1982). Collective Responsibility in Health Care. *Journal of Medicine and Philosophy,* 7(1): 11–21.

Northern Ireland Research Team (1991). *Child Sexual Abuse in Northern Ireland.* Belfast: Greystone.

O'Callaghan, D. (1996). Presentation on the G-Map Programme to the Child Concern Meeting, Sedgley Park Police Training School, Manchester, 24.1.96.

Palmer, T. (1995). *Young People who Sexually Abuse.* Report to Cleveland ACPC. 11 May, 1995.

Pearce, J. (1991). *Child Sexual Abuse: Professional and Personal Perspectives. Part 2: Inter-professional Collaboration.* Cheadle, Cheshire: Boys and Girls Welfare Society.

Peck, J.S., Sheinberg, M., and Akamatru, N.N. (1995). Forming a Consortium: a Design for Inter-agency Collaboration in the Delivery of Service Following the Disclosure of Incest. *Family Process*, 34(3): 287–302.

Perry, G.P., and Orchard, J. (1992). *Assessment and Treatment of Adolescent Sex Offenders*. Sarasota, Fl: Professional Resource Press.

Pont, C. (1992). London Borough and English Authorities Area Child Protection Committee Reports, April 1990–March 1992. London: DoH.

Rai, G.S. (1994). Complexity and Co-ordination in Child Welfare Agencies. *Administration in Social Work*, 18(1): 87–105.

Richards, M., and Payne, C. (1990). *Staff Supervision in Child Protection Work*. London: National Institute of Social Work.

Rose, K., and Savage, A. (1999). *Safe Caring*. In Wheal, A. (Ed.), op cit. 115–126.

Sanders, R., Jackson, S., and Thomas, N. (1997). Degrees of Involvement: The Interaction of Focus and Commitment in Area Child Protection Committees. *British Journal of Social Work*, 27: 871–892.

Sanders, R.M., and Ladwa-Thomas, V. (1997). Inter-agency Perspectives on Child Sexual Abuse Perpetrated by Juveniles. *Child Maltreatment*, 2(3): 264–271.

Smith, G. (1993). *Systemic Approaches to Training in Child Protection*. London: Karnac.

SSI (1993). *Inspecting for Quality: Evaluating Performance in Child Protection. A Framework for the Inspection of Local Authority Social Services Practice and Systems*. London: HMSO.

Stainton-Rogers, W. (1989). Effective Co-operation in Child Protection Work. In Morgan, S., and Righton, P. (Eds.). *Child Care: Concerns and Conflicts: A Reader*, 82-94. London: Hodder and Stoughton.

Stevenson, O. (1989). Multi-disciplinary Work in Child Protection. In Stevenson, O. (Ed.). *Child Abuse: Public Policy and Professional Practice*, 173–203. London: Harvester Wheatsheaf.

Stevenson, O. (1994). Child Protection: Where Now in Inter-professional Work? In Leathard, A. (Ed.) *Going Inter-professional: Working Together for Health and Welfare*. London: Routledge, 123–135.

Taylor, G. (1996). *Working with Denial*. Workshop at the Barnardo's conference, Learning to Change, Liverpool Town Hall, 14 March 1996.

Tibbitt, J. (1982). Working Together? Social Work Departments and Other Social Services. In Lishman, J. (Ed.). *Social Work Departments as Organisations. Research Highlights No. 4*, 41–52. Department of Social Work: University of Aberdeen.

Vince, R., and Martin, L. (1993). Inside Action Learning. *Management Education and Development*, 24(2): 205–215.

Woodhouse, D., and Pengally, P. (1991). *Anxiety and the Dynamics of Collaboration*. Aberdeen: Aberdeen University Press.

Appendix One

CITY OF SALFORD SOCIAL SERVICES DEPARTMENT
OPERATIONAL PROCEDURES

PROCEDURE FOR THE MANAGEMENT OF CHILDREN AND YOUNG PEOPLE WHO SEXUALLY ABUSE OTHER CHILDREN

1   INTRODUCTION

1.1   Working Together recommends that where abuse of a child is alleged to have been carried out by another child or young person such behaviour should always be treated seriously and should be the subject of a referral to child protection agencies. Child protection procedures would then be followed in respect of both the victim and the alleged perpetrator.

1.2   No distinction is made between cases involving abuse within the family or by a child or young person previously known to the victim and abuse by a child or young person who was not previously known. LAC(90)8 states at paragraph 10: 'Where the abuse is alleged to have been perpetrated by a person who is himself a child or a young person (i.e. under 18 years of age) whether known to the abused child or not, it is important that the Social Services Department be involved at the outset so that it may provide any necessary support.'

1.3   The report of the Committee of Enquiry into Children and Young People Who Sexually Abuse Other Children (NCH, 1992) recommends that all work with such children should take place within the context of the child protection system and should fall under the auspices of the local Area Child Protection Committee whose function would be to co-ordinate the work, to bring it into the child protection system, and to develop a strategic plan. The Enquiry Report further recommends that separate child protection conferences should be held in respect of both the victim and the alleged perpetrator. A case conference in respect of the alleged perpetrator is also recommended in 'Working Together'.

1.4   In respect of the victim the reasons for recommending that such cases should be dealt with jointly by the Police and Social Services under child protection procedures include the following:
–   to ensure that the investigation is conducted sensitively and sympathetically in accordance with principles set out in the Memorandum of Good Practice by officers who are appropriately trained and experienced and who will be alert to those child protection issues which are likely to arise in such cases;
–   to ensure that where the circumstances of the case indicate a need for protective action to be taken in respect of the child victim, such action will be taken to ensure that the child victim and his or her family receive any necessary support both during and following the completion of the investigation.

1.5   With regard to the alleged perpetrator the reasons for a joint approach under child protection procedures are:

–   to determine whether the alleged perpetrator has himself been the victim of abuse and is in need of protection;

–   to determine whether protective action is necessary in respect of any other children with whom the alleged perpetrator may be in contact;

–   to identify the need for services to the alleged perpetrator and his or her family.

1.6   With regard to the alleged perpetrator 'Working Together' recommends that following the initial child protection conference a comprehensive assessment should be undertaken. Following the completion of this assessment a planning meeting should be held to review initial plans in the light of the information obtained and to co-ordinate intervention designed to discourage the abuser from committing further abusive acts. Should the perpetrator's name be added to the Child Protection Register in response to evidence of abuse to themselves then the core group and review conference will consider the results of the assessment.

1.7   Working Together states that policies of minimal intervention are not as effective as are more focused forms of therapeutic intervention which may be supported by orders obtained via civil or criminal proceedings.

1.8   The question of appropriate intervention in cases involving children and young people who commit sexual offences against other children has been the subject of considerable debate. Traditionally no distinction has been made between these and other types of offence but recent research findings suggest the need for a different approach.

1.9   There is now a different understanding of the distinction between normal sexual experimentation and sexual abuse and growing recognition that first offences should not be regarded as isolated incidents and that re-offending is likely in the absence of effective intervention;

1.10   In contrast to the majority of juvenile offenders those who commit sexual offences are likely to grow into a pattern of offending rather than out of it (i.e. recidivism may be the norm rather than the exception);

1.11   A significant proportion of adult sex offenders report that their deviant sexual behaviour was first established in adolescence;

1.12   A significant proportion of children and young people who abuse other children have themselves been the victims of sexual abuse and may be in need of protection;

1.13   The consequences for the victim of sex offences may be much more serious both in the short-term and the long-term than has previously been acknowledged. There is a marked under-reporting of offences and a significant proportion of offenders will, in the absence of effective intervention, victimise large numbers of children during the course of their criminal careers;

1.14   Whilst intervention with adult sex offenders generally carries a poor prognosis, early intervention in adolescence can be effective in preventing the establishment of deviant patterns of behaviour;

1.15 In order to be effective, treatment programmes will generally require a high level of commitment on the part of the offender which may be difficult to secure without some form of legal mandate;

1.16 The complex nature of the problem requires a co-ordinated multi-disciplinary approach which addresses both child protection and criminal justice issues.

1.17 In response to these findings there is growing consensus that principles of minimal intervention are not appropriate to those who commit sexual offences. The following proposals are therefore recommended as the basis for agreeing a procedure for dealing with cases involving children and young people who sexually abuse other children in Salford.

2   PRINCIPLES

2.1 Work with children and young people who abuse should be co-ordinated as part of the multi-disciplinary child protection system. The Area Child Protection Committee is therefore the appropriate body to take a lead role in the development of this area of work

2.2 While sexual exploration and experimentation are a normal part of childhood development, there are circumstances in which children are abused by other children or young people and the consequences for the victim can be just as serious as when the abuser is an adult.

2.3 The primary objective of all work with children and young people who abuse must be the protection of victims and the prevention of a repetition of the abusive behaviour.

2.4 The safety of victims and potential victims must always be the first consideration.

2.5 The assessment of risk rather than the determination of guilt or innocence must be the focus of the intervention.

2.6 The aim of intervention is to control the behaviour rather than punish the perpetrator.

3   PROCEDURE

3.1 All cases involving allegations of sexual abuse by a child or young person (i.e. under 18 years of age) should be the subject of a joint investigation in accordance with agreed procedures. (This will include those cases where the alleged perpetrator is not previously known to the child and those cases where the alleged perpetrator is under the age of criminal responsibility i.e. 10 years. It will also include cases where the abuse involves children in foster care, children's homes or other residential settings.)

Where there is any doubt about the inclusion of a situation in these procedures, advice should be sought from the Child Protection Unit.

3.2 Following completion of the investigation consideration will need to be given to the need to hold an initial child protection conference in respect of both the victim and the alleged perpetrator.

3.3   With regard to the victim of the abuse a conference will only be required where there are believed to be outstanding child protection issues which remain to be addressed.

3.4   A conference should always be held where there is reason to believe that one or other of the following conditions is met. A child's parents or carers have:

–   known of the abuse and colluded with it;

–   suspected abuse and failed to protect the child;

–   not known of the abuse but demonstrated irresponsible negligence;

–   not believed the child or obstructed the child disclosing in any way.

3.5   Where there are other children in the same household as the young person suspected of abuse, consideration will need to be given either to making them the subject of a separate conference or to a consideration of their protection needs in the conference on the alleged perpetrator.

3.6   With regard to the alleged perpetrator an initial child protection conference should normally be held in all cases regardless of whether the victims were members of the same household. Where there is doubt about the appropriateness of a conference advice should be sought from the Child Protection Unit.

3.7   The timing of the conference in respect of the alleged perpetrator will depend on whether a criminal charge has been brought or whether the case has been referred to the Diversionary Panel. In either case, the conference should not normally be convened until there has been some kind of preliminary assessment. Where the case is to be considered by the Diversionary Panel the conference should be held prior to the meeting at which a decision with regard to disposal is to be made.

3.8   The purpose of the conference will be to consider the following issues:

–   whether there are any outstanding child protection issues with regard to any children with whom the alleged perpetrator is in contact;

–   whether there is any reason to suspect that the alleged perpetrator has been the victim of abuse and is in need of protection;

–   whether there is any need to provide any immediate services to the alleged perpetrator and his or her family;

–   what method of disposal is to be recommended in respect of the alleged offences.

3.9   The conference will also be required to consider the need for a comprehensive assessment in respect of the alleged perpetrator and the form that such an assessment should take. Where such an assessment has been undertaken prior to the conference the results of the assessment will provide the basis for decisions and recommendations.

3.10 Whilst the status of the conference is that of an initial child protection conference, registration of the alleged perpetrator will not normally be appropriate unless their behaviour is linked to their own abuse and the capacity of the parents to provide protection in the future is in question.

3.11 The criminal process in Greater Manchester is clear in relation to young people who are suspected of committing a sexual offence. Immediate charges can only be brought where the young person is suspected of having committed a serious sexual offence or where a remand in custody is being sought or where the young person denies the offence. In these circumstances, an initial child protection conference should be convened within 8–15 days to consider the risks that the young person may pose, issues with regard to their immediate management and any assessment work which may need to be undertaken. In all other circumstances, the police will refer the matter to the Diversionary Panel for a decision on the most appropriate disposal for the case. On receipt of such a referral the Panel will normally adjourn the matter for up to five weeks to allow for a substantive assessment and for an initial child protection conference to be held. The conference will be expected to make a recommendation with regard to disposal and a representative from the Youth Justice Team or Probation Service should always be invited. Where a prosecution is recommended, the matter will be referred back to the police for processing and the Panel advised of the outcome. Where a caution is being recommended, this will be endorsed by the Panel before being processed by the police.

3.12 Where a case is to be considered by the Diversionary Panel, any reports prepared for the initial child protection conference, together with conference minutes should be made available to the Panel and the social worker or youth justice worker responsible for the case should be invited to attend in order to represent the views of the conference.

3.13 Where it has been agreed that a comprehensive assessment or preliminary treatment work should be undertaken, the results of the assessment should be considered at a planning meeting, the purpose of which will be to review initial plans in the light of the information obtained and to formulate a co-ordinated strategy for intervention designed to reduce the likelihood of further offending and provide support to the young person and his or her family.

3.14 Where a decision is taken to include the name of the alleged perpetrator on the Child Protection Register, the process outlined in Salford's Area Child Protection Committee Child Protection Procedures should be followed in respect of subsequent assessment planning and review.

3.15 Notifications from either the Probation or Youth Justice Services with regard to young people who are charged with or convicted of sexual offences against children should be treated in the same way as other Schedule 1 notifications. Information should be entered on SOSCIS by the Child Protection Unit and the reason for referral on Screen 1 should show Code 8, 'Schedule 1 offender.'

3.16 It should be noted that under the provisions of the Sex Offenders Act 1997, young people who are cautioned or convicted for a sexual offence are subject to a registration requirement. The period of registration will normally be half that which would apply to an adult convicted of a similar offence. Where the young person receives a caution the period of registration will normally be $2^1/_2$ years.

Chapter Eight

Juveniles who Sexually Abuse:

The Relationship Between Fathers and their Sons: A Psychoanalytical View

Michael Murray

Juveniles who Sexually Abuse: The Relationship Between Fathers and their Sons: A Psychoanalytical View

Introduction

Paternal relationships among male juveniles who sexually abuse, are frequently characterised by paternal absence or the lack of paternal nurturance. For those young people who have paternal contact, the relationship with their father often lacks affection or is devoid of any attentive encouragement. These experiences go beyond the normal adolescent paternal conflicts that are equated with this period in a young person's development. The self-reported life experiences of these young people suggest that they encounter some form of paternal deprivation. Knopp (1982) first noticed this dynamic when she found that none of her subjects reported to have had a warm, close, nurturing relationship with their father.

Biller (1974) suggests that paternal deprivation is a highly significant factor in the development of serious psychological and social problems. There are, however, few recent studies that have explored paternal deprivation in the context of sexually abusive behaviour. This paper presents data from empirical research that was gathered from young sexual abusers who attended an Adolescent Psychiatric Project in Northern Ireland. This project provides a specialised service for assessing and offering therapeutic treatment to juveniles who sexually abuse. The findings are examined and explained within a psycho-dynamic framework. This particular theoretical structure is pertinent to such an investigation as it offers explanations in terms of psycho-sexual development. In addition, the attraction of such a theory places an emphasis on early parental influence and has highlighted the importance of the father/son relationship through the Oedipus Complex. A more detailed explanation and discussion of these concepts will take place later in the chapter.

It is worth noting at this early stage that the evidence presented infers that paternal deprivation is only one significant element among an array of factors which contributes to sexually abusive behaviour in young males. There is little doubt that sexually abusive behaviour is a multi-faceted phenomena which cannot be attributed to the simple equation of cause and effect. Eagle (1984) comments that, 'our behaviour, (in general) is characterised by a multiplicity of motives and aims which cannot be reduced or subordinated to one or two presumably basic underlying motive systems.' Spence (1978) makes specific reference to complexities of sexual behaviour and states that, 'sexual development involves the integration of one's self of sexuality into one's interpersonal relationship and that the integration is influenced by the demands or standards of the cultural context, sexual and interpersonal combined.'

It would therefore be misleading to suggest that paternal deprivation, per se, will lead to the development of sexually abusive behaviour. It is evident that fatherless children are not a homogenous group and an almost infinite variety of patterns and variables need to be considered when evaluating the father-absent situation.

Families

Much of the background literature gathered for this study, which informs our understanding of paternal relationships, comes from research that describes the family constellations of these young people. Due to the lack of specific reference to father/mother roles in many of these studies, the author is left to make informed deductions on specific issues related to paternal influence.

Ryan and Lane (1991) carried out a detailed study involving a thousand cases of juvenile sex offenders when they examined family function. The study highlights that parental absence was a significant factor in the life experiences of their subjects. Only 28 per cent of the juveniles were reported to be living with both natural parents at the time of their offence. 57 per cent of juveniles stated that they had experienced parental loss. Unfortunately this study does not detail how many of the absent parents were fathers and how many were mothers. For those young people who lived with both parents they highlighted experiences that are considered contra to positive role modelling. 28 per cent of the informants reported that parental violence was a major factor in family life. In terms of adverse role specific behaviour, 43 per cent reported that their fathers abused substances (alcohol and/or drugs) with 27 per cent of their mothers abusing substances (alcohol and/or drugs). In an attempt to obtain an overview of family life experiences with these young people, clinicians who had direct contact with the individual subjects were ask to give their rating on family functioning. 86 per cent of the families fell below what the clinicians would consider 'average functioning'.

In a further study carried out by Marshall and Hudson (1993), which specifically examined parent-child relationships among juvenile sexual abusers, they concluded, 'that sex offenders have a developmental history that makes them vulnerable to a variety of influences. This vulnerability we believe is driven by the failure during infancy and childhood of the parents of sex offenders to ensure that secure attachment bonds are formed between them and their children.'

Longo (1982), in a comparative study of 24 juvenile sex offenders and 24 juveniles who engaged in other forms of delinquent behaviour, who were matched for age and social class, further emphasised the significance of the parental relationship when he compared family issues. He found that family instability, psychiatric disturbance and unsatisfactory parent child relationships were more common characteristics in the sex offenders group. This research also revealed that parental absence was a factor in the subject's life experience. 79 per cent of the sexual offenders reported long-term separations from at least one parent (there is no available data on which parent was absent). In supporting previous findings on family functioning, 36 per cent of his subjects reported that they experienced their mothers to be rejecting and 63 per cent of the fathers were seen as rejecting. 26 per cent of the mothers and 50 per cent of the fathers were seen as emotionally detached from the young people.

Paternal Relationships

The evidence gathered from the available family research has given route towards exploring the relationship between young people who sexually abuse and their fathers. To date, there has been little detailed work in the field of juveniles who sexually abuse and which has concentrated on the significance of the paternal role. This apparent lack of interest in exploring paternal relationships may have been as a consequence of our preoccupation with understanding the maternal role in child development. Anna Freud and Dorothy Burlington (1944) argued this phenomenon, when they examined the rationale of providing only mother substitutes to the children, when they where evacuated during the Second World War. They criticised the authorities for focusing on maternal separation and wondered why the role of the father had been ignored. They asked why this 'conspicuous fact' had not received more attention or 'created more concern regarding the normality of the child's upbringing'.

Studies that have focused on paternal relationships demonstrate that the criticisms that Anna Freud and Dorothy Burlington (1944) levied where well founded. There is evidence to suggest a clear correlation between the nature of the paternal relationship and the manifestation of certain types of characteristics and behaviour in children. Moulton et al. (1964) commented that, 'the infants emotional relationship to its father...is an integral part of its emotional life and a necessary ingredient in the complex forces which work towards the formations of its character and personality.' He went on to state, 'that paternal discipline when combined with a high level of paternal affection, is strongly associated with male child's sensitivity to their moral transgressions. The father who is able to firmly set limits and can be affectionate and responsive to his child's needs seems to be a particularly good model for interpersonal sensitivity and moral development'.

It is also understood that the secure attachment to the father provides for the growing child a view of others that is affectionate and empathetic, which instils a desire for, and the skills necessary to, achieve intimacy with peers. It is assumed that this security and strength that is present in relationships between parent and child can be an effective basis for predicting stable adjustments.

Rutherford *et al.* (1968) reported evidence indicating that nursery school boys who perceived their father as warm and nurturing are likely to be generous with other children. They also revealed that positive paternal relationships were associated with successful peer interactions and self-confidence among adolescent peers.

Biller (1974) states that, 'the father is an important model for his child. The father's positive involvement facilitates the development of the boy's cognitive functioning, self concept, his ability to control his impulses and to function independently and responsibly and his overall interpersonal competence'. He goes on to suggest that, 'for boys, the presence of a masculine father, a positive father son relationship generates appropriate sex behaviour. The absence of a warm, affectionate relationship with an adult male, during which mutual enjoyment of sex typed interests and activities take place can seriously interfere with the boys social development.'

Much of the father's influence is related to the impact it has on the boy's sex role development. When the boy has a warm relationship with a masculine and competent father, he is well on his way to learning how to master his social and physical environment. His ability to understand the outside world, to plan for the future and to cope with crises can all be facilitated by his experiences with his father.

These studies confirm that when a male child has a positive experience of his father, then he develops the necessary personal characteristics that tend to support the development of behaviour that make it unlikely for the young person to abuse others. Equally, when the male child's experience of the relationship with their father is negative, then there emerges a greater possibility that the young person will be more likely to abuse.

Turnell (1968) in an examination of the files in child guidance clinics found that both father absence and inadequate sex role development are much more common among disturbed children than in the general population. In a further examination of children at an out-patient clinic, he found that the severity of psychopathology varied with the length of father absence and the age of onset of the father's absence. The younger the child at the onset of this absence the more serious the psychopathology. Oltman *et al.* (1967), in an examination of adult patients conferred that the effects of paternal absence could have effects that go beyond adolescence when he found particularly high rates of childhood father absence among adults who had chronically disturbed personalities and inadequate moral development.

Hoffman (1971) gave further insight into the effects of paternal deprivation on children when reported on the conscience development of seventh grade children. He found that father absent boys consistently scored lower than father present boys in a variety of moral indexes. They scored lower on measures of internal moral judgement, guilt following transgressions, acceptance of blame, moral values and rule conformity. In addition they were rated as higher in aggression by their teachers, which may also reflect difficulties in self-control. Although the influence was less clear cut, weak father identification among father present boys was related to less adequate conscience development. Boys with strong father identification scored higher on the measures of internal moral judgement, moral values and conformity to rules than did boys with low father identification.

Johnson (1987) argues that the impact of an inadequate paternal relationship is much greater in determining delinquent behaviour for both boys and girls than an inadequate maternal relationship. He comments that, 'for both boys and girls, distance from father is more predictive of theft, vandalism, and assault than is the distance from mother. Even though a youth's relationship with mother is generally more emotionally satisfying, there seem to be aspects of father's role that supersede affection in influencing delinquency.' Stern *et al.* (1984) suggested that the father serves as the prime teaching and deterrent force in the family through his roles of value transmitter and disciplinarian. Presumably, a more distant father would be less effective in fulfilling these functions.

In his experience as a psychotherapist, Meerloo (1956) found that a lack of accurate time perception, which is often associated with difficulties in self control, is common among father absent individuals. He assumed that the father represents social order and that his adherence to time schedules gives the child an important lesson in social functioning. The paternally deprived boy may find it very difficult to follow the rules of society. Antisocial acts are often impulsive as well as aggressive and there is evidence that the inability to delay gratification is associated with inaccurate time perception, lack of social responsibility, low achievement motivation and juvenile delinquency.

While these studies do not entirely concentrate on juveniles who sexually abuse, they do elicit characteristics and behaviour that are found to be common in these young people. Personal traits such as insensitivity, lack of empathy, poor self concept, impulsivity, aggression, inadequate conscience development are all found to be relevant in male children as a consequence of father absence or lack of paternal warmth. Behaviours such as delinquency, poor interaction with peers, and inappropriate sexual behaviour are found to be influenced by father absence and the lack of paternal warmth. It was within this context, that the inquiry in to the specific correlation between paternal relationships and young people who sexually abuse was undertaken.

Methodology

The study was carried out at the Young People's Centre, Belfast. This is a multi-disciplinary Adolescent Psychiatric Unit, that provides in-patient and out-patient treatment for adolescents who have a mental illness or emotional disturbance. A specialist team was set up within the unit to work with the growing numbers of referrals that were received, concerning young people who had sexually abused. A partnership arrangement between the Young People's Centre and Barnardo's was agreed, resulting in two senior practitioners being appointed to undertake this work.

The inspiration for this inquiry came from comments that young people made during a therapeutic group which focused on their abusive behaviour. The young people talked at length about their attitudes and experiences concerning their relationship with their father. All of the members in the group reported to have experienced either paternal absence or had considered their father to be emotionally distant. Given this universality, it was decided to carry out an investigation into the significance and meaning of this phenomenon.

The files of 18 young people who attended the adolescent sexual abusers programme for treatment in 1994 were examined. As a document, the files contain detailed biographical information about the young person. The strong systemic theoretical and professional practice in the unit meant that detailed accounts of family relationships were recorded in the files. Genograms along with the practitioners written descriptive accounts of family relationships were examined to extract the relevant data. These written records are long and detailed, as many of the young people who attended were receiving long-term therapeutic intervention.

A formula was developed in order to collect the data from each of the files. Factual information such as the age of the young person, who made the referral, where they lived, their relationship with the victim, category of offence, the nature of their abuse and their experience of victimisation was recorded. The information on their relationship with their father was categorised by recording if their father was absent or present. If their father was reported to be absent, then details of the absence was recorded, such as when and how long the absence was for. For those young people whose father was present, their experience of that relationship was recorded. Finally, written extracts were taken from the files where the young people had commented on their paternal relationship, particularly their self evaluation of this relationship.

Results

Subjects

The eighteen subjects for this study were all white, adolescent males, aged between 14 and 19. They were referred by general medical practitioners, social workers, probation officers, educational psychologists and psychiatrists who had serious concerns about their sexual behaviour. Using a system of categorisations, developed by Ryan and Lane (1991) (as outlined overleaf) each of the young peoples' sexual behaviour was classified by means of a behaviour/response.

Normal sexual behaviours

- Explicit sexual discussion amongst peers, use of sexual swear words, obscene jokes.
- Interest in erotic material and its use in masturbation.
- Expression through sexual innuendo, flirtations and courtship behaviours.
- Mutual consenting non-coital sexual behaviour (kissing, fondling).
- Mutual consenting masturbation.
- Mutual consenting sexual intercourse.

Behaviours that suggest monitoring, limited response or assessment

- Sexual preoccupation/anxiety.
- Use of hard core pornography.
- Indiscriminate sexual activity/intercourse.
- Twinning of sexuality and aggression.
- Sexual graffiti relating to individuals or having disturbing content.
- Single occurrences of exposure, peeping, frottage or obscene telephone calls.

Behaviours that suggest assessment/intervention

- Compulsive masturbation if chronic or public.
- Persistent or aggressive attempts to expose others genitals.
- Chronic use of pornography with sadistic or violent themes.
- Sexually explicit conversations with significantly younger children.
- Touching another's genitals without permission.
- Sexually explicit threats.

Behaviours that require a legal response, assessment and treatment

- Persistent obscene phone calls, voyeurism, exhibitionism or frottage.
- Sexual contact with significantly younger children.
- Forced sexual assault and rape.
- Inflicting genital injury.
- Sexual contact with animals.

All subjects for this research exhibited behaviours that required an assessment as they exhibited sexual behaviours that went beyond societal norms. The subjects were drawn from all those who received individual psychotherapeutic treatment.

This method of selecting subjects has disadvantages, as the criteria for selection is met with many pre-conditions. Firstly, as with most crimes involving a sexual act, it is accepted that only a small percentage are reported. This under reporting is as true for the under estimation of victims as it is for the under estimation of perpetrators. Secondly, the subjects had to be referred to this specialist unit which necessitates a referral from a statutory agency; they had met the criteria of referral set by the Young People's Centre such as appropriate geographical area and age. Thirdly, each subject had to accept on a voluntary basis the desire for therapeutic intervention.

Age

The mean age of the subjects was 16 years old: 40 per cent were aged between 12 and 16 and considered to be in their early adolescence and 60 per cent were aged between 16 and 19 and considered to be in their late adolescence.

Referral

Some 61 per cent of the young people were referred by social services agencies in the Eastern Health and Social Services Board Area. This followed decisions taken at a Child Protection Case Conference to refer the young person for a specialist assessment. In addition 16 per cent of the young people were referred by the Probation Board for Northern Ireland. All of these young people have appeared in court and received treatment under a 4th condition of a probation order. This is an additional condition that is attached to the normal three conditions that form a probation order. The consequences for the young person are that if they fail to comply with treatment then they are in breach of their order. Of the remainder 11 per cent of the subjects were referred directly by their general medical practitioner. The police, from the Royal Ulster Constabulary's, Child Abuse and Rape Enquiries (C.A.R.E.) unit referred 11 per cent of cases to the programme. These followed criminal investigations.

Residence

It was found that 83 per cent of the young people were living at home at the time of the abuse whilst 5.5 per cent lived with a blood relative following a family breakdown. One of the subjects lived in long term foster care. One of the subjects was living in residential care at the time of his offence.

Relationship of abuser to abused

In 34.7 per cent, victims were 'females not known to the abuser'. These would be incidents in which there would have been 'hands on' abuse, with one case involving rape. Others involved exposure and obscene phone calls. In 66 per cent of cases the victim was known to the abuser. In 6.9 per cent of cases the victim was the abuser's brother and in 2.7 per cent of cases the victim was the abuser's sister. Thus in 9.6 per cent of cases the victim belonged to the same nuclear family as the abuser. The results showed that when we take account of gender, 62.4 per cent of victims were of the same sex as the abuser.

Category of the offence

In 66.7 per cent of cases there was no criminal prosecution. This was due to the lack of corroborative evidence or no police investigation having been instigated. The process between an incident being reported and going to court was thwarted with many inconsistent and subjective actions, on the part of professionals, that it does not reflect the severity of the abusive act that took place. For those cases that did go to court, in 16.6 per cent of cases the young person was charged with 'gross indecency' and for 11.2 per cent the charge was of 'indecent assault'. There was one case in which the young person was charged with rape.

Nature of abuse

Some 26.7 per cent of the young people admitted to fondling their victim. Exhibitionism or exposure was the main reason for referral in 20 per cent of cases.

Masturbation of the abuser by victim occurred in 9.9 per cent of the cases. Oral sex on victim refers to such behaviour as forced fellatio on male victims and cunnilingus on female victims. In one case (3.3 per cent) the abuser forced his penis into the victims mouth. There was one case involving digital penetration. Violent anal intercourse was the main form of abuse in 3.3 per cent of cases. The one case of forced vaginal intercourse refers to an abuser raping a young female victim. Frottage, which refers to sexually rubbing up against another person without their knowledge or consent for sexual gratification was the main reason for referral in 3.3 per cent of cases.

Abusers as victims

In 50 per cent of the cases, the young person had been physically abused as defined by the Eastern Health and Social Services Child Protection guidelines. In 16 per cent of these cases, the perpetrator was the natural father, in 5.5 per cent it was the mother and in 22 per cent of cases recorded it was the step-father. In 27 per cent of cases there was confirmed evidence of sexual abuse against the young person as defined under the Eastern Health and Social Services Child Protection guidelines. In 16.6 per cent of cases the perpetrator was the young person's father and in 22 per cent it was by a perpetrator outside the nuclear family.

In one case the subject showed clinical signs of having been sexually abused and was registered under the Child Protection Register under the category of Suspected Sexual Abuse by social services. The category of Suspected, Physical, Emotional or Sexual Abuse is used for the Child Protection Register in Northern Ireland. In 17 per cent of cases there was no record that the abuser had been physically or sexually abused.

Father-son relationship

The results indicate that in all cases, none of these young people reported to have experienced a warm, close, nurturing relationship with their natural fathers. In 56 per cent of cases the young people reported that their father had abandoned the family when they were young children. The term abandonment refers to 'a total desertion' where there is no ongoing direct or indirect contact. These young people stated that they did not know or cannot recall anything about their natural father. In 50 per cent of cases the young person reported that their father had been physically abusive towards them. In 18 per cent of cases, the subjects had been sexually abused by their father. The sexual abuse was confirmed in 16.6 per cent of cases where the young person had given evidence in court that resulted in their father serving a prison sentence. In 11 per cent of cases, the young person's father had died. In one case this was a result of a poisoning after deliberately taking 'weed killer'. In the other case, death was a result of cirrhosis of the liver due to chronic alcohol abuse. In both of these cases it is assumed that the young person's father experienced emotional disturbance long before death occurred. In the two cases (11 per cent) where the father was present, the young people reported that their relationship with their father was fraught with conflict. This was due in one case to regular physical punishment and an over authoritative controlling regime in the other.

Extracts:

The following is a list of extracts taken from each of the clinical notes that describe aspects of the father-son relationship. Some of these notes are taken from the therapist's own description, while others are a monograph of what the patient or his mother stated.

Case 1 'Father left home when I was 3. I have looked for him but haven't been able to find him. I admire my father and would like to be like him.'

Case 2 'I missed him being there. Dad never got his act together. My dad has been in prison most of my life, since I was a few months old. I have fears about being a dad…would I be good enough.'

Case 3 'Father was dictatorial, extremely controlling, verbally and physically aggressive. He witnessed his father having sexual intercourse with his mother, which could be described as violent rape. P said that his behaviour towards L (his sister) had been prompted by the fact that his father had done something similar to him. P, himself, is now of

the opinion that his offending behaviour has much to do with having seen his father having sexual intercourse with his mother as well as experiencing abuse at his fathers hands.'

Case 4 'His father whom he can't remember died when he was 10 after drinking weed killer.'

Case 5 'His stepfather left for London for 2 years and never in that time did he have any contact. During this separation A found out that his dad was not his biological dad and the relationship with his sister deteriorated around this time. A is saying that he is anxious to know who his natural father is, he is angry a little with his biological father for not coming to see him and is suspicious of who he is. The assault and the splitting and the acting out in school could be perceived as angry acts and I wondered if there was any angry feelings connected with A's knowledge of his dad.'

Case 6 'I have never known my dad — I have missed out on a dad. M has five siblings all of which have different fathers.'

Case 7 'Mrs W feels G is terrified of his father — he has returned to Northern Ireland from Scotland since Christmas. Mrs W is concerned that G has been sexually abused by his father. He was sexually violent towards Mrs W and G had witnessed a lot of violence towards her. His parents were separated when he was 6 and it was only then that the bed wetting stopped.'

Case 8 'He described himself as being very angry with him. His father separated a couple of months previously and took J with him. This occurred at a time when his mother found sexually explicit written material in his room. 'I hate school. I would run away on a boat with a girl. I would have sex every night. I would kiss her and if I got fed up I would kill her then turn mad and kill everyone in that place'. On the 20/4/95 social services called a strategy meeting as J was physically assaulted by his father.

Case 9 'B shares a bedroom with his mother and father. He has a difficult relationship with his father. 'Dad calls me stupid, he feels that I can't do anything right.' Getting away from home would mean that Dad wouldn't be able to shout at him 'dopey and stupid.' He sees himself like his father. Mrs B stated that she feels that it is her husband's fault that B has talked dirty in the past as her husband often uses language and talks about girls in a sexual manner.'

Case 10 'S has never seen his dad. Mum left because he was an alcoholic and because he had sexually abused his sister.'

Case 11 'P's dad was an alcoholic and died of cirrhosis of the liver. He was extremely violent towards his mother. 'My dad once lined us all against a wall, loaded his gun and threatened to kill us all.'

Case 12 'D has had no contact with his natural dad. He was abandoned by his father at birth and expressed no wish to know who he is.'

Case 13 'I never knew my dad and have never asked mum about him.'

Case 14 'G is angry towards his mother for ruining everything. He wanted to retaliate for his father by punishing his mother. He wants to see his father more.'

Case 15 'Father has had multiple relationships and just seems to walk away. Father last week brought an 18-year old boy home and introduced him to R as his brother. He has lived in the house ever since. Father has been admitted to a psychiatric hospital with several suicide attempts since 1993.'

Case 16 'Parents marriage was annulled when 2 years old after his father left for Canada. 'I was told it was a good relationship. In 1992 I went to Canada to see him and had a brilliant time.'

Case 17 'Natural father was a soldier. I never seen him and didn't know about him until my mother told me when she was getting divorced that my step father was not my real father.'

Case 18 Father and mother divorced and went to live in England. Later the father adopted three children, one of which he sexually abused.

Discussion

This study clearly illustrates connections between male juvenile sexual abusers and the relationship they have with their father. In these eighteen case histories, none of the young people reported to have had a close, warm, nurturing relationship with their fathers. This confirmed the previous findings of Knopp (1982). In essence, the relationship these fathers had with their sons was characterised by either physical or emotional absence during their formative years. The young people experienced abandonment, physical abuse, sexual abuse or were emotionally distant from their father.

The theory of psychoanalysis offers an insight into the meaning of paternal deprivation and how this can be a crucial factor in the development of sexual deviation. The theories developed from Freudian teachings illustrate the significance of early sexual development in childhood and argue that any major disruption in this process can lead to sexual deviation. These signs are seen in early adolescence, when it is understood that a re-awakening of sexual energy, which originated in childhood, takes place. While such a theory may not be favoured by many practitioners working with male juvenile sexually abusers, it does offer insights that can help us all understand this complex behaviour.

Psychoanalysis from its inception has endeavoured to provide us with a theoretical framework in which we can understand psycho-sexual behaviour. While a lot of Freud's theoretical positions changed in other aspects of his work, this is not the case in his work on sexuality. His assumption that children are sexual beings may be difficult to conceptualise but there is clear support for his view that children have sexual experiences. He is forceful in this assumption and proclaims that 'one view of the sexual instinct, is that it is absent in childhood and only awakens in the period of life described as puberty. This, however, is not merely a simple error but one that has grave consequences, for it is mainly to this idea that we base our present ignorance of the fundamentals of sexual life.' With human sexuality as its central theme, psychoanalysis provides us with a detailed structure of psycho-sexual development. From a Freudian perspective this is marked out in the five definitive stages of the oral, anal, phallic, latent and genital.

While Freud's work seems complex and confusing at times there are two important components that arise from his sexual theories. The first is biological and the second is environmental. Whilst his biological theories have been questioned and disputed over the years, his environmental theories, particularly in relation to the parent–child relationship have remained the cornerstone of his work. His interpersonal theories and his observations of parent-child interactions have all remained credible.

Freud told us that parents have the greatest possible influence on children's development and in response, children create and develop psychic structure. He asserted that this is such a powerful and influential experience, that events and behaviours in later life can be traced back to the effects of these interactions, which occur during critical periods throughout childhood. Bowlby (1969) later supported this concept and was enthusiastic to highlight the importance of the parent-child relationship, particularly to early experiences. In his 'Attachment Theory' he stated that 'the capacity to form intimate relationships in adolescence and adulthood is understood to be largely dependent on early infant and childhood attachments.'

Psychoanalytical work has been renowned for the comments made on the importance of maternal attachments during early childhood. Melanie Klien, in her analytical work with very young children gave detailed descriptions of the first year of life which led to a greater awareness of the mothers role in psycho-sexual development. Klien did not negate the relevance of the father in this process with her attention to paternity forming part of her major theoretical contributions to psychoanalysis. She stated that fathers, like mothers, provide a model for the child. A father by his behaviour may reassure the child that firmness, authority and love can mutually coexist. Where a child is trying to create his or her identity without a good parental model, he or she may experience considerable difficulty. In the absence of a good father, children will create a fantasy, often based on views of a father at the age at which they were when he left. Their anger towards this abandoning father may make the negative fantasies very frightening. Fathers are often the focus of the child's destructive fantasies. Fathers, in Klien's view, are often more important to children than people often recognise.

The most notable and perhaps the most influential psychoanalytical theoretical position that explains the importance of the father-son relationship comes from Freud. The main theoretical reference for the investigation of this phenomena is to be found in the Oedipus Complex which occurs during the phallic stage of development. Freud discovered the Oedipus Complex in his self-analysis, which led him to conclude, that children have sexual impulses, thoughts and fantasies. From its inception, the importance of the Oedipal complex is so fundamental that Freud called it the 'core complex' or the 'nuclear complex'. In the Three Essays on Sexuality (1920) he made it clear that the Oedipus Complex is the immovable foundation stone on which the whole edifice of psychoanalysis is based. Freud (1920) states, that 'it represents the peak of infantile sexuality, which, through its after effects, exercises a decisive influence on the sexuality of adults. Every new arrival on this planet is faced with the task of mastering the Oedipus Complex; anyone who fails to do so falls victim to neurosis.' With the progression of psychoanalytic studies, the importance of the Oedipus complex has become more clearly evident; its recognition has become the shibboleth that distinguishes the adherents of psychoanalysis from its opponents.

The Oedipus Complex has come to represent the most critical period of development through which male children must pass. The term Oedipus refers to the ancient story set down by Sophocles about Oedipus Rex. In summary, the story is about the king who is foretold that his son Oedipus would grow up and kill him. The king wanted the boy disposed of, but rather than have him killed, he sent Oedipus to a foreign land. When Oedipus matured, he became a strong warrior and travelled to seek his fortune. He had an encounter during one of his journey stranger he killed. This stranger turned out to be his father. Later in the story Oedipus ends up marrying the queen who in fact is his mother. This story, like many from Greek mythology, has endured over time and has provided the main plot for such classic literature as Hamlet.

In relating this to child development, the theory advocates that the basic conflict of the phallic stage is represented in the Oedipus Complex. When the boy is 3–5 years old, he is sexually attracted to his mother. This centres on the unconscious incestuous desires that children develop for the parent of the opposite sex (a desire that is said to be stronger in male children). The type of sexuality that becomes evident during the phallic stage does not necessarily refer to the child's desire for sexual intercourse with the parent of the opposite sex, which is perhaps one of the most frequently misunderstood terms in Freud's theory of sexuality. Although the boy's feelings towards his mother are erotically tinged, this kind of sexuality is more diffuse than sexual intercourse and the child's concept of actual sexual intercourse is often undefined. This excitement and its demand for gratification are inextricably linked with his first and continuing love object, his mother, and so he wishes to take the place of his father in her life. However, being small and vulnerable his powerful father blocks his way. Any hopes that he has of possessing his mother are dashed by the threat of castration and its inevitable consequent anxiety. And so, over a period of years, he struggles to control his oedipal wishes, and will succeed, without severe damage to his masculinity, if he can learn that his sexual wishes for his mother can be deferred, to be played out on another female in later life. As this process evolves, the boys recognition of his father's greater power, coupled with his fear that his father will retaliate, generates intolerable conflict, which is resolved by renouncing the mother and identifying with the father. These feelings are of such a threatening nature they are repressed but are powerful determinants of later sexual development and adjustment. Freud postulated that the boy's identification with the father made strong by his castration fears has a number of consequences, the most notable of which is to bring about the assumption of the father's moral values. In a sense, it is a matter of realising that if he cannot beat his father he might as well join him. Through this identification with his father, the boy experiences vicarious satisfaction. He becomes more like his father and he may adopt many of his fathers mannerisms. This defence identification leads the boy to adopt masculine characteristics as exhibited by his father. These are internalised values that are the standards set by society for males. Identification with the father thus provides the impetus for the development of the boy's super-ego or conscience.

Of all the stages in child development, this undoubtedly is the most crucial when it comes to understanding sexual behaviour. It is during this period of psychosexual development that curiosity about sexual matters, sexual fantasies, sex role identification patterns and sex play emerge. Masturbation, accompanied by sexual fantasies, is normal at this stage of the child's development. Children become curious about their bodies, they desire to explore them and to discover differences between the sexes. Childhood experimentation is common, and, as many attitudes toward sexuality originate in the phallic period, the acceptance of sexuality and the management of sexual impulses are vital at this time. During this period the conscience develops and the children learn moral standards. In essence, during this period children are forming attitudes about physical pleasure; what is right and wrong, what is masculine and feminine.

If the Oedipal conflict is properly resolved, the boy replaces his sexual longing for his mother with more acceptable forms of affection. With passing, the turbulence of the first expression of the Oedipus complex and the combined stresses of the oral, anal and the phallic stage of psychosexual development, the individual can enjoy a period of relative rest. The major structures of personality (id, ego and superego) are largely formed by this time. The post Oedipal child is believed to express the components sexual instinct, oral, anal and phallic, and is prepared at an unconscious level for sex appropriate aims and object choices in adulthood.

It is understood that if a child does not successfully negotiate the 'Oedipus complex', it can give rise to psychological disturbance or inappropriate sexual behaviour. Anna Freud (1972) states that 'from their patients, they (psychoanalysts) had learned, that every adult neurosis was preceded by a childhood neurosis and that the emotionally stormy conflicts of the phallic-oedipal period, that is the Oedipal Complex, and the problems attached to its resolution, formed the core of both infantile and adult neurotic disturbance'. Chasseguet-Smirgel (1985) stated that one of the big risks of not resolving the Oedipal Complex is the 'risk of believing one can be an adult without growing up emotionally'.

Psychoanalysts place much importance on the Oedipal Complex to explain many forms of difficult behaviour. It is therefore appropriate to focus on this period of development in the lives of young people who sexually abuse. This small and limited piece of empirical research does support a hypothesis that suggests that sexually abusive behaviour in young males can be linked to unresolved issues from the Oedipal period.

Conclusions

The juvenile who sexually abuses presents society and those who are charged with correcting this behaviour with many dilemmas. One of the most fundamental being the ability to understand the cause of such behaviour (see Epps' review of causation in Chapter 1). This paper has attempted to understand one of the crucial dynamics in the life experiences of these young people. Their experience of paternal deprivation, particularly in childhood, in whatever form, must play a crucial role in their subsequent sexually abusive behaviour.

Whatever contribution this paper makes towards opening up the debate on the relationship between juvenile sex abusers and their fathers, the key question to be answered is: 'Was Freud right when he stated, 'that the absence of a strong father in childhood not infrequently favours the occurrence of inversions'.

References

Biller, H. (1974). *Paternal Deprivation*. Lexington, MA: Lexington Books.

Bowlby, J. (1969). *Attachment and Loss*. New York, Basic Books.

Burlington, D., and Freud, A. (1944). *Infants Without Families*. London: George, Allen & Unwin.

Chasseguet-Smirgel, J. (1985). *Creativity and Perversion*. Free Association Books.

Eagle, M.N. (1984). *Recent Developments in Psychoanalysis*. McGraw-Hill Books.

Freud, A. (1972). The Infantile Neurosis: Genetic and Dynamic Considerations. In *Problems of Psychoanalytical Technique and Therapy*, 1966-1970. London: Hogarth.

Freud, S. (1920). *On Sexuality*. Penguin Books (published 1977).

Hoffman, M.L. (1971). Father Absence and Conscience Development. *Developmental Psychology* (a) 400–406.

Johnson, R. (1987). Mother Versus Father's Role in Causing Delinquency. *Adolescence*, 66: 304–316

Klien, M. (1952). The Origin of Transference. *International Journal of Psychoanalysis*, 33: 433–438.

Knopp, F. (1982). *The Youthful Sex Offender*. NY: Safer Society Press.

Longo, R.E. (1982). Sexual Learning and Experience Among Adolescent Sexual Offenders. *International Journal of Offender Therapy and Comparative Criminology*, 26(3): 235–241.

Marshall, W., and Hudson, S. (1993). The Importance of Attachment Bonds. In Barbaree, H. Marshall, W., and Hudson, S. (Eds) *The Juvenile Sex Offender*. NY: Guilford Press.

Meerloo, J.M. (1956). *The Father Cuts the Cord: The Role of the Father as Initial Transference* Figure. *American Journal of Psychotherapy*, 10:, 471–480.

Moulton, P.W, Burnstein, E., Liberty, D., and Altucher, N. (1964). The Patterning of Paternal Affection and Dominance as a Determinant Guilt and Sex Typing. *Journal of Personality and Social Psychology*, 363–365.

Oltman, J.E., and Friedman, S. (1967). Parental Deprivation in Psychiatric Conditions in Personality Disorders and Other Conditions. *Diseases of the Nervous System*, 28: 298–303.

Rutherford, E., and Mussen, P. Generosity in Nursery School Boys. *Child Development*, 39: 755–765.

Ryan, G., and Lane, S. (Eds.) (1991). *Juvenile Sex Offending: Causes Consequences and Corrections*. Lexington, MA: Lexington Books.

Spence, J. (1978). *Masculinity and Femininity*. NY: Universal Press

Stern, M., Northman, J.E., and Van Slyck, M.R. (1984). Father-absence and Adolescent Problem Behaviours: Alcohol Consumption, Drug Use, and Sexual Activity. *Adolescence*, 19: 301–312.

Turnell, T.L. (1968). The Absent Father's Children's Emotional Disturbance. *Archives of General Psychiatry*, 19: 180–188

Acknowledgements

I wish to thank Dr. Ewen McEwen and the staff at the Young People's Centre for their encouragement in undertaking this research. To Mandy Coleman who was a close and supportive colleague. To Raman Kapur, whose clinical supervision and encouragement helped me make the links between psychoanalytical theory and practice.

Chapter Nine

A Description of a Community-based Project to Work with Young People who Sexually Abuse

Dr. Rachel Leheup and Steve Myers

A Description of a Community-based Project to Work with Young People who Sexually Abuse

Introduction

The issue of sexual offending/abuse by young people is one which has engaged childcare and criminal justice workers for a relatively short period of time. Barbaree *et al.* (1993) conducted a literature search and identified that prior to 1970, only 9 major papers were published on this issue. In the 1970s, 10 further papers were published but between 1981-85, 28 papers appeared followed by a further 60 up to 1993. The vast majority of these were based on information from the United States and it is only in the 1990s that any significant body of information has been developed in the United Kingdom. Projects, consultancies, protocols, procedures and conferences have since mushroomed all to deal with the problem of young people who commit sexual abusive acts (Masson, 1995).

The research highlighted several important issues of concern. There was a recognition that up to one third of all sexual assaults on children were committed by young people under the age of eighteen (Finkelhor, 1996). It was also found that the range of sexual aggressive behaviours mirrored that of adults (Ryan, 1988) and that there was a tendency to minimise some of these behaviours as adolescent experimentation (Ryan, 1986).

This chapter will describe the Thorneywood Project for young people who sexually abuse. We will explore the rationale for establishing it; the theoretical and research base informing it; the practice undertaken and information on the young people who attended.

Rationale for Establishment of the Project

The establishment of projects to work with any discrete group of people is predicated on identified need. The Child and Adolescent Psychiatric Services have for many years assessed and worked with young people who exhibit sexually abusive behaviour within the general client population and this is true of the Thorneywood Unit. The specific interests of the staff team had led to involvement in this area and the development of a local perception of expertise in providing services by child care agencies, general practitioners and the courts. These services included court reports, therapeutic intervention, consultancy and training.

Nottinghamshire has, like many other local authorities, been increasingly aware of the issue of young people who sexually abuse, in part due to high-profile cases, but also due to a general raising of concern, particularly since the publication of the NCH report in 1992. Changes in child protection procedures were introduced following the publication of the Department of Health guidance in the document 'Working Together' in 1991. This highlighted concerns about young people who sexually abuse and identified the need for services for this group, including assessment and intervention. In particular the need for a multi-agency approach was identified, partly based on existing good practice in child protection decision-making.

Structure of the Project

Planning for the Project began in 1995 and led to the appointment of a half-time project worker funded by the Nottingham Health Authority Health Investment Programme (HIP). This worker was located within the Child Mental Health Service for Nottingham. The functions of the worker included direct work with young people and their families; managing the database on referrals; co-ordinating a core group of people from the multi-disciplinary sector teams in this service who were interested in giving some time to the Project; liaising with potential referrers (mostly social workers) and attending case conferences. The project worker has a background in the probation service and the NSPCC.

Referrals for the Project were invited from any source. This could be from professional agencies or self-referrals in line with general child mental health approaches. Information about the Project was disseminated through the Area and District Child Protection Committees and also through the existing networks developed by the core group members. The only criteria were geographic; the children/young people had to be under 18 and there had to be an allegation of sexually abusive behaviour. No guidelines were given for defining this behaviour to maximise referrals.

The core group consists of two consultant child and adolescent psychiatrists; one social worker and one clinical nurse specialist. Previous experience of working with sexually abusive young people was varied and therefore the core group recognised the need to establish a shared knowledge and value base within which to assess and work with the young people and their families.

Theoretical and Research Base

To provide an effective service considerable effort was spent in exploring the theoretical and research base of the problem. This was felt to be central to the proper functioning of the Project and, particularly given the nature of some of the statements being made about young people who sexually abuse, it was felt important to be clear exactly what the original research was claiming.

The Project holds a philosophical view which is child centred and locates young people in their familial and social structures, with an acceptance that childhood is a period of dynamic change influenced by these environmental features. This position may appear innocuous, yet it made the acceptance of some of the conclusions from research problematic.

There is a growing amount of literature on young sexual abusers which has informed policy and practice. Research in this area seems to have challenged established assumptions about working with problematic behaviour. In particular, the following specific conclusions have been drawn which have dominated the approach to these young people:

- Recidivism is to be expected.

- Abusive acts will escalate in seriousness over time.

- Specific treatment, usually cognitive-behavioural group work, is necessary to prevent the behaviour continuing.

The above issues clearly impact on the management of these young people and have influenced the development of policies and practices in the UK. The creation of the above points has led to a drive to identify and treat all those young people who exhibit sexually inappropriate behaviour on the premise that any demonstration of such behaviour indicates an inevitable progression to an adult career in sexual offending.

Publications such as the NCH Report (1992) have highlighted this perceived difference between sexual abusers and other anti-social behaviour by young people. The construction of sexual offending in this context appears to be based on models of explaining adult abusive behaviour. The initial findings of working with adult abusers were indeed stark, indicating that this behaviour was entrenched, progressive and compulsive and that it had a genesis in adolescence (e.g. Abel *et al.*, 1985). The research on adult abusers is often cited as evidence for a more intensive and intrusive approach to young abusers, couched in language such as 'breaking the cycle of abuse', 'correcting deviant thought patterns' and 'preventing future victims'. This language may indicate a genuine anxiety about the prognosis for young people and the need to intervene to prevent an otherwise inevitable future life as an abuser. It is also a very powerful discourse, which responds poorly to challenge and is rigid in its application, as it has as its central premise the sole knowledge of how to prevent future child abuse, with all the moral authority ascribed to this 'truth'. One of the consequences of this discourse has been the development of programmes of intervention which have been functional in their intent and content. The abusive behaviour becomes the prime definer of that young person which can only be corrected through cognitive-behavioural approaches. Focus is on dealing with that visible and measurable abusive behaviour and its supporting attitudes. This compartmentalisation of the behaviour has led to the minimisation of, for example, the victim status of many of these young people as this is seen as less of a priority than managing the abusive behaviour. This approach potentially excludes or devalues any holistic method of working as being ineffective or irrelevant.

It also implies a homogeneity to all abusers in their motivation for and understanding of the behaviour they exhibit, which allows for the application of discrete models of intervention. Assessment is often seen in terms of fitting an expected pattern of behaviour or having particular personality traits which does not allow for the unexpected nor the developing, changeable nature of young peoples' personalities.

These general assumptions about working with young sexual abusers needed to be explored by the Project to be clear that the more holistic and multi-model approach already established in work with other young people could be effective with this client group.

Recidivism

It has earlier been identified that one of the assumptions was that young people who exhibit inappropriate sexual behaviour will go on to re-abuse and that this is to be expected. However, the research base for this is less clear on investigation. For example, the NCH Report (1992) states that most workers in this field believe that young people go on to re-offend, but accepts that there is little evidence to substantiate this. There has been little research on following cohorts of young people who have abused through time to identify recidivism. Where there has been an attempt, the recidivism rate has been remarkably low when compared with other offending behaviour (e.g. Smith, 1984; Smith and Monastersky, 1986; Davis and Leitenberg, 1987 and Furby *et al.*, 1989).

Recidivism tracking is fraught with difficulties as we are aware of the problems of disclosure around sexual abuse. However, this leaves us with the worst-case scenario that young people who sexually abuse may go on to repeat their behaviour, rather than the assumption that this is inevitable. The notion of likely recidivism seems to have stemmed from work with adult offenders, where retrospective studies were pointing to some (though not the majority) of the adult offenders beginning their abuse in adolescence.

Conclusions were drawn from this that a large percentage of abusive young people would progress to being adult offenders. There are methodological problems with this as retrospective studies cannot take into account those young people who abused but then did not go on to be adult abusers. The translation of retrospective study conclusions into longitudinal expectations is not a good indicator. What we can say is that in the absence of thorough longitudinal studies we do not know if young people who sexually abuse are more likely to continue this behaviour than other young people who become involved in problematic behaviours.

Career progression

Studies with adult abusers indicated that many of those apprehended for serious offences admitted to beginning a pattern of abusive behaviour when they were adolescents, starting with less serious offences and over time progressing to more serious categories of sexual crime (e.g. Abel *et al.*, 1993). From this it has been extrapolated that young people will develop sexual offending careers if they are identified as having committed any sexually abusive act. Again this retrospective analysis is problematic for juvenile prognosis and is contradicted by the longitudinal evidence. For example, Prentky and Knight (1993) found no correlation between the age at which a person committed their first offence and the frequency or seriousness of future offending.

Treatment protocols

There is some evidence that specific forms of work can be effective with young people who exhibit sexually abusive behaviour (e.g. Ryan, 1995). However, the relative infancy of this field of study has made problematic the availability of longitudinal studies, which could be the most favoured method of assessing effectiveness. Cognitive Behavioural Therapy (CBT) seems to be the most commonly used method (Ryan and Lane, 1997) yet this may be due to professional cultural factors rather than proven effectiveness. Knopp and Freeman-Longo (1997) reviewed 1,074 programmes for young sexual abusers in the US and found that 40 per cent described their work as primarily CBT based. However, this was a description of content rather than an analysis of effectiveness which the authors acknowledge by calling for thorough longitudinal studies to determine re-abusing rates. The evidence for the effectiveness of CBT is ambivalent, with Brannon and Troyer (1995), for example, finding little difference in recidivism outcomes between offence-specific, cognitive-behavioural programmes and more generalised, holistic, welfare based approaches.

Lab *et al.* (1993) were more pointed in their criticisms. After reviewing the literature evaluating juvenile sex offender programmes they stated that:

> ...*the growth of new treatment modalities might be extending the net of social control over many youths who might not need help.* (p 552)

They were concerned that there seemed to be two main assumptions made about these programmes. First, that there is an assumption that we know what causes this behaviour and second, that we know how to successfully treat this behaviour. Lab *et al.* were clear in their criticism that neither of these assumptions were supported by definitive research.

Discussion

The exploration of the available literature allowed the Project to retain a holistic and flexible approach to working with the young people referred as it was clear that many of the assumptions about this client group were less solid than had been indicated. The reasons for this anomaly remain speculative, but may be related to a combination of anxiety about sexual offending; notions of childhood; the desire to prevent victimisation; drawing conclusions from limited material and working with unrepresentative samples of young people.

This latter issue was central to the functioning of the Project which had decided to keep the filtering process to a minimum. Referrals would be taken from all the usual child and family psychiatric channels with the only criteria being geographic and an element of concern at the sexual behaviour from the referrer. This potentially opened the Project to a wide range of young people with very different behaviours, backgrounds, ages and

status, rather than a selected sample of, for example, court-mandated clients or those where the behaviour was of extremely serious concern. The Project had to develop a range of responses to this spectrum of young people which more selective projects would feel unnecessary, so that the five year old who has been involved in exploring another's body can be managed along with the fifteen year old who is alleged to have committed a rape. The space created by a critical analysis of the research allowed some confidence in utilising a range of methodologies and remaining focused on the needs of the child, rather than being led primarily by anxiety about re-abusive behaviour.

The Organisation of the Project

Every referral is discussed at a core group meeting and allocated to two workers. This allows for some flexibility to attend network meetings and also gives one person to the child and one to the family/carers.

The initial assessment is undertaken like any other Child and Adolescent Mental Health Assessment. The history of the young person and their family is taken and there is a clinical assessment of the social and emotional development of the young person together with their psychological functioning.

If they are living with their family, an assessment of family structure and relationships is undertaken, otherwise a history of the family is ascertained from the professional network. The young person and their family are seen both together and separately. The standard assessment is expanded to explore more fully issues concerning sexual aggression and attitudes and behaviours towards sex. The assessment is discussed in the core group and the intervention planned around the perceived needs of the particular child and family. The work with the young person is focused on developing an understanding with them about their sexual behaviour in the context of their social and family life.

Some aspects of cognitive behavioural work are used to explore areas such as the thought processes leading up to a sexually abusive act; what elements may be planned and their attitudes to what has happened. Alongside this, the therapeutic relationship is understood to be a central part of developing the work. Psycho-dynamic theory is used to think about and explore this relationship in the sessions. This allows the relationship between the therapist and the child to be explored in a way that gives more understanding of the nature of the child's experience of relationships. If the feelings evoked in the worker can be understood, it can help to differentiate between the privacy of a therapeutic relationship and the secrecy of an abusive one (Furniss, 1991).

Some young people are able to vividly evoke feelings in others of what their experiences have been and this can be an important avenue of communication but can be misunderstood unless there is a framework within which to think about it. Individual therapy needs to remain firmly within the context of the system where the therapist and the individual therapy is related to child protection, the family process and the integrated multi-professional intervention (Furniss, 1991).

With younger children, this psycho-dynamic framework is used to understand play and drawing material. This combination of therapeutic models allows for controlled flexibility within each session. Each session can begin and develop around the theme the young person brings to it rather than rigidly adhering to a framework already decided upon by the therapist. For example, the young person's position as a victim and an aggressor of sexual behaviours can thus be explored together, the framework protecting the therapist from confusion rather than confining the thoughts and feelings of the young person.

Using the relationship as a tool can effectively allow for the exploration of values, attitudes and a developing awareness for the young person of how they see themselves and how others see them.

It is the therapist's role to thread this sometimes disjointed discourse together and to help the young person make connections. It is also the role of the therapist to pick up on issues not directly raised by the young person themselves. By having a well-structured framework that includes the facility for looking at the therapeutic relationship itself, there is protection from being drawn into a relationship of collusion, denial or punishment.

With the relationship formed slowly in this model, it has proved possible, for example, a white middle-aged woman therapist to engage with a young, African-Caribbean, working-class male about his sexual fantasies, masturbatory habits and experience of pornography.

While the young person is being seen separately, the parents/carers are seen by the second worker. This allows space to think about what has happened from their perspective, to develop strategies to keep other children in the household safe and to help the young in difficulty to avoid future situations where the sexual acting-out can occur. Some of the parents have a history of sexual abuse themselves and this can be brought up again in a confusing way when one of their children has been sexually aggressive. For some, it is the first time they have spoken of their experiences.

A proportion of the families referred also have difficulties in a range of other aspects of family functioning as well as the problems of the sexual abuse. In these families we have regular whole family meetings to address issues in relationships and other behaviours. Negotiations are made with the young person and the parents about what is to be shared with the wider family and what can stay in the separate sessions.

If the case is seen before a court appearance and a report is needed, this is made clear to the young person and their family. In other cases a risk assessment may be done and placed on the social services file. This has proved to be a helpful exercise with some older teenagers who are concerned about the implications for their future. They are aware that allegations of child sexual abuse are recorded by social services and can generate future investigations and therefore have a negative impact on future relationships.

Initially, the Project deliberately decided not to offer group work until the range of referrals had been established. The Project reviewed this at the end of the first and second year. The wide range of difficulties, cognitive ability and social functioning of the young people has meant that there has not been the opportunity to provide a group work programme.

Results

Although the Project was prepared to see any referral from the Nottingham Health Authority catchment area referred by any agency there may be factors operated by potential referrers, which act as a filter. There are relatively few girls or young women, which is counter to emerging evidence about the proportion of female abusers, particularly in the younger age group (e.g. Bonner, 1998).

The information about the Project distributed within the professional networks may need revisiting and the general issue of referral bias needs further investigation. The majority of cases were referred by social services and 86 per cent lived within the City boundaries, not the surrounding suburbs. There have been 49 referrals to the Project in the first two years.

Age

The age range is 3 to 18 with the majority in the 12 to 15 age group.

Gender

Only two girls have been referred although in an Area Child Protection Committee survey undertaken in Nottinghamshire over a six month period during the first year of the Project, 19 per cent of sexually aggressive acts against children were by girls under 18. The difficulty in acknowledging sexual aggression by women has been researched elsewhere (see Saradjian, 1996) and this may be a factor here.

Ethnicity

Six cases (12 per cent) were Black or mixed Black/White parentage. This is higher than the 5 per cent of people from non-White backgrounds in the demographic data for the health authority. It is unknown whether this reflects a higher level of anxiety about sexual activity in the Black population by referrers or whether the over-representation of inner-city referrals accounts for this.

Education

Forty (82 per cent) of the referrals were in mainstream school. Of the remainder, seven were in schools for Moderate Learning Difficulty (M.L.D.) and two in schools for children with Emotional and Behavioural Difficulties (E.B.D.). The local education

authority has a vigorous policy of integration of children with special needs into mainstream schools so there are few children in 'special' schools. A further seven referrals had known learning difficulties and were given extra assistance within mainstream school. Therefore a total of fourteen (28 per cent) had learning difficulties. Whether these young people generate more concern, are easier to detect or some other factor is at work is unknown. Some of this group were referred with concerns that may not have arisen outside the context of their learning difficulties. For example, a thirteen-year old boy with general developmental delay and a very protective family was extremely socially immature. He was referred after he had gone to his friends house nearby, wearing just his underpants as a much younger child could have done. The neighbours perceived this as indecent exposure. The area had concerns about recent adult paedophile activity.

Referred incident

This information has been included to illustrate that although the Project had very open referral criteria and only a small number of cases were involved in Court proceedings, the incidents precipitating the referral were often of a serious nature:

- Twenty (40%) touching breasts or genitalia of another child.
- Fourteen (28%) anal or vaginal penetrative acts.
- Nine (18%) oral-genital contact.
- Four (8%) indecent exposure.

Victim data

All except two of the victims were known to the perpetrator. These two were the subjects of indecent exposure.

- Nineteen (40%) were siblings or other relatives.
- 31 (65%) of the victims were female and 17 (35%) male.
- 14 (29%) victims were in the 0-5 age range
- 13 (27%)   "   6-11   "
- 18 (37%)   "   12-18   "
- 3 (6%)   "   adult

Disposal

The referrals demonstrated a wide range of post-incident disposals.

35 (71%) No police involvement or no further action.

This group formed the largest single referral category, which consisted of young people who were either too young to be charged with offences (under age 10), or where there were concerns about behaviour which did not have the substantive evidence to pursue a caution or prosecution.

7 (14%) Caution.

Cautioning for an offence means that there should have been some admission of guilt and that the young person was over the age of 10. It is formally recorded and becomes a criminal record.

4 (8%) Supervision order.

Of these four, only one was given a supervision order with specific conditions to attend the project for treatment. The others had no such conditions attached. Assessments were made on a further 3 young people, two of whom received custodial sentences and a third case resulted in a mis-trial and in no further action. In spite of the low number with a legal mandate to attend, only five cases (10 per cent) failed to attend. This is a lower rate of non-attendance than for general child and adolescent mental health referrals which can be as high as 20 per cent. This could be for a number of reasons. There may be high levels of concern among families especially as sexual abuse of children currently carries a high level of publicity and social disapproval. The Project members have all been in the area for a number of years and have worked hard to have good relationships with other agencies which refer. Training has also been undertaken locally so that other agencies are clear about what the Project can offer. The way people are prepared for a referral is known to influence the attendance rate.

Previous history of abuse

There has been an assumption that children who are sexually aggressive to other children have been sexually abused themselves. This has entered popular consciousness and both the authors have anecdotal evidence from young men who have waited years to talk about their experience of childhood abuse in case people thought they may be child abusers themselves. More recently, the findings from the Great Ormond Street research (Bentovim, 1997) suggests the strong association of a young person being sexually aggressive with being physically abused, a witness to domestic violence and being emotionally abused. The 49 cases had the following abuse histories:

- Fourteen (29%) had specific histories of sexual abuse.
- Seventeen (35%) had a mixed history of physical abuse, emotional abuse and neglect.
- Six (12%) had a history of emotional abuse.
- Twelve (24%) had no known history of abuse.

Of the cases with no known history of abuse, three had not attended the Project and not enough was known. The remainder were such a wide range of different situations and clinical problems that it has not been possible to draw any overall conclusions.

Recidivism

Monitoring the cases over the three years of the Project, there have been no reported cases of re-abusing either through formal or informal channels. It is hoped to continue to monitor the young people as far as is possible given the complexity of existing systems and the ethical issues involved.

Discussion

It is not clear to us how decisions are made to refer some cases to the Project and not others. Some of the families referred had been known for a number of years to all the local agencies involved with children and mental health and had produced a feeling of hopelessness in all of them. A sexually abusive act by a child seems to have served as a trigger to have these families referred again in the hope that something would change. This could have a different effect to previous experiences. For example, one family whose chaos and violence had invalidated any previous intervention, took the sexual aggression of one of the adolescents against one of the young children very seriously and for the first time have worked persistently and with good effect to introduce better family boundaries and to reduce the chaos in their previously event-filled life.

Alternatively there were some cases where it was only when the concerns became sexual rather than physical and emotional that resources were put in for the children. For example, the child mental health service had long-standing contact with other agencies over one family where the focus had been on an alternative placement for a child with uncontrollable aggression. There were great concerns about the level of violence, substance misuse and sexual acting out between the adults. It was only when one of the children acted in a very sexually aggressive way that the plight of all the children was taken seriously and services provided. This use of the 'trigger' of sexual abuse to intervene may have consequences for other children where preoccupation with that particular threshold may exclude the need to take other abusive factors as seriously. In this case, a child in need became a child abuser before services were offered, thus potentially stigmatising him for life.

Sexual behaviour is currently a major preoccupation in our culture. This could potentially change the presentation of children in difficulty. Several of the children seen described revenge as their main motive for a sexual assault on a child they saw as usurping their place or being their rival. They had learned that sex was the worst thing they could do to another child.

Developments

The Project has developed good working links with other local agencies. Out of this has developed a multi-agency consultancy group that offers consultation to workers who have a case involving sexual abuse by one child to another. This is co-ordinated by a youth justice worker and is meeting on a regular basis.

The Project is currently discussing the possibility of sharing staff and cases with other local agencies in order to make group work part

of the package available to these young people and their families. The Project has been impressed by the willingness and honesty of most of the referrals seen. We want to repay them by developing knowledge in this area so that we can become clearer about the risk factors for re-offending and therefore to make more accurate predictions of dangerousness. It is hoped that by keeping good records and looking at our data and others in an open-minded way we will come to some better understanding of this difficult area. As the research base improves we will hopefully gain more insight into the interventions which assist the wide range of young people who sexually abuse in order to give them some hope for the future.

To illustrate some of the points made, we wish to present a case from the Project. It does not cover all the issues or ways of working as one of the findings we have been increasingly aware of as the Project develops is that these cases differ widely in their presentation and needs.

Case Study

Jo was first seen just before his sixteenth birthday. The therapist had been contacted by a range of professionals about him for some time before this, but because of his unstable circumstances previous referrals had come to nothing. Jo was also aware that the therapist had been contacted. This seemed important when he first came, as in spite of a range of difficulties, he had made up his mind to use the opportunity and work towards change.

Jo came when he realised that he was perceived to be a sexual threat to younger children by the social services department. He had been involved sexually with an older woman and was prevented from continuing to live with her, not to protect him (he was under the age of consent), but to protect the younger children in the house.

When he was aged twelve, a female relative one year younger had accused him of forcing her to have sex. They were living in the same household at the time. The allegations were investigated but no charges were brought.

History

Jo came from a large, dysfunctional family with regular violence between the parents and towards the children. There was alcohol and substance misuse and periodic imprisonment for both parents. During one of these crises, a sibling was injured and the parents split up.

Jo and some of his siblings stayed with the mother and a series of violent partners and Jo was taught to shoplift and burgle for the adults. In this situation Jo became increasingly out of control, violent and disruptive in his sporadic appearances at school. He moved between various extended family members. He came into local authority care after the allegations of sexual aggression were investigated. Over the next few years Jo was involved with a heavily delinquent peer group in multiple car crimes and property offences. He was also a heavy drinker and misused substances, especially amphetamines. His explosive temper led to regular contact with the police and to court appearances. Just before coming to the Project, Jo had disclosed sexual abuse by one of the adults he lived with as a young boy.

Therapeutic work

Jo was very committed to coming from the first time he was seen. The journey to the clinic is not easy but he was a regular and punctual attendee over the two years he was seen. It was not easy for him to trust people and the framework of assessing his sexual behaviour was helpful although uncomfortable for him. The trust in the working relationship was consolidated by spending two days together in court, when the case against his abuser was heard, and in the genito-urinary clinic when there were concerns about his HIV status.

The links between his early abuse and much of his subsequent behaviour was worked on by moving between these two areas. Jo had been very ashamed and humiliated by his own abuse and preoccupied by what others would think of him if they knew. As his sexual abuser had been male, he worried about his sexuality. This led both to him being extremely violent to any man he thought was looking at him and also to multiple sexual relationships with girls.

Because Jo had a range of difficulties and was not supported by a family, it took some time to piece together his sexual thoughts, feelings and behaviours. The therapist and Jo had developed a close relationship and the therapist was concerned that the risk assessment could be compromised. The project group discussed this and the Ross and Loss Risk Assessment schedule was used to formalise the findings about his sexual aggression. Jo was scored as low risk for sexual aggression and a report was put on his social services file.

A year and a half later, Jo has not been accused of any other sexual aggression. He is no longer substance misusing or offending and is in a stable relationship with a young woman of a similar age.

References

Abel, G., Mittelman, M., and Becker, J. (1985). Sexual Offenders: Results of Assessment and Recommendations for Treatment. In Ben-Aron, H., Hucker, S., and Webster, C. (Eds.). *Clinical Criminology*, 191–205. Toronto: M.M. Graphics.

Abel, G., Osborne, C., and Twigg, D. (1993). Sexual Assault Through the Life-span of Adult Offenders with Juvenile Histories. In Barbaree, H.E., Marshall, W.L., and Hudson, S.M. (Eds.). *The Juvenile Sex Offender*. New York: Guilford.

Barbaree, H.E., Marshall, W.L., and Hudson, S.M. (Eds.) (1993). *The Juvenile Sex Offender*. New York: Guilford.

Bentovim, A. (1997). *Results of the Great Ormond Street Hospital for Sick Children Young Abusers' Project*. Paper presented at the National Conference of the British Association for the Study and Prevention of Child Abuse and Neglect. Edinburgh. July, 1997.

Bonner, B. (1998). *Children with Sexual Behaviour Problems. Two Approaches to the Problem.* Paper Presented at the 12th International Congress on Child Abuse and Neglect, Auckland, New Zealand. September, 1998.

Brannon, J., and Troyer, R. (1995). Adolescent Sex Offenders: Investigating Adult Commitment Rates Four Years Later. *International Journal of Offender Therapy and Comparative Criminology*, 39(4): pp 317–326.

Davis, G., and Leitenberg, H. (1987). Adolescent Sex Offenders. *Psychological Bulletin*, 101: 417–427.

Finkelhor, D. (1996). Keynote Address. Presented at the 11th International Congress on Child Abuse and Neglect, Dublin, Ireland. August, 1996.

Furby, L., Weinrott, M.R., and Blackshaw, L. (1989). Sex Offender Recidivism — A Review. *Psychological Bulletin*, 105: 3–30.

Furniss, T. (1991). *The Multi-professional Handbook of Child Sexual Abuse*. London: Routledge.

Kahn, T.J., and Chambers, H.J. (1991). Assessing Re-offense Risk with Juvenile Sex Offenders. *Child Welfare*, Vol. LXX, No. 3. May-June, 333–345.

Knopp, F.H., and Freeman-Longo, R., with Lane, S., Programme Development in Ryan, G., and Lane, S. (Eds.) (1997). *Juvenile Sexual Offending*, 183–200. Jossey-Bass. San Fransisco, USA.

Lab, S., Shields, G., and Schoel, C. (1993). Research Note; An Evaluation of Juvenile Sex Offender Treatment. *Crime and Delinquency*, 39(4): 543–553.

Masson, H. (1995). Children and Adolescents who Sexually Abuse Other Children: Responses to an Emerging Problem. *Journal of Social Welfare and Family Law*, 17(3): 325–35.

National Childrens Home (1992). *Children who Sexually Abuse Other Children*. London: NCH.

Prentky, R., and Knight, R. (1993). Age of Onset of Sexual Assault. In Nagayama Hall, G., Hirschman, R., Graham, J., and Zaragoza, M. (Eds.). *Sexual Aggression: Issues in Etiology, Assessment and Treatment*. Washington D.C.: Taylor & Francis.

Ryan, G. (1986). Annotated Bibliography: Adolescent Perpetrators of Sexual Molestation of Children. *Child Abuse and Neglect: The International Journal*, 10: 125–131.

Ryan, G. (1988). *The Juvenile Sex Offender: A Question of Diagnosis*. Presentation of Unpublished Data at the National Symposium on Child Victimisation, Anaheim, CA: USA.

Ryan, G. (1995). *Treatment of Sexually Abusive Youth: The Evolving Consensus*. Paper presented at the International Experts Conference, Utrecht, Netherlands.

Ryan, G., and Lane, S. (Eds.) (1997). *Juvenile Sexual Offending* (2nd edition). Jossey-Bass, San Francisco, USA.

Saradjian, J. (1996). *Women who Sexually Abuse Children*. London: Wiley.

Smith, W.R. (1984). Patterns of Re-offending Among Juvenile Sexual Offenders. Cited in Davis, G.E., and Leitenberg, H. (1987). Adolescent Sex Offenders. *Psychological Bulletin*, 101: 417–427.

Smith, W.R., and Monastersky, C. (1986). Assessing Juvenile Sexual Offenders Risk for Re-offending. *Criminal Justice and Behaviour*, 13: 115–140.

Chapter Ten

A Psycho-educational Support Group for a Neglected Clinical Population:

Parents/Carers of Young People who Sexually Abuse Children and Others

Loretto McKeown and Jacqui McGarvey

A Psycho-educational Support Group for a Neglected Clinical Population: Parents/Carers of Young People who Sexually Abuse Children and Others

General Importance of Working with Parents/Carers

In developing and researching material to begin this group, it quickly became apparent that there was very little published in this area of work with this population. It is generally recognised that parents need to be involved, if possible, in any therapeutic treatment programme for their children. Furthermore, it would seem that it is of the utmost importance that parents be involved in a treatment programme for their children who have sexually abused

> ...parent groups work to create an environment which supports the treatment process (National Task Force Report, 1993).

Philosophy

Young abusers do not operate alone; they are part of a family. The parents/carers, being the primary unit within the family, need to have an understanding of the dynamics of sexually abusive behaviour, the implications of treatment or non-treatment, and adapt a supportive role in the programme of work. Parents are the gatekeepers in supervising and monitoring the young person's behaviour, and so are a major factor in preventing re-offending.

The objectives of the group included:

1. To promote a group support network for parents of adolescent offenders.

2. To explain the process and content of the young persons' group, which is structured around the Smets and Cebula Five Step Process (1986).

3. To offer a psycho-educational approach to understanding the cycle of offending.

4. To address the emotional/psychological needs of the parents/carers, resulting from the impact of the allegation of sexual abusive behaviour/s.

It was envisaged that the psycho-educational approach would address the emotional needs of the parents and, also, help them gain an insight into the cycle of abuse. Evidence from young people who have been treated in a group treatment programme, and experience over four years in group work with parents, has shown that the presence of parents in a parallel group programme is a strong motivating factor for the young peoples' attendance and participation in their own treatment programme.

Questionnaires were sent out to all young people who had come to the attention of the Juvenile Perpetrators Project from January 1995–December 1997 (Appendix 1). Of 53 questionnaires sent out approximately 40 per cent were returned. These were analysed by the NSPCC Practice Development Unit in London. In looking at sources of support during and after treatment, e.g. parent, friend, school, social worker; parents were the most frequently cited group who had been of help. Due to the limitations of the research by questionnaire, particularly for this age group, a further sample of six young people aged between 14 and 19 years were interviewed. These interviews were unstructured and of 20/30 minutes duration. The analysis of the interviews further supported the findings of the questionnaires.

Perhaps most important of all is the fact that parents who attended the group programme have a much better understanding of how their child offended. They can also develop skills in communicating with the young people about their treatment programme, their problems or concerns, and tend to be overall more supportive and understanding at this crucial time in the young person's life. In the course of this work various other adolescent and family issues often surface and can be appropriately addressed.

> I spent 6 months in total confusion before I joined the Parents' Group. I really didn't know anything about the subject, and the information supplied has been

very helpful. This, together with the experiences of the group leaders in dealing with other cases, has been very helpful indeed (quote from parent who attended the Group at the termination of the programme).

Establishing the need

In 1988, the National Society for the Prevention of Cruelty to Children (NSPCC) Craigavon Team, in collaboration with the Child and Family Clinic Multi-disciplinary Team, jointly developed a group treatment programme for adolescent perpetrators in the Southern Health and Social Services Board in Northern Ireland (described in the next chapter). To date seven Young Persons' Groups have been successfully completed (all referrals have been male). The age range of the young people is 12–17 years. The co-workers of the Young Persons' Groups became increasingly aware during groups 1, 2 and 3, that the parents of the young people were experiencing the need/desire to be kept au fait with issues arising in the group sessions with the young people. These parents had been getting consistent messages from the Royal Ulster Constabulary Child Abuse and Rape Enquiry Unit (RUC CARE Unit), the consulting psychologist and psychiatrist, probation board and social workers, about the importance of their role and responsibility in understanding and supporting the young offender during the treatment programme.

> *Parental supervision and monitoring are imperative when sexually abusive youths are in out-patient treatment, and cannot be assumed adequate without parental involvement in the treatment programme (National Task Force, 1993).*

Parents who brought their son to the group were frequently requesting time to discuss their son's progress and/or explanations of the programme from the already busy group facilitators. While many parents had received some professional support at the time of the investigation, and were still receiving support from social workers, issues concerning their son's current status in the group programme kept surfacing for them and they needed answers. Many of the parents also expressed a desire to become involved in some way in their son's treatment.

In view of this two workers agreed to develop a parallel support group for parents, to coincide with the young people's group.

This initiative was enthusiastically supported by the two co-workers of the Young Persons' Group, and also received the endorsement of other professionals, agencies and senior management.

The consensus of opinion was that it is important for the parents to be cognisant of the process and content of the Young Persons' Group, which is modelled on the five step Smets and Cebula model (1987). This model has been adapted to a six step process to suit the needs of the young people in the group— see McGarvey and Lenaghan, (1996). To date four Parents'/Carers' Groups, which have run parallel to the young people's groups, have been completed.

Literature

The decision to develop a psycho-educational group for parents/carers led to a review of literature in this area of work. Much was written on assessment and treatment of the adolescent offenders, i.e. Becker (1991); Bentovim, Elton, Hildebard, Tranter, Vizard (1988) Bremmer (1991); Calder (1997); Giarretto (1992); Ryan and Lane (1991); Schacht; Kerlisky; Carlson (all 1990). Despite the apparent depth of information on offer, little refers to the treatment of the parents/carers of young people who sexually abuse. Three articles which were helpful are detailed as follows: Gist and Taylor (1994); Griggs and Boldy (1995); and Ryan and Lane (1991). These articles were useful in helping the authors understand family variables, characteristics and patterns frequently identified in the families of young people who sexually abuse. After an extensive library search it seemed there were no published studies specific to this area of work. Consequently, the group facilitators looked to existing group work models for guidelines. Whilst no working model seemed to totally encapsulate the desired philosophy and objectives drawn up by the facilitators, various aspects of the programme used in the Giarretto Institute, San Jose, California, and in the North-Side Inter-agency Project, Dublin, did appear to meet some of the needs. Having studied and discussed both programmes a new model emerged, and this became the framework for the first group. This model, adapted over a period of 4 years, will be elaborated on later in the chapter.

Screening criteria

A structured interview was undertaken with most of the participants prior to inclusion in the group programme. Screening criteria for inclusion in the group included: no prior history of abuse, a willingness to discuss the impact of the offending behaviour on themselves and their families, and a commitment to attending and participating in the group process.

Selection criteria

- Parents/carers of young people attending the group (extra-familial and intra-familial).

- Parents of young people who have sexually abused others but who were not included in the young people's group.

- Foster carers/residential keyworker for the young person in the group.

- All perspective group participants were required to have completed an individual assessment and, if possible, a comprehensive family assessment.

Initially, in discussion among the facilitators of the young people's group and the Parents'/Carers' Group, it was decided to limit admission to the Parents'/Carers' Group to those parents whose sons were attending the young people's group. Attendance for the parents/carers was not mandated. During the course of the second Parents'/Carers' Group, a request was made for admission to the group from a couple whose son was not attending the young people's group programme. This couple, however, were seeking help in understanding their son's behaviour and in supervising him, as they considered him to be at risk of re-abusing. On consulting with the other group members, the inclusion of this couple did not pose a problem.

Also in the second group were two young people who were in residential care. Here was another area of need, i.e. for someone from the residential facility to be with these young people as they went through the group

process. It was, indeed, important for the residential workers to understand the process of the young people's programme, and to act in a supportive capacity should the need arise. However, the impact of the abusive behaviour and subsequent family fall-out did not affect them to the same extent.

The group facilitators recognised the importance of a comprehensive family history, which often revealed a pattern of inter-generational family dysfunctions and/or offending, such as alcohol abuse, domestic violence, rigidly religious, mental health problems, bereavement. Within the experience of the groups, all of these were factors which impinged on the sexually abusive behaviour of the young person. When a comprehensive assessment has been completed, information about the family dynamics is easily assessed, and needs can then be addressed in the group programme and in the follow-up. These findings confirm what has been mentioned in the National Task Force (1993):

> *family dysfunction revealed in the juvenile's history can undermine the treatment process if left untreated… family systems often share the same dynamics as the offenders, and support the offending by their denial and resistance to change.*

During the initial sessions of the first Parents'/Carers' Group, there was a realisation that even several years after the disclosure of abuse, these parents were still suffering the trauma of disclosure, and seemed blocked in moving forward and coming to terms with their feelings of shock, shame and embarrassment. Some were still partly in denial and minimisation. As child protection workers, the facilitators were able to relate these reactions to similar ones from parents of victims, who can be deeply traumatised by the realisation that their son/daughter has been sexually abused. It was necessary, therefore, to listen to the concerns which the parents brought to each session, and re-adjust the planned programme if necessary to meet the here and now needs. It was also recognised that where parents have multiple problems additional to the offending behaviour, they may be unable to sustain the structure and momentum of the group programme. Such parents are offered long-term individual work to address their particular needs. This may be followed by family work and the option of group work is still available to them.

Jane's Story

Jane is the mother of five children — two young people aged 16 and 14 years, and three younger female siblings aged 8 years, 6 years and 3 months. Jane was divorced and in a second relationship with Dan. The 16 and 14 year old young people abused their 8 and 6 year old sisters. In the course of investigation of the sibling abuse, both young people disclosed that they had been sexually abused by a friend in the neighbourhood (described as the 'Pied Piper' by Jane). In addition, both young people were involved in drug and alcohol abuse, and were experiencing problems at school and in the neighbourhood. Jane came to the first session of the group, accompanied by her partner Dan. Jane spoke very little but Dan seemed very supportive. At the second group session a week later Jane was alone. In a very distressed and tearful way she spoke of her problems with her children and her growing concern with her partner's attitude. Dan apparently did not want to be involved or associated with Jane's children. Jane appeared to have no support from her extended family (one of whose children her oldest son had also sexually abused); her partner was talking about moving out and she seemed almost overwhelmed and unable to cope. While all were saddened, no-one was surprised when Jane did not continue to attend the group. When it was recognised that group work was not appropriate for Jane's needs, an individual work programme was offered.

At this stage in the development of the project there were insufficient instances of extra or intra-familial abuse to warrant a group based exclusively on either type of abuse. As figure 1 depicts, each group has varied in respect of the balance of intra and extra-familial abuse.

Group make-up and attendance

There was a combination of couples and individual parents in all 4 groups, and the social, economic and educational levels varied widely. A percentage of the parents were very committed and, consequently, attended all sessions. Others attended sporadically and some others attended 1 or 2 sessions, and were either too traumatised to continue or were hindered by work commitments. Recent feedback came from a parent who was unable to attend due to work commitments. Her husband did attend the group and relayed feedback and literature to her. Retrospectively, she is demonstrating a level of anger that her husband's needs were met by the group, but she still has many unresolved issues, and hopes to attend the next planned group.

The Programme

The first group for parents/carers commenced in 1993. Sessions ran concurrently with the adolescents programme and were 1½ hours in length. Originally it had been anticipated that the parents' group would meet as often as the young peoples' group, but after the initial session the feedback from the parents indicated that they would prefer to meet every 2–3 weeks, or more often if particular concerns or worries were surfacing.

The planning for the group process focused on understanding the steps of the young

Figure 1: Composition of Parents' Groups (1993–1998)				
Group	1	2	3	4
Parent group	9 sessions	10 sessions	9 sessions	9 sessions
Young people in group	5	5	6	6
Types of abuse perpetrated by young people	4 Extra-familial 1 Intra-familial	1 Extra-familial 4 Intra-familial	3 Extra-familial 2 Intra-familial 1 both categories	4 Extra-familial 2 Intra-familial
Parents attending group	4	8	4	10

people's programme, the needs which were being expressed by parents (i.e. coming to terms with the disclosure of the abusive behaviour and its repercussions on the family), and addressing the parents' feelings of isolation, confusion, stigmatisation and guilt.

At the beginning of the groups, the facilitators felt that the groups would have a significant psycho-educational component. The need for flexibility quickly became apparent, as the parents brought their own issues to each session and time and priority needed to be given to these concerns. As a result the parents were asked early on in the group's process what they hoped and needed to get from the group. The content of the groups was 'present' focused, and parents' current issues and concerns were addressed in the various sessions. Time was also given at the beginning of each session to discuss issues and/or concerns, which had arisen for the parents since the last session.

In the initial session of each group a facilitator gave an overview of the steps of the young people's programme, and explained that each step would become the focus of a session during the life of the group. The parents were informed of the upcoming step prior to the young people working through it. It was made clear that while the parents were being made aware of the young people's progress in the steps, they would not be given details of what the individual young people had shared or worked through in their progress of the steps.

The co-workers from both the parents' group and the young people's group met on a regular basis to share perceptions of each group's progress. These meetings facilitated the adjustment and adaptation of the programme, keeping the focus on issues relevant to these young people and these parents. The facilitators thought it essential for the parents to be advised prior to the young people moving on to a new step, as some of the steps were more challenging and the parents needed to be aware of possible behavioural changes during this process e.g. being quieter, moody, aggressive.

As already indicated, a new step was presented to the parents at each session and a brief outline of the content thereof was given to the parents. Of the six steps, the impact of Step

4 was very significant in the parents' group. This is the step where the young person gives details how they planned, selected and groomed their victims. The parents in the group were well aware that the young people had committed various offences and had, in most cases, multiple victims. They accepted this as they thought the offences were opportunistic, but the realisation that often the offences had been planned and the victims had been selected was very difficult for the parents to accept.

Up to this point the parents had vacillated between minimising the extent of their son's abuse and denial of some aspects of it. However, with the disclosure of times, victims and incidents which came as a result of understanding Step 4, the last vestiges of their defence crumbled. At this stage of the programme the facilitators were aware of the need to be sensitive, supportive and empathic towards the group members, as they struggled with this pain and their feelings of inadequacy as parents.

As evidenced in the composition of the Parents' Group diagram (Figure 1), there was on average 9 sessions. The content of each session was based on the following outlines:

Content of the parents groupwork programme

Session 1 (often repeated because all parents do not always attend the first night).

- Introductions: the co-facilitators introduce themselves and outline their professional backgrounds. This is followed by the participants introducing themselves, giving as much or as little of circumstances, background, reasons for attending the group, as they feel comfortable with at this point in time.

- Explanation of the group content and soliciting parents' wishes for developing the programme further. Opportunity to ventilate feelings about coming to the group.

- General group rules, with special focus on confidentiality.

- Brief overview of the content of the young people's group.

- Importance of supervision of their son.

Session 2

- Check in and opportunity for parents to talk about any issues or concerns which have arisen from the last session (this was a feature of every session).
- Recap of last sessions and any questions regarding content of last session.
- Sexual abuse definition: awareness of the problem of young people sexually abusing.
- Importance of parents'/carers' support for young people in treatment.
- Parents discuss investigation process, its impact and implications.
- Focus on importance of supervision/monitoring behaviour of their son, i.e. babysitting rules.

Session 3

- Check in and recap on last session.
- Extended family/community response to the disclosure/allegation of sexual abuse regarding their son.
- Update on progress of young people's group: making parents/carers aware in advance of upcoming areas of work.
- Discuss policies and procedures, structure of professional agencies involved, e.g. case conference.

Session 4

- Check in.
- Recap.
- Cycle of offending.

Session 5

- Check in.
- Recap.
- Update on progress of young people's group.
- Introduction of the concept of empathy: viewing the video *'The Nightingale Roars'*.
- Discussion following video.

Session 6

- Check in.
- Recap.

- Sex education video *'What's Happening To Me?'*
- Discussion following video.

Session 7

- Check in.
- Recap.
- Visit and talk given by member of Royal Ulster Constabulary Care and Rape Enquiry Unit (RUC CARE Unit) re investigation process, Police, long-term implications of legal system, e.g. name placed on Sex Offenders' Register.
- Discussion.

Session 8

- Check in.
- Recap.
- Relevant literature.
- General feedback on progress of young people's group by co-facilitator of young people's group.

Sessions 9/10

- Check in.
- Recap.
- Coping strategies for the future.
- Overview of all the sessions.
- Evaluation of group process.
- Close.

Other key considerations

Confidentiality

The issue of confidentiality was paramount and, for the group to proceed, the facilitators felt it needed to be addressed. For various reasons some of the parents were unable to seek support from, or even tell, extended family or friends. They came into the group fearful that someone in the room might recognise them (since the Southern Health and Social Services Board is a relatively small area, approximately 300,000), and also wondering how they could explain to neighbours and friends where they were going every Thursday night.

The facilitators stressed the confidential nature of the group and assured the participants that steps had been taken to ensure that no-one else would be in the building except the parents, the young people and the group facilitators. It was agreed that since Thursday night was late night shopping this could provide a possible explanation for curious neighbours. The group agreed that the issues discussed and shared would be kept confidential within the group i.e., 'what is shared here stays here', the exception being disclosure of additional abuse — this would be reported to relevant agencies. The facilitators presented the point that outside the group if any of the members met the facilitators or each other that there would not be any social recognition. The members agreed with this and seemed relieved, as recognition could cause difficulties in everyday situations. However, the possibility of members supporting each other outside group was left as a viable option.

Group rules

The facilitators presumed that the parents of the offenders would be aware of basic rules.

- The adolescent perpetrator must not have any contact on his own with his victim(s).
- He must not babysit under any circumstances, either within or outside his family.
- He must not be left in charge of younger children at home, in school, at church, or in his workplace.

At the third session of the first group one of the parents inadvertently mentioned that his son was playing with his victims in the street. This drew attention to the need to list and emphasise the basic rules regarding contact with the victim.

It is not clear to facilitators why the parents would not have realised these basic rules. However, experience with the 4 groups has highlighted that one cannot assume the parents/carers understand and implement these necessary precautions. When this issue was first raised with the parents it became apparent that in some cases the parents were abiding by the rules in relation to the young people being alone with their victim(s), but were allowing him to play with and/or babysit other children. If the abuse happened within the immediate family some parents felt it was fine for the perpetrator to babysit for extended

family or friends. The parents did not seem to understand the wider/fuller implications. On reviewing how the parents reacted throughout the group, their reactions about the rules would be consistent with their responses to other areas of the group programme, so, therefore, the facilitators had again to be very careful and explain and monitor every detail, constantly reviewing and checking emotional reactions and understandings. This area of work is perceived to be vital in assessing the parents' ability to supervise and monitor their son's behaviour, and to help in relapse prevention and recidivism.

Reactions/feelings expressed

The feelings of the parents fluctuated depending on the stage of the process. It was very evident that at the first session the parents were tense, nervous and anxious. In some cases these feelings manifested themselves through bouts of crying, angry outbursts and controlled or rigid postures. Feelings of depression resulting from being almost overwhelmed by the disclosure of abuse and consequent helplessness were frequently evident. From the outset the parents became supportive of each other and considerate of each other's needs at the time. The cohesiveness and mutual support established in the first session deepened in ensuing sessions, and continued to be a feature through the life of each group.

Victimisation

At the very first session, in asking the parents to express their feelings about coming to the group and the impact of their son's offending behaviour on themselves and their family, it quickly became evident that many of the parents viewed themselves as victims, and were totally unprepared for the emotional and practical problems following on the disclosure of their son's abusive behaviour. The parents saw the need for attending the group, but thought that they themselves were not a factor in the inappropriate behaviours of their son(s). The facilitators recognised the need to respect their strong defences.

John's Story

John and his wife Jill were the parents of three children, aged 24, 17 and 15 years. Their 24 year old daughter was married and had a 3 year old daughter. John and Jill's 15 year old son sexually abused his niece, the couple's 3 year old grand-daughter. John was quite vocal in the group, and at the first session while group members were expressing how they felt about attending the Parents'/Carers' Group, John spoke openly 'Well, I feel like a victim'. Upon being asked to talk further on this, he continued 'It's my daughter who should be here, if she had been looking after her child my son would not have abused her, and Jill and myself would not have to be here tonight'.

It was important to listen to the expressed views of the parents and not to rush in here in a confrontational fashion, but, rather, to allow the parents their space and within the forthcoming sessions, through the process of explaining the planning, grooming and cyclic nature of the abusive behaviour, to allow them to come to an understanding of their role/responsibility in their son's behaviour. It was also important to educate the parents as to how abuse occurs in order to help them relate this to their own family situation. While we were aware that procedures had been clearly explained to the parents, they were unable to take these on board and internalise them because of the shock and trauma of the disclosure of abuse.

Isolation/stigmatisation

Over the groups there were three distinct categories of feeling isolated and stigmatised, which parallel with the feelings expressed by parents of victims of sexual abuse. These were:

1. When the abuse occurred within the family there was usually an inclination **not** to talk to extended family members or friends or take them into their confidence. Therefore, the nuclear family struggled in their isolation to keep up the pretence that things were fine and they were coping. Unfortunately this very pretence sometimes enabled secrecy to be maintained, and only a 'piece' of abusive family history came to light occasionally. In ongoing individual/family treatment, the whole inter-generational nature of abuse was uncovered and appropriately treated. It was evident from the participants of the 3 groups that they were unable, or unwilling, to get emotional

support from family, friends or neighbours. Consequently, when they came into the group there seemed to be an almost overwhelming need/urge to unburden themselves and to talk constantly during the session.

2. When the abuse was extra-familial but within the local community, the parents and family members felt isolated and stigmatised and some had on occasions been verbally assaulted. The community seemed to be divided; some took the side of the victim and some sympathised with the perpetrators family.

3. Sometimes the community was made aware through the media that an allegation of sexual abuse had been made against someone in the area. Even though neither the victim nor the perpetrator were named, the respective ages were given. In a small community both were easily identified and often suffered isolation.

Confusion

There was always the inevitable question, 'Why did my son do this?' or 'How could this have happened?' Most parents thought that they were fairly well aware of their children's activities and whereabouts. At no time had they noticed any change of behaviour, physical or emotional, in their son. A number of parents felt they had been duped and deceived because the abuse often happened within their home, and even when they were in close proximity.

Some of the parents expressed confusion about the roles of the various professionals, i.e. social worker/NSPCC/care unit/health visitor/probation officer, and their interactions with each other, with the parents and sometimes with the school. Many parents indicated that the presence of so many professionals (most of whom they had never heard of or met previously) was invasive and daunting, and added to their confusion, anxiety and bewilderment at the early stages of disclosure and Initial Child Protection Conference. A parallel can be drawn with Scott's (1996) work with parents of victims, she writes 'the victims' parents were highly anxious what police, social workers, doctors and others intended to do to their child'. However, it was important and necessary to keep before the parents an awareness of the criminal nature of the abusive behaviour and its very serious impact on the victim(s).

Divided loyalties

In cases where the abuse was intra-familial the parents, especially the mother, felt torn between her love for her son and anger at the abusive behaviour, and at the same time wanting to believe and support the victim, who was also her child. As the parents developed awareness and understanding of their son's offending behaviour, they often had to cope with the offender's siblings or extended family members, some of whom were still denying or minimising the extent of the abusive behaviour. This is an area/issue where it is important to interact with other professionals who may be dealing with victims, siblings and other family members. The model of family intervention as exemplified in the Giarretto Institute, San Jose, California, has been studied with a view to future development. Unfortunately this model is not feasible with the present population and resources.

Guilt

Guilt was intermingled with the parents' feelings of confusion and inadequacy. Many of them blamed themselves for not recognising signs and symptoms of changed behaviour, often having attributed it to school concerns. On reflection, some of the parents had indicated they recognised warning signs which had given them a sense of unease, e.g. use of telephone chat lines, pornographic magazines, inappropriate videos, obscene telephone calls. Seen in hindsight the parents realised these signs were the precursors to more serious sexual abuse.

Literature/reading

At session 1 of Group 1 the parents expressed their frustration at their lack of being able to access written information regarding their son's offending behaviour. The facilitators realised that there was limited resource materials suitable for parents. Fortunately they were familiar with 2 booklets: Gil, 1987 and Pithers *et al.*, 1993. Copies of these were made available to the parents before the termination

of the first group. Attention was drawn to the difference in terminology as these booklets are American publications. In Groups 2 and 3 the parents referred to the literature 'From Trauma to Understanding' being more helpful in their understanding of their current situation.

A leaflet entitled 'Guide for Parents Whose Children Have Sexually Abused' (Appendix 2) was written by 2 members of the project team, and is given to parents/carers at the end of the second parents' group. Feedback from the parents/carers has been very positive as it is given to them during the investigative process. Key headings from this leaflet are: 'What is sexual abuse?; Effects on the victim; How parents feel; Why concern?; Confidentiality'. A similar leaflet entitled 'Information for Young People' (Appendix 3) has been written by the authors. This is made available to the young people during the investigation process.

RUC CARE Unit

For many of the parents their son's offending behaviour was their first experience with the police and juvenile criminal/legal proceedings. On reflection many of the parents indicated that they were still unsure of the long-term consequences of their son's offence. Consequently, all 4 groups agreed that it would be helpful to have a representative from the CARE Unit to talk and explain: the role of the CARE Unit; investigative procedures; positive outcomes of the investigation; legal consequences; and long-term effects.

This clarified a number of worrying issues for parents. They also appreciated the commitment made by the CARE Unit to visit their group, as the member of the CARE Unit explained the legal procedures and gravity of the offending behaviour. Many of the parents realised for the first time the possible long-term effects on the young person concerned, i.e. he/she might have a criminal record which would not expound, i.e. Schedule 1 Offender.

Cycle of offending

As one could expect, the parents did not realise the cyclic/addictive nature of the offending behaviour. The facilitators found Ryan's 'Cycle of Offending' to be a particularly helpful visual aid when explaining this to the parents. A useful technique in explaining the cycle of abuse was to relate it to other behavioural disorders, such as gambling, alcohol, and eating. At this point in the group it was observed that the parents began to re-examine their belief systems and recognised links to their own family dynamics, sexual behaviours and attitudes. On reflection they saw that previously isolated and apparently innocent episodes were linked to the development of the abusive behaviour of their sons.

Victim empathy

Since victim empathy is regarded as an important part of the young person's treatment, it is continually linked throughout the entire 25-session process. The video 'The Nightingale Roars' by Constance Nightingale was particularly effective in helping to develop victim empathy. In this video Constance Nightingale, as a survivor, revisits the scene of her childhood abuse, and clearly expresses the long-range effects of her victimisation by her father and his friend. She outlines the importance of counselling in helping her survive her child experiences. This is shown to the parents prior to Step 3. This video was found to have a long lasting salutary effect on the parents. It evokes a wide range of emotions in the parents, and for the first time a significant movement from token awareness of the victim's feelings to the beginning of sincere empathy was evident. In discussing empathy it was noticeable that in families where the abuse was within the family the parents were more empathetic and understanding and, so, were able to help the other parents move forward and understand the victim's perspective.

Another technique which was helpful in moving the parents towards a deeper understanding of the impact of sexual abuse, not only on the victim but on the parents and entire family, was an anonymous letter written by a parent of a victim. In this letter the parent describes graphically and in detail an insight into the deep and far ranging effects of the abuse, not just on the victim but on her marital relationship and her relationship with extended family.

A second video is shown prior to young people entering Step 5 in relation to the young person's sexual development. This video is called 'What's Happening to Me?' It is a cartoon type portrayal of the sexual development of young males and females. This has been received positively by the parents, with some wanting to show it to other siblings in the family.

Issues for Facilitators

The 4 groups were facilitated by the same 2 people, both being females. While a mixed gender would undoubtedly make for an ideal situation, this was not possible. The 2 facilitators had prior experience working both individually and in groups with young people who have sexually abused, with parents of young people who have sexually abused, and with victims of abuse and parents of victims of abuse. In anticipation of meeting the needs of the parents the first group was structured as a psycho-educational support group. On the whole the overall plan did meet the needs and expectations. However, some of the reactions and responses by the parents were very different from what had been anticipated. Therefore, the prepared plan was adapted, and the facilitators recognised the need to be extremely patient and sensitive, and not to rush in and try to change the parents' perceptions, but, rather, help them see other viewpoints. Over time they gained insights and in some cases even seemed to change 360 degrees in their thinking. If the co-workers had been too confrontational and had not given time to listen to the parents' pain, it is possible that the parents would not have co-operated, nor would the groups have developed into the powerful cohesive supportive network which did evolve. Prior planning was essential, as was processing following the group. The meetings with the co-workers of the young people's group and, on occasions, consultant psychiatrist and consultant psychologist, were invaluable. The purpose of these meetings were two pronged: structure of the programme and progress; and support and affirmation of the work in both groups.

Networking: professional

Networking played a vital component due to there only being one parents' group running in the Southern Health and Social Services Board area. A network liaison was established with a Dublin project, and other centres were visited, e.g. Giarretto Institute, San Jose, California, USA; The Pines Treatment Centre, Tucson, Arizona, USA.

Parent to parent link-up

By the beginning of the second group for parents it was possible to establish a link-up network among parents, i.e. a parent whose son had completed the group work was asked to link-up with a parent whose son was preparing to join a new group. This link-up network has proved to be very effective in helping to reduce anxiety for parents coming to groups, as well as being a sounding board for them as they in turn attend the group and follow the progress of their son in the young people's group. This link-up is modelled on the Giarretto Parents' United concept in San Jose, California, which is a self-help component of the programme.

Evaluation

Evaluation of the parents' support group is three-pronged:

1. Questionnaires given to the parents at the conclusion of each group (see below for parents' comments). Feedback from this helps to improve the programme.

2. Feedback received from the Juvenile Perpetrators Project Team, group facilitators, i.e. young people's group and parents' group, case conferences, GPs, probation and the RUC CARE Unit.

3. Accountability given to the Steering Group of the Juvenile Perpetrators Project Team, who in turn report to the Area Child Protection Committee and receive feedback.

Some quotes from parents who attended the Parents'/Carers' Group:

- *Everything in the group helped — from the first night realising we were not alone — the cycle of abuse, and everything else.*

- *The group was very helpful to my wife and I and our son. I would strongly recommend it to future people in the same situation.*

- *This helped me cope with the shock and get my feelings and thoughts in order. Other families had experienced similar happenings.*

- *What was most helpful? The views of the parents, the knowledge of the facilitators, both videos, the cycle of abuse — I find it difficult to pinpoints one area as they were all so relevant, helpful and important.*

- *My feelings were very mixed up, and by attending the group I began to understand things better.*

Future Developments

Future developments will include:

- More systematic development of the parent link-up network, and public awareness talks given by parents via anonymous audio and video recordings.

- The facilitators engaging in public awareness education through multi-disciplinary inter-agency training programmes and media coverage.

- Annual recall of the parents' support group to ascertain the effectiveness of the programme and future needs.

- Pre and post tests in relation to parents' experiences of:

    - Marital happiness scale (to be developed by authors).

    - Sexual functioning scale (to be developed by authors).

    - Beck Depression Inventory (Beck, 1978).

Conclusions

This chapter has highlighted the importance of a therapeutic group treatment programme for parents/carers of young people who sexually abuse. The original aim of this programme was to help the parents/carers understand the process of the young people's treatment group. Clearly this end was achieved, as, in general, the parents/carers were highly motivated to help these young people and prevent further abuse. It is the opinion of the authors that an equally significant outcome of the programme was that these parents/carers were enabled to work through their own trauma and to develop adequate coping skills. This was achieved through their expression of fears, feelings and concerns, in an atmosphere of trust and confidentiality.

This population had been offered individual treatment following allegations of abuse, However, experience of group work seems to indicate that many of these parents/carers are still exhibiting post-traumatic stress disorder symptoms 1 to 1½ years later. Peer understanding helped validate particular situations, and the group leaders were sensitive to the needs of, and nuances expressed by, the parents/carers. The experience of the group leaders enabled the development of a careful balance of support and confrontation when necessary.

A third issue which surfaced during the first group, and which has continued to be a significant issue, is the need for community education on what sexual abuse is and what resources are available for the victims, perpetrators and their families. An often repeated refrain from the parents/carers was that until the allegation of sexual abuse landed on their doorstep, their awareness of sexual abuse and its consequences was minimal. Their recommendation, therefore, was for the development of community awareness and prevention programmes. For the group leaders this recommendation led to the development of networks for the parents/carers. It is envisaged that some form of sponsor programme would be developed in the near future.

A positive outcome arising from the development of the Young Persons' Group and the Parents'/Carers' Group, has been the setting of a standardised assessment and treatment programme for the young people and their families within the Southern Health and Social Services Board in Northern Ireland. All referrals are made to a central agency and all follow standardised procedures.

The support group for parents/carers is a part of a larger multi-disciplinary inter-agency project within the Southern Health and Social Services Board in Northern Ireland. The work with parents/carers has been fully understood and supported by those in positions of management, without whose endorsement this work could not have progressed this far.

References

Beck, A.T. (1978). *Beck Depression Inventory*.

Becker, J.V. (1991). Working with Perpetrators. In Murray, K., and Gouge, D. (Eds.). *Intervening in Cases of Child Sexual Abuse*, 157–165. Edinburgh: Scotish Academic Press.

Bentonin, A., Elton, A., Hilderbrand-Jitranter, M., and Vizard, E. (Eds.). *Child Sexual Abuse Within the Family: Assessment and Treatment*. London: Wright.

Bremner, J.F. (1991). Intervention with Juvenile Sex Offenders. *Human Systems*, 2: 235–246.

Calder, M.C. (1997). *Juveniles and Children who Sexually Abuse: A Guide to Risk Assessment*. Dorset: Russell House Publishing.

Gerdes, K.E., Gourly, M., and Cash, C. (1995). Assessing Juvenile Sex Offenders to Determine Adequate Levels of Supervision. *Child Abuse and Neglect*, 19(8): 953–961.

Giarretto, H. (1992). *Integrated Treatment of Child Sexual Abuse: A Treatment and Training Manual*. Palo Alto: Science and Behaviour Books Inc.

Gil, E. (1987). *Children who Molest: A Guide for Parents of Young Sex Offenders*. Rockville: Launch Press.

Gist, R., and Taylor, J. (1994). *Family Assessment Programme: Working with Parents and Carers of Young People who Display Inappropriate Sexual Behaviour*. Coventry: NSPCC.

Giggs, D.R., and Boldy, A. (1995). Parallel Treatment of Parents and Abuse Children. In Hunter, M. (Ed.). *Child Survivors and Perpetrators of Sexual Abuse: Treatment Innovation*, 147–165. Thousand Oaks, CA: Sage.

Hunter, M. (1995). *Child Survivors and Perpetrators of Sexual Abuse: Treatment Innovations*. Thousand Oaks, CA: Sage.

Kaplan, M.S., Becker, J.V., and Martinez, D. (1990). A Comparison of Mothers of Adolescent Incest versus Non-incest Perpetrators. *Journal of Family Violence*, 5(3): 213.

Mayle, and Robins, A. (1986). *What's Happening to Me?* — video.

McGarvey, J., and Lenaghan, M. (1996). A Structured Group Approach with Adolescent Perpetrators. *Child Abuse Review*, 5: 203–213.

National Task Force Report (1993). *Juvenile and Family Court Journal*, 44(4).

Nightingale, C. (1988). *The Nightingale Roars* — video.

NSPCC (1995). *Guide for Parents Whose Children Have Sexually Abused Others*.

NSPCC (1997). *Information for Young People*

Pithers, W.D., Gray, A.S., Cunningham, C., and Lane, S. (1993). *From Trauma to Understanding — A Guide for Parents of Children with Sexual Behaviour Problems*. Brandon, VT: Safer Society Press.

Ryan, G., and Lane, S. (Eds.) (1991). *Juvenile Sexual Offending: Causes, Consequences and Correction*. Lexington, MA: DC Heath.

Scott, D. (1996). Parental Experiences in Cases of Child Sexual Abuse: A Qualitative Study. *Child and Family Social Work*, 1(2): 107–114.

Smets, A.C. and Cebula, C.M. (1987). A Group Treatment Programme for Adolescent Sex Offenders: Five Steps Towards Resolution. *Child Abuse and Neglect*, 11: 247–254.

Vizard, E., Monck, E., and Misch, P., (1995). Child and Adolescent Sex Abuse Perpetrators: A Review of the Research Literature. *Child Psychology/Psychiatry*, 36(5): 737.

Appendix One

Please answer the following questions as best you can.

REMEMBER, DO NOT PUT YOUR NAME ANYWHERE ON THE QUESTIONNAIRE

1. **HOW ARE THINGS GOING FOR YOU NOW?**
   (please tick one box)

   Very well   ☐
   Well   ☐
   Not good   ☐

2. **ABOUT HOW MANY FRIENDS DO YOU HAVE?**
   (please tick one box)

   None   ☐
   1   ☐
   2 or 3   ☐
   4 or more ☐

3. **ABOUT HOW MANY TIMES PER WEEK DO YOU DO THINGS WITH FRIENDS OUTSIDE SCHOOL/WORK?**
   (please tick one box)

   Less than 1 ☐
   1 or 2   ☐
   3 or more   ☐

4. **COMPARED WITH OTHER YOUNG PEOPLE YOUR AGE, HOW DO YOU GET ALONG WITH:**
   (please tick one box on each line)

	Worse	Same	Better
Other young people?	☐	☐	☐
Your parents/carers?	☐	☐	☐

5. **SINCE OUR TIME AND WORK TOGETHER HAS FINISHED, WHO HAS BEEN OF HELP TO YOU:**
(please tick appropriate boxes)

      Parent ☐
      Friend ☐
      School ☐
      Social worker ☐
      Other ☐
      No-one ☐

6. **DO YOU EVER THINK OR WORRY ABOUT THE SAME THING HAPPENING AGAIN?**
(please tick one box)

      Always ☐
      Often ☐
      Sometimes ☐
      Never ☐

7. **HAS THE SAME THING HAPPENED?**
(please tick one box)

      Yes ☐   No ☐

8. **DO YOU THINK THE SAME THING COULD HAPPEN AGAIN?**

      Yes ☐
      Maybe ☐
      No ☐

9. **HOW HELPFUL DID YOU FIND OUR WORK TOGETHER?**
(please tick one box)

      Not very helpful ☐
      Helpful ☐
      Very helpful ☐

10. **WHAT WAS THE MOST DIFFICULT FOR YOU?**

      Telling about what happened ☐
      Talking about what happened ☐
      Understanding the effects on others ☐
      Learning how to stop the same thing happening again ☐

DO YOU WANT TO SAY ANYTHING MORE?

....

....

....

Thank you for your help in completing this questionnaire.

Guide for Parents Whose **CHILDREN** *Have Sexually Abused Others*

GENERAL INTRODUCTION

*This short leaflet has been written for parents whose child has sexually abused another child. A child is anyone under the age of 18. The leaflet gives brief information to help parents understand why young people sexually abuse others and how parents can help their own child and indeed themselves through what is a very **difficult, stressful, painful and confusing time for all.***

WHAT IS SEXUAL ABUSE?

The sexual abuse of a child occurs whenever any person persuades, forces, tricks or threatens a child in order to have sexual contact with him or her. Sexual contact can include touching the child's genitals and can progress to more extreme forms of sexual behaviour. Sometimes there is no direct physical contact, but the child/young person is shown pornographic materials (including photographs and books or films).

In all cases of child sexual abuse the child is being used as an object to satisfy the adolescent/adult's sexual needs or desires.

EFFECTS ON THE VICTIM

A child victim is damaged by their experiences, even if no force was used. The victim frequently suffers emotional disturbance such as:

- *embarrassment, fear, confusion*
- *guilt, anxiety, sense of rejection*
- *distrust of adults and strangers*

Some of these effects may be long lasting, and some of these symptoms of emotional harm may not be evident for years, often not until some time in adulthood.

Help for the victim can alleviate these effects.

HOW PARENTS FEEL

The first reaction of most parents when they learn that their child has abused is one of disbelief. The news of what a child has done comes as a great shock and parents will find themselves with many difficult thoughts, questions and mixed up emotions.

Parents may find themselves defending their child with other explanations for what has happened especially when the child denies what they have done, because they too are feeling ashamed, embarrassed and afraid.

It is important that parents do not simply accept that their child could not have abused. Although it will be very difficult it is essential that parents stand by and support their child during this difficult time and help their child to talk about what they have done.

One of the best ways to do this is to use the help that is available for the child and for parents.

Family members have an important part to play in giving support and ensuring that their child receives the help which is necessary. It is important for everyone to look honestly at how the abuse happened and to try to help one another, to work with others, to correct the situation.

Parents can make a vital contribution by working closely and in co-operation with the professionals who provide counselling and treatment.

Parents will also need some time for themselves so that they have the chance to talk about their own thoughts and feelings, to try and find some answers to the many questions they may have.

This time and help is available for parents.

WHY CONCERN?

Sexual abuse by young people is unfortunately not uncommon. It is of growing concern to everyone who works with children, both with children who have been victims of abuse and also with those who abuse.

There are many reasons for this concern, some of which are given below:

1. We know that many adults who sexually abuse begin offending in their teenage years and even earlier. This early abuse often goes undetected or is dismissed as of no real concern. Help is not then given. Unfortunately many of these young people then continue to abuse into adulthood, when the abuse is exceedingly more difficult to stop.

2. Sexual abusing is caused by problems in the way the young person thinks and feels about themself and others. These problems are not often obvious or easy to see. If they are not understood and help is not given then these problems will lead to more abuse.

3. Sexual abuse has a damaging effect on the person who is abused. Almost always the young person who abuses is not aware of this and as a result they go on abusing.

4. Sexual abuse very quickly becomes an addictive behaviour and one which the young person finds difficult to control and stop, even when caught.

Many parents question the need for their child to have help. Concerned parents may fear that dwelling on the matter will make things worse, that things are better 'left alone'. As a result they may resist the idea of help for their child.

Without fully exploring the problem with the possibility of help for the young person the risk of more abuse is great. The danger is that the young person will find the behaviour beyond his control so that control by others is needed.

Assessment, which aims to understand the underlying problems that led to the abuse and treatment/intervention to provide help with these problems are essential.

Assessment and treatment is available from a number of people and agencies working with young people who have sexually abused.

CONFIDENTIALITY

The information made available by any young person and their family during exploration of the problem and treatment will be shared among those people directly involved in taking decisions about the young person.

An exception to this may be in the event of a young person disclosing information such as further sexual abuse which would need to be shared with other agencies, namely Social Services and/or Police, in order to protect that young person themselves or others who may be at risk.

Appendix Three

Information for Young People

The Children's Centre, Craigavon

NSPCC

'It was scary going into the group at first, but the group has helped me to understand the effects of what I have done and how not to abuse in the future.'

Comment from a young person.

Introduction

The Children's Centre is a project jointly run by the National Society for the Prevention of Cruelty to Children (NSPCC) and the Southern Area Child Protection Committee.

The Centre has qualified trained staff, who work with young people. They will listen to, talk to, advise and respond to you to help in your treatment.

Welcome

Welcome to **Craigavon Children's Centre**. You have probably been asked to come here because it is believed that you have sexually abused someone. You are probably feeling confused, upset and frightened. This booklet has been written to explain what might happen now and how you and your family can be helped.

The most important thing for you to remember is that you must not continue to sexually abuse anyone. If you do, there will be very serious consequences, like going to prison or becoming an outcast from society.

What is sexual abuse?

Sexual abuse occurs when you persuade, force, trick or threaten a child or someone else to have sexual contact with you. Sexual contact can include fondling and touching private parts and can often lead on to more extreme forms of sexual behaviour.

Always remember that sexual abuse is a criminal offence and you can work to change this behaviour.

What happens to me?

Police Officers, who work with young people, will interview you to find out what happened and how you sexually abused your victim. This interview will be in a Police station. The officers are attached to the Child Abuse and Rape Enquiry (CARE) Unit.

The CARE Unit will already have interviewed your alleged victim and will have sent a report to the Department of Public Prosecutions (DPP) who will decide if you should go to Court. As a result you may be directed to attend the Juvenile Perpetrators Project Treatment Programme.

Who is going to help me?

You and your family will get help from people who have worked with other young people in similar situations. Your worker could be a Social Worker, a Therapist, a Probation Officer, a Psychologist or a Psychiatrist.

How long will this work take?

It depends on you and how hard you are willing to work. It is important to remember that your case will be reviewed throughout your time here. In general, you can expect to be in the programme on a weekly basis for a year, but sometimes it takes longer.

How can I get help?

After your interview with one of the Police Officers from the CARE Unit, you will begin an **individual programme of work** with an experienced member of staff. This work will also involve your parents and other family members.

Later on you may become involved in a group programme with other young people who have also sexually abused.

Yours parents or carers will also have the opportunity to attend a group to help and support them.

This programme for young people has been developed over a number of years. Some of the young people, who have been through this programme, have told us that it will help you to:

- take responsibility for your abusive behaviour
- understand how you sexually abused
- understand how your victim feels during and after the abuse
- stop abusing children
- avoid placing yourself in risk situations
- understand your own feelings

Remember - it will take a lot of hard work and co-operation from you, if you are to work through this problem.

What do I have to do?

You will have to:

- be honest and co-operate with your worker
- take responsibility for your offending behaviour
- understand how the sexual abuse has affected your victim(s)
- understand and manage your own feelings
- talk about the full details of the abuse
- talk about your personal issues
- look at consent and mutuality
- learn about sex education and how to develop appropriate relationships
- talk about your home, friends, school and work (if relevant)
- learn to recognise and manage risk situations
- look at supports for you and your family

These are the main areas of work, but there may be others depending on your own situation.

Important reminders

- You **must not** have any contact on your own with your victim(s).
- You **must not** babysit under any circumstances, either within or outside your family.
- You **must not** be left in charge of younger children at home, in school, at church, in your workplace or anywhere else.

Privacy rules in your family must be respected:

- *Bathrooms are private* - before entering knock on the door to be sure no-one else is in there.
- *Bedrooms are private* - do not enter a younger child's bedroom under any circumstances at any time.

Where can I get further help and information?

If you need help or more information you can write to:

The Children's Centre
NSPCC
Moyraverty Centre
Craigavon
Co Armagh
BT65 5HX

or call   **01762 341 338**

Chapter Eleven

Developing Groupwork with Young People who Sexually Abuse

Kate O'Boyle, Kevin Lenehan
and Jacqui McGarvey

Developing Groupwork with Young People who Sexually Abuse

Background to the Groupwork Programme

Davis and Leitenberg (1987) report that in the United States about 20 per cent of all rapes, and 30–50 per cent of all cases of child sexual abuse, can be attributed to adolescents. Further, approximately 50 per cent of adult sex offenders report that their first sexual offence occurred during their teenage years. Consistent with this, Kennedy *et al.* (1990), in their Northern Ireland study, highlighted that some 36 per cent of cases of sexual abuse involved young people as perpetrators, and most adolescent sex offenders are male (Calder, 1997). Experience, through referral to the Juvenile Perpetrators Project, would seem to be consistent with this. Current research identifies most abusers as being male but with a growing realisation that females also sexually abuse. At the time of writing the referral system does not reflect this realisation.

Currently it is acknowledged that, in working with this particular client group, the groupwork process and individual work can compliment each other in the effective treatment of these young peoples' behaviours.

This groupwork programme has developed from 1989, when professionals interested in this area of work had already noted an increasing number of adolescent males coming to the attention of child protection services as a result of their sexually abusive behaviour. With consultation and discussion between the National Society for the Prevention of Cruelty to Children (NSPCC) and the Department of Child Psychiatry, a group treatment programme for these adolescents was proposed and developed within the Southern Health and Social Services Board (N. Ireland). To date seven group programmes have been completed.

With the more recent development of the Juvenile Perpetrators Project Team (JPPT) the term adolescent has been replaced by juvenile, but for the purpose of this paper we refer to group members as young person/people.

How then do we define young people? Within the procedures of the Southern Board Area Child Protection Committee (SACPC), young people are those between the ages of 10 and 18 years. However, in acknowledging the variance of developmental stages within this age group, consideration is given to the particular 'age mix' of referrals, to decide the optimal age range for each group programme.

Defining Sexually Abusive Behaviour

In order to arrive at a definition, it is imperative to have an understanding of the research base which has been developed and the concepts formulated that enable professionals to define normal, problematic or sexually abusive behaviours. The concepts of consent and power underlie Calder's (1997) definition of sexual abuse:

> *Young people (below the age of 18 years) who engage in any form of sexual activity with another individual, that they have powers over by virtue of age, emotional maturity, gender, physical strength, intellect and where the victim in this relationship has suffered a sexual exploitation and betrayal of trust. Sexual activity includes sexual intercourse (oral, anal or vaginal), sexual touching, exposure of sexual organs, showing pornographic material, exhibitionism, voyeurism, obscene communication, frottage, fetishism and talking in a sexualised way. We should also include any form of sexual activity with an animal, and where a young person sexually abuses an adult.*

> (Adapted from Palmer, 1995)

Such a definition determines the referral format to the JPPT and thus for consideration to the group programme.

Since the inception of the groupwork Programme in 1988, the process and development has been reviewed by McCune and Scott (1994) and McGarvey and Lenaghan (1996). The timing of this latter review coincided with the launch of the JPPT. The project incorporated the groupwork programme as an integral and complementary part of working with young people who sexually abuse. Such work includes an individual and/or groupwork component within the treatment aspect of the programme. This will be discussed in more detail in the paper.

It is the intention of this paper to give a descriptive and analytical account of the groupwork programme from the perspective of two group workers who were new to this particular programme. One worker is a full-time member of the JPPT and both have been working in child protection with a social work background in family and child care. Both workers were able to avail of the previous group experiences of colleagues and of Jacqui McGarvey, co-ordinator of the JPPT.

The developed group treatment programme is based on a model by Smets and Cebula (1987), and comprises six steps as follows:

Step 1: Getting to know each other.

- Group introduction.
- Beginning of group identity.
- Development of trust.

Step 2: Why am I present in the group?

- I am willing to co-operate without having to be asked.
- I have helped others to participate in the group process.

Step 3: I am now ready to think about, to try and understand, how the children I sexually abused were affected by what I did.

- To raise intellectual awareness of the impact on the victim.
- To develop emotional understanding and an awareness of the impact on the victim.

Step 4: I am now ready to tell the details of what I did.

- Full description of the sexual abuse.
- How the sexual abuse was planned and carried out.
- Assessing the presence of denial, minimising and justification.
- Challenging the above.

Step 5: I can talk about sex and sexuality.

- Sexual knowledge and understanding.
- Appropriate understanding of physical/sexual development.
- Relationships.
- Mutuality and consent.
- Disclosure of own sexual abuse or other forms of abuse.
- Review of victim empathy.

Step 6: I understand and know how to deal with my own sexual desires. I have a vote of confidence from the group and leaders. I understand about inappropriate sexual thoughts, fantasies, masturbation and the links between these.

- Raising awareness of risk situations, emotions and thoughts.
- Skills for managing risk factors.
- Letter to victim(s).
- Support networks.

We would propose to describe and raise issues relevant to this work and, in particular, to the groupwork process involving two groups over a 2-year period.

Why groupwork?

The therapy of groups is likely to turn on the acquisition of knowledge and experience of the factors which make for a good group spirit.

(Bion, 1943)

Research programmes acknowledge that the groupwork process is an effective means of promoting awareness, tolerance, developing relationships and, indeed, mirroring community and social dynamics. Sharing and development of knowledge and appropriate information optimises the learning potential.

As the aim of working with sex offenders is to develop increased responsibility for controlling the sexually abusive behaviour, and given that their initial motivation may be poor, and their levels of denial and distorted thinking may be high, the choice of appropriate Group Models needs to take these factors into account.

(Clark and Erooga, 1994)

As such, the development of the group programme model can address these factors.

In the experience of facilitating the group, it has been noted that the young people have little or no insight into their abusing behaviours, beyond acknowledging that it is 'wrong'. As a result, the programme has been formulated and developed from the premise that the young people are lacking in insight with regard to their behaviours. They also present as having little insight into the consequences of such behaviours i.e. from family, child protection procedures, RUC CARE Unit (Royal Ulster Constabulary Child Abuse and Rape Enquiry Unit).

Such a premise has helped avoid any underlying assumptions regarding the young people's knowledge/understanding of issues/facts, and has enabled the development of a more comprehensive programme. Pre-group individual work with the young people has promoted an increased awareness of their own individual strengths and weaknesses; which has, in turn, effected increased responses in relation to: peer presence, peer experience, peer prejudices, peer pressure, and peer insight within the group format.

This has provided more scope in developing the young people's ability to make sense of their abusive behaviours. In concluding, it is worth noting the importance within the group setting of developing the young people's perception of the group having *one presenting problem*, i.e. sexually abusive behaviour. This focus promotes group unity and support and avoids minimisation.

Selection

Individual work with the young people is the beginning phase of intervention, i.e. the assessment of the young person in relation to their sexually abusive behaviour. This assessment uses the model as outlined by Loss and Ross (1988). This intervention is complimented by a series of psychological questionnaires, which can give some insight into the young person's self-perception. Outcomes for such work establish the criteria for group membership.

It has been recognised that the success or otherwise of the groupwork programme is strongly reliant on the multi-disciplinary and inter-agency network of professionals, and this is particularly so in relation to the selection process. Experience has confirmed the importance of this initial stage if the programme is to have optimal benefits for the young people. Selection for the programme is agreed through meetings of JPPT and appropriate use of consultation with psychologists/psychiatrists attached to the project. Factors considered in the process are:

Group members	Six group members have proved to be an optimum number, in terms of process/behaviour management.
Age	While referrals to the Project fall within the range of 10–18 years, the average age of the young people in the two most recent groups is 15.5 years, the youngest being 14 years and the oldest 17 years.
Level of ability	Each young person's selection into the group programme is affected by the pre-group assessment, undertaken on an individual basis and discussed within the JPPT and with other appropriate professionals. John (17 years) has a learning disability and was a group member. In discussion with other professionals, and in consultation with the clinical psychologist, it was felt that John's 'disability' could not only enhance the group process, but could also be compensated for by the group process and by individual group members. Experience within the programme was consistent with this opinion.
Behavioural difficulty	In order to maximise the benefits for the young people within the group process, it has been necessary to pay particular attention to this aspect of selection. Past experience has allowed for the acceptance of only one young person into the group who presents as having significant potential/actual behavioural problems. This is also influenced by the overall 'mix' within the group, where peer pressure can influence such behaviour as effectively as leaders' intervention, as was the case with Paul (15 years), who was particularly disruptive during Step 5. Leaders had to challenge Paul about this and remind him of group rules and group objectives. This was supported by the other young people. Paul subsequently missed the next session, but later acknowledged his inappropriate behaviour and conformed to agreed boundaries.
Denial	The issue of denial forms an important part of the pre-group individual assessment. As such, young people who do not acknowledge their sexually abusive behaviour are not selected for the groupwork programme. It is however acknowledged that young people will minimise, justify or project blame, but such issues can be addressed within the process.
Family denial/support	During the 2 groups there has been no outright family denial, rather, as with the young people, there have been levels of minimisation, justification and projecting blame. Given that young people are not operating within a vacuum, it makes sense to promote family support, whether through the field social worker and/or through the Parents' Support Programme. Facilitators would make the point that the groupwork programme is part of the continuum of the overall intervention. As such, the pre-group individual work is an important aspect of this intervention. It has been the experience to date that in the initial stage of intervention by JPPT members, the acceptance by parents/carers of the need for work is vital in enabling the young person to engage in the assessment/treatment programme. Within the groupwork programme, commitment and developed understanding by parents within the Parents' Support Group, places them in a better position to support the young person in the ongoing involvement in the work.

Nature of offences	In the 2 most recent groups the sexually abusive behaviour has ranged from: touching private parts (both children and adult), forcing children to have oral sex, attempting anal/vaginal intercourse; to bestiality. With 12 young people in the 2 groups, the nature of their abusive behaviours ranged from:
	Victims: aged 4 years to adult.
	Gender: 11 female children; 10 male children; 1 adult female; one young person also sexually abused animals.
	Intra/extra familial: 8 young people abused extra-familial; 4 young people abused intra-familial; 2 young people abused both intra and extra-familial.
	Previous offending: One young person had previously sexually abused.
	Multiple abuse: One young person had 4 victims.
Mandated treatment	It is recognised that for many young people who sexually abuse a legal mandate for treatment is recommended. This is a recognition that there is often an initial reluctance on the part of these young people to attend voluntarily, and some degree of external pressure is useful. However, in the 2 groups, none of the 12 young people who attended did so because of a legal mandate, but 4 of them were subsequently mandated through the courts to complete the programme.

It is important to note that some of the young people have themselves been victims of sexual abuse. Peter, during Step 3, disclosed to the group that he had been sexually abused by his mother. This was sensitively acknowledged within the group, and identified as a separate piece of work to be undertaken on an individual basis with Peter, outside of the group programme.

The issue of confidentiality and limits of same is addressed with the young people at the outset of the group programme, i.e. in respect of passing new information to appropriate agencies.

It was also noted that with the recent development of the JPPT, individual pre-group assessment work with the young people has enabled a 'fine tuning' of the selection process using the above criteria. Such individual work acts as the preparatory stage for treatment work, in that it enables the young person to begin to accept their abusive behaviour and the need to change. Such a development has ensured a more effective selection, and also ensures that those young people not taken into the group programme have the opportunity to address their sexually abusive behaviour

through ongoing individual programmes.

The table below highlights such a development; comparing 1992 selection and 1997 selection to the group:

	1992	1997
Number in denial	2/6	0/6
Mandated	0/6	0/6
Family denial	1/6	0/6
Family minimisation	3/6	0/6
Behavioural disturbance	2/6	0/6

The combination of denial, family minimisation and behavioural disturbance as evidenced in 1992 Group, proved to be a very difficult 'mix' for effective running of the group.

In order to promote confidentiality and avoid collusion, in so far as is possible, there are a number of other factors which would not merit selection to the group: members of the same family, young people at the same school, and young people living close to each other/knowing each other.

It has to be recognised that, despite using the above guidelines, there are no guarantees that the young people meet such criteria. Indeed, in the 1996 group it became apparent in Session 1 of the programme that 3 young people knew each other, despite wide geographical distances between them. Fortunately, this did not appear to hinder the group process.

Attendance

In planning for the practice of the group programme, there was an awareness of issues, which would impact on the subsequent attendance by the young people at the group. These include:

Planning and supports

It has been recognised that the success or otherwise of the groupwork programme is strongly reliant on the multi-disciplinary and inter-agency network, from the selection process throughout the duration of the programme.

The planning process begins with the decision to run a groupwork programme, a decision taken within the multi-disciplinary arena of the now established JPPT. At this stage the importance of selecting a 'good mix' of young people takes priority. Whilst the intention is to run a programme yearly, it was found last year that there was not sufficient young people using the selection criteria. Good practice dictated that the programme be delayed for some two months.

Timing of group	In order to accommodate young people at school/work, the groups ran in the evenings, i.e. 6.30–8.00 pm.
Transport	Given the wide catchment area this was of particular importance, necessitating agreement with the field social worker to arrange transport as appropriate. Absences from the group tended to result from a breakdown in such arrangements.
Carer/parent support	Experience would suggest that where such support was positive young peoples attendance was enhanced.
Group process	The young people can readily identify Step 4 as being the most difficult part of the work. In the first group this factor did not affect attendance. In the most recent group, Peter did not attend for several weeks because of an inability/reluctance to go through this step. It was noted that this absence affected responses from the other young people, including frustration, intolerance and irritation.
Groupwork venue	Whilst acknowledging the venue for the programme as being neutral, the young people, on occasion, did recognise school peers, particularly as the programme continued in the light nights. Given the nature of the programme, it is deemed inappropriate for anyone else to be on the premises during the sessions e.g. service users, cleaners, etc.
Agreed rules	It is important that the young people have a sense of ownership re the ground rules that apply to the programme, i.e. the young people understand and acknowledge the importance of commitment to the work. Confidentiality within the group is discussed and agreed at the outset.
Group responsibility	In the experience of the 2 groups, positive group spirit was acknowledged. This was established from the outset by encouraging the young people to take individual/group responsibility which was promoted in a proactive way e.g. through the use of role play exercises to encourage and demonstrate openness, honesty and trust.

In selecting the young people, contact is then made with field social workers/parents/carers/young people, to discuss the details of the process, both professional and practical. Both group leaders then meet with each young person to introduce themselves and reinforce/encourage them to attend. As to be expected, there was reluctance from some young people to attend, but pressure from parents/carers and professionals, alongside an explanation of the benefits of the group participation, has been successful in engaging the young people.

Current policies and procedures within the multi-disciplinary arena are explained to the parents and young people. This includes information, both verbal and in writing, regarding open access to records, complaints procedure, and the purpose and process of sharing information which is appropriate, both to the parents and other professionals. This can be done through direct contact with or through the forums of formal meetings, e.g. case plan, case conference.

Planning for the programme takes place on a weekly basis to:

- Plan the content, not only of the individual session, but also within the context of each step and, indeed, the whole programme.

- Agree co-working roles and responsibilities (see paragraph below).

- Agree the varied techniques, skills etc., that facilitate the work content, but mindful of alternative strategies that might be used.

- Record and review previous session. It is acknowledged that the recording of information is imperative, whether through the use of video and/or written recording, the purpose being:

  – To record details of the young peoples' progress.

  – To identify and confront denial and minimisation etc.

  – To facilitate, review and overall evaluation.

- The use of video to record each group session has been a valued feature of the process. Benefits include:

  – Checking inconsistencies in detailing the young peoples' behaviours/taking responsibility.

  – Highlighting development of self-esteem through the programme.

  – Useful for training purposes.

  – If further abuse is disclosed the tape can be given to the RUC.

In the practice of facilitating the two groups, more details of already known abuse has been recorded on tape. While such information was passed onto the appropriate agency, no requests for the actual tape has been made. Facilitators, agencies, parents and young people are aware that in using video recording, such tapes are 'discoverable', as indeed are written records.

An important pre-requisite of the group programme is the availability of positive support mechanisms, ranging from the field social workers on an ongoing basis, to the more formal supervision from within NSPCC and the JPPT. Such support and supervision is experienced on an informal and formal basis. At the informal level the group facilitators continually highlight and explore the pertinent issues, both at a practice and personal level. This carries through to ongoing liaison with facilitators of the parents' group and, where appropriate, other professionals. At the formal level, individual monthly supervision with the team managers addresses relevant issues, again at a practice and personal level. This is further enhanced through weekly cases meetings within the NSPCC team itself, and through monthly meetings of the JPPT. Where felt necessary, facilitators have been able to access consultations with appropriate professionals, e.g. psychologist/psychiatrist.

Practical considerations in respect of the group programme are important to the smooth running of the group, ranging from the provision of light refreshments for each session, to ensuring that social workers/parents/carers/young people receive the same written information. A further practical consideration is a commitment to the planning process. Experience has shown that setting aside one morning every week to review, record and plan was very effective. It is acknowledged, however, that maintaining this commitment can be difficult, given the nature of case work demands.

While the programme is planned within the general framework of the groupwork model, it is essential that a flexible approach is adopted, to account for individual/group needs. At times, specific issues have taken precedence over the planning objectives. An example of this was, on two occasions, when issues of bullying were noted and had to be addressed within the programme.

Co-working

The current groupwork programme has evolved with an acknowledgement and understanding that co-working is therapeutically beneficial to the process, as well as being an important factor in reducing isolation, secrecy and stress. In support of this method of working, there has also been an awareness of the same benefits applying to mixed gender co-working.

> ...*Given the complex demands on those leading groups of this nature, mixed gender co-leadership offers the best opportunity to maximise the potential of the group, and reduce the possibilities of collusion of deflection and minimise potential negative effects on staff.*

(Clark and Erooga, 1994) (8)

In the context of the overall programme, the effectiveness or otherwise of the co-working relationship is dependent on co-workers exploring and developing shared professional and personal objectives. Such objectives include:

- Shared value stance, i.e. non-judgmental approach to the young people, coupled with openness and honesty, that can be demonstrated to them in the process.

- Shared confidence in identifying behaviours and attitudes as unacceptable without being punitive.

- An understanding of each others values, feelings, fears, skills and behaviours, thus promoting and developing trust.

- Agreeing appropriate moral codes, particularly within the context of sex and sexuality.

- Agreeing appropriate language and how

to respond to inappropriate language.

- Developing strategies to deal with unpredicted/unexpected issues that undoubtedly occur e.g., sick leave.

- Shared awareness that for some young people, the leaders can be perceived as role models.

Within the Groupwork Programme, where peer support, competition and confrontation are promoted, the application of these objectives enable co-workers not only to challenge young peoples' prejudices, but also to positively present important knowledge and experiences which will, hopefully, promote young peoples' insight and awareness.

Within the practice context of the work, it is important to adopt the specific gender roles, particularly in relation to challenging prejudices/attitudes, e.g. 'Women are only out for one thing: sex and money', and 'A woman doesn't always mean no even when she says no'. It proved effective that such attitudes/prejudices be challenged in the first instance by the female worker, and reinforced by the male worker, and, in providing information, e.g. in the context of sex and sexuality, such information was provided from both the male/female perspective.

Development of the 6 Step Programme

A groupwork model developed by Smets and Cebula (1987) was chosen to form the basis of the treatment programme for the young people who sexually abuse. Originally a five Step process over a 12-week period, the model was adapted to the current six Steps and, at present, runs over an approximate 26 week period.

The current model consists of six Steps, as outlined and detailed below:

1. Developing group identity, trust and calm.

2. Developing individual commitment to the group process, i.e. engagement, co-operation, voluntary contribution, disclosure, challenging, commitment to change, reviewing.

3. Developing intellectual and emotional understanding of the impact of abuse, i.e. empathy.

4. Enabling young people to talk through their offence cycles with facilitators, challenging inconsistencies, minimisation, justification and denial.

5. Developing young peoples' knowledge of sex and sexuality.

6. Raising awareness of young peoples' own sexual desires and risk situations, and developing skills to manage such risks.

It is worth noting that while the structure of the process is clearly defined, the practice can often require the group to address specific issues as and when they arise. Progress through each step is dependent on all the young people completing each one together, as agreed by the young people themselves and the facilitators.

John, for example, was able to acknowledge to the group that he hadn't completed Step 5, as others had done, because he had been in 'bad form' in one of the sessions, had attempted to disrupt the session; had not attended the next session because facilitators had challenged him. In this situation the other young people were irritated by John's attempted disruption, and were able to confirm to facilitators his non-completion of the step. The group re-visited the content of this session and agreed that the identified work be completed on an individual basis.

Where a young person has opted not to attend certain sessions, facilitators have used the group to 'inform' the young person about what they have missed, to review already developed learning and to reinforce the importance of group members moving the process forward. It is noted that in such situations peer pressure has been both significant and effective in maintaining group commitment.

While the structure of the current model remains intact, the practice has naturally developed and adjusted, as no group remains static. This has resulted from reviewing previous programmes and learning from same. The skills and individual strengths of facilitators and the co-working relationship are also an important factor in such development. For example, one of the current facilitators is experienced in dance movement, and such experience has been used to positive effect in the group process.

The model is time-limited and has historically run over an approximate 6-month period of weekly sessions. In the most recent group programme the use of full day sessions in completing Steps 4 and 6 has proved successful, in terms of group continuity, support and optimal learning. This development arose out of liaisons with colleagues in the Galway Project.

In previous groups the young people have always identified Step 4 as the most difficult and, indeed, facilitators have always acknowledged this. In the 1996 group programme this step took eight sessions to complete, and a build up of tension among the young people was noted, both in the weeks preceding and during the weeks of the step itself. As such it was discussed and agreed that the young people complete this step in a full day session, consideration having been given to effects of missing school or work. Starting at 10.00 am, five of the young people had completed the Step at the end of the session, i.e. approximately 5.00 pm. In reviewing this process both facilitators and the young people noted the positive aspects including better, continuity, enhanced sense of togetherness, and a feeling of 'acceptance', in that the group has 'a problem' not 'six individual problems'. On the negative side, everyone was able to acknowledge that it was a 'long day', albeit interspersed with breaks/refreshments.

Peter did not attend this session, later acknowledging his fear of having to confront his sexually abusive behaviour, and accepting the criticism and irritation of the other young people in not attending. He completed this step in the subsequent session.

During the two most recent groups consideration has been given to the possible development of a 'rolling group', but this has been set aside, mainly on the basis of an acknowledgement that the geographical catchment area is 'rural', and the numbers of young people would not be sufficient to proceed with such a development. Similarly, consideration has been given to an 'open group', but this has also been set aside given the structure of the model. By definition, an open group allows for young people to join at any stage of the process, e.g. at Step 4. However, given the identified need for young people to work systematically through all six steps, and the nature of the steps themselves, i.e. progressive, the 'open group model' would not be conducive to this process. Hence, the decision to opt for the 'closed group model' was apparent where the young people come together and remain together through the progressive Steps of the work.

A dynamic of the group process is the use of peer interaction and a system of incentives to move on in therapy. To enable the young people to progress through the steps, i.e.

- To acknowledge the reasons for being in the group.
- To detail their abusive behaviour.
- To acknowledge their personal sexual development.
- To enhance insight into such behaviour and their own sexuality.
- To avoid re-abusing.

It is important that the facilitators adopt varying styles to ensure optimal responses. Such styles include:

- Supportive and encouraging.
- Sharing.
- Supervising.
- Directional and educational.
- Investigatory.
- Confrontational.
- Challenging.

Given the reason for the young people being in the group, i.e. their sexually abusive behaviour, facilitators would be clear that the use of all of the above styles is imperative throughout the 6 steps, but particularly so in Step 4, which makes the young people confront their behaviour.

Step 1

The aim of this step is to introduce the young people to each other, to identify the group objectives and process, and to begin the development of trust and communication. The young people were able to identify their own feelings with regard to being in the group, i.e. strange; nervous; embarrassed; worried; scared, and how such feelings might be overcome, i.e. talking 'it' over; build up trust; talking to all the people here. Group rules and

need for same are discussed and agreed, particularly with regards to confidentiality.

At this introductory stage there is an awareness of a common group dynamic, i.e. tension and impulsivity. An ability to work through this dynamic with the use of physical 'ice-breakers' and role plays is very important. This has the added and very positive benefit of introducing the young people to safe physical boundaries.

The use of the 'parachute' exercise was particularly beneficial in this process, enabling the young people to identify this tension and impulsivity and, through their control of the 'parachute', reduce same. The group members 'billow' the 'parachute' (large silk sheet) and facilitators encourage them to slowly walk under same, slowly passing each other, introducing themselves to others, and greeting each other as they pass with a handshake. The young people found this exercise both enjoyable and beneficial, confirming a reduction of impulsivity, tension, and the development of trust and communication. Facilitators were aware from previous individual work with John, that he had significant difficulty being in close physical proximity to anyone, including family members. However, he was able to say that he enjoyed this exercise and felt more at ease with himself and other group members.

Step 2

This step continues to develop group cohesion and promotes co-operation and active participation within the group process. It incorporates a 2-day residential programme early in this step enabling the young people, through organised physical activities, to address and promote a sense of personal sharing and trust. The activities also enable them to confront and understand their own feelings, particularly of fear and anxiety, allow them to discuss same and examine their own coping mechanisms.

John, for example, could not complete a particular activity in the Outdoor Pursuits Programme, despite encouragement from all the other young people. He was able to acknowledge fear as the reason, but also guilt that in taking so long to attempt, and finally refuse to do the activity, he had wasted the group's time.

This residential aspect of the programme is a very important and positive aspect of the group process, promoting the young peoples' self-esteem and confidence, which in turn enhances co-operation, participation and peer support in the group. It does, however, require careful planning, with facilitators meeting with the centre's manager to outline the nature of the group and its aims and objectives. A further meeting with the manager occurs to confirm dates, costs and accommodation arrangements. Facilitators then meet with centre leaders (usually two and preferably a male/female mix) who are designated to the proposed programme, and an agreed programme is constructed. Only the centre manager and designated leaders are aware of the nature of the group, with the young people only being identified by first names. The young peoples' individual behaviours are not discussed. Facilitators then meet and agree the practical arrangements, e.g. transport, sleeping arrangements, use of 'free time', supervision at night etc.

The final part of this step, usually on the second evening, is a formal group session to review the residential, and the young people are then required to make a short factual statement as to why they are present in the group. John stated 'I am in the group because I abused my 2 sisters: J who was 9 years old and P who was 6 years old'.

Facilitators at this stage of the programme begin to share personal experiences in an objective manner, thereby creating positive relationship boundaries, which can develop through the duration of the group.

Step 3

The focus of this step is to enable the young people to begin to develop intellectual awareness and emotional understanding of the impact of their sexually abusive behaviour. It is important that these issues are addressed from the premise that the young people may know their behaviour was wrong, but may not know why, i.e. lack of insight. **Empathy** is explained and nurtured, and such cognitive work is reinforced by past experiential influences and use of appropriate resource material.

Revisiting the young peoples' experiences and feelings enables them to begin to consider how a victim might feel. Responses were encouraging and relevant, e.g. hurt, disgusted, frozen, scared, unloved, humiliated, to note but a few. Following discussion of same the young people watch and discuss a video called 'The Nightingale Roars'. This video recounts the personal experiences of a victim of incest as a child, and the long-term consequences in terms of her physical, social and emotional development. Her story is told through the medium of visual and poetic expression, where the expression of feelings, thoughts and behaviours are vividly depicted.

In the most recent group it was decided to show this video twice, with the young people indicating that it was more difficult to view the second time, given the heightened impact for them. In discussing this it was evident, through verbal/non-verbal and physical responses, that the viewing of the video had significantly heightened awareness of empathy, and had also effected a remorseful response to the young peoples' own abusive behaviour.

Paul, at the end of the second viewing, walked out of the room and didn't return for some 5 minutes. He was later able to say that he had gone to the toilet and cried, such was the impact.

It was evident that revisiting this theme had promoted not just the intellectual understanding, but, crucially, the emotional development of **empathy.**

Step 4

The development of the preceding steps enhanced the young peoples' contribution and completion of this step. The young people perceive this as the most difficult. Each young person is required to talk through the details of their own sexually abusive behaviour, with the facilitators enabling this through a structured set of questions that reflect the offence cycle. This also helps to acknowledge and challenge any minimisation, justification or inconsistencies in the young peoples' accounts. Foreknowledge of victim statements is obviously crucial for facilitators to ensure that the young people take responsibility for their sexually abusive behaviour.

As noted earlier in the paper, facilitators had experienced in the 1996 group the tension and irritation amongst the young people during this step, which had taken eight sessions to complete. Having discussed this with other professionals and colleagues in the JPPT, and with the young people themselves, it was decided to complete this step in a full day session.

In reviewing same it was concluded that this was beneficial to the process and enhanced the young peoples' sense of continuity, peer support and, at times, peer confrontation. It also reinforced the premise introduced at the beginning of the programme the fact that the group had one problem, i.e. sexual abuse. Both young people and facilitators found the day stressful and physically tiring, but all were of the opinion that it was positive.

It was noted that despite the young people having pre-group individual assessment work, which had addressed their abusive behaviour, most of them found it very difficult to talk through their behaviours. Facilitators had mistakenly assumed that the opposite would be the case. In discussing this with the young people they cited two reasons for this: having to talk in front of peers, and it being more difficult to talk about their behaviour for a second time.

Peter, during this step, disclosed to the group more serious abuse than had been hitherto known. He explained the reason for this as 'wanting to get everything out'. This new information was passed onto the field social worker in line with procedures. The RUC CARE Unit and mother of the victim were informed of this additional information. The mother chose not to make a formal complaint — Peter's attendance at the group was therefore not affected. However, facilitators would note that in the event of a formal investigation of any new information, the young person may be precluded from continuing with the group process, e.g. in the event of prosecution the young person may be remanded in custody, or a solicitor may advise no further contact until the case is dealt with.

Step 5

This step enables the young people to develop an understanding of sex, sexuality and relationships. Again experience has shown the benefits of addressing this step from the premise that young people may not have the basic knowledge and/or experiences. As such, this aspect of the work was developed through the building blocks of:

- Basic needs — physical, emotional, intellectual, social; all group members contribute to the development of comprehensive groupings of identified physical, emotional, intellectual and social needs. The facilitators use this exercise to assess the young peoples' knowledge and provide them with further information on basic needs. Further discussion develops around the issue of how to meet these basic needs.

- Body parts — public, private; all body parts are named and classified as 'private' or 'non-private'. Group discussion includes reasons why differentiation is made and issues are developed later in the context of developing relationships and intimacy.

- Psychological changes — male, female; physical changes in males and females are identified in the context of stages of development, with emphasis being placed on adolescence and puberty. Associated emotional and psychological changes are highlighted and discussed in relation to the development of sexuality.

- Sexual arousal/feelings — sexual, non-sexual; the young people are encouraged to think about non-sexual feelings — physical and emotional. This area is explored through discussion of life experiences and further developed by the young people identifying changes in their physical, mental and emotional states when sexually aroused. Inappropriate associated responses are identified and discussed, linking same to preceding building blocks.

- Relationships — On the basis of all the preceding stages the young people are encouraged to apply thinking, and developed awareness into issues of developing positive relationships with others, from platonic to more intimate and sexual levels.

- Consent/mutuality/agreement. Intimacy and appropriate sexual behaviour. Legal/moral aspects of sexual behaviour — group members are encouraged to first of all define/explain the concepts of consent, mutuality and agreement. Facilitators then enable the young people to apply developed insights to their life situations, both sexual and non-sexual. Group members presented as gaining more clarity and insight generally in this area. Facilitators differentiate very clearly between personal, moral, societal and legal boundaries in relation to behaviours. It is reinforced to the young people that they need to take responsibility for their feelings, thoughts and behaviours in line with all of the above. This issue is similarly clarified with parents/carers through the parallel parents' support group.

- Prejudice and stereotype — the use of male/female facilitators is a very useful method of identifying and challenging same. The young people are encouraged to identify their own prejudicial stereotypes in the context of male/female relationships. Facilitators then enable the young people to consider them and reframe their personal perceptions in order to reduce the degree of such prejudice and stereotype. In addressing such issues, facilitators were ever aware of their own use of language, and the importance of clarifying meaning in young peoples' use of language, e.g. 'shifting girls', and encouraging them to become more responsible about how they use such language. David was able to tell the group that he had sexual intercourse with a girl of his own age, with consent. In discussing this David was able to describe and acknowledge that this experience was one of 'having sex' rather than 'making love' and was able to differentiate between the two experiences.

Step 6

In Step 6, care is taken in encouraging the young people to openly discuss sexual desires and fantasies. Despite highlighting that these issues are normal and healthy within appropriate boundaries, the young people were initially very reticent to contribute. However, after discussion and clarification of appropriate/inappropriate sexual desires and fantasies, the young people were encouraged to identify their own risk situations enabling them to 'move on' and focus on strategies and skills which will help them better manage these risk situations.

Paul, who was 'in care', talked about an incident while he was visiting home. He went out of the house and over to friends. He saw them teasing younger children and trying to pull their trousers down. Paul recognised that this was a potential risk situation and went back and told his mother. He then walked back to the children's home and explained to staff regarding his early return. He could explain the risks:

- He might have became sexually excited and been tempted to re-offend.

- He might, if he had remained, been blamed for what was happening, given the nature of his previous offending behaviour.

The young people are encouraged to identify and discuss the antecedents of their offending cycle in terms of feelings, thoughts and behaviours and through discussion to develop skills which will hopefully enable them to escape/avoid such antecedents in the future, e.g.

T — Think differently
E — Escape
A — Avoid
R — Remember consequences
S — Stop thoughts

In the most recent work, the facilitators introduced body-based exercises to support and develop the cognitive work done on:

- Feelings — thoughts and behaviours.

- Safe/unsafe boundaries.

Given the context of the work i.e. sexual abuse, pre-conditions were identified prior to using this method:

- Workers need to be comfortable in their own bodies.
- Workers need to have developed a sense of being able to identify physical/emotional states and changes in their own bodies.
- Awareness of potential for physical boundaries not being respected in certain situations.
- The need for good supervision to ensure safety (e.g. within the co-working context).
- The need to clearly explain the process to the young people involved.

The young people were encouraged to lie or sit in their own chosen relaxed position with eyes closed. They were then taken through a guided visualisation whereby they were encouraged to focus on separate parts of the body. In so doing the young people were encouraged to develop awareness of physical sensation and emotional feelings throughout their body. There was consensus after this stage that the young people had not enjoyed such a relaxed state previously.

The second part of the exercise involved one young person at a time pairing off with a facilitator in an exploration of personal boundaries. Facing each other each young person gave permission for the facilitator to approach him very slowly but instructed them to stop when any change in body sensation was felt. This change was identified before the facilitator was given permission to approach further, the process continued until the young person clearly described it as no longer comfortable for the facilitator to move any closer to him.

The young person then felt and very clearly identified his own personal space and boundary in relation to the facilitator. The exercise was repeated with reversed roles. In discussion afterwards the young people were able to relate to:

- Positive effects of increased body awareness.
- More acute recognition and identification of physical and emotional feelings.
- Increased awareness of the relationship between feelings/thoughts/behaviours.

- Increased assertiveness in saying 'No' or 'Stop'.
- More positive responses to hearing 'No' or 'Stop'.
- A strong sense of physical/emotional boundaries.

Parallels were drawn between the young person's experience of another person 'closing in on' them and the impact of their physical intrusion and sexual abuse on their victim. The issue of empathy was revisited. It was evident that this exercise and the subsequent discussion had a strong impact on the young people.

John refused to participate in the exercise but was able to identify the appropriate feelings, thoughts and behaviours of this situation i.e. he felt sick in his stomach, thinking he was afraid to participate, and behaving by saying 'No'.

In assessing what the young people have learned and retained, facilitators ask the young people to 'write a letter' to their victims. While obviously not sent, the letters are used by facilitators to gauge each young person's level of empathy, sense of responsibility and more general learning from the group process. Excerpts from these include:

- I am extremely sorry for sexually abusing you.
- I did it because I was angry and I took it out on you.
- I know now that it was very wrong of me to hurt you in this way.
- I know it's going to be hard for you but I'm sorry for what I did and I hope you can forgive me.

On completion of this step the group programme is drawn to a close. Facilitators meet with relevant professionals, parents/carers and young people to discuss the need or otherwise of further individual work. Where appropriate, work plans are formally agreed and developed to meet the needs of individual young people. Informal contact is not considered appropriate.

Two of the 12 young people in the two groups, as far as is known, have sexually abused again. One young person self-reported during post-group individual work. Reunions of the young people are organised to enable them to review the programme and discuss their own personal situations

Evaluation and Future Development

Formal reviewing, through agreed procedures with field social workers and parents, has indicated positive developments for the young people in terms of insight into their abusive behaviour, and their ability to control such behaviour. However, of the 12 young people who participated in the group programme over the last two years, six were identified as requiring further individual work. This was to revisit areas of:

- Anger management.
- Empathy.
- Risk situations.
- Relationships and sexuality.

It is worth noting that in identifying such areas of work, none of the young people refused to participate. During this ongoing period of individual work, one young person self-reported that he had sexually abused again. It has also been reported that a second young person has been involved sexually with an adult, the circumstances of which are currently being investigated.

In the most recent group programme, two full day sessions were built in to address Steps 4 and 6. Whilst acknowledging the beneficial effects of such a process, it was found

important to monitor group responses throughout the day, given the foreseen impact of the subject matter on young peoples' 'energy levels'. The use of physical exercises/short breaks can effectively redress this imbalance.

Given the very personal, intimate and abusive nature of the group context, it was noted that an essential element for facilitators is balancing the support/respect that each young person needs, at the same time attempting to eliminate any collusive relationship. As such, the importance of the early steps of the work in achieving that balance is recognised.

Having completed two group programmes, the facilitators are able to acknowledge the benefits of having worked together during the two programmes in terms of developing their professional relationship, which they believe has enhanced the group process. They would also conclude that the pre-group individual work within the JPPT created significant awareness of the potential of the group process and content. This evaluation was arrived at following discussions with previous group facilitators, who did not always have the benefits of this preceding preparatory work.

Another tangible benefit of the JPPT has been the standardised and co-ordinated referral system, resulting in 59 referrals over the 2-year period. Such a referral system has promoted a more co-ordinated and systematic intervention, reflected in the selection variables over the two most recent group programmes:

	Group 96/97	Group 97/98
No. in denial	0/6	0/6
Mandated	4/6	0/6
Family denial	0/6	0/6
Family minimisation	1/6	0/6
Behaviour disturbance	0/6	0/6

The homogenous make-up of the group enables facilitators to maximise the potential of the young people.

With the development of the JPPT, the group programme has become an integral part of the project, in terms of effective practice with young people who sexually abuse. As such, future development must address how to more effectively evaluate the groupwork aspect of the whole project programme and include more structured methods to assess:

- Young person's/parents' expectations of the groupwork programme.

- Motivation.

- Were expectations met? — How/how not?

- Young people at end of group.

As part of the overall evaluation of practice, it is important to be aware of the need to constantly review and acquire updated resources.

From a practice base, facilitators would envisage the group further developing the co-ordinated and comprehensive nature of the programme, which was first initiated in 1991/92 with the setting up of the first group. They would recognise the importance of the group programme providing a learning style that accommodates the young peoples' needs, that employs techniques which can address the varied aspects of the programme, and includes a cognitive behavioural approach which can challenge young peoples' attitudes/values and beliefs which affect anti-social behaviour. Such techniques

...should be structured and adopt a building block approach which includes the use of role play, skills enhancement, etc....and systematically focus on those factors which are related to the reasons for offending rather than general personality disorders which are not offence related (Gendreau and Andrews, 1981).

In adopting the cognitive-behavioural approach alongside such techniques, facilitators and young people appropriately explore their life experiences/ knowledge, as identified in the building blocks of Step 5. Such exploration allows the facilitators to enable the young people to understand the nature of their abusive behaviour, and move on to more effectively control and change such behaviour in the future.

In order to support such developments with the young people it is important to identify and continue to liaise with other professionals and groups who work in this field e.g. Northside Inter-agency Project, Dublin and the Galway Adolescent Project.

Experience has shown that an openness and willingness to share has enhanced the development of learning in this area of work.

Groupwork intervention has now become a very important and complimentary aspect of the therapeutic work with young people who sexually abuse and it is hoped that development of such work will continue in the spirit of openness and sharing.

> *I have been given a lot of help as I attend the Boys Group from November, and am finding it very useful information. (John — group member)*

References

Bion, W.R. (1943). Intra-group Tensions in Therapy. *Lancet*, 27, November.

Calder, M.C. (1997). *Juveniles and Children Who Sexually Abuse: A Guide to Risk Assessment*. Lyme Regis: Russell House Publishing .

Clarke, P. , and Erooga, M. (1994). Groupwork with Men who Sexually Abuse Children. In Marrisa, T., Erooga, M., and Beckett, R.C. (Eds.). *Sexual Offending Against Children*, 102–128. London: Routledge.

Davis, G.E., and Leitenburg, H. (1987). Adolescent Sex Offenders. *Psychology Bulletin*, 101(3): 417–427.

Kennedy, M.T., Hanwell, M.K.C., Blaney, R., Chivers, A.T., May, I., and Vincent, O.E. (1990). *Child Sexual Abuse in Northern Ireland — A Research Study of Incidence*. Antrim: Greystone Books.

Loss, P., and Ross, J. (1988). *Risk Assessment/Interviewing Protocol for Adolescent Sex Offenders*. London, CT: Loss and Ross Inc.

McCune, N., and Scott, F. (1994). Group Treatment Programme for Adolescent Sex Offenders. *Child Care in Practice*, 1: 1–9.

McGarvey, J., and Lenaghan, M. (1996). A Structured Group Approach with Adolescent Perpetrators. *Child Abuse Review*, 5: 203–213.

Moore, S., and Rosenthal, D. (1993). *Sexuality in Adolescence*. London: Routledge.

Morrison, T, Erooga, M., and Beckett, R.C. (Eds.) (1994). *Sexual Offending Against Children: Assessment and Treatment of Male Abusers*. London: Routledge.

Smets, A.C., and Cebula C.M. (1987). A Group Treatment Programme for Adolescent Sex Offenders: Five Steps Towards Resolution. *Child Abuse and Neglect*, 11: 247–254.

Sutton, D. (1995). *The Essential Ingredients of Offender Programmes: A Paper on the Latest Research Findings Relating to the Content of Offending Programmes*. Paper 1. The Cognitive Centre/Foundation.

Chapter Twelve

Young Abusers with Learning Disabilities:

Towards Better Understanding and Positive Interventions

David O'Callaghan

Young Abusers with Learning Disabilities: Towards Better Understanding and Positive Interventions

Introduction

G-MAP is an independent service based in the North-West of England, offering assessment and therapeutic services to young people of all ability levels who sexually abuse. The projects history dates back to the late 1980s and we have attempted in recent years to develop a strand of our service specifically for young people with learning disabilities. The response we have nationally suggests this is an area of particular unmet need. This chapter reflects the development of our thinking and the issues we have faced when attempting to provide a positive response to the young people, their carers and the responsible agencies. It will also aim to review some of the available research in this area. There is though, as yet, limited available data specifically relating to young people with learning disabilities who sexually offend. As within the wider body of research in the field of sexual aggression, we should be cautious in assuming findings concerning adults can be generalised to young people.

Throughout this chapter I shall refer to males with a learning disability who sexually abuse. The available literature and the experience of G-MAP as a service would indicate the 'male monopoly' on sexual offending, identified by Finkelhor (1984), is as true for abusers with a learning disability as within the broader population of sexual offenders.

Methodological Difficulties

Any discussion of the relative prevalence of sexually abusive behaviour by individuals with a learning disability needs to be placed in the context of definitions, terminology and an appreciation as to sources of information and their particular bias:

1. *Definitions as to the nature of sexual abuse and sexual offending.* This may have particular salience in the arena of learning disability as certain forms of learning disability as certain forms of behaviour not usually viewed as problematic in the general population e.g. excessive masturbation, may become an issue within the care settings provided for individuals with learning disabilities. In contrast, certain forms of sexual behaviour, such as sexual assaults upon women service users, are less likely to be formally reported and subject to the scrutiny of the criminal justice system (McCarthy and Thompson 1997; Verberne 1990).

2. *Definitions of 'learning disability'.* As Fryers (1997) comments, professional literature on learning disability 'reveals a remarkable variety of incompatible terms, inconsistent categories and ambiguous concepts'. Within the UK 'learning disability' refers to an impairment of intellectual functioning and an impairment of social functioning. A measure of intellectual functioning is most commonly based on an assessment using the Wechsler Adult Intelligence Scale, Revised (WAIS-R). An assessed Full Scale IQ of 70 or less is seen as the basis for an intellectual disability. There is less agreement as to the basis for evaluating social functioning. Individuals functioning at an assessed IQ of 70–80 are not infrequently brought into learning disability services and included in studies of those reporting on 'learning disabled' abuser/offenders. Potentially this inflates the figures relating to the proportion of men who have sexually offended and are identified as learning disabled.

3. *The nature of the sample.* The variety of available figures relating to the proportion of sexual abusers who are learning disabled relates in part to the nature of the sample. Studies of sexual offenders within the prison and probation services are likely to under-represent the learning disabled as a total proportion of sexual

offenders, due to the reluctance of the criminal justice system to act in relation to this group (see discussion later in this chapter). Information from settings such as special hospitals and regional secure units may lead to an over-representation, as they will deal disproportionately with individuals with a 'mental impairment' who have offended against the person. Services addressing 'challenging behaviour' within the learning disability network are likely to respond to a very broad definition as to what constitutes 'problematic sexual behaviour' and may relate primarily to what care staff regard as problematic (Thompson, Clare and Brown 1997).

The presence of clients with learning disabilities in the services for sexual offenders

Whilst research would suggest that the learning disabled are no more or indeed, less likely to be involved in criminal behaviour in general, a number of studies have suggested that offenders with a learning disability are disproportionately identified as having perpetrated sexual crimes. Gross (1985), found that 50% of imprisoned learning disabled offenders had been sentenced for sexual crimes and that this was true of 35% of such offenders in a community sample. Home Office statistics (1995) report 12% of detained mentally disordered patients as being sexual offenders. Murrey, Briggs and Davies (1992) found one-third of male sex offenders at Rampton Special Hospital to be assessed as having a learning disability. Thomas and Singh's (1995) survey of referrals to an out-patent learning disability service, found that of those referred for offending behaviour, sexual offenders constituted the highest proportion, (30%). Day's (1993) review of studies concerning intellectually disabled sex offenders that had been published over a 40-year period, identified percentages as reported for sexual offending as between 12–46%.

As projects have developed specifically for those who have sexually offended, there appears to be an increased awareness of those offenders with a intellectual disability. Northumbria Probation Sex Offender Team reported that 10% of their client group are identified as having a learning disability (Doyle and Gooch, 1995). A recent review of one of the UK's most extensive probation sex offender programmes in the West Midlands (Allam, Middleton and Browne, 1997), found that 8% of men referred were identified as learning disabled.

Victim surveys

In respect of victims with a learning disability in the largest UK survey to date, Brown, Stein and Turk (1995), identified other service users as perpetrators in 53% of identified cases. Beil and Warden (1995), similarly found other people with learning disabilities as the identified abuser in the majority of those who reported experiences of sexual victimisation. Thompson's (1997) survey found fellow learning disability service users as the identified perpetrators of abuse in 42% of female victims and 21% of males victimised.

Intellectual disability and sexually abusive behaviour amongst young males

Studies have frequently reported that learning difficulties and educational problems are over-represented amongst samples of adolescent sexual abusers. Kahn and Chambers (1991) found half their sample had histories of disruptive behaviour at school; one third a history of truancy and 39% were considered learning disabled. Epps (1991) found that 44% of his sample had learning difficulties, half having attended special school. The London based Young Abusers Project recently reported that 53% of the young people referred to them were categorised as subject to learning disability (Hawkes *et al.*, 1997). A survey of 121 young sexual offenders referred to an adolescent forensic service (Dolan *et al.*, 1996), found 46% of the sample to be identified as learning disabled, whilst the majority (36% of the total sample), were assessed as having a mild learning disability, 5.8% moderate and 1.6% severe.

Knight and Prentky's (1993) studies of the developmental history of adult sex offenders identified intellectual and social competencies as a key factor influencing whether sexual offending in adolescence would be formally identified and recorded. It may well be that many services responding to young abusers are biased towards those who are the most identifiable due to lack of sophistication in offending, as well as a frequent constellation of problem behaviours.

It may be that there is an over representation due to a number of factors, which include:

- The imprecise use of language. As identified above definitions concerning learning disability are complex, particularly in respect to social functioning. Many studies fail to differentiate between young people with educational problems and those who are assessable as having a formal degree of intellectual impairment.

- Young people may be categorised as having a degree of learning disability without a thoroughgoing psychological assessment or Statement of Special Educational Needs.

- Certain young people may perform below their ability level within formal settings.

- Impaired educational and social functioning may relate to the impact of abuse and neglect on many young people, as opposed to an organic basis for developmental impairment.

It is difficult therefore to make any definitive statement as to the presence of young people with learning disabilities within the general population of adolescents who sexually abuse. It seems reasonable to judge however, from the available data that as a group they are no less likely and possibly more likely to present with sexual behaviour problems.

The nature of sexual offences perpetrated by men with intellectual disabilities

Given the paucity of research in this area to date, generalised comments concerning this group of offenders must be taken cautiously. Available information comes mainly from those referred to specialist services. G-MAP's experience and anecdotal evidence would support the view that learning disabled

offenders present with as heterogeneous an offending and personality profile as the mainstream of sexual offenders. Within the available literature a number of distinguishing features are suggested:

- Serious offences are less commonly recorded, with a greater proportion of 'non-contact' behaviours such as exhibitionism (Murrey, Briggs and Davies, 1992). As with the Thomson (1997) study, Thomas and Singh (1995) found a relationship between the degree of disability and offences committed, with the most serious contact offences being committed by men assessed in the mild/borderline disability range.

- It is suggested that repeat offending in this group is less discriminate in terms of victim profile and nature of offence. Opportunity appears more frequently to be the primary factor in shaping offence behaviour. Thompson (1997) however, found a distinct pattern in which the more vulnerable and less able (children, women, more intellectually impaired service users) were targeted by sexually abusive men with learning disabilities.

- Substance misuse, particularly alcohol, appears to be an infrequent associated factor (Day, 1994) in contrast to non-disabled offenders. This would seem a reflection of more limited social networks, social skills and low income.

- Offence patterns of sexual abusers with learning disabilities have been reported as more frequently impulsive and with less attention to planning opportunities to offend (e.g. Cullen, 1993; Knopp, 1990). Whilst this is reflected in the experience of Allam and her colleagues, they recognise the danger of generalising and comment that:

  the experience of the SOU (Sex Offender Unit) is that some individuals (with a learning disability) are capable of undertaking meticulous 'grooming' behaviours, particularly of children. However, they are seemingly able to move much more readily from situations which trigger arousal, into committing the abuse, in a very short space of time. (Allam et al., 1997)

  Thompson (1997) found a distinct pattern of predatory sexual behaviours amongst a number of the male abusers in his survey.

- Day (1994) found that there was a more limited range of paraphillias (sexually deviant behaviours) amongst his sample. A contradictory view is put from Griffiths, Hindsburger and Christian (1985) who found a similar diversity of offence pattern in their disabled and non-disabled sample.

Day (1994) has proposed two general categories of learning disabled sex offender:

1. The first group, those who only commit sex offences, are described as being biased towards the lower end of the mild LD range, show little sophistication, more frequently commit less serious offences and demonstrate little specificity in victim selection and offence type. Day suggests this groups behaviour reflect maladaptive responses to normative sexual impulses.

2. The second group, is distinguished by allied offending, disruptive and developmental features, including early onset of aggressive and problematic behaviours. Day suggests this group represents a major challenge to service providers and requires extensive, specialist and long-term intervention, with a recognition of a poor prognosis for change.

Do we have positive goals for young people with intellectual disabilities in terms of their sexuality?

As a service we have increasingly become conscious of the context of the referrals to us. Agencies and carers appear clear on what sexual behaviour they view as problematic and wish to eliminate, for example, public masturbation, inappropriate touching of others. It is often less clear as to what would be seen as an acceptable, non-problematic expression of the young man's sexuality.

A key question is the extent to which society accepts those in the community with learning disabilities as having sexuality form as significant part of their expression of self, as those of us without such a disability. Schilling and Schinke (1989) have identified four

external boundaries of opinion which shape the development of sexuality for an individual with a learning disability;

1. *Strong advocacy* — demands full rights for those with learning disability, including support to facilitate sexual expression and the development of relationships.

2. *Moderated advocacy* — perhaps the most common view amongst parents and carers, agrees to education around sexual and personal relationships whilst viewing supervision and some restrictions as important. Full sexual relationships would be viewed with some reluctance from this stance.

3. *Value free position* — advocates that individuals sexuality is a private matter and that adults/young people with a learning disability should experience no greater or lesser restrictions on their behaviour than the general population.

4. *Negative position* — those with a learning disability should be activity discouraged from engaging in sexual activity.

Against this background, parents and carers are having to make immensely difficult decisions concerning the extent to which they acknowledge the developing sexuality of young people whose functional age does not correlate with biological/physical changes. A useful concept is that of developmental suspension (Fairburn, Rowley and Bowen, 1995), in which young people with a learning disability are 'held' at a certain age in the minds of parents and carers. The problems associated with puberty and sexual maturity in relation to those with a learning disability appear so immense, that parents and carers may adopt a tactic of psychological denial. Parents, carers and young people themselves may require particular support to manage a transition through puberty into sexual maturity. Education for learning disabled teenagers needs to be as much concerning relationships, the context of sexual behaviour and issues such as consent and safe and responsible sexual behaviour.

What are the obstacles to promoting positive opportunities for young people with learning disabilities to express their sexuality?

A number of themes are relevant when considering the particular constraints upon the psycho-sexual development of young people with learning disabilities:

- The extent to which there are *opportunities for sexual and personal relationships* and the degree to which those with a learning disability are integrated into our community will have a major influence on psycho-sexual development. The social networks of those with a learning disability remain restrictive and detached from the mainstream of their communities. Social networks created and supported by professionals are viewed (by professionals) as primarily for friendships, not the development of sexual relationships. Parents/carers protectiveness may stifle opportunities. G-MAP's experience is that many of the young people with a learning disability referred to us, lead very restricted and impoverished lives.

- *The issue of vulnerability, perceived risks and their consequences.* Traditionally the most serious concern in relation to sexual activity amongst individuals with a learning disability was likely to have been unplanned pregnancy. Today we are increasingly aware of the sexual abuse and exploitation of the more vulnerable members of our community, including those with a learning disability (Cooke and Sinason, 1998). Furthermore, the sexual health risks involved in unprotected sex have themselves changed significantly with the advent of HIV and AIDS (Cambridge, 1997). Past 'solutions' such as sterilisation and long-term use of the contraceptive pill, are seen more clearly to have, at the very least, limitations, in terms of protection.

- *The operational policy of services*, particularly residential settings, will have a major impact the opportunities service user have for personal and sexual relationships. Many services shy away from developing a clear sexuality policy which acknowledges the needs of service users in relation to sexual expression as part of any individual's overall functioning (Cambridge and McCarthy, 1997). Buildings used as care settings are seldom designed or organised to facilitate privacy. The concept of the 'intermediate zone' (Parkin and Green, 1994) reflects the group care settings uncertain position as neither a fully 'private' or fully 'public' space. McCarthy and Thompson (1996) have illustrated how the physical nature of buildings as well as staff practice can impact on the risk of abuse.

- *Staff attitudes and support* is critical, in that many individuals with a learning disability experience staff as having an almost total power over their lives and available choices. Fairburn, Rowley and Bowen (1995) contest that it is the ethical dilemmas which staff face, concerning issues of sexuality and choice, rather than the practical difficulties, which most challenge staff.

Fairbairn *et al.* suggest three key principles to addressing the complex issues raised by this area:

1. For those with a learning disability to be subject to the same restrictions and responsibilities, as the majority community.

2. Those with a learning disability have no more rights to have their sexual needs and wishes met than the rest of the community.

3. Those with a learning disability have the right not to engage in sexual activity.

Cambridge and McCarthy (1997) provide an excellent description of one services development of a sexual policy through a process of discussion, the use of external consultants and the involvement of both service users and carers. Their model emphasises the need for agencies to address difficult issues related to sexual behaviour and value of including services users/carers as opposed to a 'culture of protection'. Cambridge and McCarthy suggest services will increasingly be expected to have developed the policies, structures and skills to positively manage this aspect of service users' lives.

Are there differential routes into sexually problematic behaviour for young males with a learning disability?

Current theoretical perspectives would emphasise integrated models (e.g. Epps, Chapter 1; Hawkes *et al.*, 1997) which operate at individual, familial, situational and communal/societal levels. A number of factors have been associated with the development of sexually aggressive behaviours, for example, traumatic sexualisation (Watkins and Bentovim, 1992); exposure to violence and poor attachments/disruption in care (Bentovim and Williams, 1998), difficulties with intimacy and empathy (Lisak and Ivan, 1995) and attitudes supportive of coercive sexual behaviour (Segal and Stermac, 1990). The 'diathesis stressor paradigm' (Davidson and Neale, 1990) views the development of problematic behaviours from the perspective of the interaction between personal vulnerabilities and external stressors, which assists us to recognise the dynamic nature of risk. This body of research is of relevance in understanding the aetiology of sexually abusive/problematic behaviour by young people with learning disabilities. However, whilst we should be cautious about over-emphasising factors suggested as specific to men with learning disabilities who sexually abuse, it does seem evident there are themes which have a particular relevance.

Thompson and Brown (1998) note they had not expected medical factors to be as prominent in their small sample of sexually abusive men as proved to be the case. Literature has identified chromosonal disorders, in particular Klinefelters syndrome, as a potential causal factor in the development of problematic sexual behaviours (Epps, 1996; Gannon, Clayton-Smith, Bailey, 1997; Herzog and Money, 1993; Hummel, Ashcroft, Blessman and Anders, 1993). Comprehensive multi-disciplinary assessments should be open to this aspect and ensure that appropriate professional assessments are undertaken to determine the possible impact of such physical influences on behaviour.

Fairburn *et al.* (1995) suggest the concept of 'abuse without abuser' to describe sexual behaviours in which the initiator of an unwelcome sexual interaction does not understand the concept of consent or the impact of the behaviour on others. This is clearly particular to conceptualising abuse perpetrated by individuals with a significant degree of learning disability. Whilst there is some validity in this perspective it would seem inappropriate to automatically assume that young people with learning disabilities have no understanding that their behaviour is viewed negatively and impacts upon others. As Thompson and Brown (1998) identify, the response of carers and professionals may lead to a recognition that such behaviour is viewed as a problem or disapproved of, but be insufficient to clearly identify the behaviour to the individual as harmful and illegal. Limited education by schools and parents concerning sexual development may further leave young people with learning disabilities bereft of a model for appropriate sexual behaviour.

It has been suggested (Hayes, 1991; Murrey *et al.* 1992) that some adults or adolescents with learning disabilities may relate to children of similar developmental age. This appears a variation on Finkelhor's concept of 'emotional congruence' (Finkelhor, 1984), posited as a factor in the development of sexually abusive behaviour directed towards children.

The lack of opportunities for acceptable sexual expression (Brown and Barrett, 1994: Fairburn *et al.*, 1995) is a situation common to many young people with learning disabilities. The absence of private space, limited social networks and poor social skills may leave a developing adolescent with little direction for non-problematic sexual expression.

Sobsey (1994) outlines an ecological model to identify factors, such as patterns of substitute/respite care, about why individuals with a learning disability are particularly vulnerable to sexual abuse, frequently by other service users. McCarthy and Thompson (1996) have used the phrase 'abuse by design' to comment on how the systems and physical structures of many care settings may increase the risk of sexual abuse.

Our experience at G-MAP would suggest that the factors commonly associated with the development of sexual aggression are equally applicable to understanding this behaviour in young people with a learning disability. However, it is important to apply these in the light of an understanding of the differential life experiences of young people with a learning disability. For example, issues of intimacy, attachment and loss are significant factors in the development of problematic sexual behaviour as identified by Santry and McCarthy in Chapter 5. As Thompson and Brown (1998) identify, children and adolescents with learning disabilities may be at increased risk of experiencing rejection and separation due to the additional strains in caring for a disabled child. The arrangement of respite care is an experience of separation and substitute carers common to many children/young people with disabilities. Corbett (1996a) identifies a chaotic or insecure attachment history as a feature of all the learning disabled sexual abusers referred to the Respond project.

Respond, a psychotherapeutically based service for people with learning disability, focusing on issues of sexual abuse, have found a history of sexual abuse to be almost a universal feature of the men referred to them for problematic sexual behaviour (Corbett, 1996b). There is evidence to suggest that incidence of physical and sexual abuse is higher amongst children and adults with a learning disability than in the general population (Cooke and Sinason, 1998; Sobsey 1994).

Faulk (1994) emphasises the learning disabled child's early childhood experiences in 'failing' within school and in relation to the achievements of peers as a predominant factor in the low self-esteem of many individuals with intellectual impairment. This is supported by the research of Stanley, Dai and Nolan (1997) who found learning disabled adolescents significantly more likely to report low self-esteem and depression when compared with young people within the special school system for behavioural problems.

Approaching Assessments of Young People with Learning Disabilities

What are the key goals for assessments?

For G-MAP, functioning primarily as a provider of long-term therapeutic services to young people, our assessments contribute by providing the foundation for that intervention by addressing the following questions:

- *Problem formation* — how can we best understand this young person's sexual

behaviour. How does it relate to his overall psycho-sexual, emotional and social functioning?

- *Risk formulation* — what features in the individual's presentation and behaviour are relevant in considering risk? (recognising this must be related to our best understanding currently)
- *Risk management* — what degree of control, restriction or supervision is required to manage this young person safely?
- What do we consider to be the main areas of change for this young person? *(treatment goals)*?
- How do we propose to promote those changes *(treatment and intervention plan)*?
- How will we measure the extent of any change — what will be our *evaluation criteria*?

Planning assessments

Noelly, Muccigrosso and Zigman (1996) describe a comprehensive multi-dimensional assessment procedure for sexual abusers with mild-moderate learning disabilities. This includes:

- Written historical information (case notes; prior reports/assessments; direct observation).
- Family interviews/completion of questionnaires.
- Observations and views of professional carers (residential; day care staff etc.).
- Statements of victims, witnesses, police and medical reports.
- Direct observation by the assessors of the client in different settings.
- Assessment of social and interpersonal skills.
- Assessment of understanding as to culturally acceptable behaviours.
- Assessment of intellectual functioning and adaptive behavioural milestones to evaluate degree of learning disability.

As Briggs, Doyle, Gooch and Kennington (1998) identify, an assessment of cognitive functioning will provide assessors with crucial information as to memory, attention/concentration span, perception, language skills and ability to use conceptual thinking.

We have found that formal information on the abusive behaviour may be less accessible in the case of young people with a learning disability, as there is a bias away from involving the criminal justice system and a frequent inclination of that system (police, CPS, courts) to divert offenders with learning disabilities. When victims are young children or less able service users, it may be difficult to establish a full account from the victim's perspective.

When behaviour is overt and repetitive it may be of value to provide staff with structured formats to record behaviour in order to establish an objective baseline in terms of frequency, context and the nature of the behaviour itself (see Brown and Barrett, 1994).

What is the assessment for?

Good communication as to the purposes of an assessment is crucial if the process is to make any positive contribution to the care and management process. Our experience as a service is that many young people referred have often been the subject of a number of 'assessments' relating to specific decisions which may have been made upon them; e.g. for court proceedings, relating to child protection decisions, or to decide upon placement options (discussed in Calder, 1997; and by Lindsay in Chapter 15.) Often these are referred to generically as 'risk assessments'. Our practice at G-MAP is to begin the assessment process with professionals meeting to identify the context of the assessment and explore the expectations of those involved with the young person. If prior assessments have been undertaken it is important to avoid duplicating areas already explored. This allows us to identify what is and is not feasible (e.g. a definitive statement as to whether the young person will re-offend). Clarity as to the hoped for outcomes also facilitates professionals and carers identify to the young person the relevance of the assessment for them.

Is the behaviour sexual?

Evaluating whether a given behaviour is indeed sexually motivated can frequently be extremely complex. Behaviour may reflect a number of potential needs or responses (Brown and Barrett, 1994), for example,

- Attention seeking.
- Distress.
- Avoidance.
- Control.
- Stimulation.

There is a need to consider incidents and behaviour on a number of dimensions, though the internal dimension (fantasy, thoughts, attributions) may be more difficult to access with individuals who have intellectual disabilities. Traditionally functional analysis has been used within learning disability services to provide a model for understanding challenging behaviour (Carr and Durand, 1985). The emphasis is on establishing the more immediate environmental contingencies associated with behaviour and thus establishing the meaning and function of the behaviour. Corbett (1996b) suggests that one role for the assessor in the case of a client with a learning disability is that of 'translator'. Thompson and Brown (1998) caution about too swift judgements as to the internal meaning of behaviour, particularly in ascribing a distinct sexual interest in children, as they suggest this may have an especially negative consequence for men with learning disabilities.

The experience and understanding of the individual being assessed

Although a relevant issue for any young person, it is particularly important to consider how a teenager or young adult with a learning disability may best make sense of any assessment process. In particular;

- Does the process promote greater clarity for the young man as to why others are concerned?
- How can this experience act to support motivation to work further on the problematic sexual behaviour?

- Is the overall process empowering or does it leave the individual feeling 'done unto'.

We find it is helpful to make time at the outset of the assessment to provide information to the young person and allow them an opportunity to ask questions, for example concerning with whom we will share the information gained in the assessment. Where we are aware of a history of professional interventions we ask the young man to share with us their view of these and what aspects they found helpful and less so. It is important to establish the reason for this assessment and any decisions which may be related to it. If there is room for flexibility on the practicalities (time of day/week; who brings the young person, etc.) the young person's wishes should be ascertained, and a clear explanation given if his wishes are not practical. These considerations are not unique to assessments involving young men with learning disabilities, though assessors involved with this client group do need to ensure a particular focus upon how they address these issues.

The pace of the assessment process

Many services organise assessments within a fixed format of contact sessions. Whilst there is a danger of an assessment becoming a never-ending process, it is important to adjust your framework to the ongoing experience of how the individual is responding. It may be that a considerable part of the earlier stages of the assessment are taken up with establishing a mode of communication and developing a self comfort for the individual in communicating at any level. Respond, a psycho-therapeutically orientated service working with individuals with learning disabilities on issues of sexual abuse, writes persuasively of the need to allow clients the space to develop a working relationship based on trust and honesty (Corbett, 1996a). Many of the young men referred to G-MAP have developed tried and tested tactics for keeping professionals at some distance. Attention spans are frequently poor, with a need to structure sessions in such a way as to maintain participation and interest, for example, by constructing certain exercises as games, using pictures or building in breaks for alternative activities.

Assumptions

As with the issue of suggestibility (see below) it is important to build into your assessment tactics to validate the assumptions you may have as to what the client is communicating. A frequent issue is that of sexual knowledge, and the use of words which may have a number of potential meanings. It is our experience that young men are likely to use either definitions given to them e.g. 'I sexually abused... I did an indecent assault'; or rely on words heard from other young people which they may or may not have a clear understanding of e.g. 'I shagged...'. Spending time prior to addressing the abusive behaviour in detail, considering the young man's own sexual experiences and knowledge, and agreeing terminology (for parts of the body; types of sexual behaviour) will repay itself in aiding clarity subsequently.

Communication issues

Clare (1993) highlights a number of aspects to the intellectual functioning of individuals with a learning disability which may impact upon their participation in an assessment and will need consideration by assessors.

- **Poor memory:** Given that a psychological defense and tactic for young people reluctant to discuss sensitive or embarrassing matters, is to respond with 'I don't remember', this will need careful evaluation. We have found it helpful to check with carers as to the young person's general ability to recall past events. In the context of assessment sessions, time can be spent on considering less threatening aspects of the young person's life and evaluating their response. Psychological assessment can also provide guidance on the young person's functional ability. It is important neither to take the young person's initial response at face value or categorise it as 'denial'. Our experience at G-MAP is that many young people present with an initial statement of not being able to remember events, but with time and the space to work, the development of trust and the use of motivational approaches and imaginative communication techniques, are able to develop a fairly full account of their behaviours and associated feelings.

- **Acquiescent and suggestible responding:** A number of connected themes identified in the response to interview, particularly interrogatory, of individuals with learning disability (Clare and Gudjonsson, 1993) need to be considered. It has been found that respondents with a learning disability have a greater likelihood to find open-ended questions confusing; a bias to answer closed (yes/no) questions in the affirmative and increased vulnerability to a suggestible response to leading questions. We have found it important to work methodically through responses, and frequently return to issues to ensure our understanding of a young person's response is accurate. It is often helpful to offer a young person some choices, including a 'none of these' or 'not true for me'. Language and tone is important to ensure a young person does not feel a particular response is the most desired. We frequently use pictorial or graphic formats to allow the young person to locate themselves along a continuum, or use size, colour etc., to communicate meaning.

- **Reading difficulties and problems in understanding complex language and concepts and in discriminating responses:** In the assessment and evaluation of sexual offending, psychometric testing (the use of written questionnaires) is much used and considered by some to have advantages over direct questioning for generating certain types of information. Psychometric tests may be able to provide 'normed' samples to offer a statistical comparison of the individual with a certain group and offer an important evaluation of change pre and post -intervention. Most questionnaires, however, are designed for those with an average literacy and frequently ask the respondent to analyse a number of choices. Basic literacy and sexual knowledge may also impede responses to questionnaires designed to explore sexual attitudes, interests and preferences. Whilst it is possible to simplify certain measures and re-format using pictures, stories or graphics, there is yet to be adequate research into the value

of these attempts to adapt measures not originally designed for those with a learning disability. Clare's comment that; 'assessment of test-retest reliability over short periods suggests that, even when simplified, the majority of standard measures remain unsuitable for most people with a mild learning disabilities' (Clare, 1994), reflects much of our own experience. Within G-MAP we have a substantial commitment to the use of psychometric measures for assessment and the evaluation of progress. In working with young men with learning disabilities we have invested time in working through questionnaires directly in sessions and in using keyworkers to do so in relation to general, non-sexual measures. It is an open question for us at present if this and is extremely resource intensive process is productive. Is the experience of questions, most particularly with regard to sexual issues, being read out loud, so different to reading them to yourself that the response is distorted beyond viable use?

It is important to recognise that learning disability can disguise the complexity of the behavioural pattern. Our experience at G-MAP is that sexually aggressive young men with learning disabilities present with as complex a pattern in the development and maintenance of this behaviour as with the full spectrum of our client group. There is a tendency within the field of sexual aggression to see 'learning disabled sex offenders' as a sub-group in themselves. Whilst issues relating to functioning, social exclusion and restricted lifestyles are common presenting features, so are many others relevant to the development of sexual aggression in the general population. We find each young person we see has a unique and individual account relevant to more fully understanding how they have arrived at this point in their lives.

The system response to young males with intellectual disabilities who sexually offend

There are a number of reasons why abusive sexual behaviour presented by individuals with a learning disability may be less likely to be formally investigated and processed to within the criminal justice system.

- **Informal management by parents and/or carers.** We have frequently experienced a system of management that places a young man under total or almost total supervision and restriction. This is not on the basis of any legislative or procedural system, but assuming a level of compliance that would be unlikely, to say the least, in respect of most adolescents or young adults. Whilst recognising that such responses are often seen as the only way of protecting others and preventing the young person from the consequences to himself of any offending, the often compliant nature of those with a learning disability can mean such informal arrangements can continue for substantial periods, without review or attempts to address the underlying problem.

- **Lack of services.** Our experience of meeting colleagues across the UK would suggest, at the very least, a variable ability to access services for those with a learning disability and problematic sexual behaviour. There is perhaps a need for services concerned with sexual offending and those with learning disability to share expertise and resources to develop specific provision. The Reed Review of services for mentally disordered offenders (Department of Health/Home Office, 1992) emphasised the importance of a more clear and consistent partnership between criminal justice and social care agencies. It encouraged generic mental health services to adapt to allow the delivery of services to offenders and the development of some new specialist services to address specific areas of need. McCarthy and Thompson (1996) note an unintended consequence of the changes introduced in response to Reed,

The Reed Committee's concern to keep mentally disordered offenders away from the prison system has had the effect of introducing men with either very mild or arguably no learning disability into the (learning disability) system.

Frequently these men represent a significant danger to other, more vulnerable, service users.

- **A principal of diversion.** In September 1990 the Home Office issued circular 66/90 'Provision for Mentally Disordered Offenders'. This sets out the legal powers available and emphasises the need for informed decision making between agencies. In reviewing developments since issuing this circular the DoH and the Home Office restated that:

It is the Government's policy that those suffering from mental disorder who require specialist medical treatment or social support, should receive it from the health and social services... (those) committing criminal offences should be prosecuted where this is necessary in the public interest. In deciding whether a person should be charged, it is essential that account is taken of the circumstances and the gravity of the offence, what is known of the persons previous contacts with the criminal justice system and the psychiatric and social services.

There are real problems for the criminal justice system in how it can respond appropriately to offenders with learning disabilities. We must, however, discriminate between the practical e.g. the information available is insufficient to lead to a conviction; and the philosophical e.g. young people with learning disabilities cannot be held responsible for their actions. When dealing with individuals and agencies within the criminal justice system who express ambivalence or outright resistance we must push them clearly to articulate their assumptions and the barriers they perceive to making a contribution. The better we understand the criminal justice system in general, and the particular problems it has responding to learning disabled abusers, the better able we will be to engage with the system pro-actively and emphasise its potential contribution.

- **Victim communication.** In Hilary Brown and colleagues recent update on the largest UK survey of sexual abuse amongst a sample of people with learning disabilities (Brown, Stein and Turk, 1995) they identified half of the perpetrators as being fellow (male) service users. The largest proportion of those victimised, whether female or male victims, had been assessed as in the severe to moderate range. A third of the sample were also noted to have communication problems. It is perhaps unsurprising that these most highly vulnerable of victims are amongst the least likely to have their abuse formally responded to.

- *System denial/minimisation.* A consistent theme amongst the literature is the reluctance of agencies and structures to respond pro-actively to difficult/abusive sexual behaviours presented by those with a learning disability. This is certainly reflected in the case histories of many of the young men referred to G-MAP. It is worth emphasising Day's (1994) finding that those offenders with the most persistent and serious offence patterns most frequently began in adolescence. As Brown and Barrett (1994) comment:

  people with learning disabilities whose sexual behaviour crosses acceptable limits are not helped by a strategy of ignoring the problem until it goes away — it rarely does.

Treatment and Intervention Approaches

As O'Connor (1997) identifies, the fields of sexual aggression and the management of challenging behaviour presented by individuals with a learning disability, have derived their main theoretical models from distinct areas. Work with sexual aggressors has been influenced primarily by cognitive-behavioural theories and an emphasis on the use of thinking skills to develop self-control. Within learning disability, challenging behaviour has been addressed primarily by applied behaviour analysis, which focuses on immediate contingencies and positive interventions in behaviours. An increasing consensus has been emerging that treatment interventions with intellectually disabled offenders need to be multi-dimensional and involve a variety of modalities which reflect whole life functioning (Griffiths, Quinsey and Hingsburger, 1989; Haaven, Little and Petre-Miller, 1990: Lund, 1992; O'Connor, 1996). Frequently, groupwork is seen as a potentially valuable element to the overall service package (Swanson and Garwick, 1990; Cox-Lindenbaum and Lindenbaum, 1994). Lund (1992) has commented that these programmes often emphasise the control or elimination of abusive sexual behaviours without identifying

positive goals for non-problematic sexual expression or enhancing social and relationship skills to facilitate this. Relapse prevention (Laws, 1989; Pithers, 1990) has become the primary treatment model for sex-offender programmes across the UK and North America, and is predicated on the individual being able to transfer knowledge and skills from the therapeutic setting to external community situations. Barber (1992), writing more generally on relapse prevention, has suggested that the quality of an individuals social network is the primary factor influencing whether skills and knowledge are maintained post-treatment. Demetral (1994) proposes that practitioners working with intellectually disabled sex offenders should be particularly sensitised to establishing a supportive framework around the individual to monitor and reinforce key messages. O'Connor (1996) describes a 'problem-solving' approach in which a variety of treatment modalities were combined with environmental strategies to promote lifeskills and phased community access. Whilst O'Connor reports that a number of clients could not replicate control skills in community settings over which they demonstrated verbal mastery, evaluation suggested this broad based approach can be successful in enhancing mobility and independence for a number of clients. Murphy (1997) suggests interventions should be considered in terms of three areas:

1. *A lifestyle component* — improving opportunities for appropriate social and recreational activities.

2. *A direct treatment component* — specific therapeutic components aimed for example at developing greater control skills or promoting understanding of the appropriate boundaries to sexual behaviour

3. *A staff action component* — liaison with staff to influence overall care and management, and feedback on response to the treatment component

In developing intervention packages for learning disabled young men referred to the service, G-MAP's approach aims to reflect these holistic approaches. Our strategy has been to draw upon ideas from the spectrum of work within learning disability and sexual aggression. I will consider below some of the key areas in which our practice has needed to develop and reflect on ideas currently in the literature.

Strategies to redirect behaviour

Most reports in the literature describe single case interventions in which a set of behaviours has been targeted and a specific individual programme devised. A key element is frequently an assessment as to the function of the behaviour. A typical example is an intervention described by Wright, Herzog and Seymour (1992) in working with a young man with Down's syndrome who exhibited sexualised and other inappropriate behaviours. An analysis of the behaviour suggested it occurred under two conditions (a) when staff made demands upon the young man and (b) in order to gain attention. A programme was developed directing response amongst staff as to how to ignore attention seeking behaviour and reward more appropriate behaviours. This was allied with social skills input and cognitive-behavioural therapy. Dowrick and Ward (1997) outline an innovative intervention with a young man with mild learning disabilities who demonstrated predatory sexual behaviours towards children in the community. This involved the use of short video clips which had been prepared (involving the young man in question) showing him undertaking the desired behaviours e.g. reporting deviant fantasies, using agreed tactics if encountering children. The strategy was based upon a prior experience of the use of video 'self-modelling' with learning disabled clients to support the development of pro-social behaviours. The authors term this technique, a variation of self-modelling, as 'feedforward'. A detailed, and exceptionally resource intensive, monitoring/ evaluation programme was undertaken. Dowrick and Ward found that the technique rapidly generalised behaviour across settings, and that this continued over the follow-up period. The authors conclude this approach may be valuable in offering an alternative, non-verbally based approach to promoting desired behaviours.

As with the examples described above we have found it important to design specific interventions which target discrete behaviours. For example, collecting pictures of children or inappropriate touching of care/teaching staff. It is important to develop expectations which are concrete, specific and achievable. Ideally we aim to frame these positively: 'I will' rather than 'I will not'. The role of carers is critical in supporting and monitoring. We have found such approaches work best if feedback, rewards or sanctions operate on a short cycle e.g. between one day and a week. Positive outcomes may be fairly simple, such as access to a desired activity. Simple token economy systems (e.g. star charts) may support the process with a clear visual message as to progress.

Addressing deviant arousal

Where there is evidence of distinct arousal to abusive sexual thoughts and fantasies, we have employed behavioural techniques aimed at decreasing arousal to problematic/abusive sexual fantasies and in promoting a sexual interest in, and arousal to, appropriate non-deviant sexual fantasies. Techniques such as verbal satiation and covert sensitisation are less frequently used with young people than adults, even in North America where such approaches are more commonly accepted (Freeman-Longo, Bird, Stevenson and Fiske, 1995). Weinrott, Riggan and Frothingham (1997) outline a variation of adversive procedures for use with adolescents, which they term 'vicarious sensitisation'. This involves exposing the young person to an audio taped description of the factors leading up to his offence, stopping short of the assault. He then views a series of video clips dramatising the negative consequences of sexual offending. The authors provide data to support this method and has an impact on reducing deviant arousal. Fisher and McGregor (1997) provide a detailed review of the applicability of these treatment methods with non-disabled adolescents. They identify the relevant features of an 'appropriate' sexual fantasy which any programme should be promoting:

- full consent

- equal power relationship

- mutual agreement

- positive emotions
- no coercion
- that the focus of the fantasy should not be an individual the client is angry with

There is as yet a limited literature base on the use of these approaches with learning disabled adolescents. Haaven, Little and Petre-Miller (1990) report using directed fantasy to encourage clients to masturbate to non-abusive images as part of a broad based intervention programme with learning disabled sexual offenders. In O'Connor's (1996) programme she describes using a simplified version of covert sensitisation to associate an aversive image with deviant sexual arousal. Withers and Gaskell (1998) recently reported the use of a 'minimally aversive' cognitive-behavioural intervention to eliminate the inappropriate masturbation of an 11 year old boy with mild learning disabilities. This was supported via education and the use of distraction and positive reinforcement. We have found verbal satiation (Laws, 1995), a useful approach with young men and applicable to some of our learning disabled clients. This procedure involves identifying in detail the deviant fantasy and then arranging for the young person to repeatedly read a script of this onto a tape daily (e.g. 10–20 times). This process is allied with an 'escape scene' in which the individual rehearses how to get out of the risk situation and work on promoting non-problematic arousal. We have also used covert sensitisation in which an adverse consequence is paired with a deviant fantasy. It has been our experience that both approaches can be of value with learning disabled clients though it is vital that care be taken to ensure the process is understood and adhered to correctly. We should stress that these methods are highly individual and require considerable time input from therapists and those supporting the young person.

The use of such intrusive techniques with young people needs to be approached with caution, particularly so when they have a learning disability, and we have found the following criteria to be relevant:

- The young person experiences the arousal as problematic and is motivated to work on this area.
- Experience would support a view of the

young person as open and communicative about their sexual drives and interests.

- The pattern of deviant sexual fantasy is reasonably distinct and consistent.
- The young person is supervised and receives considerable support from carers.

To monitor sexual arousal/masturbation patterns we have designed daily diary sheets employing language or symbols agreed with the young person. We have found that such techniques can be applicable to young people with a learning disability, though are most likely to be viable with the more able and those most highly motivated.

Working to alter cognitions

Lindsay, Neilson, Morrison and Smith (1998) describe a groupwork programme for adults with learning disabilities which targets attitudes towards sexual contact with children. The authors describe positive results, but an idiosyncratic pattern of attitudinal change suggests that certain areas were more conceptually accessible for group members. The programme was more successful at educating clients on issues such as the basic boundaries to sexual conduct (ages of consent) and the negative consequences for themselves. Attitudes towards blame and harm were the most resistant and in particular a belief by the men that children had power over them. They found that treatment length was a critical variable, with 24–36 months duration producing the most demonstrable degree of change. Our own experienced has echoed those of Lyndsay and his colleagues, both in groupwork and individual programmes.

Groupwork with Young Men with Learning Disabilities who Sexually Abuse

Groupwork has emerged as the predominant treatment method for those who display sexually aggressive behaviours. In a survey of North American treatment providers undertaken by Knopp and colleagues (Knopp *et al.*, 1992), 98 per cent of programmes identified peer groups as the preferred treatment model in work with adults and adolescents who had sexually abused. In the

UK, Allam and Browne (1998) found cognitive-based sex offender groups to be operating in 97 per cent of probation departments. However, there is little supportive empirical evidence in existence. Lab, Shiels and Schondel's (1993) comparison of a structured group programme with generalised non-specific therapy, found no measurable advantage in terms of re-offence data. The Home Office project known as the STEP research (Beckett *et al.*, 1994; Hedderman and Sugg, 1996) has offered support to the impact of such programmes. Craissati and McClurg (1997) provide one of the few British studies comparing individual and group interventions with sex offenders (albeit adults), based on psychometric measurement and re-offence data. Finding greater evidence of positive treatment change in the group sample, they concluded that their study would 'tentatively support the policy of group treatment, currently in vogue'.

Although in the UK the number of groupwork programmes for adult sex offenders has increased dramatically throughout the 1990s, groupwork programmes for young people who abuse are much less in evidence and are confined predominantly to specialist projects (Hird, 1997). The recent thematic report (HM Inspectorate of Probation, 1998), examining work with sexual offenders within the Probation Service, found only two of the ten areas inspected to be running programmes for (adult) offenders with learning disabilities. A major theme of the report concerned the need to develop greater interagency services to young sexual abusers. The lack of any specific programmes for young abusers with learning disabilities appears implicit in the report.

As a therapeutic medium for children and young people, several advantages have been cited for groupwork techniques (Carrell, 1993; Dwivedi, 1993; Duboust and Knight, 1995; Malekoff, 1997). A summary of their findings includes:

- For young people who have difficulties in expressing emotions and experiences the group offers a potential to learn from others whilst developing competency in self-disclosure.

- Groups can reduce a sense of isolation, particularly for young people whose problem has a degree of social stigma.

- The group environment can become a safe psychological space in which to explore difficult or anxiety provoking issues.
- Important interpersonal and social skills can be rehearsed in a group setting.
- Groups allow a range of experiential activities which actively engage children and young people that are not practical within an adult-child interaction.
- Peer education and reinforcement is seen as particularly effective for adolescents.

Background to Developing a Groupwork Programme for Young Abusers with Learning Disabilities

G-MAP began in 1988 as a multi-agency project, whose primary aim was to provide a groupwork service for 13–18 year old males in the Greater Manchester region who had sexually abused. The content and structure of the programme reflected the predominant theoretical model of cognitive-behavioural therapy (see O'Callaghan and Print, 1994). Over time the programme devolved a more specific relapse prevention; (Pithers, 1990) focus. G-MAP was re-launched at the beginning of 1996 as an independent project. Our experience suggested that a significant gap in the provision of services existed in respect of young men with learning disabilities who displayed inappropriate or sexually aggressive behaviours. Previously we had attempted to integrate young men/boy   s wi mild learning disabilities into our existing programme. This proved problematic and we considered that content, delivery and social interaction within the group disadvantaged these young men. With the projects expansion one of our aims was to develop a strand of the service for young people with learning disabilities, and both learn from and contribute as a service to this developing area of practice. As the project has devoted time and resources into this service, the proportion of our referrals concerning young people who could be defined as falling within the learning disability spectrum has grown steadily, to being currently around 50 per cent of our referrals.

A core element of our provision is the groupwork programme we run for young men with learning disabilities. The group meets weekly for 2 hours, with a break. The age range accepted is 16–21 years. We have placed a maximum number of eight to group entry and consider an optimum number to be six participants. There is a staff group drawn from health (a clinical nurse specialist in forensic psychiatry); learning disability services (worker for learning disabled offenders) and specialist practitioners for sexually abusive young people. Two (mixed gender) staff members facilitate the group, with one other as observer.

The structure of the group is consistent, in that we consider news from the week; review key learning points from the last session; introduce the content for this session; run the session and review behaviour, contributions and learning points at the conclusion. There is a written record of the session evaluating group functioning, response to content and co-working issues. An individual write-up is produced relating to each young person and forwarded to professional carers and case managers (social workers, probation officers). This offers a summary of the session content, the young person's response and performance/contribution to the group and any issues we consider requires follow-up or reinforcement.

It is preferred for young men in the group to have concurrent individual work, undertaken by G-MAP practitioners This individual programme both supports and reinforces the group programme and addresses work not applicable within the group e.g. family issues; sexual arousal patterns; specific social skill input and personal victimisation issues.

Many of the young people who attend the group are resident in a supported setting of some kind, e.g. social service care placement, health provision or probation hostel. We find it is important to meet with care staff to set, and then review, progress in both the group and the individual work.

The programme curriculum

The programme curriculum takes on average 12 months to progress through. There is some flexibility to allow us to adequately cover each content block. Group size and the ability mix will influence the speed in which topics can be addressed. The general assessed ability span of young men attending the group is within the mild to moderate range. The group runs on an open basis with young people entering at various points following assessment and pre-group preparation. The groups rolling programme is structured as follows:

Figure 1: Group programme for young men with learning disabilities

Introduction of new group member *(to be repeated on entrance of any new member)*	• Who are we and why are we here? (group members introduce themselves). • What is important to now about me? (new group member provides some basic personal information). • How does this group work? (group members explain the purpose of the group and how we work together e.g. basic rules). • Why have I joined this group? (new group member makes first introduction). • What is my problem (new group member identifies basic areas he hopes to progress on over time in group e.g. better control over sexual behaviour; gaining others trust, greater freedom etc.).
Block One *Sexuality and development*	• What do we need to know about sex and the way our bodies develop? • Where do we learn from? (friends, family, education, media, direct experience etc.). • What kinds of things do you learn from these sources? • What is sexual behaviour? (different aspects of touch etc.). • What are sexual feelings? (how can you differentiate between sexual and non-sexual feelings).
Block Two *Boundaries to sexual behaviour*	• How do we decide if sexual behaviour is OK/not OK? (use of case studies based on pictures; role play and story telling). • What rules should there be for sexual behaviour? (amalgamate themes from previous sessions into set of statements which allow group to define OK/not OK sexual behaviour). • How did my sexual behaviour break these rules? (detailed debrief on each group members sexual offence in which they and other group members identify elements which made the behaviour unacceptable). • How to keep to the rules (some preliminary ideas on keeping safe).

Block Three *A model for understanding*	• Why do people sexually abuse? (reference back to materials used in Block Two).
	• Going up the Four Steps (use of adapted Finkelhor model as a basis for understanding behaviour).
	• Why did I abuse? — my journey up the Four Steps.
	• How honest have I been able to be so far? (open door for revision and addition).
	• What is still hard to understand about my sexual abusive behaviour? (further work to do in and out of group).
	• How honest am I able to be? (final introduction to be presented to family, carers etc.).
Block Four *The consequences for me and others of my sexual behaviour*	• What have I lost by sexually abusing? (experiences of criminal justice system, restriction, move away from home, impact on relationships etc.).
	• Who else has been hurt or harmed by my sexual behaviour? (visual metaphor e.g. ripples in a pond/branches of tree, to illustrate this).
	• What would I lose in the future if I abused again?
	• How does it feel to the victim of abuse? (drawing on group members own experiences).
	• What might this tell me about the person I abused? (establishing links between individuals or other group members experiences of abuse and that of their victim).
Block Five *Control plan*	• What rules will help me keep my sexual behaviour OK? (when not to be sexual; who not to be sexual with; where it's OK to touch people etc.).
	• What's risky for me? (activities; feelings; being out alone etc.).
	• Who can help me keep my sexual behaviour acceptable? (what do I want from other people?).
	• Putting my control plan together (getting it ready to present to family/carers etc.).

Block Six *Social and personal skills*	• Relationships and how they work (skills in interacting with others).
	• How I have got on with people in the past ('voices' of family, teachers and carers).
	• How do I get on with other people now? (examples of current relationships).
	• What it's like to be with me (behaviour in group, with other people I live with).
	• What changes do I want to make? (specific skills in social or independence skills).
	• How will these changes help in managing my sexual behaviour? (link with carers to consider how these changes may be promoted).
Block Seven *Revising my control plan*	• What is safe for me?/what is not safe for me at present? (boundary setting through explicit scenarios; promoting of group honesty e.g. over risk, sexual thoughts).
	• Who can help with keeping me safe? (testing out whether group members are in fact using others).
	• What skills do I have in controlling my sexual behaviour? (demonstrable).
	• What do I need to keep working on? (skills audit, use group to role play risk scenarios).
	• How can I improve these skills? (agreed plan, rehearsal, maintenance).
	• Earning trust and keeping safe (explaining my control plan for others; using group as a safe venue to work to this).

Lessons learned from running the group

Our experience in running the group would echo a number of themes present in the literature, relating either to groups for learning disabled sex offenders or those for learning disabled adolescents generally. These include:

- The length of time it is likely to take for group members to integrate key messages is considerably longer than for non-learning disabled clients (Lindsay *et al.*, 1998).

- should recognise the need for concrete, focused sessions, of a reasonably short duration (Gardiner *et al.*, 1996; Chapman and Clare, 1992; Swanson and Garwick, 1990). We have found ninety minutes to be a feasible time for the length of a group session. Sessions appear to work better when the theme is clearly stated, and re-emphasised throughout, and where group members can clearly relate the content/exercise to the theme being addressed.

- It is important that group facilitators employ a variety of therapeutic mediums e.g. use of drama/role play, art based exercises, visual and video material (Allam *et al.*, 1997; Chapman and Clare, 1992; Gardiner, Kelly and Wilkinson, 1996). Within the G-MAP group it has been our experience that dramatic exercises are particularly successful in relating the content of the group programme to the 'real world'.

- Other practitioners in this area (Jones and Bonnar, 1996; Gardiner *et al.*, 1996; Cormack, 1993) have commented on the difficulties in establishing group cohesion, the lack of mutual support between group members and reliance of group members on group facilitators to maintain group interaction and direction. Unlike our experience of running groups with non-disabled young people, this group were not able to take on responsibilities for tasks independently and group facilitators found it necessary to support even basic social interactions.

- Group facilitators should be prepared for boundary challenging and negative interactions between group members (Cormack, 1993; Jones and Bonnar, 1996;). Young people with learning disabilities may be less inhibited about behaviour within groups and, overtly less tolerant of their peers. In debriefing with young people a consistent message was their expectation of group facilitators to manage disruptive behaviour firmly and consistently. It was viewed as a failure on our part if we allowed rules to be flouted. We have also learned the importance of having explicit rules governing behaviour, particularly of group members to each other, available (e.g. a poster with symbols) and restated at regular intervals.

- That the therapeutic factors most positively regarded by the participants are not always those most obvious or foreseen by the facilitators (Jones and Bonnar, 1996; Mishna, 1996). For example a number of young men who have been involved in the group have viewed it as an important social opportunity.

- Although it may take longer to establish when participants have a learning disability (and may possibly be more fragile), a group environment can be developed where challenging and sensitive issues can be constructively addressed (Chapman and Clare, 1992; Cormack, 1993; Mishna, 1996; Swanson and Garwick, 1990). For example, we have experienced young men being able to share their own experiences of abuse, and work towards making important connections between this and their own abusive behaviour.

Developing Services to Young People with Learning Disabilities who Sexually Abuse

Our experience in the last three years has demonstrated that approaches can be developed which promote change or at the very least a more effective, less oppressive management strategy. There are a number of themes, which have been central to G-MAPís work with learning disabled young people, which we would suggest as relevant to the development of services in this area:

a) It is important for therapy not to be seen as the primary change medium and for practitioners to view problem behaviour from a social perspective. Interventions should be designed on a holistic basis with effective communication to ensure a co-ordinated approach.

b) Carers should be seen as central to the process of management and change. They have the potential to support, motivate, reinforce and monitor and need to take a centre place in the design of any individual programme.

c) There is an urgent need for the development of appropriate skills, resources and techniques. For example visual and dramatic mediums which are more accessible and memorable for individuals with impaired intellectual functioning.

d) Within this area of work we must articulate realistic change goals, which are less likely to reflect the concept of total 'self-management/relapse avoidance' seen in the mainstream of work with sexual offenders. For a number of clients intervention may be about a reduction, rather than elimination, of problematic sexual behaviours.

e) Purchasers will need to recognise resource implications, which reflect the intensity and duration of interventions necessary to manage and change behaviour. We have found programmes to require minimum periods of 18–24 months, with high levels of contact and liaison required to manage the more complex of clients.

f) No professional group has a monopoly on skills in this developing area and the

emphasis should be upon a multi-
disciplinary approach with practitioners
sharing ideas and skills.

g)   There is a need for greater research and
evaluation to expand our current limited
knowledge base.

As a service G-MAP has found that our
intervention packages have contributed to
young people, about whom there are
significant concerns, being able to lead less
restrictive lives, without placing those
vulnerable in the community to undue risk.
Longer-term evaluation will assist us in
establishing whether such positive changes
translate into long-term gains. To date our
experience reflects that of Thomas and Singh
(1995), who provide one of the few available
follow-up studies of learning disabled sexual
offenders managed in the community. They
conclude that:

> *a planned and structured treatment programme
> formulated and implemented by a well organised
> community support team can significantly reduce the
> need for secure placements. At present services for
> young people with learning disabilities who abuse are
> sparse and many projects may find it difficult to
> devote resources into what is maybe a small minority
> of their overall client group. As with all services to
> young people who abuse, there is a need for greater
> strategic and interagency planning to develop
> initiatives in what is a complex and resource
> intensive area of practice.*

References

Allam, J.A., and Browne, K.D. (1998). Evaluating Community-based Treatment Programmes for Men who Sexually Abuse Children. *Child Abuse Review*, 7: 13–29.

Allam, J., Middleton, D., and Browne, K. (1997). Different Clients, Different Needs?: Practice Issues in Community Based Treatment for Sex Offenders. *Criminal Behaviour and Mental Health*, Vol 7: 69– 84.

Bancroft, J. (1989). *Human Sexuality and It's Problems*. London: Churchill Livingstone.

Barber, J.D. (1992) Relapse Prevention and the Need for Brief Social Interventions. *Journal of Substance Abuse Treatment*, 9: 157–8.

Bentovim, A., and Williams, B. (1998). Children and Adolescents: Victims who Become Perpetrators. *Advances in Psychiatric Treatment*, 4: 101–107.

Beail, N., and Warden, S. (1995). Sexual Abuse of Adults with a Learning Disability. *Journal of Intellectual Disability Research*, 39(5) October: 382–387.

Beckett, R., Beech, A., Fisher, D., and Fordham, A.S. (1994). *Community-based Treatment For Sex Offenders: An Evaluation Of Seven Treatment Programmes*. London: Home Office

Briggs, D., Doyle., P., Gooch, T., and Kennington, R. (1998). *Assessing Men Who Sexually Abuse: A Practice Guide*. London: Jessica Kingsley.

Brown, H. (1997). Introduction to Special Issue on Sexuality. *Journal of Applied Research in Intellectual Disabilities*, 10(2): 80–82.

Brown, H., Stein, J., and Turk, V. (1995). The Sexual Abuse of Adults with Learning Disabilities: Report of a Second Two-year Incidence Survey. *Mental Handicap Research*, 8(1): 3–24.

Brown, H., and Barrett, S. (1994). Understanding and Responding to Difficult Sexual Behaviour. In Craft, A. (Ed.). *Practice Issues in Sexuality and Learning Disabilities*. London: Routledge.

Calder, M.C. (1997). *Juveniles and Children who Sexually Abuse: A Guide to Risk Assessment*. Lyme Regis, Dorset: Russell House Publishing.

Cambridge, P. (1997). At Whose Risk? Priorities and Conflicts for Policy Development in HIV and Learning Disability. *Journal of Applied Research in Intellectual Disabilities*, 10(2): 83–104.

Cambridge, P., and McCarthy, M. (1997). Developing and Implementing Sexuality Policy for a Learning Disability Provider Service. *Health and Social Care in the Community*, 5(4): 227–236.

Carr, E.G., and Durand, V.M. (1985). Reducing Behaviour Problems Through Functional Communication Training. *Journal of Applied Behaviour Analysis*, 18: 111–126.

Carrell, S. (1993). *Group Exercises for Adolescents: A Manual for Therapists*. London: Sage.

Chapman, T., and Clare, I. (1992). An Education Group for Male Sexual Offenders with Mild Mental Handicaps. *Mental Handicap*, 20, June: 74–80.

Clare, I. (1993). Issues in the Assessment and Treatment of the Male Sex Offender with Mild Learning Disabilities. *Journal of Sexual and Marital Therapy*, 8(2): 167–180.

Clare, I.C.H., and Gudjonsson, G.H. (1993). Interrogative Suggestibility, Confabulation, and Acquiescence in People with Mild Learning Disabilities (Mental Handicap): Implications for Reliability During Police Investigations. *British Journal of Clinical Psychology*, 32: 295–301.

Cooke, L.B., and Sinason, V. (1998). Abuse of People with Learning Disabilities and Other Vulnerable Adults. *Advances in Psychiatric Treatment*, 4: 119–125.

Corbett, A. (1996a). *Trinity of Pain: Therapeutic Responses to People with Learning Disabilities who Commit Sexual Offences.* London: Respond.

Corbett, A. (1996b). The Role of Attachment in Working with People with Learning Disabilities who Commit Sexual Offences. *NAPSAC Bulletin*, March: 14–17.

Cormack, E. (1993). Group Therapy with Adults with Learning Disabilities who have Sexually Offended. *Groupwork*, 6(2): 162–176.

Cox-Lindenbaum, D., and Lindenbaum, L. (1994). A Modality for Treating Aggressive Behaviours and Sexual Disorders in People with Mental Retardation. In Bouras, N. (Ed.). *Mental Health and Mental Retardation: Recent Advances and Practices.* Cambridge: Cambridge University Press.

Craissati, J., and McClurg, G. (1997). The Challenge Project: A Treatment Program Evaluation for Perpetrators of Child Sexual Abuse. *Child Abuse and Neglect*, 21(7): 637–648.

Cullen, C. (1993). The Treatment of People who Offend. In Howells, K., and Hollin, H. (Eds.). *Clinical Approaches to the Mentally Disordered Offender.* London: Wiley.

Davidson, G.C., and Neal, J.M. (1990). *Abnormal Psychology*, 5th edn. New York: Wiley.

Day, K. (1993). Crime and Mental Retardation. In Howells, K., and Hollin, C. (Eds.). *Clinical Approaches to the Mentally Disordered Offender.* London: Wiley.

Day, K. (1994). Characteristics, Management and Treatment of Mentally Handicapped Sex Offenders. In *Mentally Handicapped Sex Offenders: A Symposium.* Supported by Schering Health Care. Merit.

Day, K. (1994). Male Mentally Handicapped Sex Offenders. *British Journal of Psychiatry*, 165: 630–639.

Demetral, G.D. (1994). Diagrammatic Assessment of Ecological Integration of Sex Offenders with Mental Retardation in Community Residential Facilitates. *Mental Retardation*, 32: 141–145.

Department of Health and the Home Office (1992). *Review of Health and Social Services for Mentally Disordered Offenders and Others Requiring Similar Services.* Final report summary (The Reed Committee Report). London: HMSO.

Dolan, M., Holloway, J., Bailes, S., and Kroll, L. (1996).

The Psychosocial Characteristics of Juvenile Sex Offenders Referred to an Adolescent Forensic Service in the UK. *Medicine, Service and the Law*, 36: 343–352.

Dowrick. P.W., and Ward, K.M. (1997). Video Feedforward in the Support of a Man with Intellectual Disability and Inappropriate Sexual Behaviour. *Journal of Intellectual and Developmental Disability*, 22(3): 147–160.

Doyle, P., and Gooch, T. (1995). The Mentally Handicapped as Offenders. In *Forensic Aspects Of Mental Handicap*, Supported by Shering Health Care. Merit.

Duboust, S., and Knight, P. (1995). *Group Activities for Personal Development.* Bicester: Winslow Press.

Dwivedi, K.N. (Ed.) (1993). *Groupwork with Children and Adolescents: A Handbook.* London: Jessica Kingsley.

Epps, K.J. (1996). Sexually Abusive Behaviour in an Adolescent Boy with the 48, XXYY Syndrome: A Case Study. *Criminal Behaviour and Mental Health*, 6: 137–146.

Epps, K. J. (1991). The Residential Treatment of Adolescent Sex Offenders. In McMurran, M., and McDougall. C. (Eds.). Proceedings of the DCLP First Annual Conference. *Issues in Criminological and Legal Psychology*, 17(1). Leicester, England: British Psychological Society.

Faulk, M. (1994). *Basic Forensic Psychiatry.* London: Blackwell Scientific Publications.

Fairburn, G., Rowley, D., and Bowen, M. (1995). *Sexuality, Learning Difficulties and Doing What's Right.* London: David Fulton Publishers.

Finkelhor, D. (Ed.) (1984). *Child Sexual Abuse: New Theory and Research.* New York: Free Press.

Fisher, D., and McGregor, G. (1997). Behavioural Treatment Techniques. In Hoghughi, M., Bhate, S.R., and Graham, F. (Eds.). *Working with Sexually Abusive Adolescents.* London: Sage.

Freeman-Longo, R.E., Bird, S., Stephenson, W.F., and Fiske, J.A. (1995). *1994 Nationwide Survey of Treatment Programs and Models.* Brandon, VT: Safer Society Press.

Fryers, T. (1997). Impairment, Disability and Handicap: Categories and Classifications. In Russell, O. (Ed.). *The Psychiatry of Learning Disability.* London: Gaskell.

Gannon, L.E., Clayton-Smith, J., and Bailey, S. (1997). *Sexual Offending as a Presentation of Sex Chromosome Abnormality in Adolescence.* Unpublished research paper. Manchester: Prestwich Hospital.

Gardiner, M., Kelly, K., and Wilkinson, D. (1996). Group for Male Sex Offenders with Learning Disabilities. *NAPSAC Bulletin*, March. 3–6.

Griffiths, D., Hingsburger, D., and Christian, R. (1985). Treating Developmentally Handicapped Sex Offenders. *Psychiatric Aspects Of Mental Retardation*, 4(1): 49–52.

Griffiths, D., Quinsey, V., and Hingsburger, D. (1989). *Changing Inappropriate Sexual Behaviour.* New York: Brookes.

Gross, G. (1985). *Activities of the Developmental Disabilities Adult Offender Project*. Olympia, WA: Washington State Developmental Disabilities Planning Council.

Haaven, J., Little, R., and Petre-Miller, D. (1990). *Treating Intellectual Disabled Sex Offenders: A Model Residental Programme*. Orwell, VT: The Safer Society Press.

Hawkes, C., Jenkins, J., and Vizard, E. (1997). Roots of Sexual Violence in Children and Adolescents. In Varma, V. (Ed.). *Violence in Children and Adolescents*. London: Jessica Kingsley

Hayes, S. (1991). Sex Offenders. *Australia and New Zealand Journal of Developmental Disabilities*, 172: 221–227

Hedderman, C., and Sugg, D. (1996). *Does Treating Sex Offending Reduce Reoffending?* Home Office Research and Statistics Directorate, No 45. London: Home Office.

Herzog, D., and Money, J. (1993). Sexology and Social Work in the Case of Klinefelters (47 XXY) Syndrome. *Mental Retardation*, 3(3): 161–162.

Hird, J. (1997). Working in Context. In Hoghughi H., Bhate S.R., and Graham, F. (Ed.). *Working with Sexually Abusive Adolescents*. London: Routledge.

HM Inspectorate of Probation (1998). *Exercising Constant Vigilance: The Role of the Probation Service in Protecting the Public from Sex Offenders*. Report of a Thematic Inspection. London: Home Office.

Home Office (1995). *Statistics of Mentally Disordered Offenders: England and Wales 1994*. London.

Home Office (1990). *Circular 66/90: Provisions for Mentally Disordered Offenders*. London.

Humel, P., Ashcroft, W., Blessman, F., and Anders, O. (1993). Sexually Aggressive Acts of an Adolescent with Klinefelter Syndrome. *Uprax-Kinderpsychologie-Kinderpsychiatrie*, 42(4): 132–138.

Jones, A. M., and Bonnar, S. (1996). Group Psychotherapy with Learning Disabled Adults. *British Journal of Learning Disability*, 24: 65–69.

Kahn, T.J., and Chambers, H.J. (1991). Assessing Reoffence Risk with Juvenile Sexual Offenders. *Child Welfare League of America*, 70(3) May-June: 333–345.

Knight, R., and Prentky, R. (1993). Exploring Characteristics For Classifying Juvenile Sex Offenders. In Barbaree, H., Marshall, W., and Hudson, S. (Eds.). *The Juvenile Sex Offender*. New York: Guilford Press.

Knopp, F.H., Freeman-Longo, R., and Stephenson, W.H. (1992). *Nationwide Survey of Juvenile and Adult Sex Offender Treatment Program and Models*. Orwell, VT: Safer Society.

Knopp, F.H. (1990). Introduction. In Haven, J., Little, R., and Petre-Miller, D. (Eds.). *Treating Intellectually Disabled Sex Offenders*. Vermont: Safer Society Press.

Lab, S.P., Shiels, G., and Schondel, C. (1993). Research Note: An Evaluation of Juvenile Sexual Offender Treatment. *Crime and Delinquency*, 39(4).

Laws, D.R. (1989). *Relapse Prevention with Sex Offenders*. New York: Guilford Press.

Lindsay, W.R., Neilson, C.Q., Morrison, F., and Smith, A.H. (1998). The Treatment of Six Men with a Learning Disability Convicted of Sex Offences Against Children. *British Journal of Clinical Psychology*, 37: 83–98.

Lisak, D., and Ivan, C. (1995). Deficits in Intimacy and Empathy in Sexually Aggressive Men. *Journal of Interpersonal Violence*, 10(3) September: 296–308.

Lund, C.A. (1992). Long-term Treatment of Sexual Problems in Adolescent and Adult Developmentally Disabled Persons. *Annals of Sexual Research*, 5: 5–31.

Malekoff, A. (1997). *Group Work with Adolescents: Principles and Practice*. New York: Guilford Press.

McCarthy, M., and Thompson, D. (1996). Sexual Abuse by Design: An Examination of the Issues in Learning Disability. *Disability and Society*, 11(2): 205–217.

McCarthy, M., and Thompson, D. (1997). A Prevalence Study of Sexual Abuse of Adults with Intellectual Disabilities Referred for Sex Education. *Journal of Applied Research in Intellectual Disability*, 10(2): 105–124.

Mishna, F. (1996). In Their own Words: Therapeutic Factors for Adolescents who have Learning Disabilities. *International Journal of Group Psychotherapy*, 46(2): 265–273.

Murphy, G. (1997). Treatment and Risk Management. In Churchill, J., Brown, H., Craft, A., and Horrocks, C. (Eds.). *There Are No Easy Answers*. Nottingham: ARC/NAPSAC

Murrey, G.H., Briggs, D., and Davies, C. (1992). Psychopathically Disordered, Mentally Ill and Mentally Handicapped Sex Offenders: A Comparative Study. *Medicine, Science and the Law*, 32: 331–336.

Noelly, D., Muccigrosso, L., and Zigman, E. (1996). Treatment Successes with Mentally Retarded Sex Offenders. In Coleman, E., Dwyer, S.M., and Palone, N.J. (Eds.) *Sex Offender Treatment: Biological Dysfunction, Intrapsychic Conflict, Interpersonal Violence*. New York: Haworth Press.

O'Callaghan, D., and Print, B. (1994). Adolescent Sexual Abusers: Research, Assessment and Treatment. In Morrison, T., Erooga, M., and Beckett R. (Eds.). *Sexual Offending Against Children*. London: Routledge.

O'Connor, W. (1997). Towards an Environmental Perspective on Intervention for Problem Sexual Behaviour in People with an Intellectual Disability. *Journal of Applied Research in Intellectual Disabilities*, 10(2): 159–175.

O'Connor, W. (1996). A Problem Solving Intervention for Sex Offenders with an Intellectual Disability. *Journal of Intellectual and Developmental Disability*, 21(3): 219–235.

Parkin, W., and Green, L. (1994). *Sexuality and Residential Care: Research in Progress*. Paper presented at the

British Sociological Association Annual Conference Sexualities in Context, University of Central Lancashire, 28–31st March 1994.

Perry, B.D. (1994). Neurobiological Sequelae of Childhood Trauma: PTSD in Children. In Murray, M. (Ed.). *Catcholamines in Post-Traumatic Stress Disorder: Emerging Concepts.* Washington DC: American Psychiatric Press.

Pithers, W.D. (1990). Relapse Prevention with Sexual Aggressors: Method of Enhancing Therapeutic Gain and Enhancing External Supervision. In Marshall, W.L, Laws, D.R., and Barbaree, H.E. (Eds.). *Handbook of Sexual Assault, Theories and Treatment of the Offender.* New York: Plenum.

Schilling, R.F., and Shinke, S.P. (1989), Mentally Retarded Sex Offenders: Fact, Fiction and Treatment. *Journal of Social Work and Human Sexuality*, 7: 33–48.

Sigelman, C.K., Budd, E.D., Winer, J.L., Schoenrock, C.J., and Martin, W. (1982). Evaluating Alternative Techniques of Questioning Mentally Retarded Persons. *American Journal of Mental Deficiency*, 86(5): 511–518.

Sobsey, D. (1994). Sexual Abuse of Individuals with a Learning Disability. In Craft, A. (Ed.) *Practice Issues in Sexuality and Learning Disabilities.* London: Routledge.

Segal, Z.V., and Stermac, L.E. (1990). The Role of Cognition in Sexual Assault. In Marshall, W L, Laws, D.R., and Barbaree, H.E. (Eds.). *Handbook of Sexual Assault, Theories and Treatment of the Offender.* New York: Plenum.

Stanley, P.D., Dai, Y., and Nolan, R.F. (1997). Differences in Depression and Self-esteem Reported by Learning Disabled and Behaviour Disordered Middle School Students. *Journal of Adolescence*, 20: 219–222.

Suzer-Azarott, B., and Mayer, G.R. (1991). *Behaviour Analysis for Lasting Change.* Fort-Worth: Hott, Rinehart and Winston.

Swanson, C.K., and Garwick, G.B. (1990). Treatment for Low Functioning Sex Offenders: Group Therapy and Interagency Co-ordination. *Mental Retardation*, 28(3): 155–161.

Thomas, D.H., and Singh, T.H. (1995). Offenders Referred to a Learning Disability Service: A Retrospective Study from One County. *British Journal Of Learning Disability*, 23: 24–27.

Thompson, D. (1997). Profiling the Sexually Abusive Behaviour of Men with Intellectual Disabilities. *Journal of Applied Research in Intellectual Disabilities*, 10(2): 125–139.

Thompson, D., and Brown, H. (1998). *Response-ability: Working with Men with Learning Disabilities who have Difficult or Abusive Sexual Behaviours.* Brighton: Pavilion.

Thompson, D., and Brown, H. (1997). Men with Intellectual Disabilities who Abuse: A Review of the Literature. *Journal of Applied Research in Intellectual Disabilities*, 10(2): 140–158.

Thompson, D., Clare, I., and Brown, H. (1997). Not Such an 'Ordinary' Relationship: The Role of Women Support Staff in Relation to Men with Learning Disabilities who have Difficult Sexual Behaviour. *Disability and Society*, 12(4) September.

Verberne, G. (1990). Treatment of Sexually Deviant Behaviours in Mildly Mentally Retarded Adults. In Dosen, A., Van Gennep, A., and Zwanikkeen, J. (Eds.). *Treatment of Mental Illness and Behavioural Disorders in the Mentally Retarded.* Leiden, The Netherlands: Logal Publications.

Watkins, B., and Bentovim, A. (1992). Male Children and Adolescents as Victims: A Review of Current Knowledge. In Mezey, G.C., and King, M.B. (Eds.). *Male Victims of Sexual Assault.* New York: Oxford University Press.

Weinrott, M.R., Riggan, M., and Frothingham, S. (1997). Reducing Deviant Arousal on Juvenile Sex Offenders Using Vicarious Sensitisation. *Journal of Interpersonal Violence*, 12(5): 704–728.

Withers, P.S., and Gaskell, S.L. (1998). A Cognitive-behavioural Intervention to Address Inappropriate Masturbation in a Boy with Mild Learning Disabilities. *British Journal of Learning Disabilities*, 26(2): 58–61.

Wright, G., Herzog, D., and Seymour, J. (1992). Treatment of a Constellation of Inappropriate Sexual and Social Behaviours in a 20 Year-old Man with Down's Syndrome. *Sexuality and Disability*, 10: 57–61.

Chapter Thirteen

The Young Person with an Austistic Spectrum Disorder and Sexually Abusive Behaviour:

Themes Around Asperger's Syndrome and a Case Study

Graham Birtwell and Andy Bowly

The Young Person with an Austistic Spectrum Disorder and Sexually Abusive Behaviour: Themes Around Asperger's Syndrome and a Case Study

Introduction

This chapter is based on intervention with a service user that resulted in the development of a professional partnership between a scheme that specialises in services for adolescent abusers and a residential school providing education for young people with Autistic Spectrum Disorders, in order to meet this service users needs. The case of James highlighted specific challenges for a range of professionals due to his specific needs and is substantiated by Mortlock (1998). This was due to the fact that James' case challenged the traditional models of intervention with young abusers and required a creative and innovative approach.

The following account is not intended to give a definitive model of intervention with young abusers who are themselves Autistic, but is intended to raise a set of questions we had as professionals involved in the facilitation of a programme aimed at reducing James' level of risk. The chapter aims to provide the reader with a good model of practice based on research and theoretical models in both the disciplines of adolescent abusers and Autism. It is also designed to offer a critique of our practice in relation to James.

In James' case we strongly hold the view that James is a young person with Asperger's Syndrome who was displaying a range of abusive behaviour to others and was in need of a service to reduce both the risk to himself and others. The form and type of intervention was therefore determinate on adopting the programmes that are used with other adolescents. Poor empathetic skills displayed by people with autism (Mortlock, 1998) were echoed by James 'when will I feel what sex is like...what is a relationship and will I have one'. It is important to note that all young men with Asperger's Syndrome do not behave in a sexually abusive manner. James' case highlighted the specific needs of a young man who had both behaviours within the autistic spectrum and displayed abusive sexual behaviour to others.

In line with the Philosophy of Intervention outlined by Morrison and Print (1995), our intervention was legitimised by the following statement:

> Adolescents who sexually abuse may be of either gender, any race, culture, class, sexual orientation and learning ability. The position of an abuser as a member of an oppressed group does not take away from their individual responsibility.

We had to consider the differing philosophical approaches from those working purely with adolescent abusers and to those working with adolescents within the Autistic Spectrum, i.e. did James have the ability to understand and accept responsibility for his behaviour? This question will be answered during discussion of the case study.

The chapter that follows was based on a seminar presentation to the NOTA National Conference in Glasgow 1998.

The diagnostic criteria, prevalence and principle defining characteristics of Asperger's Syndrome will be outlined. Issues relating to social impairment, overtly sexualised and sexually abusive behaviour in particular will be discussed in the context of a case study. Consideration will be given to models of intervention and societal attitudes to sexuality for those with learning difficulties.

Themes around Autism and Asperger's Syndrome

Asperger's Syndrome was first described by the Austrian Physician Hans Asperger in 1944 and subsequently in 1968 and 1979. The patterns of abnormal behaviour which he outlined he considered constituted a specific personality variant which he termed autistic psychopathy. Asperger suggested six diagnostic features the first of which, the inability to relate normally to other people, being potentially the most handicapping

(Gillberg, 1985). Other features which he identified included abnormalities in speech, being often pedantic, monotonous in tone, repetitive and stereotypic (Wing, 1981). Non-verbal communication skills are often impaired, there may be little facial expression and an inability to understand and interpret the facial gestures of others. In some people with Asperger's Syndrome there may be a marked resistance to change, motor co-ordination may be poor but many may have special interests or skills. According to Gillberg (1985), one could be given the impression of marked eccentricity in those with Asperger's Syndrome. This is further illuminated by Gillberg (1989) who commented that there was a tendency for the individual to impose routine or their special interest on their entire life.

Burd and Kerbshian (1987) offered five features as defining characteristics of Asperger's Syndrome:

1. Speech — pedantic, stereotyped, prosodic.

2. Impaired non-verbal communication.

3. Social interaction — peculiar, lacking in empathy.

4. Circumscribed interests — repetitive activities or savant skills.

5. Movements — clumsy or stereotyped.

The above criteria link very closely with those described by Wolf and Cull (1986) for Schizoid Personality Disorder:

1. Solitariness.

2. Impaired empathy and emotional detachment.

3. Increased sensitivity, amounting to paranoia.

4. Unusual styles of communication.

5. Rigidity of mental set, e.g. single-minded pursuit of special interests.

Indeed Wolf and Cull (1986) use the term Schizoid Personality Disorder synonymously with the term Asperger's Syndrome.

In an extensive study by Wing (1981) 17 per cent of her sample were found to be psychotic (manifesting delusions/hallucinations, catatonic stupor and schizophrenia) and in fact did not encounter the exceptionally gifted 'schizoid' young people described by Asperger (1944).

The American Psychiatric Association (1987) use defining criteria for the Autistic Spectrum (ICD-10) but do not differentiate a separate category for Asperger's Syndrome unlike the World Health Organisation which includes Asperger's Syndrome as a distinct category within those disorders defined as developmentally pervasive (1990).

In detail the criteria for diagnosis are (W.H.O., 1990):

A. A lack of any clinically significant general delay in language or cognitive development. Diagnosis requires that single words should have developed by two years of age or earlier and that communication phrases be used by three years of age or earlier. Self-help skills, adaptive behaviour and curiosity about the environment during the first three years should be at a level consistent with normal intellectual development. However, motor milestones may be somewhat delayed as well as motor clumsiness (although not a necessary diagnostic feature). Isolated special skills, often related to abnormal preoccupations, are common, but are not required for diagnosis.

B. Qualitative impairments in reciprocal social interaction (criteria as for Autism). Diagnosis requires demonstrable abnormalities in at least three out of the following five areas:

1. Failure to adequately use eye to eye gaze, facial expression, body posture and gesture to regulate social interaction.

2. Failure to develop (in a manner appropriate to mental age, and despite ample opportunities) peer relationships that involve a mutual sharing of interests, activities and emotions.

3. Rarely seeking and using other people for comfort and affection at times of stress or distress and/or offering comfort and affection to others when they are showing distress or unhappiness.

4. Lack of shared enjoyment in terms of vicarious pleasure in other people's happiness and/or a spontaneous seeking to share their own enjoyment through joint involvement with others.

5. A lack of socio-emotional reciprocity as shown by an impaired or deviant response to other people's emotions; and/or lack of modulation of behaviour according to social context, and/or weak integration of social, emotional and communicative behaviours.

C.   Restricted, repetitive and stereotyped patterns of behaviour, interests and activities (criteria as for Autism; however it would be less usual for these to include either motor mannerisms or preoccupation with part-objects or non-functional elements of play materials). Diagnosis requires demonstrable abnormalities in at least two out of the following six areas:

1. An encompassing preoccupation with stereotyped and restricted patterns of interests.

2. Specific attachments to unusual objects.

3. Apparently compulsive adherence to specific, non-functional routines or rituals.

4. Stereotyped and repetitive motor mannerisms that involve either hand/finger flapping or twisting or complex whole body movements.

5. Preoccupations with part-objects or non-functional elements of play materials (such as odour, the feel of their surface or the noise/vibration that they generate).

6. Distress over changes in small, non-functional details of the environment.

D.   The disorder is not attributed to the other types of pervasive developmental disorder, schizotypal disorder, simple schizophrenia, reactive disinhibited attachment disorder or childhood, obsessional personality disorder, obsessive compulsive disorder.

Prevalence

It is estimated that 36 per 10,000 of the population have Asperger's Syndrome. The 1991 census estimated that there were 47,400 children with Asperger's Syndrome and 160,000 adults (National Autistic Society, 1991). In relation to the gender of those people who are diagnosed within the Autistic spectrum, the ratio of males to females is 4:1.

Acknowledging the prevalence of problematic sexual behaviour presented by young people within the Autistic Spectrum

From extensive literature and research in recent years we are now more aware of the prevalence rates relating to sexually abusive behaviour involving young people and adolescents. Research studies have consistently found that over 30 per cent of child sexual abuse was perpetrated by young people under the age of 17 years (Horne *et al.*, 1991). Furthermore, studies of adults who have committed sexual offences reveal that over 50 per cent began their behaviour in adolescence (Abel *et al.*, 1987), we are also aware that in relation to gender, the vast majority of abusers are male. The findings of the few studies on female abusers suggests that between 2–7 per cent of adolescent abusers are female (Fehrenbach *et al.*, 1986; Matthews, 1987).

In relation to the statistics regarding the prevalence rates of adolescents with an autistic trait who display problematic sexual behaviour, what numbers are we looking at? From research (O'Callaghan, 1997) there appears to be a number of indicators relating to the numbers of learning disabled men who display problematic sexual behaviour. However, due to the limited research in relation to autistic young people who display this kind of behaviour, we were drawn to research relating to statistical prevalence rates in learning disabled men who display problematic sexual behaviour. From this perspective it may be inferred that people within the autistic spectrum could be included within this group. As Bishop (1989) states:

> Autism is often accompanied by learning difficulties but a significant number of individuals have average to above average intelligence. In the latter case the condition is often referred to as Asperger's Syndrome. However there are no clear-cut boundaries. There are various references to there being an autistic continuum encompassing Autism, Asperger's Syndrome and semantic-pragmatic disorder but clinical accounts of conditions resembling Autism do not differ just in terms of severity but also in the pattern of symptoms

O'Callaghan (1997) outlined the following:

In respect of young people with sexually aggressive behaviours there appears an even higher percentage who are identified as learning disabled or those presenting with learning difficulties. Studies generally note that the adolescent sexual abuser is likely to struggle with the educational system, often presenting as a low achiever or having learning difficulties. (Fehrenbach et al., 1986; Saunders and Awad, 1988); although this has not been a consistent finding (Institute of Child Health, 1995; Oliver et al., 1993). Kahn and Chambers (1991) found half their sample had histories of disruptive behaviour at school; one third a history of truancy and 39% were considered learning disabled. Epps (1991) found that 44% of his sample had learning difficulties, half having attended special school. The London based Young Abusers Project recently reported over half (53%) of the young people referred to them were categorised as subject to learning disability (Hawkes et al., 1997). Our study (ibid) has highlighted that whilst half the sexual abusers perceived themselves as having learning difficulties as compared to 19% of non-sex offenders their general intelligence level was very similar to the non-sex offender group. Ford and Linney (1995) found that neither assessed I.Q. nor referral to special education discriminated between adolescent rapists, child abusers, violent non-sex offenders or other delinquents. A survey of 121 young sexual offenders referred to an adolescent forensic service (Dolan et al., 1996) found 46% of the sample to be identified as learning disabled, the majority (36% of the total sample) were assessed as having a mild learning disability, 5.8% moderate and 1.6 severe.

From information previously highlighted, 10–15 in 10,000 of the population have Autism (Lones, 1996). Within the referral rates at the Barnardo's Scheme, three out of 140 cases were considered to have autistic traits, representing 4.2% of the total.

The problems relating to the identification of prevalence rates for young people with learning difficulties, learning disabilities and behaviour problems relate to what O'Callaghan (1997) states as:

- Those with learning difficulties or behavioural problems, as opposed to children/young people with a learning disability are often referred to indiscriminately in samples.

- Infrequent lack of a thorough psychological assessment or educational statement of special needs.

- The difference between performance and ability.

- The impact of abuse and neglect on many young people's development, as opposed to an organic base for developmental impairment, also confuses the issue as to what percentage of sexually aggressive young people could most accurately be termed as learning disabled.

Given these points, it does appear that young people at the low functioning/learning disabled end of the ability spectrum are disproportionately represented in services for young abusers.

Furthermore, Clare (1994) states the following reasons why intervention with abusers with a learning disability may be problematic and therefore affect our overall knowledge of prevalence rates:

1. *In contrast with 'mainstream' work where referral normally follows police investigations and criminal conviction, the referral of perpetrators with learning disabilities sometimes takes place without the facts being established. Detailed information about the abuse is absolutely essential in order to minimise denial by the perpetrator and avoid pantomime exchanges of 'oh yes you did, oh no I didn't'.*

2. *Many perpetrators have a long history of receiving inconsistent messages about their abuse. When they finally receive an unmistakable negative response they may be overwhelmed by feelings of resentment and victimisation.*

3. *Despite the rhetoric about sexual rights there are few opportunities for perpetrators with a history of sexual abuse to form intimate relationships. In reality, stopping their sexual abuse often means practising lifelong abstinence from sexual contact with another person — inevitably a discouraging prospect.*

What is apparent is the lack of statistically based research on the prevalence rates relating to those with Autism and Asperger's Syndrome who are displaying sexually abusive behaviour. This in itself has practice implications for the planning of services for such service users and creates a professional fear of the unknown around prevalence rates.

James: a retrospective case history

James is a 16-year old young person with a diagnosis of Asperger's Syndrome. He had attended a local junior school's language unit prior to transferring to a residential special school for children with Autistic Spectrum Disorders. His Statement of Special Educational Needs highlighted his communication difficulties associated with Asperger's Syndrome and special educational needs in the areas of learning, behaviour and language.

To the average person, James presents as a pleasant, amiable, well-mannered young man whose communication skills, though impaired, enable him to manage to some degree in most everyday situations.

James is independent in his personal hygiene skills and can travel independently in the community to attend a local FE college one day per week, he uses public transport if necessary, crosses busy roads and shops independently.

However this pen picture hides a young man who has problems making and sustaining relationships, who can be repetitively obsessive in his use of language e.g. in respect of T.V. programmes, films, buoys on the sea and most alarmingly with matters of a sexual nature, often overtly so. Increasingly over the last 3–4 years these latter problems have resulted in him attempting and committing a series of sexual behaviours that were seen as abusive.

When reflecting upon the diagnostic criteria for Asperger's Syndrome, it is the imposition of special interests/or single minded pursuits of them by James that became highly problematic to the extreme. He could take on the persona of a film or cartoon character or be so enraptured by matters of a sexual nature, talking incessantly, pacing up and down and becoming extremely agitated. Often he could not distinguish between fact and fiction and could only be brought out of this almost 'psychotic' state by very firm and consistently applied rules with no margin for negotiation. This behaviour could last for days and be extremely disruptive, not only to his own education but to that of others as well. He could, on occasions, be physically aggressive, steal and be verbally and explicitly abusive.

Throughout the ensuing discourse it will be illustrated that James' impaired empathy, emotional detachment, impaired social interaction and the imposition of special interests often upon his whole persona, seriously affected his whole life and his striving for an understanding of the world around him. It could be conjectured that James' special intensive interests were matters of a sexual nature.

Gillberg (1983) highlighted three major problems that one normally encountered with autistic people and their sexuality:

1. A tendency to masturbate in public.

2. A tendency to demonstrate inappropriate behaviour towards other people.

3. Many use a self-mutilating technique when masturbating.

Dewey and Everard (1974) suggested that autistic people can feel attracted by other people but that the expression of their sexuality is often naïve, immature and inexperienced.

Haracopos and Pedersen (1992) stated that: 'Many autistic people display abnormal sexual behaviour and have problems in satisfying their sexual needs. Inappropriate sexual behaviour and attempts to make contacts often place a very considerable strain upon the immediate surroundings'. Indeed Haracopos and Pedersen (1992) go on to state that:

> The lack of ability to empathise can lead to a young autistic person trying to kiss or hug strangers…and can be just as easily attracted by small children as by peers. In spite of the fact that the young person lacks the means to maintain a love affair, the desire for a boyfriend or girlfriend can develop into an obsession.

These latter points are extremely relevant to the case study to be outlined.

It was during a case conference organised by social services, prior to transfer to the special school that attention was drawn to James' overtly sexualised behaviour. It was at this time that the need for a specialised sex education programme and input in the area of psycho-sexual development was suggested for James. A number of strategies were implemented with little success over the next few years. It was not until five years later, as will be described, that a specialised service became available, by which time a number of serious incidents had taken place.

During his initial years at the school, James was increasingly displaying self-stimulatory behaviour within the school environment, not an uncommon feature with a number of students with Autism related disorders.

At his mother's request, a meeting was convened to discuss James' deteriorating behaviour in the home. His deviant sexual behaviour in that environment warranted police involvement but following investigation it was decided that no legal action be taken but that the situation be closely monitored in all environments.

Over the next two years there was a steady increase in the number of incidents of a sexualised nature in which James was the main instigator. These ranged from attempted intercourse at a play centre for children during school holidays, exposing himself, masturbation in public, the use of explicit language, writing about his sexual fantasies with females of all ages and questions relating to intercourse in particular.

In relation to James' own victimisation, there were concerns raised but none of these could be substantiated.

Over the next few months conversations with James contained increasing numbers of questions from him concerning masturbation, intercourse, feelings and relationships. There was a serious danger of these questions becoming obsessive. At a further case conference it was recommended that a referral be made to a specialised team from Barnardo's and subsequently a joint project was instigated in order to provide a service for James to address his emerging abusive behaviour.

The Joint Project

Profile of Barnardo's scheme

The scheme was developed in September 1994. The scheme is a jointly funded initiative again between Barnardo's and a social services directorate in the North-West of England, with a remit to provide a systematic response to young abusers and further develop services on a city-wide basis.

The scheme is staffed by a co-ordinator, with overall responsibility for the scheme, two practitioners, (including a senior practitioner) who undertake the majority of the direct work and scheme administrator who carries out the secretarial and administration duties.

The scheme works closely with social services youth justice and child protection sections both to influence policy and procedure and provide appropriate direct work interventions with young people. Direct work, usually in the form of risk assessments and long-term interventions are carried out in a gender balanced co-working format; with co-workers usually drawn from social services.

In addition the scheme provides consultancy support and training to social services and Barnardo's staff involved in the work at some level.

The scheme aims to work with young people between the ages of 10 and 17 years, who are displaying inappropriate or abusive sexual behaviour.

The primary aim of the scheme is to effect early intervention with sexually abusive young people to control their illegal, inappropriate or abusive sexual behaviour, and to promote the opportunity for change and the acquisition of acceptable patterns of behaviour. The secondary aim of the scheme is to provide consultation, advice and support to key workers undertaking direct work with sexually abusive young people. Finally, the scheme aims to evaluate the effectiveness of this method of intervention with young people.

Profile of the school

The school provides a 24 hour curriculum which aims to meet the individual needs of each student who has a diagnosis of an Autistic Spectrum Disorder and which is clearly stated on their Statement of Special Educational Needs.

The quality of both day and residential provision is of the highest quality (substantiated by excellent reports from OFSTED, social services and the National Autistic Society) and maximises the potential of each student in order to enable them to become participating and contributing members of society.

The school has clearly stated aims, which respect the rights of each individual. The school has the capacity to provide education and care for over 50 students on a daily or weekly basis.

Model of intervention

In order to meet James' needs, the
professionals involved in his case made the
decision to create an innovative model of
intervention. This involved marrying two areas
of expertise with the aim of providing James
with an assessment programme. The work
involved developing a model of intervention
outlined in Morrison and Print (1995) which
suggests working in a mixed gender co-
working model. The model utilised the direct
practice skills and theoretical knowledge of the
residential school staff on Autism, who
facilitated a mixed gender co-working
assessment programme. This was supported
by the theoretical knowledge base and models
of intervention with adolescent abusers that
was provided by Barnardo's scheme with the
scheme working in a consultancy basis in the
development, planning, facilitation and
evaluation of the direct work with James, that
was completed by the school. (This is outlined
within the direct work section further on
within the chapter).

Essentially we were recognising that the
most effective model to meet James needs was
a multi-agency model as stated in a NOTA
briefing paper (Dec. 1993):

> A strategic response to sexual abusers should be
> located within an overall strategy for dealing with
> sexual abuse, and should be viewed as an important
> objective of multi-agency work.

Furthermore, The NCH (1992) Committee of
Enquiry Report, 'Continuum of Care Model of
Intervention' was adopted by ourselves in
order to set out good practice guidelines for
our work with James. The NCH report states:

> Practice guidelines

- Be multi-disciplinary and therefore apply to any
  professional embarking on an intervention with a
  child or young person who has sexually abused.

- Ensure that a full assessment is undertaken in
  each case on the basis of which decisions could be
  made regarding treatment or other appropriate
  interventions.

- Set standards, within the limitations of present
  knowledge, for the content of assessment and the
  nature of intervention, as well as its appropriateness
  in certain circumstances.

- Recommend the levels of knowledge, experience and
  consultation needed in order to undertake various
  activities.

- Establish ethical guidelines with respect to this work.

- Give guidance or appropriate networking with all
  relevant agencies.

Such guidance would need to be endorsed
by all relevant disciplines, making it acceptable
across disciplinary boundaries.

Due to the marrying up of a social work
based project with an educational
establishment, the residential school staff were
able to legitimise their role in James'
assessment programme by working once again
within the continuum of care model (NCH,
1992), which states:

> The role of the school in the continuum of care

> As indicated elsewhere in the report, the role of
> education in preventing the development of sexually
> abusive attitudes and behaviour cannot be
> underestimated. More specifically, schools have a
> significant role to play in recognising abusive behaviour
> when it occurs and in taking appropriate action, and
> also in supporting any child or young person who has
> been involved in sexually abusive behaviour and is
> involved in a programme of intervention.

> The committee recommends that where it has been
> established that a child or young person has been
> involved in sexually abusive behaviour, the school
> must be informed. If the recommendation of the
> committee and the guidance in Working Together are
> followed, then a child protection conference will be
> held in which representatives of the school would
> have an important contribution to make.

Societal values and beliefs in relation to James

Another factor within the planning of
intervention with James was located within
general societal attitudes in regard to the
sexuality of those with learning disability. As
Mesibov (1982) states:

> Sexuality is a highly personal matter... The use of
> sexuality requires us to examine our personal values
> and how they might, or might not, apply to people
> with autism. Because they will not form our society's
> traditional sexual unions, consisting of marriage and
> family, we must evaluate our feelings about possible
> alternatives, weighing the needs of people with
> autism against the values and morals of society'.

(Mesibov, 1982)

Furthermore, O'Callaghan (1997) poses the question that as a society, do we still hold onto the myths that those with a learning disability are either 'childlike or over-sexed'?

The continuum which exists from society is that of 'the *liberal view points* of no restrictions on sexual expressions…to that of a *conservative or protectionist* view of sex as too problematic for the learning disabled'.

Within our planning of intervention with James, we were mindful of the influences that can shape professional opinions relating to the development of any intervention that involves the sexuality of those with a learning disability. In respect of this we were mindful of Schilling and Schinkle (1989) a model which identifies four external boundaries of opinion:

1. Strong advocacy — demands full rights for those with learning disability, including support to facilitate sexual expression and the development of relationships.

2. Moderated advocacy — perhaps the most common view amongst parents and carers, agrees to education around sexual and personal relationships whilst viewing supervision and some restrictions as important. Full sexual relationships would be viewed with some reluctance from this stance.

3. Value free position — advocates that individuals sexuality is a private matter and that adults/young people with a learning disability should experience no greater or lesser restrictions on their behaviour than the general population.

4. Negative position — those with a learning disability should be actively discouraged from engaging in sexual activity.

Bearing in mind the subjective societal and professional values and beliefs that are prevalent in relation to the debates around sexuality and those with a learning disability, and being torn philosophically between a 'strong advocacy' stance in regard to developing and meeting James' needs on one level, to a 'negative position' in relation to our need to protect and reduce risk to others from James' behaviour, it was important that we were able to legitimise our intervention with James. For those who have been working with adolescent abusers since the 1980s, the parallels between this innovative work with a young man with Autism and the similar anxieties felt in the early development of work with adolescent abusers by practitioners was apparent. This was highlighted in the NCH (1992) enquiry report and in our concerns during the planning of work with James. The NCH report states:

> 5.16 *Managerial and professional peer group denial of the 'problem' as an area for legitimate professional involvement was certainly raised as a significant hindrance in the development of services. Indeed, for reasons stated above, it appears reasonably easy for the existence of the problem to be denied altogether.*

> 5.17 *This lack of legitimisation of the work with young abusers has meant an absence of agreed guidelines on dealing with issues, and no established policy on joint working. It has also meant a lack of support, supervision and training for the work.*

Consultation

The consultation model adopted by the scheme to support the development of the direct work with James is similar to that outlined by Morrison (1998). Here, consultation is defined as:

> *Consultation: a structured negotiated organisational process involving two or more staff in which one person, the consultant, is identified as having some expertise, either subject or process expertise, or both, which is used to facilitate a developmental or problem solving process regarding a work related issue with the consultee(s). The aim of the consultation process is to promote and support the effective management of sexual abusers so as to control and reduce the risk they pose to others.*

As a joint agency initiative we adopted the following consultation practice model in order to facilitate the direct work with James taken from 'The Practitioners Tool Kit' (from Morrison, 1998), which suggests that the following are essential elements in any piece of good practice.

- Supervision.
- Clinical accountability.
- Clear case or programme targets.
- Co-working/team building preparation.
- Personal preparation.
- Ethical basis.
- Sex offender intervention techniques/skills.

- Mandate, role clarity and resource to do the work.
- Value base.
- Knowledge base.

These elements were negotiated, planned and evaluated during monthly consultation sessions and bi-monthly case reviews.

Direct work

The aims of our assessment with James were reflective of those in Respond's 'Trinity of Pain' publication, which were:

- to evaluate risk and dangerousness
- to predict recidivism
- to identify needs
- to decide who is suitable for treatment (group and/or individual)
- to recommend necessary restrictions (e.g. regarding contact, babysitting etc.) (Corbett, 1996).

At a recent conference, entitled 'Offending behaviour in people with learning disabilities: Prevention and Treatment', which was organised by The Hester Adrian Research Centre, University of Manchester (October 1998), two presentations raised specific caution to those of us facilitating any form of assessment around offending behaviour with those service users who have a learning disability. Firstly, Steve Turner set out the following points that may be important for consideration when engaging in an assessment. He states that the limitations and dangers of risk assessments are:

- Offending is rare in this group — so risk is over estimated.
- Much offending behaviour never reaches the court.
- Defining the population at risk (the impact is that there are higher detection rates, rather than incidence rates for this group).
- Whether the prediction of future behaviour possible.

At the same conference Dr. Tony Holland of Cambridge University highlighted the following ethical and legal dilemmas for intervening with such service users as being

'Care versus Autonomy, Safety versus Risk, and Control versus Choice'.

We would advise the readers to be mindful of the above points when planning any intervention with a service user with a learning disability, and specifically with a service user such as James.

The direct work began with the mixed gender school staff, following a three month planning period with all professionals involved. Organised sessions could last up to half an hour in duration. The focus of each session was clearly outlined to James at the outset and at the end of the ensuing discussions positive feedback was always given.

The work was undertaken over a 16 month period. The earliest work which began towards the end of 1996 looked at self, feelings, likes/dislikes. After a couple of months a life map was constructed so that James could create a visual impression of the highs, lows, changes in his life and memories etc. When children with Autism/Asperger's Syndrome are in an anxious or high state of arousal they may not be at their best linguistically. Consequently they often process information more efficiently when it is presented visually. Likewise it is often easier to convey meaning through drawing, as in this case. Considerable input was necessary to aid his memory of past events as his concept of the passage of time was poor.

James was asked to list his likes and dislikes e.g. Likes — football, tennis, women taking clothes off, squash, quiche, his erect penis, chips, touching girls, seconds of pudding. Matters of a sexual nature were treated as routinely as any other topic and showed no embarrassment, no awareness of social taboos, very much 'matter of fact' — a typical feature of some people with Asperger's Syndrome.

Over the first three months James grew to trust and confide in his co-workers. He made an allegation that he had had intercourse with his sister. These allegations were investigated, but nothing was fully substantiated.

Within the confines of the school environment James was closely supervised and controlled at all times. A distinctive feature of people with an Autism Spectrum Disorder is the need for structure in their lives. Clear boundaries need to be set, for as Segar (1997) so aptly states: 'If I could explain Asperger's Syndrome in just one sentence it would be as follows… Autistic people have to understand scientifically what non-autistic people already understand instinctively'. (p 24) Fact and reality rather than the inferred or the innate.

Following consultation with the senior practitioner from the Barnardo's team, it was decided to give James a measure of control over his behaviour. Positive behaviour would be a 'green coded' route, negative behaviour a 'red code' (based on Ryan and Blum, 1988, 1993 Primary Prevention Project). Unfortunately James could not handle this sudden, immense amount of responsibility for his own behaviour. He had written a clear set of rules…red/green. He chose to behave negatively, indulging in all red coded negative behaviours. In hindsight, the measure of self control given to him was too much, too soon and he was simply not ready for it. As a consequence, a behaviour support programme was reintroduced. Within two weeks he had been enabled to regain a measure of control over his behaviour and work once again centred upon self and particularly self-image. James was encouraged to systematically work through the 'play book for kids about sex' by Blank and Quackenbush (1982), whilst still having regular discussions with his co-workers. At this time he was in a very happy, positive frame of mind openly talking sensibly about himself.

By May 1997 he was beginning to show signs of increasing anxiety related to the uncertainty of his future, post 16 and was concerned whether or not he would have relationship by 'the time he was a man' (James' words).

Via the consultation process, a sociometric exercise was conducted to support this work. James was asked to indicate his feelings towards all those he had listed according to a set of 14 very specific questions — an arbitrary but illuminating list of statements 'can you….e.g. talk to 'a', 'b' etc. His responses were recorded on a checklist for all those people he had included in the sociometric exercise. The results were then analysed by an educational psychologist who independently confirmed our beliefs that James, was lacking in social empathy and had a poorly controlled sexual arousal, and would require high levels of supervision for his own and for the safety of others. He considered James lacked appropriate boundaries towards females both verbally and in his actions, and that without appropriate supervision would pose a significant risk of engaging in sexual activities towards females of any age and without any understanding of the nature and need for consent.

During the next month, James refused to discuss any issues related to the programme, his anxiety level increased although his behaviour remained manageable. Of overriding and understandable significance to James was where he would be for the next academic year.

Plans were set in motion for James to pursue living in the community with very specialised support, for it was considered that the school's FE unit, with its philosophy of independence, would not be appropriate given the maximum level of 1:1 supervision that would be needed, coupled to the serious threat James posed to staff and pupils alike, particularly female.

Throughout the next few weeks school continually sought progress and confirmation of the plans for supported living to be provided by a local society. Unfortunately the provision failed to materialise and it was considered that a placement in school could be accommodated in the short-term but that supported living was a priority for December.

On resumption of the next school year he was happy and relaxed and ready to continue working with his co-workers. A new life map was designed for the immediate 16 plus period of his life. He drew all positive routes to travel along and for the first five weeks life was very pleasant with no problems. However by October his behaviour suddenly started to deteriorate. In order to reaffirm with James that an appropriate code of conduct was essential in the FE unit as it was in school, a 'can do' chart was constructed along the lines of the concentric circles of the sociometric study. In principle the chart illustrated those activities and interests that he most liked doing to those he least liked. This exercise was aimed at focusing his positive behaviour. James continued to be very co-operative and positive in discussion sessions but unfortunately his behaviour was rapidly deteriorating. He began targeting those females in whom he had previously shown no interest whatsoever, he had begun to seriously disrupt the education of others by comments to them which he knew upset/distressed them and was verbally abusive to staff.

His position in school became untenable and exclusion followed. After protracted discussions, planning meetings and consultation with all relevant agencies, James, after living at home for the next two months, went to live in a supported environment in the community. This placement was to progress smoothly for a couple of months until once again his behaviour deteriorated to such a level that he was placed in a community health unit for a period of assessment.

The joint project as described ceased when he moved to the supported environment in the community. The community setting was itself facilitated by a joint agency approach in order to meet James' needs and based on the concept of creating a safe environment for James to live in. Unfortunately, limitations in providing a safe environment, within an appropriate care and control ethos resulted in an increased risk behaviour being demonstrated by James in a relatively short period of time. This was in the context of the risk and self harm to others, and also in terms of physical and sexual behaviour.

At this time in his life James was now being supported by a specialist health learning disability team, with the scheme now monitoring a consultancy and information role to the new set of professionals working with James. The scheme's role formally ended on James' voluntary admission to the community mental health facility.

James' situation is one that is described in the work by Malek (1991, 1993) in which she describes the 'spillage effect' that occurs when agencies 'pass the buck' in relation to responses to controlling children with difficult behaviour. The concept develops as a response to problematic behaviour that professionals' feel inadequately skilled or knowledgeable to respond to. In relation to young people with an autistic trait who display abusive behaviour, we are not suggesting that all young people with autism display such behaviours. However what James' case has shown us are the complexities of need that such a young person presents. This resulted in a lack of awareness of how to intervene, and consequently in the spillage from one service to another.

Concluding thoughts

In the seminar paper to the NOTA annual conference in Glasgow in 1998, the authors of this paper raised the following 'points for consideration' in relation to the intervention with young people with Autism and Asperger's Syndrome who are displaying problematic sexual behaviour:

1. The definition of those young people with Asperger's and Autism is a contentious issue.

2. The lack of research specific to this group, which is presently included in the general definition of learning disability, creates problems gaining accurate facts relating to prevalence, etc.

3. There is limited research into the psycho-sexual development of this group and specifically in relation to their sexually abusive behaviour.

4. Social impairment of this group as a central defining feature limits the traditional intervention models we use with adolescent abusers.

5. A multi-disciplinary approach needs to be viewed as a model of good practice.

6. Realistic expectations around the ability of a young person with Asperger's needs to be critiqued in the context of that young person's ability to learn and control their behaviour.

7. Re-evaluation of present models of intervention needs to occur to account for specific traits and needs of those with Asperger's, i.e. cognitive-behavioural approach needs to be critiqued in this context.

8. Continuous evaluation of any innovative work with an Asperger's young person needs to occur due to their impaired social understanding.

9. Young people with Asperger's and Autism must be viewed as young people in need who have the human right to services to meet their needs as defined in the Children's Act 1989 and therefore we must strive toward developing such services.

The United National Declaration of Rights for mentally handicapped people (as authors we would point out our objection to the phrase 'mentally handicapped') state that 'The mentally handicapped person has the same basic rights as citizens of the same country and same age'.

However as Mortlock (1993, p 4) points out:

> In addition to poor empathetic skills many people with Autism have difficulty with sexual timing and with social communication, problems that can make it virtually impossible for them to access a social peer group.

The implication for James is that he may never be able to obtain and sustain a meaningful relationship.

Having devoted so much time to try to provide him with a knowledge base upon which to form meaningful relationships the nature of his rapid departure from school was so disappointing. Undoubtedly progress had been made primarily in terms of the level of trust he placed in his co-workers, the manner in which he was able to express his views, orally though more effectively through writing, and to a lesser degree his understanding of the rules of social engagement (rights and wrongs). It was considered that this work and the close involvement of the Barnardo's team be continued and that the process of change from one set of co-workers to his key workers be seen as a carefully planned transition. No time limit could be placed upon the work but that it be ongoing and subject to regular review. It is unlikely that he can be taught strategies for every eventuality for the unexpected can often occur. It is also unlikely that James will be able to achieve a true understanding of the meaning of 'a relationship' even though he has had a thorough grounding in the social rules that govern their existence. His preoccupation with matters of a sexual nature present him as a potential risk to females of all ages. His lack of empathy and his often inappropriate behaviour warrant that he be continually and closely supervised at all times, with the aim of facilitating the process of risk assessment in all situations in which he resides, works etc. in the future.

In James case, if we did not recognise and appropriately intervene to meet his needs, we essentially would have failed to meet his, society's and his victim's needs in the pursuit of reducing further risk. By not acknowledging his behaviour due to his diagnosis of Asperger's Syndrome as a 'problematic and abusive' set of behaviours, we would have failed to acknowledge that victims resulted from such behaviour. In essence we would have denied their experience and perpetuated the denial that due to his learning disability that his behaviour is not abusive, but only as a result of his Autistic Spectrum Disorder. This we do not accept because it is important to acknowledge that James was a young person who acted in a problematic sexual manner to others and had 'Autistic' traits that resulted in specific consideration for those responding, to address and control his behaviour. Not that he was purely an 'Autistic' abuser, because these two definitions have two extremely differing consequences on the way society will view this behaviour and him as a young man with Asperger's Syndrome.

We would conclude by raising the following questions for consideration by those professionals working in similar situations:

1. Did our intervention increase James' problematic behaviour?

2. What did the intervention achieve?

Essentially as professionals we believe that in regard to the first question, that our intervention raised a positive level of awareness for James and enabled him to answer the questions he was asking about his feelings, relationships etc. and facilitated a process of self risk-assessment around his behaviour.

In relation to the second question, the intervention identified the risks that are apparent in relation to James' behaviour, and the intervention informed others of the risk and facilitated the creation of a 'protective environment' (Smith, 1995) by those working and caring for James in order to reduce the risk for James and others in the future.

References

Abel, G., Becker, J., Cunningham-Rathner, J., and Rouleau, J. (1987). Self-Reported Sex Crimes of 561 Non-incarcerated Paraphiliacs. *Journal of Interpersonal Violence*, 2(6): 3 - 25

American Psychiatric Association (1987). *Diagnostic and Statistical Manual of Mental Disorders*. (3rd Edition). Washington DC.

Asperger, H. (1944). Die 'Autistichen Psychopathen' in Kindesalter. *Archiv Fur Psychiatric und Nerven Krankheiten*, 117(76): 136.

Asperger, H. (1968). Zur Diffentialdiagnose des Kindlichen Autismus. *Acta Paedospychiatrica*, 35: 136–145.

Asperger, H. (1979). *Problems in Infantile Autism Communication*, 13: 45–52

Blank, J., and Quackenbush (1982). *The Playbook for Kids About Sex.*

Bond. T. (1985). *Games for Social and Life Skills.* Hutchinson.

Burd, L., and Kerbeshian, J. (1987). Asperger Syndrome. *British Journal of Psychiatry*, 151.

Clare, I. (1994). Treatment for Men with Learning Disabilities who are Perpetrators of Sexual Abuse. Motivational Difficulties and Effect on Practitioners. *NAPSAC Bulletin* No. 8, June 1994: 3–6.

Corbett, A. (1996). Trinity of Pain. Therapeutic Responses to People with Learning Disabilities who Commit Sexual Offences. *Respond* 1996

Dewey, M.A., and Everard, M.P. (1974). The Near Normal Autistic Adolescent. *Journal of Autism and Childhood Schizophrenia*, 4(4).

Fehrenbach, P., Smith, W., Monastersky, C., and Delsher, R. (1986). Adolescent Sex Offenders: Offenders and Offence Characteristic. *American Journal of Orthopsychiatry*, 56: 225–233.

Gillberg, C. (1983). *Adolescence Autism. Awakening of Sexual Awareness.* Paper presented at the 1983 Europe Autism Conference.

Gillberg, C. (1985). Asperger's Syndrome and Recurrent Psychosis — A Case Study. *Journal of Autism and Developmental Disorders*, 15(4): 389–397.

Gillberg, C. (1989). Asperger Syndrome in 23 Swedish Children. *Developmental Medicine and Child Neurology*, 31: 520–531.

Haracopos, D., and Pedersen, L. (1992). *Sexuality and Autism.*

Horne, L., Glasgow, D., Cox A., and Calam, R. (1991). Sexual Abuse of Children by Children. *Journal of Child Law*, 3(4): 147–151.

Lones, J. (1996). Autism and Aspergers Syndrome: Implications for Examinations. *Skill Journal*, 6 November 1996.

Malek, M. (1991). *Psychiatric Admissions: A Report on Young People Entering Psychiatric Care.* London: The Children's Society.

Malek, M. (1993). *Passing the Buck: A Summary - Institutional Responses to Controlling Children with Difficult Behaviour.* London: The Children's Society.

Mathews, R. (1987). *Female Sexual Offenders: Treatment and Legal Issues.* (Report by Phase Programme of Genesis II). Minneapolis, Minnesota.

Mesibov, G. (1982). Current Issues and Perspectives in Autism and Adolescence. *Autism in Adolescents and Adults.* NY: Plenum Press.

Morrison, T. (1998). *Casework Consultation: A Practical Guide for Consultation to Work with Sex Offenders and Other High-risk Clients.* Whiting and Birch Ltd/NOTA.

Morrison, J., and Punt, B. (1995). *Adolescent Sexual Abusers: An Overview.* Hull Birenson Corporate Services/NOTA.

Mortlock, J. (1993). *The Socio-sexual Development of People with Autism and Related Learning Disabilities.* National Autistic Society.

Mortlock, J. (1998). *Sexuality and Adolescents Handicapped by Autism.* National Autistic Society.

National Children Homes (1992). *The Report of the Committee of Enquiry into Children and Young People who Sexually Abuse Other Children.* London: NCH.

NOTA (1993). *Good Practice in a Multi-agency Management of Sex Offenders who Assault Children.* A NOTA briefing paper. December 1993.

O'Callaghan, D. (1997). *Understanding and Intervening in Problematic Sexual Behaviours Presented by Young Men with Learning Disabilities.* Manchester: G.MAP.

Ryan, G., and Blum, J. (1988, 1993). *Understanding and Responding to the Sexual Behaviour of Children.* A Primary Preparation Prevention Project.

Schilling, R.F., and Schinkle, S.P. (1988). Mentally Retarded Sex Offenders: Fact, Fiction and Treatment. *Journal of Social Work and Human Sexuality*, 7: 33–48.

Segar, M. (1997). *A Guide to Coping Specifically for People with Asperger's Syndrome. Sexuality and Relationships* — booklet from the 'Love, Life and Live Curriculum' — Merseyside Youth Association.

Smith, G. (1995). *The Protectors Handbook — Reducing the Risk of Child Sexual Abuse and Helping Children Recover.* Women's Press.

Wing, L. (1981). Asperger's Syndrome: A Clinical Account. *Psychological Medicine*, 11: 115–129.

Wolf, S., and Cull, A. (1986). Schizoid Personality and Antisocial Conduct: a Retrospective Case Note Study. *Psychological Medicine*, 16: 677–687

World Health Organisation (1990). International Classification of Diseases: 10th Revision, Ch. V. Mental and behavioural disorders (including disorders of psychological development). Diagnostic criteria for research (May 1990 draft for field trials). Geneva: WHO (in Happe F. 1994 *Autism an Introduction to Psychological Theory.* UCL Press.)

Chapter Fourteen

The Significance of Trauma in Problematic Sexual Behaviour

Stuart J. Mulholland and Jeannie McIntee

The Significance of Trauma in Problematic Sexual Behaviour

Introduction

The test of a first rate intelligence is the ability to hold two opposed ideas in the mind at the same time and still retain the ability to function.

F. Scott Fitzgerald

This quote aptly summarises the difficulty of the task facing practitioners when they are required to deal with the issue of trauma in relation to young people who exhibit problematic or aggressive sexual behaviours.

At times this may be presented in terms of whether to regard the young person as a victim or an abuser. In these circumstances the task of holding both 'ideas' can be reduced to a stark choice, and the solution to this dilemma will often be described in terms that respond more to the practitioner's fear of collusion than the complexity of the young person's needs. O'Callaghan and Print (1994) highlight the dilemma for practitioners in that, to place initial emphasis on abusers own experiences of victimisation may enhance their *poor me* image and give them messages that they are not entirely responsible for their behaviour.' Resolution has not been assisted by the tendency to create separate services or different modules within treatment programmes. For such young people the experience of a discrete module relating to their own victim experiences will not necessarily promote the integrative understanding about their lives, their personality and their behaviour which offers them hope in adulthood.

Indeed, to view the effects of trauma in such a compartmentalised manner may also reduce the overall effects of treatment. Causality might not be as extraneous to the process of changing behaviours as Richardson *et al*. (1997) seem to imply when they suggest that 'identification and understanding of the learning process become the target of assessment with causes remaining conjectural'. If one of these causes relates to the experience of trauma, its significance in terms of assessing the amount of information that is likely to be retained by the young person and indeed the very way in which they learn cannot be dismissed as 'conjecture'. We would suggest that such an understanding of the role played by trauma in the development of the young person should never be considered to be 'conjecture' simply because of the difficulty in proving simple causality. It should be apparent that this information is integral to the process of assessment.

We believe that it is possible to develop a model that helps practitioners to accommodate trauma as an integral part of their intervention while still functioning in a manner which reduces the risk of harm to others. Indeed, without this understanding, it is possible that all subsequent cognitive-behavioural techniques such as relapse prevention will be critically undermined and the likelihood of predicting future risk greatly reduced.

Ward *et al*. (1996) have suggested that 'In order to be able to effectively regulate their behaviour, individuals require certain capacities and knowledge. These include intact attentional and memory processes, declarative knowledge about the work and the self, and the ability to self-reflect, use symbols, learn vicariously, evaluate options and to anticipate the likely outcomes of the actions of oneself and others'. As trauma can adversely affect the development of such skills as well as hinder the acquisition of such knowledge it is essential that we find a way to adjust our treatment programmes accordingly.

At times it may even be necessary to deal with the issue of trauma before that of the sexually aggressive behaviour in order to promote a sense of responsibility in the young person. Such considerations and judgements should properly be made in terms of an assessment that prioritises the needs of the young person and considers all aspects of their background and development in order to frame a treatment programme. Unfortunately the development of such a model of intervention has been hindered by the manner in which research has developed over the last decade. Rather than promoting understanding, the research findings have helped to create the sense of confusion and frustration that has led many practitioners to abandon the concept of causality as conjecture and instead focus on the method of intervention. It is necessary therefore to consider the extent to which research methodology has contributed to this state of affairs before proposing the basis for such a model.

The Need for Consilience

Given the fact that the first book to be written specifically by UK professionals about their practice with sex offenders was published as recently as 1994 (Morrison *et al.*, 1994) it seems strange that we have developed such uniformity in our approach to the issue of problematic or aggressive sexual behaviours.

In particular, the use of cognitive-behavioural models appears to form the basis of most intervention programmes (Knopp *et al.*, 1992). Although unable to offer predictive outcomes, the value of this model is that the success of the programme in terms of changing cognition can be evaluated relatively easily.

As this approach has the self-management of the clinical problem as its therapeutic goal, considerations about the causes of the behaviour have tended to assume less significance. This tendency to dislocate the cause from the presenting behaviours cannot be ascribed totally to the predominance of cognitive-behavioural programmes. Rather it has its origins in the failure of research to offer adequate explanations to account for the development of sexually aggressive behaviours.

As Burton *et al.* (1997) have suggested, 'Sexually aggressive behaviours by children have been treated descriptively in extant literature but to date few research studies have tested or even alluded to a theoretical explanation for such behaviour'.

Although the focus of such research has been broadened to identify multi- factorial explanations, it has proved to be impossible to reduce these ever-lengthening lists to predictive fundamental laws. The result can best be described as the 'Murder on the Orient Express' scenario as the only certainty is that they all did it! (Wilson, 1998)

At such times it can seem as if our research only serves to highlight the gaps in our understanding. Unfortunately the failure of this research to identify predictive factors has undermined our attempts to understand the significance of trauma in the development and continuance of the problematic or aggressive sexual behaviours.

Of particular concern is the assumption that we should be able to reduce such a complex phenomenon to a simple set of predictive factors. Comparison with the natural sciences shows that there has been a significant shift from the search for new fundamental laws and instead a move 'towards new kinds of synthesis in order to understand complex systems' (Wilson, 1998). Wilson argues that a balanced perspective cannot be acquired by studying disciplines in pieces but through the pursuit of the consilience among them. He suggests that consilience (literally a 'jumping together' of knowledge) offers the best way of exploring the gaps that exist in our knowledge. If we can link facts and fact based theory across disciplines it might be possible to create a common groundwork of explanation. This approach would appear to offer a better prospect of explaining causality than the current tendency to work within narrow professional disciplines.

If we seek a synthesis of research from a variety of disciplines including that of trauma it may be possible to construct a model that offers greater understanding of causality and informs our approach to treatment. Given the limitations of our understanding and the inadequacies of our attempts to formulate predictive tests within social science, we must resist any pressure to calcify our understanding of this phenomenon. The fact that the majority of traumatised children do not develop such problematic or aggressive sexual behaviours should not prevent us from trying to understand its significance in the lives of the young people with whom we work.

If we continue to use such narrow concepts of causality we may reach the verdict of Kahn and Lafond (1988). Having confirmed that 60 per cent of a sample of 350 had been sexually victimised, they could not prove that it led directly to the development of sexually abusive behaviours and therefore had to conclude that it was not a significant factor. We would suggest that the trauma reported by these young people should be integral to our understanding of their subsequent behaviour. One failing of this methodology is its inability to consider the effect of trauma as more than merely a simple relationship between sexual victimisation and sexual aggression. We must broaden our definition to include all forms of trauma if we are to begin to understand its significance in relation to sexual behaviours.

A study of adolescents in Oxford (James and Neil, 1996) found that family dysfunction or inadequate parenting including neglect and/or physical or sexual abuse was common in 85 per cent of cases. These figures correspond with that of the Halt Project where 98 per cent meet the criteria of significant trauma e.g. death of a parent, physical/emotional/sexual abuse. Research needs to be more capable of analysing complex relationships examining the presence of causal and protective factors as well as their interrelationship with the complex issue of the young person's developmental progress. If we either ignore or imply that such information is not significant because we cannot prove simple causality by empirical research we run the risk of separating causality from the provision of treatment. Consequently treatment itself can become fragmented and it may become impossible for the young person to integrate an understanding of the causes of the behaviour with the knowledge of how to control the behaviour itself.

If we consider the broad range of problematic behaviours that can result from a traumatic experience we may find that we have simply dealt with one set of symptoms without preparing the young person to deal with future manifestations of this problem. Given that the 'perception of past events may be an important factor in determining future psychological adjustment' (Varia *et al.*, 1996), this issue may have an impact on all aspects of their lives.

It is apparent that some of the issues relating to research methodology have undoubtedly influenced the way in which practitioners have attempted to accommodate the significance of trauma when dealing with young people who exhibit problematic or aggressive sexual behaviours. The lack of a consilient approach that seeks explanations from a variety of disciplines has not benefited practitioners. However, before leaving this particular topic it is important to stress that this must be viewed as more than an argument over research methodology. The type of consilient approach that we would advocate must of necessity include the discipline of ethics. When seeking the synthesis of knowledge and research to help understand the young person we should not use efficacy of treatment as the principle criteria. When Richardson *et al.* (1997) argue that the 'heterogeneity of sexually abusive adolescents coupled with the absence of adequate theories of causation suggest a 'whole' person approach to assessment' should be advocated, we would agree with the conclusion, but argue against its premise.

It should be primarily on an ethical basis that the young person's needs must be made the determinant factor in devising our treatment approach. This does not necessarily undermine or ignore the risks that the young person may present. It is possible to maintain strong external controls while still ensuring that all of the young person's needs continue to be met within the provision of treatment.

A Trauma Based Model for Understanding Problematic or Aggressive Sexual Behaviours

It is of course the task of the practitioner to hold opposing ideas even in the case of trauma and sexual aggression. Yet this task would undoubtedly be made easier if such ideas were accommodated within an overall model which promoted understanding and informed the type of treatment being offered to the young person.

The fact that this model cannot be tested in terms of simple predictive outcomes or direct causality should not be the sole criteria for determining its validity. The failure of empirical research to achieve these goals in relation to sexually aggressive behaviour should not be used to limit our understanding of causality or abandon it altogether.

It is possible to link fact and fact-based theories across disciplines to construct a model that fits the reality of the young person. Past behaviour is the best predictor of future behaviour. However, it may be necessary to include not only the past behaviour of the child but also the past behaviour the child was in receipt of from others.

Canter's (1994) examination of adult criminal behaviour has shown that the behaviour is developmental and it is causally linked to past experience. He argues that criminal behaviour shadows the individual's developmental experience not only in childhood but throughout the adult criminal career.

Recent research from Canada (Mathews, 1998) has carried out tests with a sample of 60 young people, concluding that the nature of the sexual abuse perpetrated on them by adults was significant in terms of the manner in which their own sexually aggressive behaviours developed. Researchers identified 5 major factors that seemed to be significant in terms of predicting children who would go on to develop sexual behaviour problems. These were:

- Sexual arousal during the experience of being abused.
- Sadism used by perpetrator.
- Who the child blames for their abuse.
- Physical abuse in history of child.

- Emotional abuse in history of child.

At times there may have also been a reliance on a confused moral/medical philosophical framework for understanding these problematic behaviours. If the child is not assisted to understand their own behaviour within the philosophical framework of social learning theory then the behaviour is difficult to conceptualise as separate from their sense of self. A social learning theory philosophical framework conceptualises the unwanted behaviour either acquired through imitation or as a reaction to events. This views behaviour as a concrete entity that can be analysed, understood and changed in the light of new circumstances. Furthermore, these problematic or aggressive sexual behaviours could be permanently changed since children and young people are enormously capable of making new adaptations and assimilating learning.

The following trauma-based model (see Figure 1) does not require to prove direct causality but nevertheless promotes understanding.

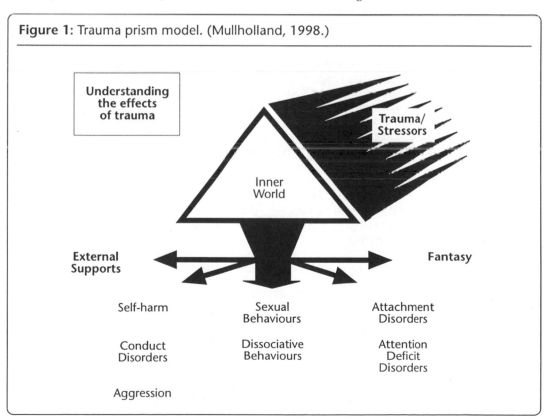

Figure 1: Trauma prism model. (Mullholland, 1998.)

If we compare the child's inner world (Bowlby, 1988) to a prism we can observe both white light and the splitting of such light into the colours of the spectrum. In this way we can compare the effects of trauma in relation to a general set of behaviours. We can observe that two seemingly separate phenomena are linked despite the complexity of the process involved.

Current research in the field of trauma would suggest that the nature and presence of external supports can play an important mediating role in preventing the development of a wide range of problematic behaviours (Irwin, 1996). This role is supplemented by the child's inner supports, in particular their creative imagination and the ability to construct a fantasy world where they can escape from the harshness of reality.

Both of these factors can mediate the effects of trauma but their success is also dependant on the age/developmental stage of the child as well as specific factors relating to the duration, frequency, nature and context of the trauma. In some circumstances these factors combine to overwhelm the child's internal and external supports resulting in the acting out of a range of problematic behaviours. Although we would not claim that such a model is predictive, it does appear to link facts and fact-based theories from a number of different disciplines in order to promote the understanding of a complex phenomenon such as problematic or aggressive sexual behaviours in cases where there is evidence of significant trauma. Although not exhaustive the range of behaviours described in the model may become the focus of our intervention. However, it also highlights the importance of understanding the effects of trauma on the child's development, and it suggests that the role played by adults in mediating these effects may be as important as the specific behavioural intervention.

If we combine this with McIntee's trauma model (see Figure 2) and examine the way in which this 'prism' works, we can begin to understand the connection between trauma and problematic or aggressive sexual behaviours in young people.

When trauma threatens, both animal and human mammals react in instinctively similar ways (Nijenhuis *et al.*, 1998). Sensory processes can signal danger even before there is conscious awareness of that danger and if the threat is great enough, conscious processing of the incoming information may be partially or almost entirely suspended, whilst instinctive behaviours prevail.

Research has not yet established exactly what happens to the delayed process data, but clinical experience suggests that the brain engages automatically in repeated attempts at processing the backlog. These may manifest as flashbacks, hallucinations, intrusive thoughts and images, obsessional and compulsive behaviours, a lack of reality testing, nightmares, uncontrollable and labile affect, rumination, dissociation, day-dreaming or psychological vacancy. In children these behaviours can often be misunderstood as conduct disorder, schizophrenia, Autism, Asperger's Syndrome and many other disorders of childhood. It is therefore imperative that a full assessment of trauma is undertaken in any child assessment, and the same is true for adults.

Under normal circumstances, where a child is not overwhelmed by trauma, the developmental process is an associative one. A child moves from single competencies to multiple and integrated competencies. The child builds up a world view or map of the objects and people in his environment and the relationships between them. Object relations theorists describe the child as moving from part objects to whole objects and eventually to complex inter-relationships (Kohut, 1984; Sterne, 1985, 1990; Winnicott, 1960).

Overwhelming trauma interferes with this developmental process (see figure 3).

In a still-developing child the biological developmental imperatives may provide little time for the processing of backlogged data and the balance between integrated data and 'still to process' data may be quite different. The child's natural tendency to make use of imaginary friends may also become distortedly attached to poorly processed data giving rise to a fragmented sense of self. Under normal circumstances, a child's creative imagination makes temporary use of imaginary companions to make up for deficiencies, or to assist in the accommodation of overwhelming affect. For a child with gross overload and backlog of information and affect, processing this normal stage of development may become too essential to relinquish. It may become distorted into fragmented self-parts that

Figure 2: McIntee's Model of Trauma and its Impact on Child Development

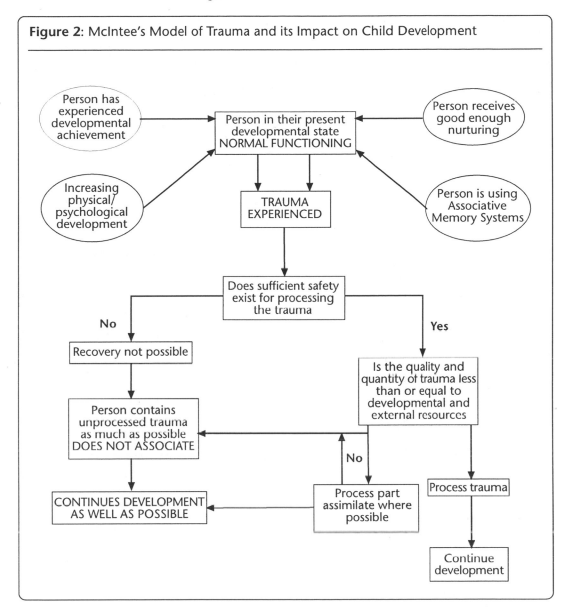

Figure 3: The Trauma Process

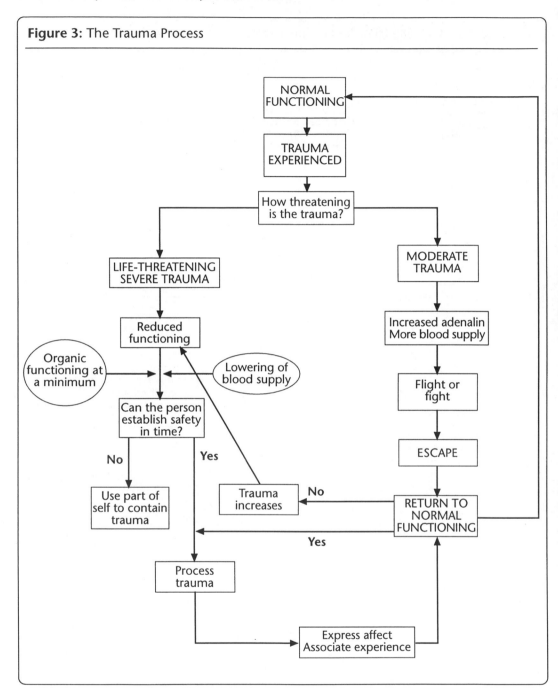

develop in their own right, rather than acting as temporary ancillary relief to the central development of self. It is difficult for a child to build associations between behaviours, consequences and affect, and even in the early years to recognise and label correctly their own affect. It is a long time before children have the capacity to recognise the building up of distress or anger and it is difficult to learn to recognise and anticipate this correctly in others. A child can only learn this through the medium of a caring adult who is able to reflect accurately the state of the child and add helpful information. The adult must be able to act like a true mirror and to reflect affect states and behaviours accurately, maintain appropriate boundaries around their own affect and not confuse the child by projecting their own feelings onto the child.

It is highly likely that any child who is in receipt of service intervention is experiencing or presenting difficulty as a result of trauma of some kind. This may be the trauma of abuse or neglect as well as accidental or medical trauma. Any unresolved trauma and affect will be likely to result in some form of developmental delay or unevenness, intellectual or motional, giving rise to problematic behaviours. Intervening with a troubled child is quite likely to fail unless there is thorough assessment of all aspects of the child's developmental unevenness, the presence of unresolved trauma and affect and an understanding of the world view or relational map the child holds. Unless such a holistic approach is adopted and the child-centred view maintained, it is likely the interventions will be insufficiently tailored to create change. The more troubled the child, the more true this is likely to be. A standard or group approach will leave untouched key elements that will militate against the success of the intervention, will waste financial and human resources and may exacerbate the child's situation.

In terms of the theoretical orientation of interventions, the complex nature of troubled children means that a cognitive behavioural intervention alone will not address the developmental delay caused by trauma. Unless there is an understanding of the various levels of functioning of the child, it will not be possible to know if the level of intervention has been correctly pitched. It will remain unknown if the whole child is responding to the interventions and how.

It is important to know if the child is dissociated so as to know how much or how little of the child is in treatment whereas other parts of the child are dominant when at large in society. Amnesia is a strong feature of trauma and dissociation, and the extreme absent-mindedness of children and adolescents takes on a new meaning when dissociated processes are more fully understood.

Unless the development of the child is addressed and maximised, intervention has a minimised effect upon a disintegrated child. An example of this is easily understood when considering a toddler. Dysfunctional parents often fail to understand that such a small child does not have a developed memory system to remember being told not to touch something before and this can lead to inappropriate chastisement. A non-integrated but chronologically older child may have just the same difficulty and they too may end up inappropriately punished for repeated violations of rules. Simultaneously the frustration level of the worker rises and there is the danger that the feelings of the worker overflow and become projected onto the child. The child becomes seen as hopeless, bad, incorrigible and intransigent. Rejection and punishment are nearby in this situation and would result in further traumatisation of the child.

The results are revolving door cases and helplessness and hopelessness amongst staff and children. The child's body goes on growing and a prominent feature is the chronological age that is becoming more discrepant over time from the hidden features of the functional ages of the self-parts of the traumatised child. As the child's chronological age increases, opportunities for resolution diminish, the problems increase and the child may learn scripts that fine tune and polish the unwanted behaviours. There is a real danger that cognitive interventions that are not linked to holistic development of the child may achieve just such a result. Successful learning of offending cycles, the skills of perpetrators etc. by part of the child's self, in the absence of the development of the whole child, is likely to produce more highly skilled abusers and criminals.

This does not mean there is no place for groupwork or for cognitive behavioural interventions. Indeed a clearly integrated programme of developmental, psychodynamic and cognitive-behavioural interventions are specifically required to maximise the possibility of optimum change as quickly as possible and to tackle the multi-level complex problem being presented by the child. In order to have a complex intervention maximally intervene with a complex child problem, full and complex assessment and continuing assessment is essential. There are very important principles in a child-centred approach to intervention. The first is that the treatment must be tailor-made to fit the particular constellation of developmental attributes of the child and their world view.

The second is that the sexual component of the treatment is fitted into a holistic intervention. To intervene primarily on a sexual level reinforces a view that the child may have already acquired that the primary feature of world interactions and the world view is sexual. It is very important that the sexual component has its full and appropriate place in the intervention but it is also important that it is a component and not the dominant component. This approach results in a correctional view that the world is about a lot of things including sex, which has its place, but the world is not about sex per se.

It is important to re-frame sexualised behaviour where appropriate. The child may be lacking the ability to label appropriately emotions like anger, frustration, boredom, power and powerlessness, and sex can become the vehicle for the expression of these emotions. It is important that appropriate psycho-educational intervention is built in so that there is a de-sexualising of the child's world.

Application of the Model: A Case Study

J is a 15 year old boy, who currently resides in a residential unit that specialises in caring for traumatised young people. His personal history can be summarised as follows:

- Mother suffered post-natal depression/early attachment difficulties.

- Incest between father/daughter, and father/J.

- J witnessed extreme violence perpetrated by father towards mother.

- J experienced extensive physical and emotional abuse.

- Multiple placements throughout early life (only 4 years spent within family by age 12 years old).

Presenting behaviours

- Chronic lying and denial of observable behaviour.

- Poor school performance.

- Episodic dissociative 'phasing out'.

- Extremely violent behaviour towards staff and residents.

- Obsessional behaviours.

- Talking to self in third person.

- Shoplifting/theft.

- Sexualised behaviours including simulating masturbation in public, inappropriate sexual behaviour towards younger children, aggressive sexual touching of adult female staff, and exposure of genitals in public.

The case was referred to the Halt Project which specialises in the treatment of children and young people who exhibit problematic or aggressive sexual behaviours. This project was set up by Glasgow City Council in 1994 to respond to the needs of young people like J. However, as it was assessed that J would require an integrated approach to meet his complex needs, it was felt that the therapist would benefit from consultation with an external agency.

Chester Therapy Centre, which is an independent multi-disciplinary service providing clinical and forensic psychological and psychotherapeutic services directly to clients, was approached to provide consultancy. It was hoped that by integrating the knowledge of the centre in relation to traumatised children and young people, with the treatment being developed by the Halt Project we could begin to address all of J's needs.

In the light of this information, J was assessed as a severely traumatised young person. It was felt that these early traumatic experiences had a profound effect on his level of cognitive and affective development, producing a number of dissociative responses. We believed that the most appropriate method of viewing his problematic and aggressive sexual behaviours was within a wider context of the effects of trauma.

Although several incidents of sexually aggressive behaviour appeared to be premeditated, most fell into the category of impulsive, opportunistic responses to stressful situations and were generally carried out with little attempt at secrecy.

A review of previous interventions indicated that cognitive-behavioural approaches had not resulted in a reduction of his problematic or aggressive sexual behaviours. Similarly, his experience of psychodynamic group-work had actually produced a deterioration in his behaviour and eventually resulted in his refusal to attend. Consequently, we assessed that the variety of interventions had not assisted J to hold a unified view of himself and had simply mirrored the fragmentation already being experienced by the young person.

The first step was therefore to limit the number of people working with J to the absolute minimum. As far as possible all of his treatment needs would be met by one therapist. It was also felt that as cognitive-behavioural approaches tend to assume a minimal level of integration, the failure of previous interventions might be attributed to his level of dissociation.

Consequently, one of the initial goals of treatment was to try to promote greater integration whilst the use of cognitive-behavioural techniques would be included within a holistic treatment approach. A similar strategy is outlined by Silberg (1996):

> Therapy for dissociative children should involve cognitive techniques that help the child learn how to cope with the after-effects of trauma, directive approaches in dealing with traumatic content, sensitivity to the family content and emphasis on the child's need for mastery of developmentally appropriate tasks.

Within this framework the needs of the traumatised young person are prioritised while relying on external controls as the main method of regulating the problematic and aggressive sexual behaviours. However, in order to prevent this process focusing solely on issues of physical safety, the care staff in J's placement were also encouraged to promote the levels of psychological and emotional safety which are essential to the treatment of traumatised young people (James, 1994). Consistent parenting is identified by Silberg as the most important factor in the prediction of successful outcomes of therapy for dissociative children and adolescents.

As such the integration of treatment techniques between therapist and care staff was accorded a high priority in terms of time and resources. The level of parental participation and involvement in therapy is also known to have affected the outcome of treatment with traumatised children (Dell and Eisenhower, 1990). Although J had maintained minimal levels of contact with his family they had not been included in previous treatment programmes, and we quickly identified that the re-engagement of the family would be accorded a high priority.

In view of the difficulty faced by dissociative young people in terms of forming intimate attachments, emphasis in the first three months of treatment was on developing a trusting relationship between the therapist and J. This entailed a great deal of testing behaviour on the part of the young person and a conscious decision by the therapist not to interpret this as either a challenge to their authority or a reluctance by the young person to deal with the sexually aggressive behaviours.

Although this work was primarily process-led and progressed at the young person's pace, it also had to achieve the intended goal of promoting integration. The solution lay in the provision of metaphor and imagery that helped to explain the young person's reality.

Kluft (1984) has suggested that metaphor and imagery are crucial in terms of promoting integration. As Silberg (1996) points out, the young person needs to develop a narrative not just in terms of their actions but also in what has happened to them in their lives. It was therefore felt that J required a pictorial narrative that could try to achieve this aim but also seek to explain the purpose and context of treatment.

Psychotherapeutic techniques may have emphasised passive non-directive approaches but trauma therapists now tend to believe that more directive approaches work better with traumatised children (James, 1994).

It is arguable that by providing a narrative which fitted J's reality, the therapist was able to gain the level of credibility which Silberg (1996) believes to be a prerequisite for helping the young person to move 'beyond the feeling of fragmentation'. The use of a narrative picture was also extremely helpful in terms of ensuring consistency of approach across all areas of the young person's life and was used with care staff and the family to explain our intervention.

The narrative picture had been devised by the therapist to assist other young people within the Halt Project and compared the sinking of the Titanic with the experience of trauma in the young person's life. However, the main focus of the narrative picture was in relation to the survivors and the fact that they had ended up in separate yet linked lifeboats. Each lifeboat contained all the components that the person thought they would need to survive. In the case of the traumatised young person the lifeboat contained the largest safe to hold all of his feelings, thoughts and memories.

As a consequence his lifeboat sat very low in the water and was constantly at risk of being swamped by the slightest wave. The prospect of being rescued or of reaching land seemed very remote and the over-riding feelings associated with the picture were those of fear, loneliness, desperation and an overwhelming sense of loss. Within this narrative J could readily identify with such feelings and was able to relate it to his own life (see Figure 4).

Our task was explained in terms of helping him to re-examine his coping strategies and to ensure that in trying to survive he did not end up 'sinking' his lifeboat. Certain items such as the sexually aggressive behaviours were identified as one particular box that would have to be jettisoned as quickly as possible. Others, such as the use of the 'safe', would require careful unpacking and examination before this could be reduced to a size that did not threaten to sink his lifeboat. As J was entitled to his own privacy he was provided with a small lockable box in which he could store his written thoughts and feelings. This

Figure 4

was kept within the residential establishment and served as a visual prompt to remind him of the size of 'safe' that we wanted him to utilise in the future.

Although this narrative picture reflected the fragmentation in terms of the family situation and J's behaviours it also provided a means of unifying his experiences. In doing so it ensured that the aim of achieving integration in terms of linking past trauma with current behaviours was always present within the process of treatment. This was not as threatening as might be expected because J could choose which aspect of the narrative picture he wished to discuss at each meeting.

He was continually reminded that any attempt by another person to climb into his boat to try to unpack the contents would have the adverse effect of sinking him. Our task was therefore explained as that of encouraging him by creating an atmosphere of trust and safety in which he would feel able to carry out this process by himself. Throughout this early stage of engagement the therapist was encouraged by the consultant to develop a range of measures designed to increase J's sense of control and thereby enhance his sense of responsibility for his behaviours.

Although the narrative contained many different components, the following themes were particularly relevant in terms of the therapeutic intervention with J.

Responsibility

The most powerful aspect of the narrative picture was the way that it helped J to understand his behaviours as a response to the effects of trauma. Instead of fostering collusion it helped to identify the choices that were available to him. At its most basic level this was the choice to survive in a way that did not involve hurting himself or others. As his level of integration developed, cognitive exercises were devised to fit his experience. The therapist had already developed a 'spiral' process rather than a cycle to work with other young people and this helped to convey J's sense of events spinning out of his control. The focus of treatment was to highlight the steps leading to such behaviours and the possible consequences of his actions.

These behaviours were so extensive and repetitive that a straightforward relapse-prevention model or cycle would have created a sense of disillusionment and failure. The 'spiral' provided a fresh start and focused J's efforts on controlling the behaviours at their earliest formation rather than accounting for lapses or relapses.

Responsibility is a concept that lacks meaning when the young person is unable to utilise a range of strategies to cope with stressful situations. Bowlby has described how a child learns to avoid testing alternative strategies to deal with the world and cuts himself off from any form of corrective feedback. This is particularly true of traumatised dissociative young people and until we have created sufficient levels of psychological, physical and emotional safety they will not test the strategies that we encourage them to use.

In order for responsibility to be a meaningful concept for J he had to experience a level of safety in which he could accept corrective feedback. Once this was achieved the change in all of his problematic and aggressive behaviours was quite profound.

Attachment

We are aware of the impact which trauma can have on the formation of secure attachments. 'Abuse is inherently tied to a lack of support and nurturance which directly impacts on the child's sense of self' (Erickson and Egeland, 1987). In J's case there were attachment difficulties within the first few weeks of life and these were compounded by subsequent episodes of abuse within the family. The development of dissociative effects and attendant behaviours ensured that all of the significant attachments in J's life were strained to breaking point.

Silberg (1996) suggests that

> the risk of not developing attachment is that the child will be doomed to feel isolated and ultimately risk becoming a perpetrator of further victimisation.

The Titanic metaphor allowed us to highlight the importance of such issues and to discuss the extent to which J's behaviour could affect these relationships. Although all of his family had ended up in different lifeboats they were still 'attached' and as such the effects of one person dealing with their 'baggage' could easily rock the others` lifeboats. This issue became extremely important when J began to disclose the extent of the abuse perpetrated by his father. It allowed us to discuss the way in which his allegations and subsequent retractions were affecting relationships within the family. It also allowed J the opportunity to state that he considered his attachment to his mother to be the most important in his life and to articulate the goal of putting their lifeboats closer together.

This proved to be an important means of re-engaging the family in the process of treatment and it afforded them the means by which they could discuss their relationships at a deeper emotional level.

Affective expression

Another use of the narrative picture was that it provided the means by which the young person could begin to accept that he had a wide range of affective experiences. The process of exploring the 'safe' and identifying a variety of emotions also assisted his attempts to regulate their expression. The use of his private 'safe' that he could choose to share with the therapist became a useful strategy in replacing the acting out of his emotions. It constantly reinforced the concept that he was in control of this process and demonstrated that he could deal with different emotions rather than be overwhelmed. As his trust developed J began to choose to keep the feelings in his 'safe' and to share them with the therapist on a regular basis.

All of these methods of encouraging affective expression were contrasted with the avoidant coping strategy of storing feelings and memories in the large 'safe'. Such avoidant coping strategies were acknowledged but never dismissed. In the context of surviving such extensive trauma the use of these

strategies could be understood. However, in the context of the narrative picture their usefulness had diminished to the point where they actually threatened his survival. In such circumstances, new strategies were employed and within the context of treatment and a safe residential environment J found the courage to test another way of surviving.

Conclusion

In our attempt to contribute to the debate concerning the treatment of problematic or aggressive sexual behaviours in young people we would like to emphasise the need for a consilient approach and more comprehensive approach.

As Wilson (1998) points out, this cannot be 'proved with logic from first principles or grounded in any definitive set of empirical tests, at least not by any yet conceived. The strongest appeal of consilience is in the prospect of intellectual adventure and given even quite modest success, the value of understanding the human condition with a higher degree of certainty.'

This approach will of necessity become a synthesis of different disciplines and approaches. We would suggest that the criteria for choosing which particular synthesis must properly be determined by the young person's needs. Where it is apparent that this includes the effects of significant trauma we must find ways to adapt our treatment programmes accordingly.

While this will undoubtedly contain cognitive behavioural models, the stage at which these are utilised and the way in which they are adapted will ultimately depend on wider considerations of their needs. In such cases we must resist the temptation to mirror the young person's fragmentation by creating services that emphasise separateness and division.

References

Bowlby, J. (1988). *A Secure Base: Clinical Applications of Attachment Theory*. London: Routledge.

Burton, D.L., Nesmith, A.A., and Badten, L. (1997). Clinicians Views on Sexually Aggressive Children and Their Families: A Theoretical Exploration. *Child Abuse and Neglect*, 21(2): 157–169.

Canter, D. (1994). *Criminal Shadows; Inside the Mind of the Serial Killer*. London: Harper Collins.

Dell, D.F., and Eisenhower, J.W. (1990). Adolescent Multiple Personality Disorder: A Preliminary Study. *Journal of the American Academy of Child and Adolescent Psychiatry*, 35.

Erickson, M.F., and Egeland, B. (1987). A Developmental View of the Psychological Consequences of Maltreatment. *School Psychology Review*, 16(2): 156–168.

Hoghughi, M.S. (Ed.), with Bhate, S.R., and Graham, F. (1997). *Working With Sexually Abusive Adolescents*. London: Sage.

Irwin, H.J. (1996). Traumatic Childhood Events, Perceived Availability of Emotional Support, and the Development of Dissociative Tendencies. *Child Abuse and Neglect*, 20(8): 701–707.

James, A.C., and Neil, P. (1996). Juvenile Sexual Offending: One-year Period Prevalence Study. *Child Abuse and Neglect*, 20(6): 477–485.

James, B. (1994). *Handbook for Treatment of Attachment — Trauma Problems in Children*. New York: Lexington Books.

Kahn, T.J., and Lafond, M.A. (1988). Treatment of the Adolescent Sex Offender. *Child and Adolescent Social Work Journal*, 5.

Kent, L., Laidlaw, J.D.D., Brockington, I.F. (1995). Foetal Abuse. *Child Abuse and Neglect*, 21(2): 181–186.

Kluft, R.P. (1984). Multiple Personality in Childhood. *Psychiatric Clinics of North America*, 7.

Knopp, F.H., Freeman Longo, R., and Stevenson, W.F. (1992). *Nation-wide Study of Juvenile and Adult Sex Offender Treatment Programmes and Models*. Orwell, VT: Safer Society Press.

Kohut, H. (1984). *How Does Analysis Cure?* Chicago: University of Chicago Press.

McIntee, J. (1992). *Trauma: The Psychological Process*. Chester: Chester Therapy Centre.

McIntee, J., and Crompton, I. (1997). The Psychological Effects of Trauma on Children. In Bates, J., Pugh, R., and Thompson, N. (Eds.) *Protecting Children: Challenges and Change*. Aldershot: Arena.

Mathews (1998). *Factors Associated with Sexual Behaviour Problems in Sexually Abused Children*. Paper presented at N.A.P.N Conference, Winnipeg, Canada.

Morrison, T., Erooga, M., and Beckett, R. (Eds.) (1994). *Sexual Offending Against Children*. London: Routledge.

Nijenhuis, E.R.S., Spinhoven, P., Vanderlinden, J., and van Dyck, R. (1998). Somatoform Dissociative Symptoms as Related to Animal Defensive Reactions to Predatory Imminence and Injury. *Journal of Abnormal Psychology*, 107: 63–73.

O'Callaghan, D., and Print, B. (1994). Adolescent Sexual Abusers: Research, Assessment and Treatment. In Morrison, et al. (Eds.), op cit.

Richardson, G., Bate, S., and Graham, F. (1997). Cognitive-based Practice with Sexually Abusive Adolescents. In Hughes, M.S. (Ed.). *Working with Sexually Abusive Adolescents*, 128–143. London: Sage.

Silberg, J. (Ed.) (1996). *The Dissociative Child Diagnosis, Treatment, and Management*. Sidran Press.

Sterne, D.N. (1985). *The Interpersonal World of the Infant: A View from Psychoanalysis and Developmental Psychology*. New York: Basic Books.

Sterne, D.N., (1990). *Diary of a Baby*. London: Harper Collins.

Varia, R., Abidin, R., and Dass, P. (1996), Perceptions of Abuse: Effects on Adult Psychological and Social Adjustment. *Child Abuse and Neglect*, 20(6): 511–526.

Ward, T., Hudson, S., and Keenan, T. (1996). *A Self Regulation Model of the Sexual Offence Process*. Paper Presented at A.T.S.A. Conference. Chicago, USA.

Wilson, E.O. (1998). *Consilience: The Unity of Knowledge*. Little Brown & Co.

Winnicott, D. (1960) Ego Distortion in Terms of True and False Self. In Winnicott, D. (Ed.) (1960). *The Maturational Process and the Facilitative Environment*. London: Hogarth Press and the Institute of Psychoanalysis.

Winnicott, D. (1971). *Playing and Reality*. Harmonsworth: Penguin.

Chapter Fifteen

Dilemmas and Potential Work with Sexually Abusive Young People in Residential Settings

Meg Lindsay OBE

Dilemmas and Potential Work with Sexually Abusive Young People in Residential Settings

Introduction

In any book on the subject of work with sexually abusive young people, consideration must be given to residential settings. Given the profile of these young people - often victims of sexual and physical abuse, frequently from disrupted family situations, having had frequent changes of carer etc. (Bentovim and Williams, 1998) — it is obvious that many will come to the attention of social workers, and of these a significant proportion are likely to be placed in residential care. In a survey of residential units in Scotland, 30 per cent of managers believed that they were definitely caring for young people who had sexually abused others, and a further 30 per cent strongly suspected that such young people were among their residents (Lindsay, 1997). Only in some cases was their sexually abusive behaviour the reason for placement. In many other cases, this will not have been known at the time of placement, only becoming apparent later. Therefore, whether deliberately placed as a result of abusive behaviour or not, significant numbers of young people who sexually abuse appear in residential settings, and present real challenges to their carers. What is surprising is not that such young people are there, but how low a priority the issue has been given in the thinking and literature around sexual abuse and sexual aggression. Yet these young people are inevitably some of the most complex and challenging to care for effectively and safely, and they are likely to continue to come into our children's homes and residential schools, possibly in ever increasing numbers, as recognition of abusive behaviour becomes more widespread. One residential school reported to us that on a randomly selected date, 17 of their 34 residents were known to have sexually abusive behaviour patterns. It is vitally important, and indeed urgent, that more effort and thought are expended on improving the ability of residential resources to respond effectively.

Why has this issue received so little attention in the vast literature on sexual abuse and in the rapidly growing discussion around the subject of 'safe care'? One of the reasons is to be found in widespread ignorance of this seriousness of the problem, arising from lack of research. Kendrick, in his literature review appended to Kent's 'Children's Safeguards Review' (Kent, 1997) comments 'There is increasing evidence of the sexual abuse of children by other residents'. He goes on to quote White (1987), who 'writing in the mid-1980s, decried the lack of attention, in terms of research, information and reports, that this subject gets…' (Kendrick, 1997; p 210). General focus on the issue of young abusers was considerably aided by the Committee of Inquiry into Children and Young People who Sexually Abuse Other Children, whose report appeared in 1992. It outlined the prevalence of the problem, but also expressed concern about the unpreparedness of staff in the residential sector to cope with it (NCH, 1992).

In addition, there has been an assumption that young people will come to the attention of the authorities as a result of convictions for sexual offences. This has meant that it is assumed that decisions about their care have been made with this as the focal point, and such literature and policy as there is, is based on this assumption. But the evidence quoted above is that these are the minority. Many more young people are becoming looked after by local authorities without their tendencies to abuse being either known or seen as the key issue at the time of placement.

Another reason for the low priority given to this topic is the generally poor status of residential work, meaning that high status tasks such as child protection overshadow it. As one residential worker commented 'Many youngsters are brought into care as a result of abuse. This is often seen as 'problem solved' — not enough work in depth is done'. (Quotes from residential staff in this chapter are drawn from the study by the author first printed in *The Tip of the Iceberg — Sexual Abuse in the*

Context of Residential Child Care (Lindsay, 1997). Some of the quotes are not directly drawn from the published study but emanate from other information gained by the author in the course of that study.) Also, high status work such as therapy is not seen in this country as something to be undertaken by residential staff. Further, because of the low status of residential care and the historically low numbers of trained staff, few external managers have experience of residential care and do not understand the particular difficulties, or the considerable potential, of this type of care.

Two main challenges face us if we are to improve the care of these young people. Firstly, we must develop safe residential care amongst the considerable difficulties and risks involved in looking after such young people, twenty four hours a day, seven days a week, along with other young people who are also highly vulnerable. The study referred to above (Lindsay, 1997) also showed that 60 per cent of managers believed they were caring for a young person who had been sexually abused and 30 per cent believed they were caring for both abused and abusing young people together. These risks must be minimised, and the best ways of providing safe care for these young people and their peers defined. Secondly, there is evidence to suggest that residential care can provide powerful potential for the treatment of such young people, and this must be explored urgently. Therefore this chapter will consider how we can care safely for sexually abusive young people in residential settings, and will then briefly consider the debate about the need to develop specialist residential care more extensively as an effective treatment setting.

How Can We Care Safely for Sexually Abusive Young People in Residential Settings?

Safe care has become a focus during the 1990s, resulting from high profile cases concerning abuse of children in children's homes by the staff employed to care for them. Kincora, Leicestershire, North Wales (Jones, 1996), and others, all created huge anxiety about the safety of children and young people in the state care. The Utting (1997) and Kent (1997)

reports studied the issues in some detail, and rafts of recommendations have been put forward as a result. Yet while it is true that abuse by staff is an appalling betrayal of trust and does inestimable damage to the victims, none the less, what little evidence has been amassed suggests that it is not a frequent occurrence, although this in no way mitigates the seriousness of this as an issue for resolution. The views of young people who live in care settings, as expressed most recently by Who Cares? Scotland (the very effective advocacy movement of Scottish children and young people in care) at the Centrepiece 1998 conference of The Centre for Residential Care, was that abuse by staff is not mentioned to them by young people living in residential care as frequently as other dangers. But one of the major concerns of these young people is abuse by their peers. Indeed, in numerical terms, there is much more chance of a young person being abused by a peer than by a member of staff, and much less protection for them both before and after the event. As Kent comments 'Abuse by peers, both physical and sexual, seems to be much more prevalent than abuse by carers' (Kent, 1997; p 98). As one residential worker said, 'This is an underestimated area of work — most alarmingly, the frequency with which children may sexually abuse others'.

In order to improve the safety of residential child care settings, it is necessary to understand the residential setting, and what poses the particular risks to safety. Then three areas must be improved — general practice, staff training and support, and managerial awareness and action.

The setting

Residential care is all about groups — staff groups and resident groups. These groups are constantly changing — staff come and go on shifts, take days off and annual leave, go to training events etc. Even small residential settings of four to six residents will require a staff team of a minimum size of about eight to ten, in order to ensure two staff on a shift at a time. That is a lot of coming and going. Young people also come and go. The speed and frequency of this will depend upon the exact type of setting — a service providing respite care will probably change its resident group twice per week, whereas some children's homes may have only very occasional changes as a young person moves on. None the less, in any setting there will be far more change than in an 'ordinary family'.

These two issues, the group, and the frequency of change, are both important when trying to provide safe care with and for young people who may be sexually abusive. It is also important to consider the nature of the resident group likely to be living in the average residential setting. The typical profile of the young people who enter residential care—high levels of previous abuse, disrupted family histories, poor self-image—makes the risk factors all too obvious. For example, the group setting provides a choice of victims for a young person who wishes to abuse. These victims may well already have been abused, and therefore be less likely to be confident in making complaints, and less likely to be believed. The setting thus provides a ready source of 'safe victims'. Also unlike an ordinary family, the young people concerned are not related, thus the group dynamic is quite different, with even more boundaries missing or blurred.

The busy schedule also means that opportunities to abuse are not hard to manufacture. One young man in a residential school was known to feign stomach upset, or to misbehave such that he was 'grounded' and not allowed to go on outings. Thus, at a time when few staff were around, he had access to another young person who was also regularly barred from outings. Young people intending to abuse can also exploit the routines of normal residential life such as staff meeting times, shift changes, etc., when they know that staff will inevitably be less able to monitor what is going on in the building.

The number of staff involved in the caring team also means that communication and the transfer of information is a constant challenge in residential settings. Staff are rarely able to meet all together and even weekly staff meetings will have staff missing, or will contain staff who are in the process of working over 24 hours non-stop and are therefore tired. The completion of the necessarily complex set of reports and logs, and the shift changeover time can easily be disrupted by crises. The close working environment and intense nature of the task may mean that tensions develop in the staff team, further hindering communication. Yet it is clear that sexual abuse thrives in settings where people do not share what they have observed. Patterns which could raise staff's suspicions early on about one young person's behaviour towards another can easily be missed as different members of the team each hold different pieces of the jigsaw, but the opportunity to put them together is difficult to manufacture, and therefore often lost.

The movement of young people through the unit also means that good information about each young person is hard to obtain. This can be worsened when field work colleagues, desperate to find a place for a young person whose abusive behaviour has made them persona non grata everywhere else, omit to pass on details of the young person's pattern of abuse, or even that they have a history of abusive behaviour at all. Given that young abusers often carefully conceal their method of approaching victims, and can be very adept at winning the trust of adults, the fact that they are not well known means again that the potential is there for them to target and groom a victim, often in ways they have previously used, but which are not recognised because information has not been transferred from their previous carers to their current carers.

The nature of the young people who enter residential care also means that they bring with them issues which make the detection and prevention of abuse difficult. Most of the young people living in residential settings are adolescents, between 14 and 16 years old. This is a stage at which young people are exploring their sexuality and sexual identity. Normal exploration and curiosity is very much a feature of adolescents in this age group. It can be difficult to distinguish between this normal teenage behaviour and potentially or actually abusive behaviour. Signs may be missed or the significance of those that are noticed may be underestimated. In addition to this, because many of the young people living in residential settings are there because they have been sexually abused, many will exhibit abnormal sexual knowledge for their age, and in many cases will exhibit overtly sexualised behaviour. This is hard for staff to deal with in a group setting, and may in itself be perceived as or actually be abusive to other residents. However, these are also clear messages which will be picked up by a young person who wishes to abuse, and make these young people especially vulnerable. As noted above, young people who have been abused may also be less confident about reporting any threat they perceive. Their understanding of normal sexual activity and the boundaries within which it should occur is already weak or non-existent. They may perceive that the last time they 'told' resulted in them having to leave home, and may fear what else can happen if they report again. Further, they may fear what the abuser will do to them if they tell, and are not believed. Their own family relationships may be fractured, or they may have been placed miles away from them. Thus the range of people with whom they have contact may be limited, making them feel and be all the more helpless. All of this represents a potent cocktail of need and risk with which residential staff have to deal.

Thus it is clear that residential care can be a difficult setting in which to care safely and productively for young people who sexually abuse. One residential worker described it as 'An explosive issue, which needs a very professional approach'. Yet these same factors of group living, frequent change and the nature of the group, can also be used positively and productively. Groups of staff who have the relevant knowledge and have developed expertise in working with these young people have the best chance of recognising and addressing abusive behaviour at an early stage. Able to support one another in what is stressful work, and able to be relieved of some of the intensity by their time off etc., an effective staff team is powerful tool. The resident group, if assisted by such a skilled staff team, and aware of the issues and problems which each of its members brings with him or her, can both protect its members and induce change in them so that residential care can be a powerful experience and an engine for change. That change may be positive or negative. In order to make for a positive experience, safety is the prerequisite, and thus all the above issues must be considered, and action taken.

General practice: issues and dilemmas

There are issues in the general practice of residential care which require careful thought and intervention if safe care is to be provided.

These cover such issues as the culture of the service, placement decisions, child care planning, confidentiality, the handling of allegations, and the provision of direct therapy. There are also very real dilemmas which needed to be recognised and tackled — the balance of confidentiality against openness, privacy against monitoring, rights of potential victim and potential abuser, amongst others. These are real dilemmas which cannot be brushed aside — difficult decisions have to be taken about them.

Culture

The culture of the service is the vital ingredient which will make the most profound difference to the safety and effectiveness of the care offered. In some ways, it does not matter how many policies and procedures are in place, or how well trained staff are, if the ethos surrounding everything is one of secrecy, bullying and distrust. If staff abuse their power and model aggressive, undermining relationships with one another and the residents, there is little chance that young people will feel confident about resisting or reporting abuse within the unit, or recognising and beginning to work on their own bullying and abuse of power, including sexual power. Yet the culture of the unit is extremely difficult to accurately define and consciously develop (Whitaker, Archer and Hicks, 1994).

However, some steps can be taken. The crucial aspect of the culture affecting work with sexually abusive young people is openness, honesty and a respect for each individual which pervades the entire service. This is not an optional extra in working with abusive young people, it is the core of everything that has to be done. Staff must display healthy and open attitudes to sex. It should not be a taboo topic, nor should it be an occasion for crude humour. Appropriate sex education, such as the 'good enough' parent would supply, is a necessary component. Young people have to know that their questions about sex will be openly received and answered. Giving young people information about normal sexual practice will help them recognise unwelcome sexual approaches from their peers. This openness should include frank discussions about how life is lived and what goes on in the unit. There must be clear understanding and agreement about what is and is not acceptable in terms of, for example, nudity, physical contact, language etc. By doing this, the residential unit is doing consciously what families do without thinking about it, by specifying the norms which exist within their living space. This ensures that each young person, and staff member, understands what these are as soon as they arrive. In this way, it is easier to see when these norms have been breached, and what should be done. This means that young people whose experience of abuse has resulted in them being unsure where appropriate boundaries are, such that they do not readily know what is acceptable and what is not, are given permission to recognise and report any unacceptable approaches from their peers. It also means that a young abuser gets an unambiguous, early message that abusive behaviour will be reported and dealt with and not remain a secret. The Centre for Residential Child has produced guidance notes (CRCC, 1995) for residential workers in dealing with these issues.

Placement choice

The issue of placement decision making is another thorny area. The Children Act 1989 Guidelines state that young people who sexually abuse others should not be placed in the same services as those who have been abused. Yet Kent (1997) notes that in reality 'it is happening all the time'. The study referred to earlier (Lindsay, 1997) demonstrates powerfully that one out of every three Scottish residential child care services were caring for both abused and abusing young people simultaneously. Keeping abusers and abused young people apart appears to be sound common sense, except that in many cases it is quite impossible to do. Many young people who abuse others have themselves been abused. Araji (1997) reviews quoted studies by Johnson (1988, 1989) and Friedrich and Luecke (1988) showing that between 50 and 75 per cent of males abusers were also victims, and 100 per cent of females. Bentovim makes similar points, giving figures of between 30 and 70 per cent (Bentovim and Williams, 1998). Thus, even if young abusers are placed in services specifically for them only, they will still be living alongside young people who have been

abused. As one worker commented 'There is a need for particular attention to be paid to working with young people who are both the victims of abuse themselves and abuse others'.

The second reason why it is not possible to totally separate young abusers from those who have been abused is, as has been noted above, that the history of abuse of young people is not always, or even usually, known before they enter the care system. In some cases it is divulged once the young person gains confidence in staff, or it comes to light as a result of an incident of some sort. Thus it will never be possible to ensure that all young people who may abuse can be placed separately from those who have been abused. However, it is possible to develop specialist services able to devote time and expertise specifically to young abusers and this will be discussed below. But even if these were readily available, difficult placement decisions would still have to be made, both at initial placement, or later when their previously concealed inclination to abuse becomes known. It is therefore essential that when such decisions are taken, as much accurate information as possible is made available. If the young person has a history of abusing others, details of this and work done or planned in relation to it must be outlined. The particular pattern of abuse must be described, and the type of victim to whom they may be drawn. It is only in the light of all this information that good plans can be made which will both address the young person's difficulties, and ensure the safety of those with whom he/she will be living.

The decision about where to place must be closely tied to a detailed care plan for the young person, covering all aspects of their care, not just their abusive behaviour. Obviously, this is simple good practice, which should apply to any young person. Unfortunately, fear of failing to find a placement at all may mean, as was noted above, that details are not given, or the seriousness of behaviour downplayed or not mentioned. This is dangerous. It is also the case that if an incident occurs, very sudden and precipitate decisions are often taken to move the young person, thus necessitating a new placement being found. Sometimes this may be inevitable. The victim may well not feel able to continue living with their abuser. Alternatively, one staff member was anxious at their 'inability to remove the abuser from the unit, if abuse takes place in the unit'. We suspect this is not unusual.

The work that is done around any move with both victim and young abuser will be crucial to the recovery of one, and in the treatment of the other. Time must be spent in creating detailed care plans for and with both. The possibility of discussion between them about what has happened should be considered, with the victim's wishes taking precedence. In the light of this work, a new placement can be sought, with specific plans in place. The staff of the future placement then know exactly what has happened and what their work with the young person will have to entail. Unfortunately, often this is not done; panic reigns, and sudden, ad hoc decisions are taken. As Epps (1997) states '...it is undoubtedly the case that the placement of sexually abusive children and adolescents is haphazard. It is likely that only a minority will be placed in ideal circumstances...' Not only does this disrupt any work being done with the young person about their abusive tendencies; it also puts the residents of their next home at risk, as they are moved into a situation where their history and pattern of abuse are not known, and therefore the risks they present cannot be assessed.

Confidentiality

This brings up another dilemma. How much of the young person's history needs to be known, and by whom? This is another one of the decisions to be made at placement. What happens to considerations of confidentiality? What indeed do we mean by confidentiality in this situation? It has been common practice in some services for young people to be told to develop a 'cover story' which can be told to peers and others to explain their reason for being 'in care'. The thinking behind this is that the stigma attached to the label 'abuser' is so intense and of such longevity that it will make present and future life impossible for the young person, and act against any change in their behaviour that they may be trying to make. Unfortunately, what the use of 'cover stories' also does is to deny other young people

knowledge which they may need in order to protect themselves. For this reason, and because one of the touchstones of work with abusers is achieving recognition by them of the effects of their behaviour on others, the use of 'cover stories' should be avoided. Young people must be encouraged and helped to work with staff and their peers in a climate of openness. None the less, it is certainly true that the stigma of having been identified as an abuser is huge, and is increasing amongst the general public, with much media hype, and even the growth of vigilante movements dedicated to 'rooting out paedophiles'. Thus while openness is the only possible approach, the care plan must also specify exactly what different groups of people need to know, and must include a clear strategy for helping the young person anticipate the difficulties they will encounter in the future as a result of their past actions.

Therapy

Other dilemmas relate to the supply of therapy. Realistically, the amount of therapeutic input available for such young people is minuscule compared with the numbers who require it; in most cases, it is simply not available. 'We are using the expertise of a new project in the area which has been inundated with referrals, thus highlighting the massive need and lack of resources', said one residential manager. However, where therapy is available, there must be clarity from the outset as to how the therapist and the residential staff will work together. Catherine McAskill (1991) in her excellent study of foster parents who have cared for sexually abused children, notes that one of the key difficulties for them was in the relationship with therapists, who communicated little, and would often not allow them to know the content of their discussions with the young person. This left the foster parents feeling undervalued and having to cope in the dark with the young person's reactions. Residential staff have often said that they feel the same. The delicacy of the therapeutic relationship cannot be undervalued. But it is also true that to let another layer of secrecy enter into work with these young people is dangerous.

Staff training and support

If a genuine difference is to be made to the care of these young people, then better training and support for front line staff is sine qua non. As consecutive government reports, Utting (1991, 1997); Skinner (1992); Warner (1992); Kent (1997), have made very clear, the training of residential staff is woefully inadequate, and the country is still expecting some of the least qualified staff to care for some of the most damaged young people in society. '…staff working in residential establishments…were worried about dealing with overt sexualised behaviour when they had little information or guidance as to how to deal with it' (NCH, 1992, p 17). Faced with little training, and often little understanding and support from management, staff often report feeling demoralised and anxious. As some members of staff succinctly put it 'Lack of expertise causes panic in staff'; 'Staff find this a difficult and painful issue'; 'An emotive and panic inducing subject in too many settings'; 'Once we have identified it, we don't know what to do about it'. That staff should feel so anxious and de-skilled in the face of caring for these young people is not surprising. The dilemmas of caring safely for this group of very damaged young people have been outlined above. Staff may feel isolated in carrying out their responsibility to care safely and effectively for them, and fear allegations against themselves. Add to this the likelihood that, as in any group of people, some staff will themselves have been sexually abused, and a potent mixture of fear and uncertainty is likely to emerge, as the above quotes demonstrate. These staff need training which will not only give them good background knowledge about normal adolescent sexual development, and about sexually abusive behaviour, but which will also be realistic and practical. 'More training is required, as lack of knowledge is a great inhibiting factor in work' and 'There is an ongoing need to heighten the awareness of practitioners with regard to this issue', said two residential managers.

It must not be forgotten that residential staff, unlike their fieldwork or therapist colleagues, live daily with these young people, assisting them with personal tasks, sitting up late listening to them, going to them when they are disturbed at night and so forth. Not only does this provide fertile fields for intervening with the young person, it also presents challenges and emotions which those in other roles simply do not experience. These staff need to know how to assess risk, ('Continuing training and support is required to enable staff to evaluate risks appropriately'), and how to work with children and young people who may potentially be abusers but who also have a whole range of other needs, problems and potential which must be recognised. In fact working with a young person who has abused others requires the same skills and abilities which good residential practitioners utilise every day, that is assessment, empathy, limit setting, use of the group etc., but they need assistance to see this, and to use these skills with confidence. This training should be delivered to a standardised syllabus wherever possible. Too often, when staff do receive a couple of days training on the topic, it is carried out by this independent trainer, or at that seminar, or on a 'tailor made' basis for the unit concerned. But what is needed is generally agreed training packages which all employers can recognise, so that precious training time is not squandered. This will enable staff to work consistently, on the basis of similar knowledge, and will gradually increase the knowledge base in residential care generally. Ideally, this type of training is so vital that it should be delivered pre-service.

Staff also need both emotional and practical support. As one described 'Dealing with abuse…can be daunting for staff, who need appropriate support'. Supervision is crucial. It not only helps front line workers to carry out their role, but also acts as one of the sources of information to allow the early identification of risk. However, support to the supervisor is essential. Senior staff in residential settings often feel a huge weight of responsibility; young people and staff in their care have so many conflicting and seemingly irreconcilable needs, and the risks are so hard to perceive and avoid. The practical support they require includes policy and procedure, which will enable them to feel that the agency for which they work both understands and shares the risk with them. They also require support in terms of the flexible use of resources. These issues will be dealt with more fully below.

Managerial awareness

Without clear definitions, administrative and clinical practices have, often in the name of treatment, denied children needed protection.

(Caldwell and Rejino, 1993)

In order to provide adequate support, management throughout the unit must understand the issues, and recognise the hugely complex task expected of residential staff, some aspects of which have been described above. This involves understanding from the inside the milieu in which residential staff work. If senior managers do not appreciate the particular practical and practice challenges of residential work with sexually abusive young people, then there is little chance of staff being adequately prepared to undertake their task, or of the general day to day practice being improved. It is vital that all managers responsible for operating residential settings are aware that it is likely that their units will be catering for young people who abuse others, whether this is their intended function or not, as described above. They must also be aware what makes the provision of safe residential care a difficult task, even in the absence of residents who may abuse. When abuses within residential settings do occur, it is all too easy to assume that these necessarily represent negligence and unacceptable lapses. What is less often recognised is that, without a detailed understanding by management of the complexity of residential care, and action on it, abuse will be more likely to occur than not. Unfortunately, such understanding is far from universal, and workers often feel that the problem is 'dumped' on them by both placing and managing agencies — 'The current trend is for social work to do the 'statutory required' and pass on...'.

As has been described, residential settings inevitably involve multiple carers coming and going on rostas at different times, and a volatile and changing resident group, all carrying with them trauma of one sort of another. In addition, the resources deployed for the conduct of residential care often bring their own problems.

Management of resources

Buildings

It is a key responsibility of management to regularly update themselves on this situation within their services, with a view towards safe care. This includes careful deployment of resources, including buildings and personnel. Most readers will recognise that much residential care takes place in often largish, older buildings, creating a complex layout, hard to monitor. Communication between carers is thus difficult, and monitoring of the group and individuals within it is hard. Even in small, modern units, based on domestic accommodation, the number of people living and working there are larger than the average family, and thus buildings have often been combined or extended resulting in a convoluted layout in which nooks and crannies provide ample opportunity for abuse. In therapy, one service for young abusers asks them to draw out a map of their unit, and mark where the 'best' places to abuse are. The young people do not find this difficult, often choosing the same venues as other young abusers do — places where staff seldom pass, e.g. bicycle sheds, cupboards, even, in the case of one residential school, behind gymnastic equipment in the sports hall. Thus managers and agencies should regularly audit the safety of their buildings with these issues in mind as well as conventional health and safety requirements, and should be particularly keen to include these considerations in drawing up architectural briefs for new-build resources. The balance must be struck between the young people's rights to privacy and a homely environment, and their right to safety. This is not easy as no-one wants to see defensive environments developing in children's homes and residential schools. But too often the issue of building design is forgotten or poorly understood by agencies which have failed to understand the complex and inherently difficult nature of residential care as described above.

Staff

The other key resource is staff. The needs of staff in terms of training and support, and management's role in supplying these has been described. The composition and lay out of the staff team also need consideration. Systems must be in place to enable managers to be constantly in touch with issues in the unit, and able to alter the numbers and skill-mix of staff working there. If the resident group contains a volatile mix of young people who may abuse and those who have been abused or are in other ways vulnerable, then it may be necessary to increase staff numbers, or to introduce staff with particular skills and confidence in this situation. To do this requires flexibility first of all at senior management level. Given the likelihood of this situation arising in any residential unit at any time, as we have shown, it is essential that systems for delivering this degree of flexibility are in place as a matter of routine, and are budgeted for. Attempting to cobble together panic measures when a situation has arisen is altogether too little, too late.

Constant and detailed awareness of what is going on in a unit at any time is vital — what is the nature of the resident group, what are the skills and morale of the staff group and how do these interplay. This is the responsibility of external management, and yet sometimes one fears that this is the role which of all the many complex roles in residential care, is least well understood, and of which least is expected.

Development of effective policy

Care of abused/abusing young people…constitutes a problem in all establishments and one which requires policy.

(a residential manager)

In any good system, a powerful loop exists linking management, policy and practice. Management consults and produces policy; it then implements the policy; policy acts to change practice; management then reviews practice, and revises policy in the light of this. When preparing units to deal with sexually abusive young people, the design of good, effective policy and procedure, well implemented and regularly reviewed and updated, is essential. Yet it has been our experience that in too many services around the country, staff are left in a policy/procedure void when it comes to this work, or are working within policy guidelines designed primarily for field social work settings. Agency child protection policies must address the practical problems faced in residential care — dealing with disclosures of abuse by one resident against another, providing intimate care to these young people, solving the dilemma of what to tell to whom etc. — and they must mesh with other policies. Individual unit policies must take into account sexually abusive behaviour between two residents. Agencies seem particularly inhibited in dealing with this most difficult situation because both young people are likely to be 'looked-after'. This adds a layer of complexity not found when the abuser is outwith the 'looked after' system. Child protection policy is usually designed in the assumption that the agency has no direct responsibility for the abuser. In this case, they usually do. The role of care planning and careful placement decision making in these situations has been described above. It is essential that agencies give serious thought in general terms to what their position will be in these cases. We have heard of cases such as one where an allegation had occurred between children placed by different authorities in the same independently run children's home. The subsequent case conference resembled a tug-o-war between the fieldworkers from the two authorities, each trying to put pressure on the independent provider to prioritise the care needs of their child. That such issues should be left to individual practitioners — field and residential — to wrestle with in a vacuum, without pre-thinking and definition of good practice by their agencies, is asking for trouble. Agencies need to provide guidelines in anticipation of these allegations arising with reasonable regularity, not once in a blue moon.

These are some of the difficult areas to be faced. They should in the first instance be faced by management, who, in consultation with their staff, should draw up policy and guidance on how to handle such tricky issues. It is not acceptable that staff in the front line are left with the burden of trying to devise policy 'on the hoof'.

Exploring the Potential of Residential Care as a Treatment Resource for Young People who Sexually Abuse

There are enormous difficulties around the practice of working with abused and abusers in the one residential establishment. Abusers have the same basic needs for care and attention as those abused and have often been abused themselves. There is, however, a difficulty in protecting others from them and in dealing with abusive behaviour, which requires different skills and possibly staffing and a different focus.

(a residential manager)

...there is a need within the continuum of care for the establishment of more specialist residential treatment facilities for children and young people who have abused other children...

(NCH, 1992)

So far we have described the frequency with which young people who have sexually abusive patterns of behaviour enter non-specific residential care. We have considered the pressure this puts on residential staff to provide a safe caring environment, and suggested key issues which must be worked on to ensure the minimum risk is encountered. However, residential care can be exploited as a dynamic treatment resource for sexually abusive young people. At present, the main concerns surround safety in mainstream settings, against a backdrop of ignorance about the numbers of such young people already in residential care. This is natural enough, given the highly publicised abuse scandals in children's homes, but it is essentially a reactive response. In all but a few cases, the potential of residential care to be used pro-actively has not been fully explored.

This is less the case in the USA and Canada, where treatment facilities specifically for sexually abusive young people are well established. Although some have been developed in the UK, they are thin on the ground, tending to be for those already convicted of sexual offences. This may be symptomatic of different approaches to the use of residential care between the UK countries and North America. Here, there has been a movement away from seeing residential care as an intervention of choice in terms of its

potential to create change in the child. Emphasis has tended to be on placements to protect the child while work is done with the family. Indeed, the use of the term 'treatment' as a stated reason for placement is regarded with some suspicion, smacking of a medical model, or of the care system as some kind an agent of social control. Fear of a return to the philosophy of the 'reformatory' has led to 'care' becoming the primary objective rather than the sine qua non of residential work which underpins all else. The design and use of 'programmes' to induce changes in behaviour is thus not part of the thinking of most residential workers. In the USA, there is unashamed emphasis on treatment programmes, and openly stated intentions to alter the child's behaviour through residential treatment, although even there, there is concern that such provision is too scarce (Matthews, 1996). Such programmes do exist here, notably Glenthorne and Aycliffe, but on the whole there is no clear pattern of development, particularly in non-secure resources. Hird (1997) gives a good summary of the history and nature of resources in the UK.

There are arguments both for and against the development of such specialist resources. Arguments against usually take two forms. The first is the anxiety that by segregating young abusers, this inevitably focuses on their maladaptive, i.e. abusive, behaviour to the exclusion of the other aspects of their lives and personalities. Given that for each individual, there are a whole complex of issues needing attention, focus and concentration on this one issue is seen as unjustifiable, and segregation as only worsening the stigma and increasing the tendency of other young people to scapegoat those thus segregated. It is also contended, with some force, that residential staff simply do not have the skills and knowledge they require to carry out such a role effectively.

Arguments in favour are the well attested powerful effect of the residential experience in engendering profound change in individuals, by using the intense living situation of the group, mixed with skilful leadership from staff. That this is seen as an effective tool evidenced by the explosion of residential management training, using outdoor pursuits as tools, to give individuals insights into their own functioning. Specialist care, it is said, means that staff can develop the skills needed to work on the issues of abusive behaviour in a whole range of ways and in all the settings that residential life provides. This has the potential to achieve far more than weekly therapy sessions, if the young person has the good fortune to even have access to these.

Intensive approaches are necessary because early intervention has the most chance of success and attempting to alter paedophile behaviour. Once it is well established in adulthood this is extremely difficult. Calder (1997) lists six reasons for investment in early intervention, i.e. deviant behaviour patterns are less ingrained; juveniles are still experimenting with patterns of sexual satisfaction, and can still select alternatives; distorted thinking patterns are less entrenched; they can still learn new social skills; future victims can be protected; and it will save money. Charles and MacDonald (1996) put it strongly 'Timing is of the utmost importance in regard to intervention. Early intervention, as soon as the offending or intrusive behaviour has been identified, is critical in terms of treatment success'.

Intervention strategies must be varied, with well matched resources. This must include residential resources, but is not to suggest that such services stand in splendid isolation. They must be part of a complex of multi-agency work and packages of care involving a range of different professional skills and consultancy. Such was recommended by the NCH Committee of Inquiry in 1992, and its relevance has not diminished. Charles and MacDonald also make the point that '...a wide spectrum of services is required to ensure that the treatment needs of each individual can be met'. However, there is a real danger that short-sighted fiscal pressure will see residential resources as too costly to develop in specialist formats. This means that young people will still be routed into non-specialist residential care, regardless of how complex and ingrained their abusive behaviour is. The fact that this may cost more in the long term, both humanly and financially, is usually ignored.

The stigma of this particular kind of deviance is extreme, and it is therefore in the young abusers' interests, as well as those of their potential victims, for an intensive focus to be given to it, and to their whole life planning

in the light of it. This is especially the case for those who have committed and been convicted of a sexual offence. For them the prospect of mandatory reporting, and the long-term effects of this on their lives is one which they need help to plan for and cope with.

It is our view that, like it or not, there is increasing public demand for those who have shown a tendency to abuse to be separated, certainly from those who have been abused (but who have not abused others), and probably from all other young people. In addition, it is likely that residential care will become increasingly the out-of-home placement choice for such young people, given the emerging problems of caring safely for them in foster care. Thus expertise in the effective and safe residential care of them must be expanded rapidly.

By introducing such specialist units, such expertise can be developed, not least in dealing with some of the dilemmas of care described above. Practice skills thus developed can then be transferred to mainstream residential child care, where without doubt the majority of young abusers will continue to live once they are looked after by the local authority.

Thus the increased development of specialist resources appears both a natural and an inevitable progression, given the challenges to the safe care of other residents and the treatment needs of these residents. The opportunity must be grasped to explore the best possible models of care for this group, and this learning should be garnered and used to improve the care of all.

Conclusion

Living in residential care, these young people present very considerable challenges in terms of risks to safety of others, and of the need to induce change in their behaviour. We need urgently to work upon both issues. It is possible to provide safer care than at present, by facing up to the very real dilemmas residential staff face daily, and providing them with the training, support and management action that they desperately require and wish. It is also essential to explore with more determination the real potential for change that residential care can present. Residential care has a vital part to play in any discussion about the management of these young people as they will in many cases become recipients of the service, whether that is the expressed plan for them or not. As such, it is a matter of urgency that the service is resourced to do the job required of it.

References

Araji, S.K. (1997). *Sexually Aggressive Children — Coming to Understand Them*. London: Sage Publications.

Bentovim, A., and Williams, B. (1998). Children and Adolescents: Victims Who Become Perpetrators. *Advances in Psychiatric Treatment*, 4: 101–107.

Calder, M.C. (1997). *Juveniles and Children who Sexually Abuse — A Guide to Risk Assessment*. Lyme Regis, Dorset: Russell House Publishing.

Caldwell and Rejino (1993). *Ensuring that all Children and Adolescents in Residential Treatment Live in a Protected, Safe Environment*. NY: Haworth Press.

Centre for Residential Child Care (1995). *Guidance for Residential Workers Caring for Young People who Have Been Sexually Abused and Those who Abuse Others*. Glasgow: CRCC.

Department of Health, *The Children Act 1989 Guidelines*, Volume 5.

Epps, K. (1997). *Pointers to Carers*. In Calder, M.C., op cit, 99–109.

Hird, J., (1997). Working in Context. In Hoghughi, M.S. (Ed.) (1997) with Bharte, S.R., and Graham, F. *Working with Sexually Abusive Adolescents*. London: Sage.

Hoghughi, M.S. (Ed.) (1997) with Bharte, S.R., and Graham, F. *Working with Sexually Abusive Adolescents*. London: Sage.

Jones, A. (1996). *Report of the Examination Team on Child Care and Practice in North Wales*. London: HMSO.

Kendrick, A. (1997). Safeguarding Children Living Away from Home from Abuse: A Literature Review. In Kent, R. (Ed.) (1997). *Children's Safeguards Review*. Edinburgh: The Stationery Office.

Kent, R. (1997). *Children's Safeguards Review*. Edinburgh: The Stationery Office.

Lindsay, M., (1997). *The Tip of the Iceberg — Sexual Abuse in the Context of Residential Child Care*. Glasgow: CRCC.

MaCaskill, C. (1991). *Adopting and Fostering a Sexually Abused Child*. London: Batsford.

Matthews, W. (1996). The Adolescent Sex Offender Field in Canada: Old Problems, Current Issues, and Emerging Controversies. *Journal of Child and Youth Care*, 11(1).

NCH (1992). *The Report of the Committee of Inquiry into Children and Young People who Sexually Abuse Other Children*. London: National Children's Home.

Skinner, A. (1992). *Another Kind of Home — A Review of Residential Child Care*. Edinburgh: The Stationery Office.

Utting, W. (1991). *Children in the Public Care*. London: HMSO.

Utting, W., (1997). *People Like Us*. London: HMSO.

Whitaker, D., Archer, L., Hicks, L. (1994). *The Prevailing Cultures and Staff Dynamics in Children's Homes*. York: University of York.

White, K., (1987). Residential Care of Adolescents: Residents, Carers, and Sexual Issues. In Horobin, G. (Ed.). *Sex, Gender, and Care Work, Research Highlights in Social Work*, 15. London: Jessica Kingsley.

Chapter Sixteen

Adolescent Sex Offenders:

Characteristics and Treatment Effectiveness in the Republic of Ireland

Audrey Sheridan and Kieran McGrath

Adolescent Sex Offenders: Characteristics and Treatment Effectiveness in the Republic of Ireland

Introduction

This paper will describe the first systematic evaluation in the Republic of Ireland of a group of sexually abusive adolescents who attended the Northside Inter-Agency Project (NIAP), a joint venture between staff at the Children's Hospital, Temple Street, the Eastern Health Board and the Mater Hospital in Dublin between 1991 and 1996. The paper also looks at both the characteristics and treatment outcome of this group. The social context in which child sexual abuse (CSA) has been addressed in the Republic of Ireland is examined, as well as a brief look at the methodological problems associated with this type of research. Unless otherwise stated, the findings of this chapter are reported by Sheridan *et al.* (1998).

Child Sexual Abuse in the Republic of Ireland

In looking at sexual offending in the Republic of Ireland, it is essential to place it in its social context. The past thirty years have brought enormous social change. The Republic had traditionally been a country where much of its social policy was influenced by the Catholic Church. From 1960 onwards socio-economic change radically altered perspectives on issues such as women working outside the home, contraception and divorce. However, the beginnings of a new awareness of child sexual abuse came in 1983, in the form of a seminar entitled 'Incest', organised by the Irish Association of Social Workers (McKeown and Gilligan, 1991). The following year the first national statistics were collected, when 33 confirmed cases were identified from a total of 88 referrals (see Table 1 below).

Table 1: Reported and confirmed cases of child abuse 1984–1995

Year	All reports of child abuse	Reports of Sexual Abuse	Confirmed child abuse	Confirmed sexual abuse
1984	479	88	182 (37.9%)	33 (37.5%)
1985	767	34	304 (39.6%)	133 (56.8%)
1986	1015	475	495 (48.7%)	274 (57.6%)
1987	1646	926	763 (46.3%)	456 (49.2%)
1988	2673	1055	1243 (46.5%)	465 (50.2%)
1989	3252	1242	1658 (50.9%)	568 (45.7%)
1990	N/A	N/A	N/A	N/A
1991	3856	1507	1465 (37.9%)	599 (39.7%)
1992	3812	1362*	1701 (44.6%)*	587 (43.0%)*
1993	4110	1791	1609 (39.1%)	681 (38.0%)
1994	5152	1816	1868 (36.2%)	557 (30.6%)
1995	6415	2441	2276 (35.4%)	765 (31.3%)

(* Figures for one health board on child sexual abuse not available - included in overall total.)
(Source: Department of Health)

The mid 1980s saw a huge upsurge in suspected cases, and by 1987 the number of cases reported to health boards had risen to 926. This led to the publication of new child abuse guidelines which, for the first time, specifically addressed the issue of child sexual abuse (Department of Health, 1987).

It had traditionally been the case, as Gilligan (1991) has remarked, that 'child-centred provision in public policy in Ireland is more the exception that the rule' (p 225). However, in the 1990s the care of vulnerable children was to become a highly charged political issue (Ferguson, 1995). The case that started this process, more than any other, was the so called 'X-Case' in 1992. This involved a 14 year old pregnant rape victim, who was prevented from leaving the country, to obtain an abortion in the UK, by a High Court injunction initiated by the Attorney General. In doing so the court was interpreting Article 41:3:3 of the Irish Constitution (on the right to life of the unborn child) in a way that had never been anticipated. The idea that the forces of the state could be brought to bear on a teenage victim of rape, in such circumstances, shocked the whole country. This led to unprecedented political controversy, both in Ireland and internationally. The social effects of all this have been long-lasting. This case was hugely significant in changing many people's attitudes, not just to social reform in general, but specifically towards child abuse. It brought home to the whole population that child sexual abuse really did exist and that the law was a very blunt instrument for dealing with it.

One of the by-products of this widespread social upheaval has been that it has created room for a deeper examination of the position of vulnerable children in society generally. This was long overdue. Even with massive social change from the 1960s onwards child care still had a very long way to go to become a high-profile issue.

Since 1992, there has been a series of child abuse scandals, followed by official inquiries and a raft of policy changes in the area of child protection. There has also been a steady flow of cases involving sexual abuse by priests and members of religious orders, which has seen over 30 of them being imprisoned.

If proof was needed that child maltreatment had become a major political issue it can be found in the fact the mishandling of the extradition to Northern Ireland, of a priest who had molested many children in both parts of Ireland, led to the fall of the government led by Albert Reynolds in 1994 (McGrath, 1996b).

Structural Responses to Sexual Offending

With regard to the treatment of sex offenders in Ireland, this was recommended by a number of child abuse inquiry reports, (see, for example, Department of Health, 1996; McGuinness, 1993). However, policy development 'has been cautious, fragmented and incremental' (Geiran, 1996, p 151). The huge rise in cases of sexual offending being prosecuted has led to a sharp increase in the number of men being imprisoned for such crimes. They now constitute approximately 10 per cent of the entire prison population (Murphy, 1998). Two community-based treatment projects for adults emerged in the Central Mental Hospital, Dublin, and one in the North Western Health Board (Travers, 1998) as well as one prison-based project in Arbour Hill Prison, Dublin. There are now four community-based treatment programmes aimed at adolescent sex offenders, two in Dublin: Northside Inter-agency Project and the Southside Inter-agency Treatment Service, as well as a project based in Drogheda, run by the North Eastern Health Board, and one in Galway run by the Western Health Board.

Legal changes

The first serious review of child sexual abuse in Ireland occurred in 1990 with the publication of a report by the Law Reform Commission (1990). This recommended many changes, some of which were incorporated into the 1992 Criminal Evidence Act, which, for example, allowed children to give evidence in sexual abuse cases via video link. Sentences for sexual offences have been increased. For example, following the controversy over the Kilkenny Incest Case (McGuinness, 1993), incest was reclassified as a felony rather than a misdemeanour. Further reforms are envisaged following the recent publication of a discussion document on sexual offences (Department of Justice, Equality and Law Reform, 1998) which sought responses on a wide variety of topics including legal changes, the treatment of offenders, sex offender registers and electronic tagging. Another recent initiative is a European Research Project under the DAPHNE Initiative which will examine, among other issues, legal obstacles to the rehabilitation of sex offenders in three EU countries, Spain, the Netherlands and Ireland (Samper-Ramos, 1998).

Introduction to the study

The Northside Inter-agency Project (NIAP) was the first of the treatment programmes for adolescents to be established in the Republic of Ireland. It is a small community-based therapeutic programme providing weekly outpatient cognitive and behavioural therapy to groups of sexually abusive adolescents (Bruen, 1994). Five years after the group was first established, all of the youths who attended for therapy (thirty in total at that point in time) were invited to return to participate in a review and of this number, twenty-two youths returned voluntarily. Although methodologically flawed due to the absence of an untreated control group, this study was a first of its kind in Ireland. We looked at treatment outcome and characteristics of the adolescents in the following ways:

- Through behavioural indicators.
- Through self report of re-offending, and
- Through seeking the views of the treating therapists.

What are the characteristics of sexually abusive adolescents?

Adolescents who sexually offend not only merit intervention from the point of the damage they can do, but also as we shall see in this study (pp 286–7) from the evidence of the difficulties that they experience in their own right. According to Camp and Thyer, (1993), 'the magnitude and significance of the myriad problems associated with these youths has not been fully recognised or appreciated'. One example of findings from studies which investigate such difficulties is Ryan, Myoshi, Metzner, Krugman and Fryer's (1996) study which collected data from 90 service providers in 30 states in USA who provided information on over sixteen hundred adolescents within

their services. The results found that sexually abusive youths were themselves often victims of physical and sexual abuse, neglect and many had experienced loss of a parental figure through marital breakdown, bereavement or through abandonment or neglect. This study also found that though the youths had experienced 'reasonable academic success', a large number (60%), 'were known to have truancy, learning disabilities and/or behaviour problems at school. Only 28% were reported as having no record of problems at school.' (p 18). Ryan *et al.* reported that many of the youth experienced abuse or neglect themselves and cited a range of traumatic experiences which the youngsters who sexually offended had been subject to in their young lives. These were; physical abuse (41.8%), sexual abuse (39.1%), neglect (25.9%) and domestic violence in the family home (63.4%). Clinical impressions on 774 of the youth was obtained and in most cases, the therapists and evaluators considered that the youths were 'treatable' (72%) despite the youths at times being seen as having low motivation to participate in treatment.

Does treatment work?

When therapists provide therapy for either adult or juvenile sex offenders, they rarely expect a cure, but hope for sufficient changes to occur either within the person themselves or within the environment in which they live or both, to reduce the probability of re-offending. It is well documented that adolescents do great harm and perpetrate approximately one third of all sexual offences against children, (Fehrenbach, Smith, Monastersky and Deisher, 1986; Kennedy and Manwell, 1992; McKeown and Gilligan, 1991; Vizard, Monck and Misch, 1995). Bremer (1992) comments that 'given the potential pool of adult sex offenders these juveniles represent, it is a social imperative to intervene' (p 327). Martin Calder (1997a; 1997b) has extensively reviewed the statistics and looked at the consequences of failing to intervene early with this group. Myers (1998) and Leheup and Myers (Chapter 9) have challenged the selectiveness of these figures and offered a new viewpoint. Some of the reasons that treatment may be more effective with adolescents are that they are still in a developmental and transitional stage, where sexual patterns may be less fixed, family support may be available and where positive changes within the family system may still have influence.

Measuring whether or not treatment is effective can be beset by difficulties. Camp and Thyer (1993) note that 'research on the effective treatment of adolescent sex offenders is still in its infancy' (p 200). They point to the limitations of each of the standard ways of evaluating treatment change, such as recidivism, self-report, and questionnaire measures. It is a real dilemma for clinicians if they have a belief in the value of therapy yet cannot argue for resources for services due to a lack of convincing data on the potential efficacy of their approach. Barbaree (1996) cautions against both pessimism and optimism and argues that these are equally dangerous perspectives when looking at treatment outcome. He cautions against a Type 1 error (of concluding that treatment works, when in fact it doesn't) and against a Type 2 error (of concluding that treatment does not work, when in fact it does). The challenge for therapists and researchers is 'to take a balance between these two types of error, while maintaining scientific rigour' (1996 ATSA Conference).

Some of the difficulties reported by commentators on treatment outcome are:

Low base rates. It is easier to prove that an intervention is effective if the behaviour occurs frequently. Sexual offending, while common, occurs rarely and intermittently, consequently it is more difficult to demonstrate a 'treatment effect' (Barbaree, 1996; Hall, 1995).

Denial and concealment of re-offending. By its nature, sexual offending is illegal, secretive and taboo. Perpetrators often go to great lengths to remain undetected. It is possible that this seriously hinders estimates of the incidence of offending and re-offending.

Re-arrest rates. Many studies focus on re-arrest rates as a measure of whether or not treatment was effective. It is known that the majority of sexual offences remain undetected (Elliot, Huizinga and Morse, 1985) and re-arrest rates are likely to considerably under-represent the incidence of re-offending and possibly exaggerate the effect of treatment in the process.

Follow-up periods are too short. Some studies have shown that untreated sex offenders can remain at risk of reoffending for over 20 years (Hanson, Steffy and Gauthier, 1993) with some serious sexual offenders reconvicted between 10 and 31 years after their release. Marshall and Eccles (1991) note that many studies have follow-up periods which are far too short to reveal effectiveness of treatment.

Questionnaire measures. These are often used before and after a programme of treatment to examine attitudes potentially correlated with abusive behaviour. While useful, it is possible that an experienced attendee at group will spot the 'correct' answer, giving a response bias (e.g. Stermac *et al.*, 1990).

Length of time at risk (LAR). The longer an offender is discharged from treatment, the greater opportunity he has to recidivate/re-offend. When follow-up studies take a short time between treatment and follow up, there is less opportunity to show that treatment has been effective. Where studies have follow-up intervals of over five years, the possibility of showing a significant treatment effect is greater (Hall, 1995).

Risk of re-offending. Some offenders are of much higher risk of re-offending than others. The key factors associated with higher rates of recidivism are; severity of sexual assault, violence used, marital relationships or their absence, relationship (or its absence) to victim, criminal histories, male psychopathy, disinhibition through impulsivity or alcohol use, fewer environmental supports, fewer social supports, repeated sexual crimes and multiple forms of sexual assaults or crimes, personal histories of caregiver inconstancy and institutional placement (Becker and Hunter, 1993; McGrath, 1991).

Programmes. Not all programmes have sexual offenders with similar levels of severity of abusive histories and relative levels of risk. Community samples tend to have fewer high-risk offenders as these may have already been incarcerated. It is difficult to compare the effectiveness of a programme of treatment in an institution with one in the community by virtue of the clients they serve and the nature of the programme (Scott-Fordham, 1993). In this sense, it is often confusing to interpret the information on treatment outcome from various programmes of therapy as they may vary in the kind of offender presented.

Variables. Programmes in themselves have differing components, duration, models of therapy, and treating therapists. Within a programme, therapists may have different levels of experience and support (Scott-Fordham, 1993), empathy and motivation. Research reports rarely examine these variables in their evaluation of treatment outcomes.

Programmes of treatment for adolescent sexual offenders show a range of outcomes of therapy. It must be borne in mind that the follow-up periods for these youths is often short rather than long term. Some programmes which have reported recidivism data are:

- Borduin *et al.*'s study, (1990) showed that with just 16 cases yielded multi-systemic therapy recidivism rates of 12.5% after an average length at risk (LAR) of 37 months compared with individual therapy which had recidivism rates of 75%.

- Schram *et al.* (1991) reported that 10% of their 197 adolescents re-offended sexually over an average LAR of 6.8 years. In a residential treatment programme, Bremer (1992) found that 6% had re-offended with LAR between six months and eight and a half years. However, when she sought to ask the youths confidentially, almost twice that number reported they had re-offended, (11%).

- Kahn and Chambers (1991) found that with 221 adolescent sex offenders during a 6-month period follow-up, that 7.5% had re-offended.

- Fehrenbach *et al.* (1986) followed 223 adolescents over 12 months and found that 7% had committed another sex offence.

- Knopp (1982) found that of 80 juveniles attending programmes, that 5% had re-offended.

Until this study, on which this chapter is based, was published in 1998 by Sheridan *et al.*, there was no information available on therapeutic outcomes with sexually abusive adolescents in Ireland. Travers (1998) notes that of attenders at their treatment programme for adult incest offenders in a rural community, 3% had re-offended, though the total number who received treatment is not mentioned.

Encouraged by Bremer's (1992) assertion that 'recidivism (conviction post-treatment) alone cannot be prima facie evidence of success' (p 327), we chose to include an anonymous self report as part of the present study on the youths who attended NIAP.

Method

The present study addresses two broad questions: (1) what are the characteristics of adolescents who present for treatment for sexually abusive behaviour in an Irish context, and (2) how effective is treatment for the youth in question? A parallel study was conducted simultaneously by a research assistant (O'Reilly, 1996) who examined the characteristics of the youths who attended treatment compared with a community sample of youths matched for age and demographics. (The comparison of treated with untreated sexually abusive youth has yet to be undertaken in an Irish context.)

The areas investigated were as follows:

1. Interview with the adolescent.

2. Clinician consultation A, historical and familial factors.

3. Clinician consultation B, response to treatment.

4. Self -report of sexual re-offending.

5. Parallel characteristics study.

1. Interview with adolescent

We attempted to address the emotional and situational precursors to sexual offending with reference to the well known 'Four Factor Theory' of Finkelhor (1984). These include: emotional factors, removal of internal barriers to offending, removal of external barriers such as access to victims and babysitting. Each adolescent was interviewed about their lifestyles, and about the possible risks he might be taking which may place him at risk of re-offending sexually.

2. Clinician consultation A — historical and familial factors

The treating therapists filled out a questionnaire covering historical and familial information (adapted from McKeown's 1988 census questionnaire), covering the young offender's personal and family histories including his sexual offences.

3. Clinician consultation B — response to treatment

The treating therapists also completed questionnaires covering:

- Family support.
- Completion of steps of the programme (adapted from Smets and Cebula, 1988).
- Difficulties encountered during treatment.
- Impressions of clinical change.

4. Self-report of sexual re-offending

Each youth was asked to fill out a simple 'yes/no' questionnaire while alone and then to place the uncoded sheet of paper into a sealed, unmarked envelope.

5. Parallel characteristics study

O'Reilly undertook the sourcing of materials across a range of key issues and compared the NIAP youths with a community sample matched for age and socio-economic status, (O'Reilly, 1996; O'Reilly *et al.*, 1998). Some of the key areas investigated by him are reported in this paper.

Characteristics of the Youths and their Families.

- The youths in the sample and their families were heavy users of social services prior to the disclosure of sexual abuse by the youth in question. In 18% of cases, prior to disclosure, the youth and or their family had attended a Child Sexual Abuse Assessment Unit. In 41% of cases, the youth or his family had attended the local Child Guidance Clinic. In 42% of cases, the family were known to Community Care Services. Together, a majority had attended assessment or therapeutic services in the past (59%) though 41% of families' first contact with the services was in relation to their son's sexually abusive behaviour.

- Parental separation and loss of a parent was common among the families of the

youths in the sample (41% and 9% respectively). In some cases, significantly acrimonious marital relationships existed in the families where parents remained together. A few families (9%) had no obvious problems prior to their son's sexual offences coming to light.

- In their commission of sexual offences, the 22 youths in the sample abused 40 victims, mostly female (78%) with approximately one in four victims male (23%). The victims ranged in age from one year to adolescence, mostly coming from within the youth's own family, (over half of the victims were abused by brothers or step-brothers). The number of times the sexual abuse took place ranged from once to fifty times, with an average of eleven sexually abusive incidents per child. The full range of sexual behaviours was evident in this sample of abusive adolescents, ranging from exposing themselves to violent sexual intercourse and all types of sexual contact in between these extremes. In over forty percent of cases the adolescent attempted sexual intercourse with their victim. In over a quarter of cases (27%) the adolescent used physical violence and/or the threat thereof as part of the sexual abuse. The age of first known sexual offence was typically aged fourteen for this sample but ranged from eleven years upwards. Many of the youths engaged in sexual offending during a time when they were baby-sitting (68%).

- Many of the youths experienced adverse life circumstances themselves. Most of them were considered to have been emotionally abused prior to coming to treatment (86%). Many had experienced physical abuse in the past (64%). Approximately a quarter experienced sexual abuse (23%). While attending the programme, just over a quarter of the youths (27%) lived away from their families in either residential units or foster homes. Although most of the youths were living with their parents when they came to the programme (73%) almost half had lived away from home at some point.

- Aside from sexually abusive behaviour, the youths presented with a range of difficulty in other areas. In therapy, those which presented most commonly were; anger management (37% of sample), conflict with significant others (50%), depression (23%), impulsivity (23%), hostility within family (29%), low intellectual functioning (19%). In comparison with a community sample, these youths had significantly more physical abuse in their histories (p<0.01), had greater behaviour difficulty in school resulting in expulsion, (p<0.01), and were more likely to have parents who were separated, (p<0.5), (O'Reilly *et al.*, 1998).

- All of the sexual offences were reported to the Garda (police). In a large proportion of the cases (68%), referral was made to the Director of Public Prosecutions. In only one case was the decision taken by the DPP to prosecute (5%). Approximately half of the youths were known to have been visited by the Garda Juvenile Liaison Officer (JLO). Not all of the youths had access to JLO services however. Some parents were reluctant to bring charges against their sons. The one youth who was referred to the courts by the DPP, a sentence was passed of 18 months imprisonment.

Effectiveness of Treatment

We will discuss treatment effectiveness from the following vantage points:

- Levels of relative risk of re-offending post-treatment.
- Completion of steps of the therapeutic programme.
- Clinical impressions of therapeutic outcome.
- Behaviour and lifestyle post-treatment.
- Familial support during treatment.
- Incidence of re-offending.

Levels of relative risk of re-offending post-treatment

Assessment of risk of re-offending sexually was made as a team decision by all of the NIAP members using the protocol in Table 2

(O'Reilly, 1996). The breakdown of relative risk was as follows:

14	(64%)	low risk
6	(27%)	high risk
2	(9%)	unknown risk.

When analysed statistically, O'Reilly (1998) found that these youths tended to have a greater range of psychological difficulties (depression, anxiety, internalising and externalising problems, somatic complaints, aggressiveness, self-destructiveness and withdrawal). They experienced less social support and their self-esteem was less robust. Family relationships were characterised by poorer quality attachment and greater family dysfunction. This information reflects the assessment of the clinicians.

Completion of steps of the programme

Most of the youths co-operated well with treatment (87%), acknowledged that they had sexually offended (77%), with just under a quarter being reluctant participants in the therapeutic process. A large portion (72%), were seen as attaining some degree of victim empathy during treatment, though fewer were able to identify their own thinking errors, with a substantial 41% seen as having difficulty in this area. 68–73% of the youths were able to develop and implement a relapse prevention plan at the end of therapy. Table 3 below sets out the full findings.

Clinician's impressions of therapeutic outcome

In 91% of cases, the clinicians indicated that clinical change had occurred during the course of therapy, with just two youngsters who had dropped out of treatment seen as not having demonstrated clinical change. The clinicians observed increases in insight, victim empathy, ability to express feelings, social skills, greater control of problems and improvements in self-esteem. Greater insight was more commonly indicated for the youths in the low risk group, (86%) compared with the high-risk group (25%). Table 4 sets out in detail the potentially risky behaviours of youths, post-treatment.

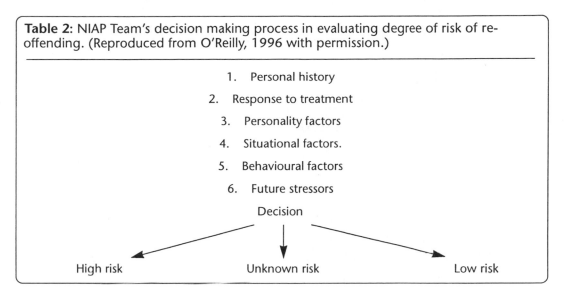

Table 2: NIAP Team's decision making process in evaluating degree of risk of re-offending. (Reproduced from O'Reilly, 1996 with permission.)

1. Personal history
2. Response to treatment
3. Personality factors
4. Situational factors.
5. Behavioural factors
6. Future stressors

Decision

High risk   Unknown risk   Low risk

Table 3: Completion of Steps of the Programme, NIAP, Dublin, 1991–1996. Devised and adapted from Smets and Cebula's (1987) Programme.

	Poor/ Very Poor	Fair, Good or Very Good
Willingness to co-operate with programme of therapy	13%	87%
Participation in group	23%	77%
Taking responsibility for abusive behaviour	23%	77%
Taking responsibility for actions in everyday situations	41%	59%
Development of victim empathy and awareness	28%	72%
Ability to identify his own thinking errors	41%	59%
Ability to identify the thinking errors of others	41%	59%
Ability to identify and describe his own cycle of abuse	32%	68%
Understanding of sexuality both positive and negative aspects	32%	68%
Development of relapse prevention plan in relation to the abuse	27%	73%
Ability to take positive action in risky* situations (*i.e. risk of re-offending)	32%	68%

Table 4: Potentially risky behaviour of youth post - treatment, NIAP, Dublin, 1991–1996

Emotional Blockages	% (N=22)
Discontent with job or schooling	23%
No involvement in steady relationship (Duration less than 1 month)	57%
Unhappy with relationship with potential partner(s)	14%
Daily conflict with family	14%
Weekly conflict in other relationships	19%
Feelings of depression (frequently)	0%
Feelings of depression (occasionally)	43%
Feelings of anger (frequently)	14%
Feelings of anger (occasionally)	43%
Feeling as if could seriously hurt or kill someone, (frequently)	5%
Feeling as if could seriously hurt or kill someone, (occasionally)	23%
Disinhibition of conscience/increase of deviant arousal	
Preference for younger sexual partners	0%
Occasional viewing of 'blue movies'	23%
Occasional viewing of 'sexy' magazines	33%
Ever drunk or high while viewing pornography	19%
Use of sex lines since treatment	5%
Thoughts about sexual contact with victim	9%
Engaged in prostitution	0%
'Drunk' on weekly basis	33%
'High' on weekly basis	27%
Access to victim/potential victims	
Babysitting/childminding	27%
Babysitting victim	14%
Impending parenthood	14%

(Reproduced from Sheridan *et al.*, 1998).

Behaviour and lifestyle risks of re-offending

Emotional factors

While most of the youths reported satisfactory work, family and heterosexual relationships, a significant proportion continued to experience some emotional difficulties after treatment. The most frequent were occasional feelings of depression (43%), anger (43%) and rage (23%). The most frequently occurring risk was lack of involvement with steady relationship (57%). However, it is probable that this indicator should be applicable only to adults as developmentally, the younger teenagers in the sample would not be expected to have formed exclusive relationships at their age. Fourteen per cent of the sample argued with their family on a daily basis mostly with their parents. While conflict with family is a normal and common experience for adolescents generally, daily conflict for youths who are emotionally vulnerable is a source of ongoing emotional stress.

Behavioural factors

Few of the youths appeared to have the 'drifting' lifestyles that Marshall and Eccles (1991) refer to, whilst 77% were gainfully occupied and happy with their daily activity. While most reported that they did not use pornography or become intoxicated regularly, between one quarter and one third did engage in these activities. Two youths admitted to having sexual fantasies about their victims.

Situational factors

Most of the sexual abuse occurred within the youngster's own family (74%), so frequent contact with their victim is unsurprising for the youths in this sample. Some 45% continued to have daily contact with their victims and a further 14% had weekly contact. However, 27% of the sample had babysat or minded children since attending treatment and 14% had babysat their victim. A further 14% were due to become parents and were expecting their first child. These findings highlight the practicalities of follow-up in a very real manner. The youths we see in treatment will get on with their lives

regardless. The question is how do we ensure that those who need supervision and ongoing therapy remain connected to services? One or two of the youths who returned were still defensive about their sexual offending and had families who did not support treatment. If such youths are in roles of baby   sittin cause for alarm. Others really did consider themselves to have moved on in their lives. Several of the youths who returned to participate in this research reported that they had been doing well in their relationships and were getting on with their families and to some extent had left the idea of themselves as an abuser behind them. Coming in again to NIAP they said, brought back the pain of how difficult it was when the abuse came to light both for them and for their families.

Familial support

Many of the boys' families had numerous stressful life experiences to cope with. Despite this, the parents impressed as extremely supportive of their son's attendance at therapy, although at a practical level, it was sometimes more difficult for them to follow through on that support. The clinicians reported the following findings (see Table 5).

One part of the decision about risk of re-offending is dependent on the support the youth receives during treatment from his family which may not only place effective controls on his behaviour but will also help him to integrate the effects of treatment. However family support alone is insufficient, as a supportive family may still have an impulse ridden youngster who remains at high risk of re-offending despite their best efforts.

Incidence of re-offending

None of the twenty-two youths who were the subject of this study reported that they had sexually re-offended since attending treatment. However 44 youths have attended for treatment and one is known to have re-offended (McGrath, 1998) (see Table 6 for details).

Table 5: Familial support for treatment, NIAP, Dublin, 1991–1996

Parents availed of group therapy (one or both).	78%
Parents were in agreement with attendance at therapy.	91%
Parents strongly encouraged son to attend.	59%
Parents were able to take positive action in relation to son's behaviour.	68%
Parents did not deny or minimise sexual abuse.	50%
Parents gained an understanding of factors which influenced son's sexual behaviour.	64%
Parents learned to help young person implement relapse prevention plan.	64%

Table 6: Incidence of re-offending NIAP, Dublin, 1991–98

Year	No.	Re-offended (%)
1996	22	0 (0%)
1998	44	1 (2%)

Summary

The youths in the sample come from a range of social backgrounds, but more typically from middle to lower socio-economic groupings. Some of the youths did well in treatment, responding to the steps in treatment well and achieving each stage. Others struggled through treatment, were inconsistent attenders and less well attached to the process of therapy. The challenge to provide therapy for these youths involves catering for such diversity within each therapeutic group.

The life experiences of these youths are harsher, with somewhat less emotional involvement from others, and with significant family background stresses. The youths in this sample were more likely than the average adolescent to have experienced parental loss, physical violence, have school and reading difficulties as well as behaviour difficulties by their own report, and in this way are more likely to be marginalised at school than their peers. Their self-esteem scores are somewhat lower and they perform more poorly on tests of verbal reasoning, (O'Reilly, 1996).

We found the youths in this sample remarkably open about their current lifestyles and acknowledging feelings of depression and anger at times, reporting some conflict in their relationships, especially with parents. While most reported things were going well, there was a small proportion who experienced severe problems with anger, who were likely to get drunk and disorderly and who sometimes felt like hurting others. These youths are probably more likely to get into trouble of various kinds. The different possible triggers which are postulated to decrease inhibitions to abuse were examined. Whilst only two youths admitted to fantasising about their victims post-treatment, it is possible that more actually engaged in this activity. A large proportion of the youths in this sample engage in alcohol or drug use. A few use pornography. While this is interesting information, it does not really tell us which youth had a problem with which kinds of activity. In order for this information to be really useful, we would need to know which youths were engaging in which behaviour and under which circumstances.

It is to be expected that the youths in this sample continue to see their victims as they are siblings or step-siblings in many cases, and parents have given commitments to keeping their children safe. It is of concern though that we find abusive youths babysitting, regardless of how well they have progressed in therapy.

If these youth have not done well in therapy, this is of even greater concern.

Let us look at treatment effectiveness from the various perspectives. The clinicians assessment considered that many of the youths completed the steps of the programme well, with 87% seen as compliant with treatment, 77% participating well, taking responsibility for their behaviour well, and 72% developing good victim empathy. Over two-thirds were able to identify and describe their cycles of abuse, understand their sexuality, develop and implement a relapse prevention plan at the end of treatment. Parental support for treatment could be argued as a therapeutic outcome and looking at this aspect, 68% were considered to be able to influence their son's behaviour.

These youths still engaged in anti-social behaviour which in some areas was no different from their peers. Their history of sexual offending means they should be more cautious about their behaviour but, in all likelihood, are probably less likely to be careful. They were still likely to have rows with their parents, (arguably this is developmentally normal), they still saw their victims in many cases, and one in four had babysat. More than half (57%) said they had few emotional problems now and most were gainfully occupied by school or employment. In total, these youths still took an average of seven risks each which their therapists would not recommend. In an anonymous self-report survey none said they had re-offended sexually since treatment.

Perhaps one interpretation which helps to make sense of this data is that youths who are considered of 'high risk' and youths who are considered 'low risk' of re-offending do engage in a variety of behaviours which are seen as risky, but the relative meaning of these behaviours for any given youth may be unique. Indeed, many of these youths continue to engage in a range of behaviours which may place them at risk of sexually re-offending. However, the key to identifying who is most at risk combines behavioural, historical and clinical judgements for each individual. Clearly some risky behaviours have greater significance for some youths than for others and some behaviours are much more intrinsically risky than others. 'Drunk, babysitting and watching blue movies' may be of far greater significance for a youth as far as

re-offending is concerned than getting high on drugs in the company of his peers.

There are advantages and disadvantages to each of the ways in which we addressed assessing therapeutic outcome in this study. The most clear-cut and most commonly used measure is self-report of re-offending, although this may suffer a sample bias (only those who have not re-offended return) or else a response bias, (those who did re-offend will not admit). Clinical impression is a little used measure in treatment outcome studies, with a few exceptions as the data is 'soft' rather than 'hard'. However, the richness of clinical information from skilled therapists who know the boys intimately is invaluable and while it may be subject to methodological problems from a research point of view, it is highly useful clinical material especially when combined with harder data such as recidivism or re-offence rates.

Looking at the behaviour of the youths post-treatment is an unusual and informative way of gathering information about their lives post-treatment. It is inferential and very 'soft' as far as data is concerned, but fleshes out the practical and problematic aspects of follow-up in a very real way.

In this case, the question is 'how can youths be monitored and supervised on an ongoing basis after treatment in a way that maintains the safety of victims and potential victims in the absence of a legal mandate for therapy?' A further question arises; 'how can developmental stages through which the youth will pass at some stage after treatment, be supported so that he can negotiate these safely'. An example from this study is the impending parenthood of three of the adolescents. At the present time, once the youths have completed therapy, there is limited recourse to keep them connected to services.

Conclusion: Looking to the Future

The need to provide more and better treatment services to adolescent sex offenders is likely to become more evident in the coming years. In the USA specialist agencies and practitioners assess sexually abusive youths at the request of the courts and the youth is sent for community, residential or other treatment. There is no equivalent to this kind of disposition planning in Ireland. Sheerin (1998) argues that Irish Law can be stretched to mandate sex offenders to attend for treatment but that as yet, this rarely if ever happens.

Research into these issues is, as Camp and Thyer (1993) have pointed out 'in its infancy' and much work will be required in the future. The present study has identified some of the key issues in relation to the characteristics of, and the effectiveness of therapy with, a small group of Irish adolescent sex offenders. Many more questions remain about the futures of these young men, especially their behaviour in relationships as husbands, partners, fathers and neighbours. Of the 22 youths interviewed in this study, three were already expectant fathers, emphasising how quickly these very practical questions arise.

The attitudes of professionals are crucially important whether their focus is clinical or research oriented. McGrath (1996b) comments that 'in the caring professions we are obliged to take an optimistic and understanding view'. A realistic view of adolescence, he argues, responds to their need for care and protection as well as the awareness of their potentially abusive behaviour and the need to safeguard those at risk from adolescents. The difficulties of measuring the effectiveness of therapy with adolescent sex offenders would not be underestimated. It is incumbent, however, on clinicians and researchers to continue to find ways to obtain data that can make preventative work with this group more effective. In the Republic of Ireland this emerging field will benefit from more and better research in the interests of future generations of children and adolescents.

References

Barbaree, H.E. (1996). *Evaluating the Efficacy of Sex Offender Treatment; Realistic and Constructive Alternatives to Optimism and Pessimism.* Presentation to Association for the Treatment of Sexual Abusers (ATSA) Conference, Chicago, IL, November.

Becker, J., and Hunter, J. (1993). Aggressive Sex Offenders. *Sexual and Gender Identity Disorders*, 2(3): 477–487.

Borduin, C., Hennggeller, S., Blaske, D., and Stein, R. (1990). The Multisystemic Treatment of Adolescent Sex Offenders. *International Journal of Offender Therapy and Comparative Criminology*, 34: 105–113.

Bremer, J., (1992). Serious Juvenile Sex Offenders: Treatment and Long Term Follow-Up. *Psychiatric Annals*, 22(6): 326–332.

Bruen, S. (1994). *Juvenile Sex Offenders: Issues for Treatment and for Therapists.* Unpublished MSW dissertation, University College, Cork.

Calder, M.C. (1997a). *Juveniles and Children who Sexually Abuse: A Guide to Risk Assessment.* Lyme Regis, Dorset: Russell House Publishing.

Calder, M.C. (1997b). Young People who Sexually Abuse: Towards International Consensus? *Social Work in Europe*, 4(1): 36–39.

Camp, B., and Thyer, B. (1993). Treatment of Adolescent Sex Offenders: A Review of Empirical Research. *The Journal of Applied Sciences*, 17(2): 191–206.

Davis, G.E., and Leitenberg, H. (1987). Adolescent Sex Offenders. *Psychological Bulletin*, 101: 417–427.

Department of Health (1987). *Child Abuse Guidelines — Guidelines for the Identification, Investigation and Management of Child Abuse.* Dublin: Stationery Office.

Department of Health (1996). *Report on the Inquiry into the Operation of Madonna House.* Dublin: Government Publications.

Department of Justice, Equality and Law Reform (1998). *The Law on Sexual Offences: A Discussion Paper.* Dublin: The Stationery Office.

Elliot, D.S., Huizinga, D., and Morse, B. (1985). *The Dynamics of Deviant Behaviour; A National Survey Progress Report.* Boulder, Colorado: Behavioural Research Institute.

Fehrenbach, P.A., Smith, W., Monastersky, C., and Deisher, R.W. (1986). Adolescent Sex Offenders: Offender and Offence Characteristics. *American Journal of Orthopsychiatry*, 56: 225–233.

Ferguson, H. (1995). Child Welfare, Child Protection and the Child Care Act 1991: Key Issues for Policy and Practice. In Ferguson, H., and Kenny, P. (Eds.). *On Behalf of the Child: Child Welfare, Child Protection and the Child Care Act 1991.* Dublin: A&A Farmer.

Finkelhor, D. (1984). *Child Sexual Abuse: New Theory and Research.* New York: Free Press.

Geiran, V. (1996). Treatment of Sex Offenders in Ireland — The Development of Policy and Practice. *Administration*, 44(2): 136–158.

Gilligan, R. (1991). *Irish Child Care Services — Policy, Practice and Provision.* Dublin: Institute of Public Administration.

Hall, G. (1995). Sexual Offender Recidivism Revisited: A Meta-analysis of Recent Treatment S of Consulting and Clinical Psychology, 3(5): 802–809.

Hanson, R.K., Steffy, R.A., and Gauthier, R. (1993). Long-term Recidivism of Child Molesters. *Journal of Consulting and Clinical Psychology*, 61: 646–652.

Kahn, T.J., and Chambers, H.J. (1991). Assessing Reoffense Risk with Juvenile Sex Offenders. *Child Welfare*, 70.

Kennedy, M., and Manwell, M. (1992). The Pattern of Child Sexual Abuse in Northern Ireland. *Child Abuse Review*, 1: 89–101.

Knopp, F.H. (1982). *Remedial Intervention in Adolescent Sex Offenses: Nine Program Descriptions.* Syracuse, NY: Safer Society Press.

Law Reform Commission (1990). *Child Sexual Abuse. Report No 32.* Dublin: The Law Reform Commission.

McGrath, K. (1996a). Intervening in Child Sexual Abuse in Ireland: Towards Victim-centred Policies and Practices. *Administration,* 44(2): 57–71.

McGrath, K. (1996b). *Treating Adolescents who Abuse Within the Family.* Proceedings of the International Conference 'Violence in the Family' Amsterdam, 13–15 Oct, 1996.

McGrath, K. (1998). Sex Abuse Policies Must Focus on Reality. *The Irish Times,* 31.1.'98

McGrath, R. (1991). Sex Offender Risk Assessment and Disposition Planning. *International Journal of Offender Therapy and Comparative Criminology,* 35(4): 329–356.

McGuinness, C. (1993). *Report of the Kilkenny Incest Investigation.* Dublin: Stationery Office.

McKeown, K. (1993). *Child Sexual Abuse in the Eastern Health Board Region of Ireland in 1988.* Dublin: Eastern Health Board.

McKeown, K., and Gilligan, R. (1991). Child Sexual Abuse in the Eastern Health Board Region of Ireland in 1988: An Analysis of 512 Confirmed Cases. *Economic and Social Review,* 22(2): 101–134.

Marshall, W.L., and Eccles, A. (1991). Issues in Clinical Practice with Sex Offenders. *Journal of Interpersonal Violence,* 6(1): 68–93.

Murphy (1998). *Treating Sex Offenders.* Unpublished paper given to Irish Penal Reform Seminar, Dublin (November).

Myers, S. (1998). Young People who Sexually Abuse: Is Consensus Possible or Desirable? *Social Work in Europe,* 5(1): 53–56.

O'Reilly, G. (1996). *A Psychological Investigation of the Characteristics of Adolescent Perpetrators of Child Sexual Abuse.* Unpublished MPsych Thesis, Dept. of Psychology, University College, Dublin.

O'Reilly, G., Sheridan, A., Carr, A., Cherry, J., Donohoe, E., McGrath, K., O'Reilly, K., Phelan, S., and Tallon, M. (1998). A Descriptive Study of Adolescent Sexual Offenders in an Irish Community-based Treatment Programme. *Irish Journal of Psychology,* 19: 152–167.

Ryan, G., Myoshi, T., Metzner, J., Krugman, R., and Fryer, G. (1996). Trends in a National Sample of Sexually Abusive Youths. *Journal of the American Academy of Child and Adolescent Psychiatry,* 35: 17–25.

Ryan, G., and Lane, S. (1997). *Juvenile Sexual Offending: Causes, Consequences and Correction* (2nd edition). San Francisco, CA: Jossey-Bass.

Samper-Ramos, I. (1998). *Research Proposal to European Commission.* APREMI. Valencia, Spain.

Schram, D.D., Milloy, C.D., and Rowe, W.E., (1991). *Juvenile Sex Offenders: A Follow-up Study of Reoffense Behaviour.* Washington: Urban Policy Research.

Scott-Fordham, A. (1993). An Evaluation of Sex Offender Treatment Programmes. *Issues in Criminological and Legal Psychology,* 19: 60–65.

Sheerin, D. (1998). Legal Options in Ireland for Getting Adolescent Sex Offenders into Treatment Programmes and Keeping Them There. *Irish Journal of Psychology,* 19: 181–189.

Sheridan, A., McKeown, K., Cherry, J., Donohoe, E., McGrath, K., O'Reilly, K., Phelan, S., and Tallon, M. (1998). Perspectives on Treatment Outcome in Adolescent Sex Offending: A Study of a Community-Based Treatment Programme. *Irish Journal of Psychology,* 19: 168–180.

Smets, A., and Cebula, C. (1987). A Group Treatment Programme for Adolescent Sex Offenders. Five Steps Towards Resolution. *Child Abuse and Neglect,* 11: 247–254.

Stermac, L., Segal, Z., and Gillis, R. (1990). Social and Cultural Factors in Sexual Assault. In Marshall, W.L., Laws, D.R., and Barbaree, H.E. (Eds.). *Handbook of Sexual Assault: Issues, Theories and Treatment of the Offender.* NY: Plenum. 143–159.

Travers, O. (1998). Treatment v Punishment: A Case for Treating Sex Offenders in the Community. *Irish Journal Of Psychology,* 19(1): 226–233.

Vizard, E., Monck, E., and Misch, P. (1995). Child and Adolescent Sex Abuse Perpetrators: A Review of the Research Literature. *Journal of Child Psychology and Psychiatry,* 36: 731–756.